The Blade
of Toledo

Dedicated to all the people who have helped to make The Blade successful for its first 150 years - its employees, advertisers, distributors and carriers, and, most importantly, its readers.

The Blade of Toledo
The First 150 Years

by John M. Harrison

Toledo Blade Co.
Toledo, Ohio

1985

Copyright © 1985 by The Toledo Blade Co., 541 Superior St., Toledo, Ohio 43660. All rights reserved. No part of this book may be reproduced, stored in a retrieval system or reproduced in any form without written permission from the publisher. Made in the United States of America. Library of Congress Catalogue card number 85-4803

Library of Congress Cataloging in Publication Data

Harrison, John M.
    The Blade of Toledo

    Bibliography: p.
    Includes index.
    1. Blade (Toledo, Ohio)   I. Title.
PN4899.T65B534   1985   071'.7113   85-4803
ISBN 0-9614554-0-3

PREFACE

The history of American journalism has been written almost entirely in terms of a few newspapers and a few individuals. As might be expected, these have been confined largely to a few metropolitan areas—New York, Boston, Philadelphia and Washington—where so much of the action took place in the early history of the American colonies and the young nation that emerged from them.

Unless careful attention is paid to the footnotes in most histories of American journalism, the impression is left that almost nothing happened west of the Alleghenies. A page or two may be devoted to Chicago newspapers. Denver often gets a nod — entirely on the basis of the antics of Bonfils and Tammen of the Post. There will be almost no mention of Milwaukee, Des Moines, Louisville, or Toledo.

This is too bad. It means that many Americans know almost nothing about considerable numbers of publications with long histories, notable accomplishments, interesting and colorful personnel. This book is about one such newspaper—THE BLADE—which is one hundred and fifty years old in 1985.

THE BLADE is one of the first newspapers established west of the Alleghenies, and it is among the very few that began publication before 1850 still in existence. Its editors have included such nationally known figures as David Ross Locke and Grove Patterson. For all but the first thirty years, it has been owned by only two families — the Lockes from 1865 to 1926, the Blocks from 1926 to the present. It is Toledo's oldest business firm.

Always an issues-oriented newspaper, THE BLADE has played an influential part in many local and national crises from 1835 to 1985. And although there are a few notable exceptions, it has maintained a remarkable degree of consistency in its positions. So it was decided at the outset to tell the story of THE BLADE's first one hundred and fifty years in terms of the issues and problems it has confronted. People, buildings and equipment are not unimportant, however, and they have received attention when it has seemed essential for understanding what was going on and why.

There is relatively little published history of THE BLADE. The most ambitious undertaking, dealing with the newspaper's first one hundred years, is the dissertation prepared by Dr. William Howard Taft for the PhD program in American Culture at Western Reserve University (now Case-Western Reserve) in 1950. Dr. Taft, who is Professor Emeritus of Journalism at the University of Missouri, has been most helpful in relation to this document. It has been useful in many ways and my thanks are extended to him.

Special thanks are due to a number of members of THE BLADE staff — Mary Reddington, librarian; Jenny Mount, news editor; Bill Rosenberg, retired managing editor; and William K. Block, Jr., director of operations.

Thanks also to the University of Iowa Library for the cooperation of its inter-library loan and video film departments. And to my wife, Shirley M. Harrison, research assistant and editor extraordinary.

JOHN M. HARRISON

CONTENTS

PART I: THE EARLY YEARS

1. A Blade with No Elasticity — 3
2. The Future According to Jesup Scott — 17
3. The Blade Goes Daily — 24
4. The Coming of Civil Strife — 42
5. A Steady Voice for the Union — 58
6. A Victory and a Great Loss — 69

PART II: THE LOCKE YEARS

7. A New Man in Charge — 81
8. The Perils of Reconstruction — 87
9. The Weekly Blade—Nasby's Paper — 100
10. Years of Locke's Absence — 105
11. Busted Bankers and the Rum Power — 112
12. David Ross Locke's Last Years — 125
13. A New Generation Takes Over — 138
14. The Coming of 'Golden Rule' Jones — 147
15. A New Mayor, A New Editor — 157
16. Grove Patterson Joins The Blade — 172
17. Battling for the Lord — 179
18. The Blade in War and Peace — 189
19. Nearing the End of an Era — 201

PART III: THE BLOCK YEARS

20.	A Change at the Top	207
21.	A Stormy Transition	213
22.	The Best of Times, the Worst of Times	221
23.	Problems of Depression	230
24.	Years of Troubles	238
25.	European Interlude	245
26.	Down with the New Deal!	250
27.	The End of a Century	259
28.	A Difficult Transition	266
29.	Toledo Tomorrow—and Beyond	272
30.	The Blade and Mr. Gosser	281
31.	Years of Growth and Change	287
32.	Our Man in Europe	294
33.	Adventures in Politics	304
34.	Past the 125-Year Milestone	315
35.	Affairs of the Family	324
36.	In Matters Educational	330
37.	Liberty and Justice for All	336
38.	The Troubled Seventies	342
39.	The Arrival of Tomorrow?	348
40.	The Blade at 150	354
	Notes	362
	Sources	366
	Index	367
	Honor Roll	373

PART I
THE EARLY YEARS
1835-1865

Chapter 1

A Blade with No Elasticity

The story of *The Blade* is so closely interwoven with the story of Toledo that, as an earlier historian of the newspaper has observed, the two cannot be separated.[1] *The Blade* and Toledo came into being a century and a half ago within a few months of each other. The relationship between them has remained one of the closest in the annals of American journalism.

The Blade was, in fact, established before Toledo had been incorporated and one of the principal reasons for its establishment was to promote the municipality that was to result when the pioneer settlements of Port Lawrence and Vistula were incorporated as Toledo.

Those who brought *The Blade* into being did have other fish to fry. One of the newspaper's early concerns was the border dispute between the State of Ohio and the Territory of Michigan over an area which included Toledo, extending westward from Lake Erie to the Indiana border. Another was to provide a voice for the Whig party in its political warfare with the Democrats, assuring full operation of the two-party system in the newly formed county of Lucas, named for Robert Lucas, Ohio's governor.

The area already had one weekly newspaper — the Port Lawrence *Herald,* established and edited by Andrew Palmer, a Jacksonian Democrat. When Port Lawrence and Vistula were merged, the *Herald* became the Toledo *Gazette,* but the interests of the two settlements often conflicted. A growing belief that these could be reconciled only by a strong second newspaper, with no previous commitment to either Vistula or Port Lawrence, opened the way for *The Blade.*

Real estate investors and other leading citizens of the two villages began early in 1835 to talk together about establishing a second newspaper. These included Major Benjamin Stickney, Edward Bissell, Joseph R. Williams, W. J. Daniels, Coleman I. Keeler, and Emery D. Potter — the first local judge, who was later mayor for several terms. Stickney and Bissell called a meeting early in December at the Mansion House — a hotel and tavern on Summit Street — where the need to start a newspaper was discussed. Financial support was promised by Stickney, Bissell and others with real estate holdings, but who should be editor was the most important problem.

Several in the group, including Potter and Williams, promised to contribute material of various kinds, but a full-time editor would be needed and the founders knew the man they wanted. He was George B. Way, an attorney in Urbana, Ohio, who had visited in Port Lawrence and Vistula and had made a favorable impression on those who met him. Way was a native of Maryland who had attended Yale and Miami universities before beginning his law practice in Urbana. He agreed to come to Toledo as editor of the new Whig journal, with Dr. Wilson Everett as publisher. Dr. Everett, who had published a newspaper named the *Collustrator* at Urbana, continued to practice medicine in Toledo. A notice on the editorial page of the first issue of *The Blade* advised readers that "he may be found during the daytime at the office of the Toledo Blade, and, through the night, at the Mansion House Hotel."

Way was literate and prolific. His style, though somewhat florid by today's tastes, was lively and reflective of scholarly interests. He was also an active and successful politician. A dedicated Whig, he was named secretary of the party's Lucas County central committee when it was first organized. A member of the first city council, he subsequently served as mayor of Toledo, was elected twice to the Ohio Legislature, and campaigned actively for "Tippecanoe and Tyler Too" in the 1840 national election.

George Way has been described as "a very eloquent man who could fill the courtroom with a flood of eloquence, frequently carrying both the jurors and the court with his persuasive words."[2] He wrote with equal eloquence, but it was to the courtroom that he soon returned — in 1837. He moved in 1846 to Defiance, where he continued to be prominent in legal and political affairs in northwestern Ohio.

The only issue of *The Blade* under George Way's editorship

A Blade with No Elasticity

which has survived is the very first one, dated December 19, 1835. Special thought and care undoubtedly went into its editorial page, and insofar as it reflects Way's capacities as thinker and writer, the content is impressive. Two long editorials dealing with *The Blade* and its purposes are of special interest.

One of these is captioned "Our Name" and it provides some important indications both as to Way's editorial flair and the direction in which *The Blade* could be expected to go under his editorship:

> We are not of those who are disposed to scout at the efficiency of a name, and do not believe that "a rose by any other name would smell as sweet." Who can believe for the moment, that Andrew Jackson would have ever reached the Chief Magistracy, if he had been unfortunately christened Jonathan Sooks, or that Daniel Webster would have ever attained to his lofty distinction under an appellation such as Ephraim Doolittle. We like some quaintness, some conceit — some point, some significance concealed in the praenomen of a paper . . . Whenever we see blazoned over the head of the columns of a new paper, "Franklin Advertiser," or "Warren Press," we are provoked to write "edited by John Smith." . . .
>
> Our readers will immediately perceive that the name we have assumed was suggested by the notoriety a certain city in Old Spain obtained for a peculiar kind of manufacture, and when they are reminded that in the pending contest with Michigan, it has been and will continue to be the duty of the Toledo press to fight with that valour and ability which the justice of their cause deserves, they will not deem the selection inept.
>
> We know there is much temerity in assuming such a name; but we wish to be perfectly understood that we send forth, concealed under it, no menace, and do not threaten to be tart, smart, witty, severe, ironical, caustic, or provoking. We assume the name because it contains an apt allusion to the origin of the name of our flourishing place, and to recent occurrences in the border warfare . . . We may be accused of challenging the rest of the world. No. We should prefer to keep our blade always in its scabbard, and hope not to be compelled to use it often in the offensive. We should not like, however, to have it rust in its sheath so that it will not easily leap forth when necessity or honor demand that we should use it.
>
> Our blade has no elasticity — it will break before it will bend. Neither is it a mirror wherein every passer by may see his own peculiar and perhaps narrow whims and prejudices reflected. Neither is our blade a heavy broadsword nor a malignant little rapier; but we intend it shall be as sturdy as a Scottish claymore — an instrument better fitted for long and enduring service than for its use in brilliant exploits. We hope it will always leap from its scabbard whenever the rights of individuals, or of the community shall be infringed. Let it never make a reckless, however

inefficient a lunge at the Union of the States, or Constitution of our country, but let it always be drawn in defense of our inestimable political privileges, and against all doctrines that have a tendency to enslave the minds and free thoughts of Americans, and always ready to wage an eternal warfare with all who would attempt to smother a free discussion of any question, moral, political, or religious.

There is at least one other claimant to authorship of this editorial — Joseph R. Williams, who was an early contributor to *The Blade,* and who became its owner and editor almost twenty years later (see page 36). A second editorial in this first issue, "Our Editorial Course," seems certainly to have been written by Way. It is a remarkable document for the time in which it was written, strongly criticizing the partisanship that was characteristic of most newspapers of the period. *The Blade* was established to serve the Whig party and its editor was an active partisan, but here he plainly declares that an excess of partisan zeal in the press was endangering the nation's political and governmental processes. To avoid these partisan excesses, *The Blade* would "refrain from binding ourselves to the chariot-wheel of any political chieftain, nor shall we pledge ourselves to devote the sum total of our energies to the prosecution of any one scheme in politics, morals, or statistics; but we shall hold ourselves free to applaud any one act or principle, without exciting the expectation that we are to do the same by all that may be found in connection therewith."

Having thus admonished against partisanship in the press, Way continued to expound some positive goals toward which *The Blade* would strive under his editorship:

> At this epoch, a very necessary measure is the removal of sectional feelings and prejudices, which, all candid persons must admit, have, during late years, been too warmly cherished by those whose duty it was to pursue an opposite course, thus paving the way for a dissolution of our union into pristine elements. For the purpose of removing those sectional feelings, nothing can so much conduce as faculty of intercommunication . . . The construction of great and splendid works of internal improvement, such as Rail Roads and Canals, will have more influence in binding the separate portions of this nation indissolubly together, than all the Constitutions, contracts, and reasonings upon abstract principles that can be put upon paper . . .
>
> The diffusion of knowledge, of all kinds, should keep pace with the increase of our population; but the instruments of its diffusion should not be those whose passions or individual interest prompt them to mislead those whom they intend to instruct. It shall be our aim to seize upon every

A Blade with No Elasticity

thing which we may presume will be useful to those who may condescend to read our pages . . .

A continuous chain of foreign and domestic news will be kept up, that our readers may be advised of the sayings and doings of the great world in which they live; as also a record of the most interesting proceedings of Congress, our State Legislature, and those of the Legislatures of other states that may be thought worthy of the attention of our readers.

Also included would be "articles of a literary or *belle lettre* cast, especially such as blend instruction with amusement" and would "not even disdain to season our columns with a few sprightly anecdotes or pungent witticisms, provided we can find them manufactured to our hands," since Way laid "no claim to the faculty of originating such newspaper spices."

Thus did George Way — a lawyer with an interest in politics and a flair for literary allusion — set forth a credo to which *The Blade* has adhered with remarkable fealty over the next hundred and fifty years. Item by item, the positions Way set forth in 1835 bear a striking resemblance to those to which his successors adhere in 1985. Often the subject matter has changed; the principles have not.

In addition to the two long editorials on the name and the policies of the fledgling newspaper, this first issue of *The Blade* contained praise of "Our Village." Both its growth and its promise for the future were cited. Others were invited to "come and dwell amongst us and share in the advantages which the commanding location of the town and the enterprise of its inhabitants will, in all human probability, place within our grasp."

George Way had a sense of humor, too — something relatively uncommon among editors of the time — and he used it to good effect in a short editorial in that first issue concerning the contest between the State of Ohio and the Territory of Michigan already mentioned over the narrow strip of land — about seven miles wide — extending from Lake Erie to the Indiana border, and including Toledo. The real excitement was over, but there were still matters of concern to backers of *The Blade*, who had large investments in the disputed strip. Among their concerns were possible loss of a canal terminus and Great Lakes trade.

At the peak of the excitement, Governor Lucas had mobilized 10,000 militiamen, and Michigan's 21-year-old territorial governor, Stevens T. Mason, tried to prevent enforcement of Ohio law in the area. When a series of minor confrontations followed, the only blood spilled was drawn by Two Stickney, younger son of Benjamin (an older son was named One). A Michigan deputy sheriff was wounded slightly when Two Stickney struck him with a pen knife before fleeing the field. *The Blade* offered this comment in its first issue:

"In all our contests with Michigan, we believe no blade has been used, although there are vague reports of whistling bullets and wounded stumps. Hand to hand and hilt to hilt the combatants have never come, and the most brilliant achievements in this warfare have been some valiant assaults upon horses, hen-roosts, and the rifling of some pantries."

The Toledo War, as it came to be known, reached a climax when, just before 1,200 Michigan troops were to occupy the area, a group of Ohioans sneaked into Toledo from nearby Perrysburg, organized a Lucas County government after midnight, then fled back to Maumee to celebrate. Two federal commissioners now were able to negotiate a truce and Congress settled the dispute early in 1836, giving Michigan the Upper Peninsula when it was admitted as a state the next year, while Ohio got the 468 square miles of land that had almost caused a war. The victory was celebrated in Toledo on June 25, 1836, "with cannon fire and bells at sunrise, a parade, all-day speechmaking and a gala evening party with 26 toasts proclaiming the victory."[3] Way's comment on that occasion has, unfortunately, been lost, there being no copies of *The Blade* for the year 1836 surviving.

George Way's editorship lasted only a little more than a year, but that was long enough for him to play an important part in the election of Toledo's first mayor in the spring of 1837. He vigorously supported John Berdan, the Whig candidate, against Andrew Palmer, editor of the Toledo *Gazette*. It was the young editor's first political victory, especially sweet because Berdan, a decided underdog, defeated Palmer by a single vote.

Way had, as noted earlier, considerable help from several Toledoans during his editorship. Notable among these were Joseph R. Williams and Pierre M. Irving, both of whom became even more active in the newspaper's affairs after Way's departure.

Pierre Irving was a nephew of Washington Irving, with whom he had worked as a research assistant on the book, *Astoria*. He had been caught up in the speculative boom involving the buying and selling of land on the Western frontier, extending at this time a bit beyond the Mississippi River. Irving had lived at Jacksonville, Illinois, where he practiced law and bought real estate, before moving to Toledo in

1836. He came at the urging of John Berdan, a brother of Irving's first wife, who had died in 1832. Berdan had made an agreement to buy a one-twelfth interest in the town plat of Toledo, of which he offered to sell a one-fifth interest to his brother-in-law. The arrangement fell through, but Irving stayed on in Toledo, joining Berdan in various investments. Pierre Irving continued to contribute to *The Blade* until 1838, when his second wife became ill with what he described as "bilious fever" and refused to return to Toledo after being taken East to regain her health.[4]

Joseph Williams, who would become owner and editor of *The Blade* twenty years later, arrived in Toledo in 1835 as the agent of a New England company seeking land investments. Williams was a native of Taunton, Massachusetts, and a graduate of Harvard. He had given up the practice of law when his health failed. He moved in 1839 to Michigan, where he became active in politics; he was twice the Whig candidate for a seat in Congress and twice the opponent of Lewis Cass for the United States Senate. He became owner and editor of *The Blade* in May, 1853.

George Way's departure as editor of *The Blade* was a major blow to Whig leaders, and the situation was exacerbated when Pierre Irving left later in the same year. In a frontier settlement such as Toledo was in 1837, there were few who could match the quality of their writing talents and their perceptions. Williams stayed on for a time to help Way's successor, but some of the substance and verve that had characterized the newspaper in its first two years were lost for the moment.

Abel W. Fairbanks, who had come to Toledo from Detroit, took over as editor and publisher of *The Blade* in May, 1837. He always referred to himself as a printer, and his primary interest was in the production of the newspaper, rather than its content. He retained the city printing contract for many years, along with exclusive rights to publish proceedings of the city council.[5] Newspapers did not yet send their own representatives to meetings of governmental agencies.

Fairbanks was active in Whig political affairs and was elected city treasurer in 1848. His other community interests included the Toledo Mechanics' Library Association, of which he was treasurer for a time. He also supported vigorously many of the causes with which Way had been concerned. One of these was the dispute between Toledo and Maumee over which should be the seat of Lucas county's government. Soon after he became editor of *The Blade*, he spoke out against moving the county seat from Toledo to Maumee. He argued that Toledo was nearer the center of the county's population, that it paid two-thirds of the total county taxes, that it had good railroad facilities, and — as a clinching argument — "We want it!"[6]

Later in 1837, *The Blade* expressed other fears concerning the county's fate, including the likelihood that it "is destined to the fate of poor Poland." Citing the sources of his fear, Fairbanks wrote:

> First comes a petition from the western inhabitants to take off a portion of that quarter. These are the Russians, who choose the largest slice. Then follows an application from some "all-nameless" individuals for the opposite shore. These are the Prussians who are content with a more moderate share. Last comes the petition . . . from the authors of another project for a new county to be formed out of the north part of Sandusky and Huron counties and a small fraction of Lucas. These are the Austrians . . . Let Michigan now join the allied forces and renew her grasp upon the disputed tract and the dismemberment might be rendered totally complete.

Lucas County survived attempts at partitioning, and Toledo remained the county seat. There were innumerable battles along the way to final resolution of this rivalry in 1852, including local political skirmishes, appeals to the Legislature and the courts. In all this, *The Blade* not unexpectedly championed Toledo's interests, carrying on a running exchange of invective with the rival Maumee *Express* in which both achieved dizzying heights — or depths — of rhetoric.

Fairbanks relied during most of his years as owner of *The Blade* on a series of editors to supervise and produce the news and editorial content. In fact, the differences between reporting and editorializing were slight, and both were used to advance the cause of the political party that the newspaper served. The concept of objectivity in reporting news events would be little mentioned until some twenty-five years later, when wire services began supplying accounts of news to the press throughout the country. Since these included journals of widely varying political persuasions, care had to be taken to avoid offending potential customers.

The first of Fairbanks' editors was Andrew Palmer — the same Andrew Palmer who had been editor of the rival Toledo *Gazette*, voice of the local Democratic party. He had come over to the Whigs in the five years since *The Blade* had been established, drawn by the candidacy of William Henry Harrison for the presidency and by the

A Blade with No Elasticity

hope of tangible reward. Toledo Whigs had formed a Tippecanoe Club in support of Harrison in April, with Edward Bissell as its president. When a Democratic Reform Club was organized three months later with the express purpose of defecting to Harrison and the Whigs, Andrew Palmer was one of its members. So, interestingly enough, was Edward Bissell, already head of the Whigs' Tippecanoe Club.

Palmer, who gave rousing support to the Whigs' war hero candidate, was a native of Binghamton, New York. He was apprenticed to the newspaper business at fourteen, then with an older brother had established a weekly paper at Rensselaerville, New York, before coming to Toledo in 1833 as a speculator in land.[7] After editing the Port Lawrence *Herald*, which became the Toledo *Gazette*, Palmer bought the *Western Hemisphere* in Columbus. He changed its name to the *Ohio Statesman* and acted as spokesman for the Democratic party.

When he became editor of *The Blade* on July 14, 1840, Palmer wrote that, if his health permitted, he would devote to it the principal portion of his time, until after the presidential election. *The Blade* had already demonstrated its enthusiastic support of Harrison, who had commanded the U.S. army in the Northwest Territory in the War of 1812.

General Harrison's visit to the celebration of the anniversary of the lifting of the siege of Fort Meigs on the Maumee River near what is now Perrysburg was the highlight of that ten-day event. The account of it written for *The Blade* by Hezekiah L. Hosmer, later to be one of Fairbanks' editors, received wide circulation in the Ohio press. These excerpts from *The Blade* of June 17, 1840, reflect some of Hosmer's enthusiasm:

> The Celebration at
> FORT MEIGS
> A Great Day for the Republic — Another Bright Spot
> in the Political Horizon of Our Beloved Country
>
> Heaven never smiled on a more joyful and heart-stirring scene than was presented at the site of old Fort Meigs the 14th inst. The weather was delightful, the atmosphere was clear and the sun shone brightly and benignly, and God and nature seemed alike to approve . . .
>
> Numerous other processions, delegations and military organizations from different states continued to arrive during the day . . . there could not have been less than FORTY THOUSAND PERSONS who joined in the celebration . . .
>
> In the midst of that great mass of people, and surrounded by the

banners and devices we have been describing, and by several of the best disciplined and most beautiful independent Military Companies from this and neighboring states stood GEN. WILLIAM HENRY HARRISON, the hero of the scene. Here, upon the very grounds his own deeds of valor and noble daring had hallowed with historic reminiscences of the most thrilling and exalted character, stood the war-worn and time-honored chieftain and civilian. It was indeed a grand and inspiring spectacle, and one which it would be but mockery for us to attempt to portray.

Harrison's triumphal visit continued from Fort Meigs with a voyage on the Maumee River to Toledo. *The Blade* reported enthusiastically that the General was escorted from the landing to the American Hotel to receive congratulations from many who had not yet shaken his hand. Mayor Myron H. Tilden introduced him to his followers at the hotel. *The Blade's* account of the celebration included many excerpts from the address by the Whig presidential candidate. Each issue also contained a complete copy of "Harrison's Great Speech."

Andrew Palmer's conversion to the Whig ranks did not go without reproach from the Democrats. A letter from Palmer replying to these attacks was published in the July 1 issue of *The Blade*, which added: "Let the Van Buren men read it, and then say with what justice these attacks have been made; who it is that has changed, Mr. P. or the Van Buren party." Few may have had the stamina to read through Palmer's entire letter, which occupied four and one-half columns of space.

When he took over editorship of *The Blade* a month later, Andrew Palmer began an outpouring of editorials in praise of "Tippecanoe and Tyler Too" that all but engulfed its four pages. Beginning with the August 5 issue, editorials and local items appeared on the front page for the first time, running over to fill the space usually allotted to them on page two. Palmer's enthusiasms for the Whig candidates continued to dominate the weekly issues of August 12, 19 and 26, September 2, 9, 16, 23 and 30, and October 7. When the Whigs swept the state elections in Ohio, *The Blade* of October 14 proclaimed:

GLORY ENOUGH
FOR ONE DAY
The Buckeye Boys have done nobly. There is hardly a Corporal's Guard left of the Van Buren Party in Ohio. Such a using up of loco focoism is no where to be met with in the annals of our country.

A Blade with No Elasticity

There was further exultation in *The Blade* of October 21, calling attention to the one-sided victory of Whig Thomas Corwin over the incumbent governor, Wilson Shannon, and to other party triumphs, including the action of Lucas County voters in sending George B. Way, first editor of *The Blade*, to the Ohio House of Representatives. Joy was unrestrained:

ATTENTION THE UNION!!
Ohio, in Committee of the Whole,
Has Reported!
The Buckeye State sends to her Sisters,
Greeting:
A WHIG GOVERNOR BY
19,000 MAJORITY
Whig Gain of Five Members of Congress!

A majority of at least 25 in joint ballot in the State Legislature!

When Harrison and Tyler easily won the national election in November, the enthusiasm was even greater. Then, having completed what he had set out to do in six months as editor of *The Blade*, Andrew Palmer announced in December that "the connection which has heretofore subsisted between the undersigned and the editorial department of the Blade ceases with the present number." He went on to explain that "in assuming the editorial charge of this paper, in July last, the undersigned was impelled solely by that strong desire which has so strikingly pervaded the great mass of the American people, to contribute whatever lay in his power, to promote the grand political results with which their efforts have finally been crowned."

Andrew Palmer's expectations of reward for his editorial services to the new president were temporarily frustrated. He was to have been named postmaster of Toledo, but when President Harrison died within a month after his inauguration the appointment was delayed. In July, 1841, *The Blade* wanted to know why "there has been no appointment of Post Master in this city?" and complained of a report being circulated "that the office is to be given to a person who does not reside amongst us, and who is not even a resident of this State." Not until October 29 was it reported that "Andrew Palmer, Esq." had received the plum he had expected.

★ ★ ★

Abel W. Fairbanks continued as key figure in the operation of *The Blade* for the next three years; S. S. Blanchard, Edward A. Graves and Daniel McBain were associated with him in various capacities. The first of these arrangements was a partnership with Blanchard, announced on April 21, 1841, to publish *The Blade* and to add a book bindery "where all kinds of printing and blank work will be done on short notice." It was announced on May 21 that "the office of *The Blade* has been removed to the building two doors east of the Retail Store, and the first door west of the Franklin House, Summit Street, up stairs." There was the additional information that "subscribers will receive their papers in the Book Store."

Enthusiastically as *The Blade* had supported the election of a Whig president and his running mate, it was not long in expressing its disillusionment with John Tyler as president. When Tyler vetoed a bill to create a national banking corporation in September, *The Blade* roundly denounced him:

> Deeply as we regret the necessity of condemning the doctrines of a President elected to office by the votes of the Whig party, still we cannot falter. We have been deceived or betrayed.
>
> The victory won under the watchword of HARRISON AND REFORM is rendered almost bootless, and the alternatives of war presented, namely to submit, or fight the battle over again.

Another long editorial the next week, on September 28, renewed the attack on Tyler, examined the future of the Whig party, then asked:

> What then shall we do? Without a head, our efforts will prove unavailing — division and estrangement will inevitably ensue — the Whig party become broken, and ruin, distress and Executive misrule increased and fastened upon the country. What might be though premature under other circumstances seems to us now to have become an absolute necessity. We should have our candidate for the Presidency in the field and keep him before the people.

It didn't take long for *The Blade* to find its man. Two weeks later, at the head of its editorial columns, its choice was revealed:

For President in 1844
HENRY CLAY
Subject to the decision of the Whig party of the union

Henry Clay had long been admired by *The Blade*, which gave strong support to his candidacy in both 1844 and 1848. It is interesting to note that in this period, when both major parties sought presidential candidates among military heroes, *The Blade* was wary of them, preferring men who had come up through the party ranks to the United States Congress or a state governorship.

A Blade with No Elasticity

Of the three generals chosen as presidential candidates by the Whigs between 1840 and 1852, Harrison was the only one who excited warm support from *The Blade*, which endorsed nonmilitary figures in both 1848 and 1852 before the party conventions. *The Blade* supported Zachary Taylor (1848) and Winfield Scott (1852) only after they had been nominated by the Whigs.

There was another change in the ownership and management arrangements during 1842. This announcement appeared on July 8, over the name of Edward A. Graves:

> The undersigned has purchased of A.W. Fairbanks his interest in the Toledo Blade, and in future it will be conducted by him. The Blade will remain as heretofore, Whig. To sustain myself in the undertaking, it will be necessary to adopt the Cash System and adhere to it strictly.

Only two weeks later, a new editor was announced. He was Daniel McBain, who had no particular qualifications for the job beyond loyalty to the Whig party, having been a store clerk, deputy county clerk, and city treasurer. During McBain's editorship, which continued for only a year, the paths of *The Blade* and its onetime editor, Andrew Palmer, now postmaster of Toledo, again crossed. An editorial of October 14 describes the circumstances:

> It is well known that Mr. Palmer . . . received his appointment through the influence of his Whig friends of this town and that if it had not been for his profession of Whig principles, he never would have held the station he now occupies. Yet notwithstanding the support extended to him and the obligation he was under to the Whig party, Mr. Palmer has boldly advocated and sustained the peculiar views of the Executive by every means, both privately and officially . . .
>
> We did hope that a regard for political consistency would prevent Mr. Palmer from proving so recreant to the Whig Party as recent events have shown to be the case . . .
>
> The first intimation of the great devotion to Tylerism, on the part of Mr. Palmer, was exhibited in his taking the post office printing from this office and bestowing it upon the Register, the Locofoco organ of this place. From that time we have seen him strenuously using all his efforts to perfect the "colation" between the Locofoco party and John Tyler.

Andrew Palmer's perfidy in first giving aid and comfort to Tyler, who had appointed him postmaster, then taking the post office printing from *The Blade* and bestowing it on a rival from the Locofocos, as the Democrats often were known, was clearly more than Daniel McBain and his associates could stomach. A year later *The Blade* would allege that Palmer was, in fact, editor of the opposing Register, bringing full circle the strange relationship between the newspaper and its one-time editor.

Things went badly for the Whigs in the years 1842-43, while Fairbanks, Blanchard, Graves and McBain wrestled with the problems confronting *The Blade* and the Whig party. The Democrats elected two representatives from Lucas county to the Ohio Legislature in 1842 and a congressman from the Toledo district in 1843. Fairbanks, who became owner and editor again in July, 1843, spoke of these results as disgraceful to the Whig party and declared that he felt "angry, dispirited, humiliated." The situation was about to improve. In 1844, Fairbanks found a new editor, who would make his impact felt on *The Blade*, on the Whig party, and on Toledo.

Chapter 2

The Future According to Jesup Scott

Jesup W. Scott took over as editor of *The Blade* in March, 1844. He had an abiding faith in the future of the Midwest, and especially of Toledo, although that faith shifted easily, having been also focused on Cincinnati and Maumee. But his enthusiasm for whatever city was the current beneficiary of his encomiums knew no bounds.

Scott was much more than the traditional civic booster. He supported his claims on behalf of Toledo with detailed and well-reasoned editorials, dealing with a variety of the forces that he contended would make the city great. Scott was editor for just over three years, but in that short time he established himself as one of the handful of men who distinguished themselves as *The Blade's* great editors. He was the first to exert the kind of influence that subsequently would characterize the editorships of David Ross Locke and Grove Patterson.

Born at Ridgefield, Connecticut, in 1799, he got his first newspaper experience in South Carolina, where he had gone at the age of twenty. He tried his hand at editing the Columbia *Telescope* in 1824-25, while living in Lexington, South Carolina. Previously he had practiced both law and medicine for brief periods and had taught at the South Carolina Female College. Scott returned to his family home in Connecticut in 1830 because, he said, he was disliked in the South as a Yankee. He was an instinctive foe of slavery and had little use for the southern way of life. These convictions would play a part in establishing his unflagging opposition to the system of human servitude, an opposition that characterized *The Blade's* positions in the years ahead.

In the spring of 1831, Scott came to northwest Ohio to look after the widespread land holdings of his father-in-law, Jessup Wakeman, in Erie County. While living at Norwalk in 1832, Scott published a monthly magazine, *The Ohio and Michigan Register and Emigrant's Guide,* whose sixteen pages provided a variety of information about the western lands. It was at this time that Scott first predicted that the future great city of the world would be found in the American interior, not on the seacoast.[8] Scott persisted in this notion throughout his life, first designating Cincinnati for that honor. After he had come to the Maumee Valley in 1832, he became convinced that here was where his "great city of the future" would be. He located in the settlement of Maumee, he was elected prosecuting attorney and soon established the area's first newspaper, the *Miami of the Lake,* which first appeared on December 11, 1833. Now Maumee became his choice to become the "great city."

Few land speculators did so well as Scott. At the peak of the land boom in 1836, with holdings valued at $400,000, he retired to Connecticut to live on his fortune. When the panic of 1837 all but wiped him out, he returned to the Maumee Valley, where he made a particularly fortuitous purchase of a tract midway between Vistula and Port Lawrence. When they merged, Scott's property became part of the downtown of the new town of Toledo, which spread northwest away from the river.[9] The value of this property was to increase more than tenfold before Scott's death in 1874.

Old friends and associates in Maumee denounced Scott as a traitor when he became editor of *The Blade* and started to beat the drums for Toledo, but he was not deterred. His editorials on the forces that he believed were working to promote the new town's growth and prosperity were often interrelated, forming a series of commentaries of considerable impact.

The Wabash and Erie Canal and its importance to Toledo's future was the subject of a long editorial on January 28, 1844. It concluded: "In our next issue we propose to show that on the opening of the lake to the ocean commerce through the canals now constructing in Canada, our city will be likely to take the lead in business which that commerce will create." Then, the next week: "As the foreign commerce of the lakes is destined, within ten years, to greatly alter and modify the face of affairs over the whole lake country, we hope our readers will feel sufficient interest in the subject to read another article relating to it, which we design to give in our next."

The Future According to Jesup Scott

That editorial, which did not appear until February 16, concluded: "It seems plain to us that the St. Lawrence and Lake region are to be the great ship building, ship owning and ship navigating portion of the American continent. Our region will be to the rest of the continent what the North Sea and Baltic have been and are to Europe." Scott's vision would, in fact, be realized, though not for more than a century, when *The Blade* would take the lead in urging port development.

Scott next directed his readers' attention to the part that railroads would play in Toledo's development, then to "The State of Ohio — Its Wealth and Resources."

There is little doubt that Jesup Scott was personally convinced that Toledo and the surrounding area presented opportunities for growth and development equal to those to be found anywhere in the world. He espoused his beliefs not only in *The Blade*, but also in such popular national commercial journals as *Hunt's Merchant's Magazine* and *DeBow's Review* over a period extending from 1843 to 1860. His enthusiasm never waned, and in 1868 he published a 49-page pamphlet predicting that Toledo would, by the year 2000, be the largest city in the world. The title of the pamphlet: "A Presentation of Causes Tending to Fix the Position of the Future Great City of the World in the Central Plain of North America: Showing that the Center of the World's Commerce, now Represented by the City of London is Moving Westward to the City of New York and thence, within One Hundred Years to the Best Position on the Great Lakes.[10]

But Scott's conviction that Toledo was destined for greatness was not his only concern as editor of *The Blade*.

Its editorial page, which had been undistinguished since the brief period of George Way's editorship, improved in both substance and style. Scott was a loyal Whig, and the party's fortunes in Toledo and Lucas county showed marked improvement while he was editor. Shattered by Henry Clay's defeat by James K. Polk in the presidential election of 1844, Scott declared that "the noblest statesman of our land has been thrust aside — and by whom! Not by the patriot sons of revolutionary fathers; not by the native sons of the soil, men nurtured and educated in the principles of our free government; for of such he had a decided majority in his favor. Almost the entire vote of the least intelligent classes of naturalized foreigners was thrown against him. By the votes of such has Mr. Polk been made our President." It was an argument that newspaper editors — first Whig, then Republican, and including Scott and his successors at *The Blade* — would use more and more frequently. As the numbers of immigrants increased — first the Irish, then those from central and southern Europe — they tended, for a variety of reasons, to affiliate with the Democratic party. Whig and Republican editors were not hesitant to capitalize on suspicions of these "foreigners." Another comment on the outcome of the 1844 election suggests that other prejudices were played upon: "Illinois has gone for Polk, particularly the Mormon part of it."

The conflict over slavery was heating up during Jesup Scott's editorship, and he put *The Blade* in the vanguard among those opposed to slavery in all its aspects. Thus, reporting "The Latest News from the Lexington Mob" in August, 1845, Scott observed:

> The Slave holders have triumphed over the liberty of the press in Kentucky. The noble C.M. Clay, after a prostration occasioned by 35 days of suffering from typhoid fever, has had his press — the True American — taken from him and sent out of the state by a mob of slave holders. The press has arrived in a free state, in Ohio, at Cincinnati, and we welcome the bold instrument of freedom in our state. A still warmer welcome would be given the bold advocate of liberty, should he come to live with us.

When Texas was admitted to the Union a few months later, on terms of which Scott did not approve, he denounced the action. "With pain and humiliation," *The Blade* of January 2, 1846, declared, "we feel that the Slave power has its foot on the neck of the once free north — never to be removed as long as northern traitors are to be bought with office."

Much of Scott's attention was occupied by the threat of war with England over the Oregon border question, which did not materialize, and that of war with Mexico over Texas and related matters, which did break out in 1846. In each instance, he urged settlement by peaceful negotiation. *The Blade's* comments — especially those on the developing conflict in Mexico — were tinged with Whiggish dogma and found much to fault in the actions and policies of President Polk. There seemed, Scott wrote on May 18, 1846, "to be no room for doubt that our government placed itself in the wrong and became the aggressor, by sending our army beyond the western boundary of Texas, and into a province of Mexico."

Once war had begun, Scott gave it token support. Almost every issue of *The Blade* carried war dispatches, including reports by other

The Future According to Jesup Scott 21

newspapers — in Buffalo, Cleveland, and New Orleans. It was to the generals — especially Zachary Taylor and Winfield Scott — that *The Blade* referred favorably, not to Polk or any of his administration. General Taylor had displayed "energy, bravery and skill . . . in maintaining and giving security to his position on the Rio Grande." It might be hoped that the blows he had struck "would show Mexico how little she is likely to gain in battle with our troops, and . . . dispose her to peace."

When Mexico did not oblige by suing for peace, the war became increasingly unpopular with the public, and Jesup Scott declared in October that "the administration is heartily sick of the war" and will ask Congress, "as soon as it assembles, to appropriate a large sum of money to buy a peace." Here was an opening for a thrust at Polk and the Democrats: "The only hope now seems to be in bribing the Mexican ruler. Even this vile recourse may be less wicked and impolitic than the present mode of carrying on the war."

Jesup Scott blew his stack when the Polk administration projected politics into military affairs. Congress defeated the President's proposal to give Senator Thomas Hart Benton of Missouri, a militia colonel, command over the generals in the field, and *The Blade* exploded: "Thank God there are degrees of meanness to which the President is yet unable to bring down his partizans *(sic)* in Congress. Nearly half of the Democrats in the lower branch of Congress refused to sanction the disgraceful project, and enough Senators of that party joined the Whigs to defeat it in that body. We have it from a reliable source that Polk has even less of the respect of all parties in Congress than the base John Tyler had."

Scott severed his connections with *The Blade* six months later, after three and one-half years in which he had been responsible for changes that considerably improved the newspaper. He had become senior partner in the firm of Scott & Fairbanks as publishers of *The Blade* in 1845. The first edition of the new tri-weekly edition of *The Blade* was published, in tabloid size, on May 11, 1846. This was a "fitting occasion," Scott declared, to present a "brief notice of the place whence it comes."

This place was Toledo, where "nearly all the exchange commerce between Lake Erie and the two canals, known as the Wabash and Erie and the Miami and Erie, is transacted." Its population "is small compared to our business and our unrivalled means to support a future growth . . . but a fraction over 2,100." Most important, "measures are now in progress to remove all the local causes of disease, so that the liability of our place to severe billious disorders, so much exaggerated by common fame, aided by envious rivals, will be numbered with the things of the past."

Health was one of the problems with which Toledo's land speculators and promoters had wrestled since the first settlers had struggled through the Black Swamp, which they had to cross in order to reach the Maumee Valley. A tract of land about 40 by 120 miles, covered with dense forest, it extended along the western end of Lake Erie. It struck fear in the hearts of those who traversed it, and it was a prime factor in creating the reputation for unhealthiness that plagued Toledo and its developers for many years to come.[11]

Jesup Scott took a wide variety of approaches in his commentaries on this problem. When reports of illness and death in Toledo persisted, he finally gave vent to his frustration:

> Baron Munchausen himself, if alive, could not get up a story about Toledo's sickness and mortality too monstrous for general belief. . . . It is no testimony in our favor to deny that we are sick and dead. The public *will* make us sick and kill us off, and bury us. We can't help ourselves. It is a duty or an amusement in which the public will not deny themselves.

During his years as editor of *The Blade*, Scott's influence went far beyond political affairs. He became an admirer of "the learned blacksmith," Elihu Burritt of Boston, self-taught scholar and folk hero. Influenced by Burritt's ideas, Scott began to advocate establishment in Toledo of "manual labor schools," where workers "with stout hearts and good hands" could educate themselves. In 1846, he suggested the need for a school similar to the one founded in Troy, New York, by Stephen Van Rensselaer (which became Rensselaer Polytechnic Institute). "What noble minded man will give himself a great name and the county of Lucas the lasting benefit of an agricultural school," Scott inquired, "by donating a sufficient farm for the purpose?"[12]

This "noble minded man" proved to be Jesup Scott himself. He gave 160 acres of land, valued at $80,000, for the educational institution that was established as the Toledo University of Arts and Trades soon after his death in 1873. The school encountered financial problems for many years, but survived to become the University of Toledo. Jesup W. Scott High School provides another lasting tie between this pioneer editor of *The Blade* and education in Toledo.

The Future According to Jesup Scott

Jesup Scott's valedictory editorial of July 14, 1847, was brief. He had "endeavored to do his duty," but as to "how far he had succeeded it is not for him to say." There was a flicker of humor at its conclusion: his connection with *The Blade* as its editor would now cease, "unless for the purpose of self-defense." No such purpose arose, although Scott, as one of Toledo's most active and influential citizens during the next quarter of a century, was a frequent contributor to the editorial page of the newspaper whose reputation he had enhanced so considerably as its editor. Scott never lost his faith in the potential for building a great city on the banks of the Maumee. Late in life, he wrote:

"I think I am in exactly the best climate — on the isotherm of 50° in heat. It is the isotherm on and near which mankind have chosen to congregate in greatest numbers and built up nearly all the great modern cities. It is the climate of the best grasses, the best grain, the best fruits, and — and — and the best men."[13]

Chapter 3

The Blade Goes Daily

Hezekiah L. Hosmer, who had written of William Henry Harrison's appearance at Fort Meigs in 1840, succeeded Scott as editor of *The Blade*. He was by no means his remarkable predecessor's equal. The quality of the editorial and local page declined markedly. Hosmer boosted Toledo and the Whigs, but he had little of Scott's knowledge or writing skills. Criticism of the Polk administration and its policies continued, with an especially bitter comment on October 11: "No one who reads the history of this country for the past two years and a half will deny to President Polk the full possession of all the infamous renown which that bloody period confers upon him, as the author of the first event that marks the departure of our government from the paths of justice and virtue." The reference was, of course, to the increasingly unpopular war with Mexico.

Just a week later, on October 18, *The Blade* found more congenial and promising subject matter, and Hosmer obviously enjoyed making these observations on the further extension of Samuel F. B. Morse's wondrous invention — the telegraph.

> Well, we are soon to have a connection with the lightning line. Three weeks hence and we, the citizens of this goodly city will be able to give our thoughts not to the winds and waves, the trees and wild woods, but to the wires... To speak plainly — the telegraph will be completed to this place in about three weeks.
>
> Are we to have a connection? Who doubts it. Who that looks at our commerce, our steady growth, our harbor, our canals, our railroads, our situation with reference to the great country surrounding us.

The coming of the magnetic telegraph was, of course, an event of far greater significance than Hosmer and most others could foresee. In 1844 — the same year that Samuel F. B. Morse had sent the first

The Blade Goes Daily 25

message from Washington to Baltimore — the Magnetic Telegraph Company had been organized by Morse and two partners, Amos Kendall and William M. Swain. The company was providing news to all the New York newspapers by 1846, and had reached as far west as St. Louis by 1847.[14]

The Blade carried an almost casual announcement on February 14, 1848, of the arrival in Toledo of the most significant innovation in the history of American newspapers up to that time:

> The magic wires are here and we are in connection. We shall be able henceforth to furnish our readers with the latest news — the daily condition of the eastern market, and all that kind of practical intelligence which is now eagerly sought after by the business world. The expense incident to the employment of the telegraph, we can illy bear, but a conviction that your enterprize in this matter will not go unrewarded induces us to hazard the experiment of a trial.

This was followed by an announcement, which seemed almost an afterthought, that "it is our intention, if the increase in patronage is sufficient, to commence the publication of a daily paper by the opening of navigation — of the same size and appearance of the Tri-Weekly." There was an appeal to "send in your subscriptions, friends," and a promise to "give you the *quid pro quo* for your liberality."

The Blade first used reports received by way of the magnetic telegraph on the day this announcement was made, although the first dispatches specifically labeled "By Telegraph" are not to be found until the March 1 issue. These included reports on the war in Mexico, a fire in Albany, New York, and market reports from Buffalo. There were problems with the new service and it was announced on March 6 that "because we get the Telegraph reports between 4 and 6 o'clock p.m., which does not give us time to circulate our papers over the territory in which our subscribers are located, we have changed our publication day and issue of our paper in the morning instead of the evening." This was only the beginning of the headaches the telegraph was to cause *The Blade* and its readers. There were reports for several days in succession that there was "no telegraph news today because the wires are down to the east."

Other complaints against the wire service included the charge that the Sandusky operator was incompetent, that "on several occasions, soon after the report was commenced, and when it was perfectly intelligible to the operators here and west of us, he was unable to interpret it, and put us to the inconvenience of waiting for another transmission." The lateness of the telegraph reports caused problems in delivery of papers, and when one subscriber complained that "we frequently do not receive our paper for 2 or 3 days," *The Blade* responded that "hereafter we shall go to press at 3 o'clock, report or no report, and as soon as another line of telegraph reaches here, shall endeavor to procure reports in seasons." Most annoying of all was the kind of practice revealed in this item of August 16:

> A long report was received yesterday at the office announcing the arrival of the Cambria with seven days later news from Europe. We were requested to pay extra for it and refused. In the evening, at an hour too late for insertion in yesterday's paper, it was sent to us with a note by our operator informing us that it was all a hoax, got up in Pittsburgh. This trifling is much too common... We shall avoid it if possible when another line is established.

These and other problems and annoyances continued for many months, but despite them the magnetic telegraph was soon to effect a major change in *The Blade*. In the issue of April 12, the promise made two months earlier concerning the beginning of a daily edition was revealed to be near realization, with publication to begin on April 17. It was their purpose, the proprietors declared, "to furnish their readers with the latest Commercial Intelligence and General News, received through the medium of the Magnetic Telegraph." Toledo's growth and the future prospect of continuing business expansion in "several towns in the Maumee Valley seem to justify the enterprise, and encourage the proprietors with the belief that it will not go unrewarded."

When the first daily edition appeared on schedule the following Monday, it was acknowledged that "but for the existence of this wonderful machine (the magnetic telegraph), we should be content to travel on a year or two longer with the tri-weekly." Then followed a statement that was not typical of newspapers of the period:

> Our part in the work before us, we feel to be as important in its character as it is difficult in its performance. The day of small things and local puffery is over. Toledo must henceforth depend upon its real possessions, more than its fancied ones.

There were developments aplenty to sustain this reliance on "real possessions." Only a month after the appearance of that first daily paper, *The Blade* could announce the arrival from Montreal of an Atlantic steamer, the "Free Trader," and go on to exult: "What a world we live in! Here is over two thousand miles of river, canal and

The Blade Goes Daily 27

lake navigation; for vessels and steamships of a respectable size, and the vast increasing products of our western El Dorado, can be transported from the extreme end of Lake Michigan to any part of the world, with but a single transshipment on the Atlantic Seaboard." The visions of growth and greatness that Jesup Scott had expounded in *The Blade* only a few years earlier now seemed on the verge of realization. Toledo and its newspaper flexed their muscles and looked toward distant horizons.

★ ★ ★

The Blade had some problems deciding where to position itself in the political realignments brought on by the struggle over the slavery issue. The sympathies of its editor and proprietor were clearly with the anti-slavery forces, and they wanted to go along with the Free Soil party that emerged as the rallying point for those who opposed extension of slavery. Two barriers to all-out support of the Free Soilers presented themselves and led eventually to a break between A. W. Fairbanks and H. L. Hosmer.

The first was *The Blade's* long-standing tradition of support for the Whig party and its candidates, a tradition that the more conservative Fairbanks found it especially hard to abandon. The second was a strong dislike of Martin Van Buren, who had become an active leader in the liberal element of the Democratic party (known as the Barnburners) and was to emerge as the Free Soil candidate for President. It is likely that their mutual dislike of Van Buren kept Fairbanks and Hosmer together for a few months, but it was a temporary accommodation.

When Toledo's Free Soilers held a public meeting at the New Council Room on July 31, 1848, *The Blade* described it as "overwhelmingly enthusiastic, indeed larger than any ever held before in this City, the Hall being so crowded that numbers could not find standing room inside," being "clustered on the stairs, around the doors, and on the high ground adjacent." Richard Mott, who was later elected to Congress on the Free Soil ticket, was named chairman, and a set of resolutions was approved, including the naming of twenty-five delegates to the upcoming national convention at Buffalo. Another resolution pledged support of the nominee of that convention for the Presidency.

The enthusiasm that *The Blade* manifested here was to be short-lived. Only ten days later, on August 12, this commentary was offered at the conclusion of the Buffalo convention:

> This great assembly, composed of citizens from all the free, and the northern tier of slave states, have with singular unanimity nominated Martin Van Buren for the Presidency, and Charles F. Adams for the Vice Presidency. These gentlemen are the representatives of the bolting free soil Locos, the Abolitionists, and a few renegade Whigs . . .
> Well! we shall see what we shall see. — Mr. Van Buren is no stranger to the citizens of the United States. His career has not been one to be speedily forgotten. We must believe that a stroke of lunacy has attacked the Whigs, before we can believe that any considerable portion of them will be willing to give him their support, merely because he has added to his own principles one of the most prominent of the Whig creed, and based upon it his claims to their considerations . . .

The Blade remained loyal to the Whigs in the 1848 election. General Zachary Taylor was not its choice for the presidential nomination. That designation had gone to Henry Clay, with Daniel Webster as an alternate choice. Yet when the Whigs chose Taylor as their candidate in 1848, *The Blade* managed to overcome its previous lack of enthusiasm for military men and to summon up considerable support for him and his running mate, Millard Fillmore of New York. *The Blade* leaped aboard ship in an editorial entitled "Our Flag to the Breeze," on June 10:

> Bear a hand boys. Every man hold the ropes. Altogether now. There she goes — now she settles beautifully at the top and now her majestic folds begin to unfurl. Letter by letter streams in the sunlight, and now she is fully spread:
>
> For President
> Zachary Taylor of Louisiana
> For Vice President
> Millard Fillmore of New York
>
> And this is our flag, under which we have enlisted for the campaign of 1848 . . .

The campaign was relatively dull, despite the three-way competition among Taylor, Van Buren, and Lewis Cass of Michigan, the Democratic nominee. *The Blade* found some sport in jousting with the Detroit *Free-Press,* which supported Cass. Its case for Taylor was based on his having opposed the Mexican War, acknowledged that he favored the Wilmot Proviso, and promised to limit the exercise of the presidential veto.

Taylor's election in November, 1848, was largely a result of his having carried New York, where Van Buren's candidacy split the Democratic vote. The principal reason to rejoice, *The Blade* suggested, was "because the country has risen out of reach of" Cass's power and influence.

Hezekiah L. Hosmer severed his connection with *The Blade* only a few days after Taylor's inauguration on March 4, 1849, and his farewell editorial makes it clear that his departure was a consequence of differences with Fairbanks over the Free Soil movement. "It is supposed by some," Hosmer wrote, "that because I am to act as Commercial Reporter, for a paper of different political faith from *The Blade*, I have changed my faith. This is not so. To my Whig brethren I say adhere to the Whig faith as I shall."

The newspaper he joined was the Toledo *Republican*, with which *The Blade* carried on an almost continuous exchange of argument and vituperation for many months. The *Republican* was a leader in trying to bring together the Free Soilers (including some former Whigs) and the Democrats of Lucas County. The two groups held simultaneous conventions at nearby Swanton, on which *The Blade* commented, "These conventions did not come together, lest they should take fire and explode, or lest they should get so heated up as to burn up the dross, and thus destroy the mixture." Frequent satirical references to the Swanton conventions appeared in subsequent issues of *The Blade*, which summed them up August 18: "Married at Swanton, Lucas Co., Ohio, on Wednesday, the 15th inst., Mr. Radical M. Democracy and Miss Abby D. Freesoil, of this county."

What Hezekiah Hosmer had tried to achieve in his political maneuvering was revealed two weeks later in an announcement quoted by *The Blade* from the *Republican*. It reported that Robert A. Forsyth of Maumee City had been named Collector of the Port of Miami, but went on to elaborate:

> There were several competitors for the office, among whom we may name . . . H. L. Hosmer of this city. For a while it appeared that Mr. Hosmer would receive the appointment, but it is understood that Mr. Ewing refused to sanction his appointment, because he was commercial reporter for the Toledo *Republican*. If this be so, it is a fair specimen of the no party character of the Administration of Gen. Taylor.

To which *The Blade* responded "exactly so," adding that it should be understood "that there are enough good men and true in the Whig party to fill all the offices, without taking up a man whose politics are doubtful, to say the least of him."

Dr. Hosmer Graham, who operated the American Hotel in Toledo, became editor of *The Blade* on March 14, 1849, succeeding Hezekiah Hosmer. He resigned September 29, apparently as a result of a political disagreement with Abel Fairbanks only two weeks before the state and local elections. In the six months of his editorship, Dr. Graham seems to have been more interested in medicine and health than in politics. Long articles dealing with the circulatory system and other physiological and anatomical matters appeared in the editorial columns. An editorial on July 9 directed "the attention of our readers to the advertisement of Swaim's Panacea," citing its success in "curing diseases of the blood, liver, skin, &c, &c," and calling attention to the fact that "pamphlets showing some of the extraordinary cases may be seen at this office."

Cholera and its impact on Toledo's prospects for future growth also attracted Graham's attention. His concern was not so much with taking steps to control the disease as with minimizing the damage done by reports of its prevalence. An editorial titled "Health of Toledo" in the June 30 issue offers the following progression of arguments:

> This city has been retarded in its growth by false and exaggerated reports. It has been for several years represented by interested and irresponsible persons as one of the most unhealthy locations on the Lake shore; and for three or four years after its first settlement it was not the most healthy.
>
> The time has now come, when most of the rival cities and villages have ceased to be rivals, and the place is allowed to stand or fall upon its merits. The false and exaggerated reports of sickness have been lived down, and Toledo is now taking rank with the most healthy places . . .
>
> Real estate is rising rapidly in value and there is an increasing demand for it. Sales of real estate have been made within a few weeks showing an increase in price of three or four hundred per cent, in one year.
>
> Those who desire to secure good bargains in real estate, in this city, would do well to make their purchases as soon as possible.

Three weeks later, amid reports of cholera in epidemic proportion in various cities, listing numbers of deaths and other specific details, *The Blade* again "cautions our citizens against becoming excited and alarmed on the subject." Many persons, it was suggested, "become alarmed by hearing general conversation on the subject of cholera, or by hearing descriptions of particular cases." Finally, it was hoped that "there will be no feeling of disagreement between the Physicians and the Board of Health, but that all will act for the common good and harmony."

★ ★ ★

Abel W. Fairbanks disposed of his controlling interest in *The Blade* on November 17, 1849, and its owners and editors changed

The Blade Goes Daily

with some regularity for the next several years — until it was purchased by Joseph R. Williams in April, 1853.

Stephen T. Hosmer bought *The Blade* from Fairbanks. He had previously published the Maumee *Times,* worked as a printer for the newspaper he now owned, and had established the Fort Meigs *Reveille,* a Whig publication, at Perrysburg in 1843. Hezekiah L. Hosmer returned as editor and the business operated as S. T. Hosmer & Co.

The Hosmers had problems with the postal system and the magnetic telegraph companies during the first several months of their ownership and operation of *The Blade*. A steady stream of complaints appeared, such as this one on January 14, 1850:

> The telegraphic report for this day was arrested several times in its transmission, for a long period of time, by someone supposed to be in the Milan Office. It was probably a boy playing with the key.

The post office — specifically the Maumee post office — drew Hezekiah Hosmer's ire on February 12. The citizens of Perrysburg "say that they get the Cleveland papers with greater regularity than ours," *The Blade* declared, adding that "we are satisfied that the trouble is in the Maumee P.O. and shall proceed forthwith to enter complaints to the Department."

During the first few months of 1850, the editor's attention was drawn to such matters as the Webster-Parkman murder trial in Boston, the prospect of a concert appearance in Toledo by Jenny Lind (the Swedish nightingale), and completion of several new business buildings in the expanding downtown area. Relatively little attention was paid to political affairs, though the continuing controversy over the extension of slavery was sometimes the subject of editorial comment.

On May 21, in the course of urging approval of the Compromise of 1850, which had the support of President Taylor, *The Blade* advised its readers to "stand by Old Zack and the country is safe." Within less than two months, there was to be no "Old Zack" in the White House. *The Blade* mourned Taylor's death in the issue of July 10, its column rules reversed in the traditional tribute to an important individual at his death:

> A heavy calamity has befallen the nation! A great light has expired! Our President, in whom were centered our hopes for a successful issue of the most gloomy crisis in our national history is no more. Death has overthrown him at the moment when his usefulness seemed the greatest,

and when the hopes of the people clustered thick and heavy about him.
. . . What man so well calculated as he shall meet the present crisis in
our history! Alas! we know not, but tremble for the future while we write.

Only a few weeks previously, *The Blade* had declared of Vice President Millard Fillmore that "he has but a tittle of the influence of Gen. Taylor, either in the North or South." However, the new President's appointment of Daniel Webster as Secretary of State was heartily applauded, and his other cabinet choices were found to be "reliable, as advisers, and as Whigs."[15]

The Blade continued to say little about national politics and government during the remaining two and one-half years of Millard Fillmore's incumbency. The Hosmers' interests remained with the increasing numbers of visiting musicians, comedians and theatrical companies appearing in Toledo, as well as with civic boosterism and bickering with the Toledo *Republican*.

There was much agitation against the Fugitive Slave Law, but *The Blade*, while opposing some of its provisions, took a relatively moderate position concerning its enforcement, "so long as it is the law of the land." The *Republican's* much more radical position drew this comment from Hosmer:

> Our neighbor must excuse us from any further discussion of the Fugitive Slave Law until after the next session of Congress. We are perfectly willing that he should operate in a small way, whenever he can assemble from five to ten persons together to make a demonstration. The resolutions thus passed look as large on paper as if they had the sanction of the entire community. Go ahead neighbor. The game is too small for any one but you to play it.

Ownership of *The Blade* changed again on January 27, 1852, when it was announced that "by an arrangement, this day completed, *The Blade* will hereafter be published by the undersigned, as equal and joint proprietors, under the name of Latimer, Andrews & Co." H. L. Hosmer, P. E. Latimer and Samuel Andrews each now held a one-third interest, with Hosmer continuing as editor. Latimer and Andrews, the new partners, had each paid $2,500 for his share in the ownership.[16]

The new proprietors announced on February 4 that they had "determined as soon after the opening of navigation as practicable, to enlarge their daily paper to a size commensurate with the growth and business of the city, and the increasing wants of the community."

The promise was made good with the announcement in the issue of April 30:

The Blade Goes Daily

> Tomorrow we shall lay before our readers the first number of our enlarged daily paper. The dainty little sheet which for the past two years and a half it has been our pleasure to superintend, with this number gives place to one of more ample dimensions — an experiment, warranted as we believe, by the increasing growth and importance of our city . . . The era of newspaperial literature has just commenced. The daily press, already powerful, is to become the greatest arbiter of public opinion.

The editor's prescience about the future of newspapers in the United States should certainly be noted. As for "our enlarged daily paper," which appeared on May 1, it was printed on a larger sheet of newsprint than in the past, allowing for seven columns of type instead of five. The number of pages, however, remained at four per issue.

The Blade paid much attention in its expanded pages to the continuing expansion of the railroads, the approaching resolution of the extended fight over whether Toledo or Maumee should be the Lucas county seat, and to assorted specimens of visiting entertainers, including The Infant Drummer who was, *The Blade* assured its readers, "but three years and four months old," despite the rumor that he "has been three years old for several years past."

The national political situation in 1852 was muddled and confusing. Both major parties had lost many of their members to the anti-slavery parties; each was jockeying for position, attempting to satisfy the demands of the widely varying elements within its ranks. *The Blade* continued to avoid extensive comment. Henry Clay and Daniel Webster — both of whom would be dead before the November election — continued to be *The Blade's* favored candidates, although Clay's advanced age tended to rule him out. On April 21, Hosmer summed up the situation:

> There is no doubt that our State, in its Whig tendencies, is largely in favor of General Scott as the candidate for the Presidency . . . Although not our first choice, we shall support Gen. Scott as cordially as any other Whig, and shall go for an enthusiastic campaign if he is nominated . . .
> We have not for a moment doubted the power of the Whig party to elect their candidate, be he whom he may, and between such men as Fillmore, Webster and Scott, we have not thought that the Whig party could be dissatisfied with either. They are all proper men for the station.

Stalemate, which had been anticipated, developed in the national conventions of both major parties in 1852. The Democrats nominated Franklin K. Pierce, of New Hampshire, on the 49th ballot; the Whigs chose Gen. Winfield T. Scott on the 53rd. To give the South representation on their tickets, the Democrats chose as the vice presidential nominee William R. King of Alabama, the Whigs William A. Graham of North Carolina.

The Blade supported Scott, of course, although with no great show of enthusiasm. Having proclaimed the October state elections "a Whig triumph" — on the basis of some reduction in the Democratic margins of victory from two years previously, Hosmer insisted that the Whigs "will have less than an average majority of 8,000 to overcome with Gen. Scott — a thing so easily accomplished that it needs little more than reference." This proved harder than predicted, and Franklin K. Pierce was elected president. Hosmer called attention to the fact that "the Whigs have done nobly" in the rural districts, but "have been overthrown by the vote of the cities, where the population is of a character to be swayed by mercenary influences," which "have been employed without stint." *The Blade* would "speak more at length in a future article" of the reasons for the Whig defeat. The promised article came only two days later, providing an analysis of the tangled situation within the ranks of the Whigs, together with some candid commentary on the recent past:

> We believe that the Whig National Convention mistook the sense of the Nation, by nominating General Scott. The people were tired of the military test. It had not worked to suit them. No fault could be found with Harrison or Taylor, but both were old men when elected, both died before their policy was fairly developed, and as a whole the thing had been a failure. The administration of Mr. Fillmore had been satisfactory to both great parties. Questions both of domestic and foreign policy had been settled by it, in a manner highly creditable to the President, and honorable to the nation. Mr. Fillmore in his own person represented the opinion of a full moiety of the Whig party in the North, and all of it in the South, on the subject of Slavery.
>
> The Whigs composing this branch of the party, satisfied with his course, desired his renomination or the nomination of Daniel Webster. Either of these men would have been acceptable to a greater number of their own party than Gen. Scott. But other counsel ruled. Gen. Scott was understood to be the chosen candidate of Gov. Seward, and he was the first man to announce the doctrine that there was a law higher than the constitution, and this heretical dogma, from the supposed influence it would have in conciliating the free soil vote . . . dictated the nomination of General Scott. The effect began to develop itself in the Convention. The South withdrew and all hope of assistance from the Whigs in that portion of the Union expired before adjournment . . . That portion of the Whig party that regarded the defection of Seward on the Compromise as dictated by jealousy of Fillmore looked upon the nomination as a

stepping stone for the elevation of Seward, and from the first felt indifferent to the matter . . .

Mr. Webster, who, it was understood, would take the stump for Fillmore if nominated, was so much disappointed at the result that he by his conduct, declared his willingness that Scott should be defeated, and became himself the candidate of a large number of disaffected Whigs, who voted for him, even after his death.

The Blade reversed its column rules for Daniel Webster at his death on October 28, as it had for Henry Clay four months earlier. Of Webster, it was declared that "another Prince has fallen from Israel"; of Clay that "America has lost her most incorruptible statesman, the world one of the noblest beings that ever wore human form." Concluding its tribute to Webster, *The Blade* declared that "the last of that mighty trio — Clay-Calhoun-Webster — who for nearly half a century had occupied so large a space in the affections of the Nation, has at length departed."

One other event of 1852 that caught the attention of *The Blade* was publication of a book that was to assume particular significance in the intensifying conflict over slavery. The reviewer of *Uncle Tom's Cabin*, who used the initials P. P. D., had mixed feelings about Harriet Beecher Stowe's book. P. P. D. came to a conclusion that was very near the position *The Blade* had taken under various combinations of ownership since 1844, when Jesup Scott had resigned as editor:

> If I were asked to make a regular characterization of "Uncle Tom's Cabin," I should call it "an appeal to the passions of a political faction" — for that designates the office which it will mainly perform. It will be an inflamer of minds, already too much inflamed. It will cause men to rail loudly against an evil which they will not raise a finger to remedy in a practicable manner. — It will increase the potency of the idea that there is but "one evil under the sun," and will cause many difficulties to arise against those who wish for the happiness of all men, white as well as black, and who fully cherish the vision of America undivided, yet free from slaves, and the vision of Africa, enlightened and christianized by emigrants from our shores.

This is essentially the position taken by the more moderate elements among those who opposed slavery in the decade before the Union was all but torn apart. *The Blade* was opposed to the enslavement of human beings, but there was no talk of granting equal footing to the freed black men. It advocated sending them back to Africa as part of a grand scheme of colonization — to the greater glory of God and the nation that had magnanimously given them their freedom.

★ ★ ★

Joseph R. Williams was to take the lead in establishing *The Blade's* reputation as a leading exponent of liberal principles in this crucial period.

Williams was one of the group of land owners and businessmen who had met at the Mansion House in December, 1835, to launch the new weekly publication he claimed to have named *The Blade*. Now, returning from Michigan after almost fifteen years, he bought a controlling interest in the newspaper he had helped to establish, although his responsibilities in Michigan prevented him from taking charge as editor at the time of the purchase on April 25, 1853. Hezekiah Hosmer remained as editor until October, when he revealed in a valedictory editorial that sale of *The Blade* to Williams, for $6,000, had been forced because improvements in the paper and construction of a new building had proved too expensive for its previous owners.

In his introductory editorial, Joseph Williams provided evidence of the qualities that would bring about a considerable revitalization of *The Blade* under his editorship:

> On all topics of general interest, as they arise, on which it becomes our duty to speak, we shall speak in language that will not be misunderstood. The difficulty with us always has been, and probably will be, that we are too flatfooted . . .
> In politics it is very apparent that the people can no longer be managed by the old and corrupt devices, and machinery of parties. Men having no affinities or sympathies with each other, must in the end cease to co-operate with each other. The whole fabric of old party organizations is crumbling, and the fact is no longer concealed by honest, thinking, patriotic men.

Joseph Williams was an outspoken advocate of many positions that were regarded as radical at the midpoint of the 19th century. In an editorial captioned "The Dignity of Labor," he wrote that "terrible injuries are inflicted on society, and especially on the female sex, by the distribution, the appreciation, and the rewards of labor." And he added that in the United States "the great facts that beauty and strength, development, usefulness, and final respectability depend on labor, are not sufficiently taught." They should, he urged, "be taught everywhere, in the family, the school, and the college."

The Blade Goes Daily

Throughout his editorship, Williams kept *The Blade* in the forefront of the anti-slavery forces. Of the Fugitive Slave Law, he wrote that "every instance of its execution has made 5,000 Abolitionists." Of the Kansas-Nebraska Bill: "It may be passed. But such a storm of agitation will be raised as will never be allayed." Williams took the position from the beginning that outright abolition of slavery was impossible, and that it was unconstitutional, but he was equally insistent that the voters of the North must unite to prevent slavery from spreading to the Western territories and states.

Williams' observations in his salutatory editorial on Americans' disillusionment with the existing political parties were to prove prophetic. In the next year, both Whigs and Democrats who were opposed to the spread of slavery began to despair of accomplishing that within the system, and they began to break away from their party affiliations. A group of such dissidents in the Fifth Ohio Congressional District met at Defiance to pass a series of resolutions and to nominate a candidate for representative in Congress.

Richard S. Mott, a Quaker and a successful Toledo businessman, was that nominee. Designated an anti-Nebraska candidate, as were most Free Soilers in the 1854 election, Mott surprised everyone by sweeping to victory over the Democratic incumbent and a Whig in October. He won by 3,200 votes in a district that the Democrats had carried by 4,000 two years earlier. *The Blade*, which had supported Mott, was exultant, hailing the result as "not defeat only," but "annihilation" for the Pierce administration.

The Republican party was founded the same year, and under its banner the anti-slavery forces began to unite in 1855 and 1856. Joseph Williams was a delegate to the new party's first Ohio convention at Columbus in July, 1855, and helped nominate United States Senator Salmon P. Chase as the first Republican candidate for governor. Now *The Blade* formed an affiliation that was to dominate its political position in presidential elections from the time it endorsed the first Republican candidate, John C. Fremont, in 1856, until a century later, when it supported Adlai Stevenson, the Democrat, against President Dwight Eisenhower, seeking a second term. Only once during that period did *The Blade* fail to endorse the Republican candidate — in 1912, when it followed many Republicans into Theodore Roosevelt's Bull Moose party.

The presidential campaign of 1856, in which Fremont lost to

James Buchanan, the Democratic candidate, was the only one in which Joseph Williams took part as editor of *The Blade*. He wrote in his valedictory editorial, just a week before the election, of his experiences:

> We have controlled this organ for good or evil during a most eventful period . . . The audacious and avowed purpose of the Slave Power to usurp all the functions of the Government, and convert to its base uses the common territory, has aroused the people of the Free States to a concentration of action, which will be expressed at the polls on Tuesday next . . . To have aided in an humble way, in the revolution of opinion in Ohio, and to place this proud state in the front rank of the pending political contest, on the side of justice and truth, is a subject of proud satisfaction.

For a year before Williams sold *The Blade* to Clark Waggoner and Gideon T. Stewart, he had relatively little to do with its operation. Williams had all the qualities of a great editor and although he deserves to be ranked among the ablest men who have served *The Blade* in that capacity during its 150 years, his editorship was handicapped by two factors. One was illness; the other was that he knew very little about — and had relatively little interest in learning — the business and mechanical aspects of producing a newspaper. As newspapers developed from one-man operations into more and more complicated organizations, these were becoming matters of increasing importance.

Williams recognized these problems almost at once. As early as May 4, 1854 — little more than six months after he had taken charge of *The Blade* — he wrote: "We have found the task of managing a Daily paper as thankless and vexatious as it is declared to be by the most captious of the editorial tribe . . . The confinement and severity of the labor is such that we may be compelled to abandon the trust that we have undertaken. — Indeed that is the probability." Two weeks later, the editor apologized for "a dearth of editorial matter, and a lack of that attention in detail indispensable to a daily paper." The reason: "We find that our health is not proof against that continuous and prolonged exertion day after day necessary to sustain the several departments of the paper, in such a manner as we should prefer to sustain it." Further indication that Williams' health made it impossible for him to perform his usual activities was to be found in that letters from various prominent Toledoans, including Jesup W. Scott, often occupied the lead editorial position during much of this period.

The Blade Goes Daily

The first of Williams' several attempts to dispose of his property appeared at the head of the editorial columns on June 13, 1854: "The Proprietor of *The Blade* establishment offers the same for sale. His health is not adequate to support the duties which devolve upon him." The offer to sell appeared for several weeks thereafter, but found no takers.

Williams also was plagued during the next several months by a succession of human and mechanical failures that resulted in a series of apologies for failure to provide papers on time — or, in some instances, to provide them at all. In one instance, "a trifling yet material part of our Power Press broke" and there was no one who knew how to repair it. Less than a month later, "we have never failed to receive our regular supplies of paper till this issue." In another ten days, there was a delay "by accident" and, besides this, "two or three carrier boys are sick." A few months later: "Failed again today to receive paper till we were going to press, and therefore obliged to issue on half sheet." Next day the roof fell in:

> We began the week with one compositor short, the foreman was sick, a carrier boy tumbled into a cellar and left his papers that night near where they fell; our paper makers failed to supply us in time, because the drought has so interfered as to prevent the manufacture as fast as their customers demand . . .
>
> While we met with these casualties, we were now receiving under our new Telegraphic arrangements, a larger amount of news which required an increased skill and facility in making up the paper.

Joseph Williams went to Washington, D.C., late in November, 1855, leaving others to worry about putting out *The Blade* from day to day. The purpose of his trip was to secure from Congress its book binding contract for the coming year, a goal he finally accomplished the following February 22. The award (over more than 30 other aspirants) had been delayed by the three-month deadlock in the House over naming a Speaker — a result of a division between Republicans, Democrats, and members of the American party (often known as the Know-Nothings).

During much of this time, Williams provided regular reports from the nation's capital to *The Blade*, dealing largely with the fight over the speakership. Early in February — at about the time that the Republican candidate, N. P. Banks of Massachusetts, finally became the speaker — *The Blade* regretted the absence of "our interesting Washington correspondence," explaining that "Mr. W. has for some time been confined to his room from a severe attack of influenza."

On his return from Washington, Williams obviously had determined to extricate himself from the newspaper business. The editorial operation of *The Blade* had, by late February, 1856, been turned over to T. Spencer Sprague, listed in the masthead as Corresponding Editor, and Charles H. Sprague, designated Local Editor. An editorial six weeks later referred to the fact that "the editor of this paper has been absent from his post for a long time" and, in a following comment appeared the statement that "it is probable that we shall soon cease to publish and edit *The Blade*."

The limited evidence available suggests that Williams made a conditional sale of *The Blade* to the Spragues in April, at which time his name disappeared from the masthead as editor and proprietor. Williams returned to Washington, and reports from there (signed with his initial, W) appeared with regularity for several weeks. He came back to Toledo in July and announced an increase in the subscription price, complaining that it had been "most unwarrantedly reduced" in his absence and that "if the price were permanently reduced, the size and value would have to be proportionally diminished." An advertisement at the head of the editorial column in September announced that "The Toledo Blade Establishment Is Offered for Sale." On October 1, Clark Waggoner and Gideon T. Stewart became the new owners, but were unable to take over possession and management until November 1.

In his valedictory editorial, Williams reviewed the problems he had confronted as owner and editor of *The Blade*, restated his adherence to Free Soil principles, and concluded:

> When we surrender *The Blade*, we surrender an instrument that, for weal or woe, in the strife of the world, will be wielded for an indefinite period. While there is a Toledo, and newspapers are the instrument of business and dissemination of knowledge, there may be a Toledo Blade. Whoever wields it assumes an almost fearful trust . . . We hand *The Blade* over to our successors with the injunction, which was formerly inscribed on the exquisite and world-renowned Spanish blades of Toledo manufacture: "Never draw me without reason — never sheath me without honor."

In returning to the words that had been used in the first issue of *The Blade* more than twenty years earlier, Williams suggested a continuity that was both chronological and ideological. Over two decades, the newspaper he had helped to found had essentially lived up to the inscription on those earlier Toledo blades.

The Blade announced on May 4, 1857, that "Hon. Joseph R.

Williams, lately the editor and publisher of this paper, was to have left here today to assume the direction of Michigan State Agricultural College as its President." The investiture was to be held at Lansing on May 13, and it was announced that Williams would "set forth the design, objects and policy of the new institution more fully than they have yet been presented to the public." Williams continued as president of one of the first American colleges of agriculture and the mechanical arts until 1860, when the health problems that had begun during his stay in Toledo forced him to resign. He was elected to the Michigan Legislature and was presiding officer of its upper house when he died on June 15, 1861.

Chapter 4

The Coming of Civil Strife

The new ownership of *The Blade* provided a better balance of interests and abilities than Williams had possessed. Gideon T. Stewart was a businessman who had moved to Toledo from Norwalk, Ohio. Clark Waggoner had begun his career as an apprentice on the Milan, Ohio, *Times*. He had worked on a number of newspapers in northwestern Ohio and was for a time publisher of the *Lower Sandusky Whig* in Fremont. The political background of both men was Whig-Republican, though Stewart, an ardent advocate of prohibiting the sale of alcoholic beverages, was a sometime candidate for office on the Prohibition party ticket. In their salutatory editorial of November 1, 1856, Stewart and Waggoner declared that they would "offer no other assurances than those of their own personal sentiments and political antecedents that *The Blade* "shall be thoroughly Republican in its spirits and principles."

The same editorial did contain evidence, however, that the new owners had some ideas about the role of the American newspaper that were different from those of previous owners of *The Blade* and that they intended to put these into practice:

> After the issue of our next Weekly, we will devote more space than under the pressure of the presidential contest it has been possible to afford, to subjects and interests out of the political field. We will attempt to enlarge the amount of literary and miscellaneous reading, and to furnish matter of value to the Merchant, Mechanic, and Farmer. The local and commercial columns will be under the charge of Mr. S. G. Arnold, late Editor of the Syracuse Daily Chronicle, who brings with him a high reputation and an editorial experience of nearly 23 years.

Arnold, who had joined *The Blade* staff on October 1, promptly implemented changes along the lines indicated by the new owners. The nation stood in 1856 at the brink of an era in which such federal legislation as the Morrill Act and the Homestead Act would enhance working men's opportunities to get a better education, to become land owners, and generally to improve their social and economic lot. This was the real beginning of social mobility in the United States, translating the tenets of Jacksonian democracy into something more than universal suffrage. Already, elementary and secondary schools had begun to grow, and literacy was on the increase. Inevitably, these forces influenced newspapers. Although the party press did not disappear at this point, newspapers began to take on a much greater diversity, and *The Blade*, under its new ownership and management, provided a typical study of these nationwide developments.

Politics did not, of course, disappear from its pages. Less than a week after the new owners had taken charge, the presidential election contest involving the first Republican candidate was decided, in favor of James Buchanan, the Democrat. The owners of *The Blade*, who had supported John C. Fremont, the Republican, in his race against Buchanan and Millard Fillmore, the American (or Know-Nothing) candidate, clearly were not pleased:

> Mr. Buchanan will come into the government under very extraordinary circumstances, and we do not see how he can be anything else than a mere instrument in the hands of the Slave Power. No President was ever chosen before on a purely sectional idea . . .
> Mr. Buchanan will also go into the Government in a lean minority. We have had Presidents before who were elected by a minority, but none under any such circumstances as Mr. Buchanan. The majority against him will be overwhelming. He will not be the Executive of the people, but of a very small minority and that minority representing not the Democratic ideas of opinion and justice, but of despotism, force and brutality.

Rationalizations of Buchanan's victory over Fremont in subsequent issues are interesting. A single township in northern Illinois is cited for its overwhelming vote in favor of Fremont, and it is pointed out that the township produced huge amounts of grain crops during the past year. "Intelligence, thrift, and a love of Freedom always go hand in hand," it is observed. *The Blade* cites by way of contrast a congressional district in southern Illinois, carried overwhelmingly by Buchanan, which "contains eleven thousand one hundred and eighty-six persons who can neither read nor write."

The innovations promised by the new owners did, however, begin to make their appearance. More local news — mostly of the bits-and-pieces sort — was found in each issue. A Wit and Humor department was inaugurated. Changes in the editorial page were numerous. More news items and advertising began to appear on this second page of each issue. A number of special departments — Art and Science, Agricultural Items, Weather Items, and others — became regular features of the page. *The Blade*'s own editorial commentary, which had rarely occupied fewer than two columns, often three or four, now averaged only about a column daily.

Never in its history a sensational newpaper, *The Blade*, like other mid-19th century newspapers, did at this point reflect a kind of morbid interest in exaggerated realism in describing various disasters. An editorial captioned "Dreadful Accidents" in the December 12 issue provides grisly descriptions of half-a-dozen accidents involving fire, acid, scalding water, and other horrors, following this rationalization: "Our exchanges lately seem to abound with accounts of the most terrible casualties on land and water. Many of these have been the result of neglect and indiscretion, and such we would publish not merely as a matter of news, but as a warning to the public against similar error and disaster." Equally gruesome details in a later editorial on the punishment of participants in slave insurrections in the South were, perhaps, unlikely to serve the same purpose.

The first instance of detailed coverage of a local criminal case provided further indication of changes in *The Blade*. The telegraph had reported crime at a distance, but a murder close to home received little more than passing mention. There was no such reticence when J. M. Ward was arrested in February, 1857, for the murder of his wife, Olive, in Sylvania. Gruesome details of the way in which Ward was alleged to have slain his wife and disposed of her body were there for all to read. When Ward's trial began the next month, an editorial promised daily coverage, which was generously supplied. A full account of the testimony and arguments by attorneys, running four to six columns, appeared for each of the next several days. The jury deliberated for only half an hour on March 26 before finding Ward guilty as charged. *The Blade* editorialized that "Ward has not yet had his sentence but he will hang by the neck 'til he is dead, dead." Three full columns were devoted to the life and death of J. M. Ward — including a graphic description of the hanging — when that unjudicial prophecy was fulfilled on June 12.

On March 9, 1857, the United States Supreme Court handed down its decision in the Dred Scott case, declaring that a Negro slave was not a citizen of the United States and could not sue in a federal court. *The Blade* characterized the decision as one "that will strike the world with horror." It made the government "the instrument of oppression and despotism," declaring in favor of "attainting the blood of four millions of persons." Six weeks later, the Ohio Legislature approved a measure to prohibit slave-holding in the state. *The Blade* rejoiced, declaring that "Ohio takes the lead in condemning the action of the partizan (sic) United States Court."

In June, 1857, a young congressman from Illinois attracted the attention of the newspaper that would soon become one of his avid admirers. It offered this comment:

> Judge (Lyman) Trumbull and the Hon. A. Lincoln have lit into Stephen A. Douglas pretty severely.
>
> The latter gentleman followed the little demagogue in a speech at Springfield and walked into his positions in a way which was exceedingly cruel.
>
> He showed how exactly identical were the positions of Douglas with the divine right of kings, the aristocracy of the old world and the tyranny of all the ages.

The full text of Lincoln's Springfield speech appeared subsequently in two issues of *The Blade,* with the approving comment that "there is a smoothness, clearness and facility in Mr. Lincoln's statements which are peculiar and which make his speech one of the most readable and attractive within the range of our recollection."

The Blade regretted Lincoln's defeat by Douglas in the contest for the latter's seat in the United States Senate a year later. The series of debates between the two was followed closely, and there was never any doubt in the editor's mind that Lincoln held a decided advantage. When Douglas was elected in November, 1858, *The Blade* concluded that Illinois voters had "given him credit for the good he had done, but have failed to find that he has regular and steady principles," adding that "we shall see how he behaves now." Only a few days later, *The Blade* demanded that Douglas "give up his seat to Lincoln," having discovered that the Republican candidate had received a plurality of the popular vote and that Douglas owed his election to an unfair apportionment system in the Illinois Legislature.

★ ★ ★

Alonzo D. Pelton joined Stewart and Waggoner in partnership in 1859, remaining in the firm with Waggoner after Stewart left Toledo in 1860 to become owner of the Dubuque (Iowa) *Times.* Pelton was a businessman, member of the Toledo Board of Trade, and a prime mover in the railroad boom of the period. His initial interest in the newspaper was primarily financial, though he subsequently became involved in other aspects of its operation.

The Blade had for some time prior to 1859 been carrying on a running fight with Abner L. Backus, a member of the Ohio Board of Public Works, over a number of issues — the principal one being alleged fraud in canal construction in the state. Clark Waggoner found another point of attack when he discovered that Paul Edwards, named by Backus to be canal collector for the port of Toledo, had been twice convicted of gambling. When Waggoner raised the issue in the columns of *The Blade*, the consequences for him were considerable, as he described them in the issue of July 9:

> Leaving *The Blade* office at my usual hour for tea, last evening, I passed down the south side of Summit street alone, except for the presence of my little son, some 11 years of age. I had passed the store of W. J. Finlay but a few feet when, without the slightest warning or indication of the presence of hostile designs of any one, I was violently struck, from behind, on the side of my head, and immediately caught and held. Stunned by the force of the blow, I was bewildered and only sensible of blows and restraints. Thus, with no intelligent conception of my real situation or knowledge as to my assailant, I struggled as well as I could. While thus struggling, passersby interposed and liberated me from the grasp of the assaulter, whom, for the first time, I then found to be Paul Edwards, the Canal Collector at this Port . . .
>
> The only explanation I have from my assaulter of his reasons for this attack upon me, was afterwards received through third parties. To them he stated that it was made in consequence of the comments in the editorial columns of *The Blade* in regard to his fitness for the public situation which he occupies and which comments he attributed to my pen . . .
>
> In all that I have written in this connection, and in making the above plain statement of fact, I have sought to avoid everything in any way calculated unnecessarily to provoke any man's passions. What I have done has been under a deep sense of duty to the public and to this community . . .
>
> In conclusion, I will say that if the time has arrived in Toledo when my life as a public journalist is hazarded by denouncing the vice and crime of Gambling, it is very plain to my mind that the time has also arrived when it is time for somebody to take that hazard, and attempt to arouse the community to a sense of its true condition and great danger.

With this trumpet blast, Clark Waggoner was embarked on an attempt to arouse the community, and he enjoyed every minute of it. An editorial intended to further this campaign appeared in almost every issue of *The Blade* during the next several weeks. The captions

The Coming of Civil Strife 47

at the head of the editorials appearing in the issues of July 11-14 suggest their nature and purpose:

THE GAMBLING QUESTION
IS CRIME A MATTER OF PUBLIC CONCERN?
THAT IS THE QUESTION
ABNER L. BACKUS AND HIS APPOINTMENTS
MR. BACKUS ON CRIME — A GRATIFYING IMPROVEMENT

Waggoner's crusade went on. The minor injuries he suffered when Paul Edwards attacked him were a small enough price for his pleasure in wielding his editorial shillelagh against gambling, Abner Backus, and the unfortunate Edwards.

Then, on October 16, 1859, occurred what *The Blade* first described as a "disturbance" at Harper's Ferry, Virginia. "Not as alarming as the sensitiveness of a slave-holding community would indicate" was the way Clark Waggoner described it, but its implications were "still very serious." It was observed that "many readers will be surprised to learn that a prominent leader in these operations is Capt. John Brown, or 'Ossawatomie' Brown, as he is known in Kansas," who was "formerly an active business man in Summit county." Latest reports by telegraph, it was suggested in conclusion, "show that the insurgents have been pretty much subdued, and that order will soon be fully restored."

The Blade, like many other anti-slavery newspapers, was caught in an uncomfortable situation by the events at Harper's Ferry. Almost none could condone the assault on a federal arsenal with plans to lead a slave insurrection. Yet their sympathies were clearly with John Brown — insane or not — and they grasped for ways to rationalize his actions. Only a day after the first report, for example, *The Blade* contended:

> It hardly lies with the Democratic papers and leaders who defended all the outrages on Brown (in Kansas) now to affect a holy horror at his madness. Had the Federal Government exhibited a tithe of the anxiety to sustain the laws and protect innocent men, women and children from infuriated Missouri Border Ruffians in Kansas, that it has to quell this insurrection of twenty-two fanatics, Brown's mind would never have been distraught, as it now is . . .

The extent to which the whole fabric of the Union was damaged by the trial and execution of John Brown and his associates at Harper's Ferry is illustrated by the comments appearing in *The Blade* during the next few weeks. Here was a newspaper that had stood firmly in defense of the Constitution, even when, through the

Fugitive Slave Law, it was interpreted to place the property rights of slaveholders above the civil rights of human beings. Now it began to waver in its often expressed belief that slavery, where it already existed, was entitled to the protection of the law. At the conclusion of John Brown's trial, on November 3, *The Blade* speculated about his sentence:

> The truth is, the character of Brown's trial, together with his own manly and undaunted bearing, have raised very serious doubts in the minds of the Virginia authorities as to the policy of hanging him. It is getting to be understood more than it has been that while the mass of people at the North are firm and faithful to the Union and its compromises, and would not brook any assault upon the rights of Slaveholders, their sympathies and feelings are constantly and decidedly on the side of the Slave, and are ready for expression on any occasion which commends itself to their judgment. Their hearts are with the Slave, while their allegiance alone binds them to the Master.

It was another month before John Brown's execution, and in that time fresh doubts had grown in the mind of Clark Waggoner. *The Blade* took notice of the hanging in Virginia on the day sentence was carried out — December 2 — with these comments:

> The memories with which the second of December will be associated will long make it a notable point in each revolving calendar. Whatever may be thought of the right or wrong of the act for which John Brown today suffers on a Virginia gallows, there is that in the evident purpose of the humanity underlying it which constitutions nor compromises can induce men with hearts to condemn. That he dies, we may be bound to regard as right. Indeed, when we contemplate the apparent readiness for expiation, there is little ground left for regrets on that score. But the great and fatal cause — the cause of Slavery — which demands such sacrifices for the exercise of the clear and most humane promptings of our manhood — what shall be said of it? Shall we go on and cherish it as one of our National glories? Shall we strengthen it in its present positions and extend its power and demands to new Territories? That's a practical question to be discussed hereafter.

The Blade found little in the events of the next year to offer hope that the "practical question" of what should be done about slavery could be amicably resolved.

That same December, the U.S. House began a fight over election of a speaker that would extend to February 1, 1860. The slavery issue was at the heart of the struggle.

John Sherman of Ohio was the Republican candidate in a three-way contest involving candidates of the Democratic and American (Know-Nothing) parties as well, and a protracted debate over slavery on the floor of the House preceded the balloting for the speakership. *The Blade* observed that the debate, "disorderly and furious as it was and is in its purposes, will not be without its good fruits." It would show that the Republicans "are after all the only party to which the friends of the Union can now look for a restoration of the peace and good will, which marked the feeling of the country when Jefferson, Madison and Monroe administered the government on Republican principles."

The House was able to elect a speaker only after John Sherman withdrew. He was particularly obnoxious to Southern representatives, it was charged, because he had endorsed Hinton Helper's *The Impending Crisis of the South,* which *The Blade* characterized as combining "the most vile and atrocious sentiments." Clark Waggoner described the fight in the House as "a concentration of Southern gentlemen against Sherman." It was, as had been the case two years earlier, essentially a North vs. South conflict. Not entirely, however. After William Pennington of New Jersey — the Republican choice after Sherman's withdrawal — had been elected, the following appeared in *The Blade* of February 6:

> LET NORTHERN DEMOCRATS REMEMBER THAT
> George H. Pendleton
> C. L. Vallandigham
> William Howard
> Charles D. Martin
> and Samuel D. Cox
> Democratic Congressmen from Ohio, abandoned their party organization and went over to the Know-Nothing Caucus nominee for Speaker.

There was good news for Toledo Republicans early in April, 1860, when their party swept the municipal elections — a sharp reversal in a city where Democrats had been consistent winners. Waggoner thought this was an omen of Republican success in the upcoming presidential election, which was to get under way within the month when the Democratic convention was to be held in Charleston, South Carolina.

The disintegration of that Charleston convention was an indication of what lay ahead for the nation. When delegates from nine southern states walked out after a bitter fight over platform recommendations on protecting slavery in the territories from local interference, the convention adjourned to meet in Baltimore in June. "The result of these things cannot be otherwise than good for the country," *The Blade* declared, "and it only remains now for the Republicans to go steadily forward, make up a good ticket, maintain their present conservative position, and walk over the field."

The Blade made sure it got the full story of the Chicago convention of the Republicans in May. Plans were announced on May 15 for a Daily Extra Blade, an unusual step for a newspaper of its size at the time:

> In view of the absorbing interest felt by all classes and parties in the Chicago Convention, we have made arrangements, in addition to the regular telegraph facilities, for a Special Report to embrace a more full and complete record of the proceedings than has ever been furnished of any similar body . . .
>
> In order to get the Chicago news as early as possible to our city readers and those to be reached by the morning trains, we shall issue a Daily Morning Extra, to contain all the reports received during the night . . .
>
> This arrangement will involve no small amount of additional labor and expense, but we cheerfully meet it, believing that the interest in the expected news will ensure a proper appreciation of our efforts in the premise.

The Blade had endorsed no candidate for the Republican nomination prior to the convention, but it had made no secret of its admiration for Abraham Lincoln, having followed closely his unsuccessful campaign against Stephen A. Douglas for the Senate and having lauded his performance in the series of debates between the two in Illinois. When the Chicago convention nominated Lincoln on the third ballot, *The Blade* declared that "by this action the Great West has a candidate, one who is not afraid to work and one whom we can work for with confidence of success." Lincoln was described as "no new man, of questionable character and principles, sprung upon the people by party legerdemain; but is a statesman of known ability, a Republican firm in the faith, and in all respects reliable, and a man against whose good name the bitterest opponent has not dared to raise a suspicion."

Waggoner and his associates did have some problems with the proper spelling of Lincoln's first name. It was spelled Araham on May 18, then changed to Abram on May 19, before finally appearing as Abraham on May 21 — and thereafter. One can only speculate on the significance — if any — of the fact that most of the highly laudatory material concerning the Republican candidate which appeared on the editorial page during the next several weeks was reprinted from other sources — much of it from various Chicago newspapers. It is possible that Waggoner actually had some reservations about Lincoln as the party's candidate. More likely is that he simply did not feel sufficiently familiar with Lincoln's political and personal record to offer comments of his own.

Stephen A. Douglas was the candidate of the Northern and Western wing of the Democratic party, John C. Breckenridge, senator from Kentucky who had been James Buchanan's vice president, was the candidate of the Democratic Southern wing; John Bell, senator from Tennessee, ran as the candidate of the Constitutional Unionists, a party of former Whigs and other conservatives whose aim was the preservation of the Union.

Once the campaign was under way, *The Blade* devoted much more time and space to attacking the other three candidates than it did to lauding Lincoln. Douglas was most often the target of Waggoner's barbs. Much was made of the argument that voters whose position on the slavery issue was moderate would waste their ballots if they cast them for Douglas. If, as seemed likely, Breckenridge and Bell carried all or most of the southern and border states, Douglas would get very few votes in the Electoral College. There was, of course, a strong possibility that the election would fail to return a candidate with an Electoral College majority, throwing the decision into the House of Representatives. Waggoner sought to persuade readers that this was a Lincoln vs. Breckenridge contest and that, surely, they would prefer even a "Black Republican" to the candidate of the "Seceders."

The Blade also gave strong support in the 1860 election to James M. Ashley, who had been elected to Congress in 1858 and was seeking a second term. Although Clark Waggoner and, later, David Ross Locke were to become increasingly disenchanted with the radical Republican views of the man who came to be known in the Reconstruction era as "Impeachment" Ashley, there was no reservation in this election about the preference of Ashley over the Democratic candidate, General James B. Steedman.

There was much joy when the state and local elections in October produced a Republican sweep in Ohio, as well as Pennsylvania, Indiana, and other neighboring states. "We have met the enemy, in all their multiplied and pie-bald forms — singly and combined," *The Blade* exulted, adding that "the result of yesterday's contest is the most overwhelming victory that was ever achieved in this City and County." Congressman Ashley carried Toledo, though his margin was only 176 votes. He gained a 1,200-vote advantage in the district.

Clark Waggoner resorted to a favorite device of editorial writers of the times when, in the October 29 issue, he made his prediction about the outcome of the presidential election:

> OBITUARY
>
> DIED, at his residence in Pennsylvania, of Internal Corruption, on the evening of October 9th, SHAM DEMOCRACY, whose grandfather was Nullification, whose father was Disunion. He leaves his only son, Slavery Extension, in very feeble health. He cannot survive and his funeral will probably be attended on the Fourth of March next, at Washington. The services will be conducted by A. Lincoln. Friends of the family are invited to be present.

When Lincoln was elected, with a plurality of the popular vote and a clear majority in the Electoral College, *The Blade* proclaimed in headlines:

> THE BATTLE FOUGHT AND THE VICTORY WON
> ABRAHAM LINCOLN TRIUMPHANTLY ELECTED
> GLORY ENOUGH FOR FOUR YEARS

Lincoln had a majority of more than 1,000 votes over Douglas in Lucas County; he won Ohio by 45,000.

The Blade's post-election editorials contained almost no specific comment on Abraham Lincoln, or the problems he faced in assuming the presidency. The country was, of course, abuzz with talk of the secession of several southern states, whose spokesmen had threatened such action if the candidate of the "Black Republicans" should win the election. Waggoner may have hoped to calm the atmosphere, and he did suggest that ways might be found to resolve the conflict. Within a month, it was to be made clear that this was a futile hope.

The Blade had by now had enough of compromise. Its reaction to threats of secession being heard in Congress and in the southern capitals was predictably firm. On December 7, Waggoner wrote: "The remarkable course of the Fire Eaters in Congress and in the Cotton States, is fast bringing efforts to a crisis, and it is certainly to be hoped that those who regard the Union of our Fathers as worth saving, will stand firm and await the issue." Then, on December 12, under the headline IS IT WAR?:

> Circumstances daily occurring — well authenticated reports reaching us almost hourly by telegraph and the mails — irresistibly force us to face an unpleasant question ...
>
> Should the Secessionists, in their madness, compel an affirmative answer, History would show no clearer and nobler example of forbearance

The Coming of Civil Strife 53

under provocation than that now exercised by the Majority, who are entitled to rule this country, toward the insane Minority of Secessionists who are endeavoring to ruin it.

Newspapers had begun to use various graphic devices only recently, and *The Blade* published one of these — a sketch of Charleston harbor — on January 7, 1861, along with information concerning the vulnerable fortifications at Fort Sumter, Fort Moultrie, and Castle Pinckney. Waggoner was sure that Sumter might have been made secure with "a reasonable degree of energy and decision on the part of the Executive," meaning, of course, James Buchanan, who was still President.

The Blade saw some hope in the upcoming inauguration of Abraham Lincoln. "If the people are as true to the Constitution and the Union as Abraham Lincoln will prove himself to be, we need have no anxiety for the future," Waggoner wrote on February 9. Lincoln was inaugurated on March 4, 1861. He named Salmon P. Chase, United States Senator from Ohio, to be his Secretary of the Treasury. Some regarded Chase as too radical on the question of emancipation, but *The Blade* was pleased at this recognition of a fellow Ohioan whom it had supported in the past — first for Governor, then for the seat he now held in the Senate.

★ ★ ★

Would there be war between the Union and the Confederacy? Clark Waggoner was among many Americans who believed it was inevitable. "These piping times of Secession and threatened war," as Waggoner described them on January 3, 1861, were also a time for newspapers to expand their readership, and *The Blade* boasted that "by the present arrangement of trains, we are enabled to send *The Blade* over most of the Roads so as to furnish later news than any other paper."

On the same day he was boasting of prompt service to readers of *The Blade*, Waggoner took heart at news from Washington to the effect that "the President has determined to adopt the policy of Messrs. Holt and Stanton, the Acting Secretary of War and Attorney General, in the management of South Carolina," which meant that he had determined "to go forward in the use of means to preserve the integrity of the Union, and the enforcement of the laws."

When, on the morning of January 9, Secessionist guns fired on the *Star of The West*, a steamer carrying provisions and reinforcements to Fort Sumter, on its way into Charleston Harbor, *The Blade* described it as "an act of open war against the United States" and proclaimed THE WAR COMMENCED. There were follow-up stories on the trials of the *Star of The West,* including a first-person account by one of the ship's passengers, reprinted from the New York *Evening Post.* But war had not yet commenced, though the number of states approving resolutions of secession increased, as did reports of those states' members of Congress leaving Washington. Louisiana on January 28 became the seventh state to secede, with Texas soon to follow. Waggoner saw an occasional ray of hope, but these were few and their number dwindled.

Above all else, Waggoner and *The Blade* now opposed proposals which came from many sources to effect a compromise with the Secessionists by making concessions on protection and extension of slavery. Stephen A. Douglas was taken to task on January 28 for having declared that he was "ready to make any sacrifice of opinion or of consistency to save the Union." There was even concern about what Lincoln might do when he became President. NO SURRENDER was the headline of Waggoner's February 11 editorial:

> The deep solicitude now pervading every section of the country as to the course of the new administration in regard to the grave questions which now threaten the destruction of the government, will soon be relieved by the development of his policy. No Executive ever assumed the head of the government under circumstances so critical to the nation or so trying to himself. The anxiety and doubt as to his purposes are made the more intense by at least a seeming difference of opinions among his political friends. This state of things cannot continue long. In a few short days, the nation will know what effect treason and folly have had on Mr. Lincoln's mind, and to what extent his faith in the principles which secured his election has been affected by the assaults made and being made upon constitutional liberty and good government.

The editorial concluded: "Our confidence in his firmness and patriotism is unshaken." Certainly few editors remained so firmly committed as Clark Waggoner was to the notion that the people of the Union must adhere to the leadership of their President. Even when he might question the advisability of a specific act or policy of Lincoln's, Waggoner kept *The Blade* foursquare behind the President. Again and again, he would cite the need to support policies formulated by the nation's Commander in Chief. *The Blade's* loyalty to Lincoln in this role began on March 4, 1861, with his inauguration, and continued until April 14, 1865, when he was assassinated.

★ ★ ★

Clark Waggoner professed to take some comfort in Abraham

Lincoln's inaugural address. "Nothing like menace or ill-feeling is shown by him," *The Blade* declared on March 5, adding that Lincoln "evidently relies on the 'sober second thought' of the people of the seceding states, encouraged by a conciliatory, yet firm policy on his part, for the deliverance of the government from its difficulties." Two weeks later, Waggoner took heart in reports that seemed to suggest that neither Missouri nor Virginia would leave the Union. Signs were now "most positive" that none of the remaining Slave States could "be induced to join the Southern Confederacy." On the contrary, "Union men in the Seceded States will ere long begin to make themselves heard, and the demagogues who have dragged them into this suicidal position will be thrown overboard."

THINGS LOOK BRIGHTER was the headline for this commentary. Not for long, however. An April 6 headline declared that WAR IS COMING and, two days later, there was a report that "the anticipated blow has not yet been struck; but the preliminaries continue to go forward with activity." Then, on April 13:

THE WAR BEGUN!
STARTLING NEWS FROM CHARLESTON!

By our last night's telegraph report, we got the news of the commencement of hostilities at Charleston. The information thus received was to the effect that the battle was commenced by cannonading from Fort Moultrie and other points upon Sumter at 4 o'clock yesterday morning. — That the fire was moderately responded to by Major Anderson until 7 o'clock, when his shots were more heavy and constant.

Allowing that the reports we get are reliable, the indications are certainly not favorable for Major Anderson . . . But whatever may be the fate of the noble hero of Sumter and his gallant little band, the cause in which he fights will not perish. They may be sacrificed, but thousands of brave men will fly to fill the gap which their loss shall create.

"The blow is struck!" *The Blade* thundered. "The time when the friends of constitutional government and civil liberty must take their position for or against the government has arrived." A call to citizens to rally to the Union cause concluded the editorial. Toledo's response was immediate and enthusiastic. So was *The Blade's*. A mass meeting to demonstrate loyalty to the Union was held on April 15, of which Waggoner wrote: "It is one: One for the Right, One for the Flag; and one with a terribly meaning emphasis against the Confederate Traitors."

There were more tangible responses. Members of the Toledo Wide Awakes, a political club organized in 1860 to help elect Lincoln, were summoned to redeem their pledge that, if a rebellion should break out, they would support the President to the fullest extent. Three companies of soldiers were organized and ordered to Union Army headquarters in Cleveland. *The Blade* reported on April 18 that "work of enlistment is progressing here actively, and the enthusiasm is more general and deeper than at any former time." *The Blade* proposed a plan to raise money from local residents for families who had lost members to the armed services. Contributions the first day amounted to $3,000. A MILITARY NOTICES column was introduced in the April 20 issue for publication of meetings of military units, notices from the government, announcements of local citizens who planned to raise military companies.

When the Northwest Regiment left Toledo on April 25, Waggoner provided a graphic account, using the implications of the departure to stir patriotic sentiment:

> The leave-taking of the gallant men who left Toledo this morning, with the display of interest and sympathy for them and the noble cause in which they go, proved the most impressive scene ever witnessed in this section. With those who participated in or observed it, its memory will never be lost. Amid all the solemnity of parting friends common on such occasions, there was an evident fixedness of purpose on the part of the volunteers and a cheerful resignation among those they left which clearly marked the earnestness with which our people enter into the war, and their willingness to make any sacrifice to give the Government efficiency and success.
>
> If the Governor says so, he can have three more such regiments from the Northwest on ten days notice. One of them could easily have been raised at the depot this morning, had that vast crowd but known it was wanted.

The Blade provided its readers with extensive telegraph reports of developments in the early days of the war, including accounts of the fighting, along with items about Toledo men in army camps. But anyone looking at its front page would have had no notion that a war was in progress. The long-standing practice — carrying over from British newspapers — of reserving page one to advertising messages continued to prevail. News of the war was relegated to the third page, with an occasional overflow to page two. In most issues, a brief summary of the day's developments appeared at the top of the first column of editorials under a one-line headline, THE NEWS. This usually contained some editorial opinion or interpretation, along with news reports. Typical is the following from the issue of April 22:

> The indications are by no means favorable for an early peace. The

madness of the traitors is past conception, and the people of the loyal states may calculate that their best efforts will be called into requisition if they expect to sustain the government as it should be done. They should be prepared for further calls for troops and money, and give a response worthy of themselves and the glorious cause for which they contend.

Chapter 5

A Steady Voice for the Union

No other war in the nation's history has presented such serious problems about the role of the press and its freedom to report day-to-day developments at the front and behind the lines. There were also to be challenges to the First Amendment provisions in the matter of criticizing the Government and its policies. Was this treason?

Even before the fighting had begun, there were questions about access to information. When rumors of the evacuation or reinforcement of Fort Sumter were rife, *The Blade* reminded its readers on April 4 that "these reports have neither been endorsed nor contradicted by any member of the Administration." Nor was there, as had been the case in the Buchanan Administration, a "traitorous spy in the Cabinet to divulge its secrets to the secessionists." Clark Waggoner left no doubt where he and his newspaper stood in this matter:

> Our people have not been used to this thing of the Government keeping its own secrets, and it will take a little time for them to get out of their minds the idea which the practice of the last Administration created, that the deliberations of the Cabinet must be known to the public as soon as it closes its sessions. When this is accomplished, the public will pay less attention to the vaporing of professional newsmongers, and await with patience the announcement of the policy of the Administration.

Resolute as Waggoner was in support of the Administration's war policies — including those affecting the press — he had obvious reservations about the consequences of some of them. There is a clearly plaintive note in this EXPLANATORY on July 10:

> If from this time on, we do not furnish the usual amount of startling war news, the reader must excuse the fact on the ground that the government has seen fit, so to speak, to clip the wings of telegraphic

A Steady Voice for the Union

imagination. So, for the present, farewell to the old round of sensational dispatches! The "gentleman" who has so regularly "come in" from Fort Monroe, Richmond, Manassas, Fairfax, &c, now finds his occupation gone." We suppose the "Grand Army" will not "move forward" either "tomorrow" or "next day," now. Everything must come to a standstill. The war at once becomes prosaic and must rely upon old fogeys like Scott for its management. How gloomy the prospect!

Whatever doubts *The Blade's* editor may have had about leaving such decisions in the hands of General Winfield Scott, he had no reservations about newspapers' responsibility to avoid publishing materials that might harm the Union cause. Only six months after the war had begun, General John C. Fremont, who headed the Union forces in the West, was the subject of charges on which a court-martial was to be based. Waggoner deplored publication of the charges and Fremont's response to them as "grossly wrong, and their circulation as only calculated to provoke feeling and divide public sentiment on essential points." While General Fremont was "at the head of an army on an important march," while he was "exerting his best endeavors to drive out the rebels from Missouri, and retrieve our late reverses so far as it is within his power," *The Blade* "had not thought it fit" to circulate either charges or counter-charges.

A more blistering indictment of the performance of some newspapers in this time of national crisis was forthcoming only ten day later, on October 18. It was, Waggoner wrote, "a shame to those concerned in it and an outrage upon the country." The papers referred to, he continued, "seem to regard it as their special duty and the highest evidence of their wisdom and usefulness, to carp and cavil at every assailable step of the Government, and those of all prominent officers, except such as they may have selected as favorites and objects of their indiscriminate praise." The deplorable results were to create "a popular distrust in the capacity, if not in the fidelity of the National Government," of which a direct result was "difficulty in recruiting for the Army and a backwardness in subscriptions to the National Loan." What was the remedy? "More consideration on the part of the press and the people, and the exertion of greater patience and a more just faith in the Government," Waggoner concluded.

Neither had *The Blade* any doubt as to where the responsibility lay for General George McClellan's action, a week later, forbidding the sending by telegraph of the war dispatches of newspaper correspondents unless approved by the Government, prohibiting their transmission to the public except through the medium of the Associated Press:

> The present step has been rendered necessary by the refusal of presses represented at Washington to heed the request repeatedly made by the Government in regard to Army plans and movements. It will be recollected that Gen. McClellan not only made a general request of this kind, but a special one with reference to the naval expedition, in neither of which were his wishes regarded . . . As a result of this policy on the part of the press, we have the present censorship of the telegraph, and may yet have the same applied to the mails.

The Union press had little good news to report from the front during these first six months of the fighting. Yet Waggoner and *The Blade* never wavered in their support of the Union cause and of Abraham Lincoln as President. After a succession of Union reverses in the Peninsular campaign and on the Western fronts in September, *The Blade* insisted that perfect unity of action on the part of Government and people was essential to success, concluding that "we must have one head to control all movements, and that head must have the full and cordial support of the Army, the Navy, and loyal citizens."

There were few limits on the extent to which *The Blade* would go to preserve the Union and to deal with those whom it described on May 10, less than a month after hostilities had begun, as NORTHERN ALLIES OF TREASON. There were, an editorial so headlined declared, individuals in most cities and towns "who are rank secessionists at heart, but who manage most adroitly in gauging their treason exactly to what they regard the endurable point — that at which public law or public sentiment would chastise public outrage." *The Blade* had no doubt how to deal with these "allies of treason": "Let them be *blacklisted* — socially, commercially and politically — cut off from all intercourse with the men whose rights they violate and whose government they aid in destroying."

The death of Stephen A. Douglas in June provided another striking example of how much importance Clark Waggoner attached to keeping the Union intact. As recently as late January of the same year, *The Blade* had taken Douglas to task because "he and his followers upbraid the Republicans for not abandoning all their principles and convictions of right and duty to satisfy the Secessionists and 'promote peace'." Now, at his death, *The Blade* declared that "it will ever be a pleasing reflection with the hosts of Mr. Douglas's warm friends, that his last public appearance was distinguished by the delivery of an eloquent and patriotic defense of the Union and of the war now in progress for its preservation." There was, of course, a greater consistency in *The Blade's* position than in that of Douglas. It had stuck with its terms for preserving the Union, whereas he had changed his. Since Douglas had seen the light before he died, *The Blade* could now eulogize him.

There was consistency, too, in *The Blade's* position with respect to slavery. Clark Waggoner had been opposed to it from the time he became editor and had been active in the anti-slavery movement. He had been equally against abolition in the sense of freeing those in servitude in states where, it was maintained, the Constitution recognized the right to own and hold men in slavery. He had made this differentiation clear in the columns of *The Blade* many times, and it had put the newspaper and its editor in a difficult relationship with James M. Ashley, who represented Ohio's Fifth Congressional District. *The Blade* had supported Ashley's candidacy in 1858 and again in 1860, but Clark Waggoner had reservations about his Abolitionist zeal. Once the war had begun, the issue between them was drawn more sharply than ever.

Beginning early in June, 1861, and continuing for several weeks, an extended colloquy involving Ashley and Waggoner over this difference occupied many columns. "The main point of disagreement between us as we understand it," *The Blade* declared, "is that he sought the unconditional abolition of Slavery as an object of war; while we claimed that the sole and only aim on the part of loyal citizens should be to put down the rebellion and maintain the Union and the Constitution as they existed at the commencement of the war, and that all measures should be adopted with special reference to that single object."

In September, 1862, President Lincoln issued a proclamation declaring his intention to free all slaves within the states and parts of states then in a state of rebellion against the Federal Government, and *The Blade* could endorse his action without reservation because emancipation was being employed to preserve the Union. When the proclamation became effective on January 1, 1863, Waggoner spelled out the rationalization for Lincoln's less than entirely popular action: "The President, of course, places this important step on his authority as Commander in Chief of the Army and Navy, and justifies it as a war measure made necessary by the obstinate and persistent rebellion among the inhabitants of the territory concerned. Placed upon these grounds, we think all loyal citizens will support, and most of them approve, the step."

But Waggoner would have none of "those who especially rejoice in the name of Radicals," who were "finding fault with the President because he did not decree universal Emancipation." *The Blade* declared:

> We should certainly suppose that all Anti-Slavery men would now be satisfied. Those who are not must be regarded as impracticable and visionary. Congress is expressly prohibited by the Constitution from interfering with the local institutions of any State. This prohibition is always in force in regard to loyal States. It is only under the war-making power that the right exists to interfere with Slavery, and then simply upon the ground that it is the main support of the rebellion and that whatever furnishes assistance to the efforts to destroy the government should be removed.

★ ★ ★

An observation in *The Blade* of June 26, 1861, reflects the extent to which news of the war dominated the press during the first few months of fighting: "Our space is too much occupied with telegraph reports and other matters for comment upon their character or other subjects. Some important items will be found in the telegraph dispatches, and an interesting letter from our war correspondent, now in western Virginia." Regular dispatches from an unidentified correspondent near the front lines began to appear in *The Blade* about this time. So did letters from soldiers in the field, describing army life and providing some information about recent fighting. These latter were always signed with a *nom de plume*, rather than the name of the letter writer.

The volatility of the situation at the front and of the reactions of the press and the people is strikingly illustrated in a series of three excerpts from *The Blade* within two weeks' time in the summer of 1861:

July 12:

> We stop the press to give the following highly important news just received by telegraph, by which it will be seen that the Union forces have achieved two important victories in Virginia — one in the complete capture of the enemy's Camp at Laurel Hill, and the other at Rich Mountain, ten miles west of Beverly.
>
> This glorious news will be grateful to the friends of the Government, as it will be disheartening to the hordes of rebels now banded for the destruction of the Union.

July 18:

> The "good time" has come! The Grand Army is in motion, the rebels

A Steady Voice for the Union 63

are flying, and the blood of loyal citizens flows faster and warmer in their veins! It is hoped that even croakers will now find something to approve in the policy of the Government.

We are the more rejoiced at the great movement from Washington because we believe it is not a hasty one, dictated by the clamor of impatience and ignorance, but the result of prudent foresight and ample preparation . . . No backward step will now be taken, but each day will find the advance of the Army further South, and the flight of the rebels more rapid than the preceding one.

July 23:

The all-absorbing subject of thought and conversation now is the condition of the grand army at Washington and the extent of the disaster growing out of the stampede from Bull's Run. No event ever occurred in this country to produce so great and sudden a revulsion of feeling as did that. From the heights of joy and hope, the friends of the Union were by a single electric flash hurled down to the depth of disappointment and chagrin.

From that pit of despair (a consequence of the second Battle of Bull Run) *The Blade* rose up in relatively short time. By August 21, when a Postmaster-General's order excluded five anti-Union newspapers in New York from the mails, Clark Waggoner's terse comment was "good!" He extended this comment a few days later: "The simple announcement . . . that certain rebel journals of New York were to be suppressed, was responded to everywhere with joy, not only on account of the particular good which was to come from their suppressions, but much more on account of the assurance it gave that the government has resolved to act with increased vigor and boldness. The time when the people wanted to discuss nice technicalities is past. They care little whether the *habeas corpus* is suspended or not, so that the rebels are. The national edifice is on fire and the people are not particular whether trespass is committed or not by the firemen to get water to extinguish the flames."

This is one of a very few times in the long history of *The Blade* when it has been suggested that the constitutional rights of individuals should sometimes be sacrificed to the will of the majority. Undoubtedly Clark Waggoner meant these words when he wrote them, and it is striking testimony to the intensity of feeling that was characteristic of the time. The national edifice was indeed on fire, and few could concern themselves with the legal niceties of what actions might seem necessary to extinguish the flames.

Notice of some other matters than the war was taken in the columns of *The Blade* at this crucial period. One was the death of

Joseph R. Williams, to which the entire first column of page two was devoted, including a brief tribute by the editor, declaring that, during an editorial career of three years, Williams had "completely Republicanized the Northwestern District of Ohio." Another was an attempt by the Toledo *Times* to take the contract for county printing and advertising away from *The Blade*. The *Times* would do the advertising at one-fourth the present rate, the printing at three-fourths what was now being paid to *The Blade*. Lucas County could then pay the difference to the families of volunteers, now in need of relief, and thus both patriotic and economic ends could be served. This was, Waggoner wrote, "so clearly the work of petty spite and meanness, growing out of the fact that *The Blade*, in the course of legitimate competition, had obtained an advantage in business over their incompetence and shiftlessness, that we thought further discussion unnecessary." There was also mention of a new domestic novel, titled "East Lynne: or the Earl's Daughter." Unfortunately, there had been no time to read the book, "but with the reading public it is enough to assure its popularity to know that this book is from the pen of 'The Heir to Ashley,' 'The Earl's Secret,' and other popular tales."

★ ★ ★

It was a different Ashley who occupied much of *The Blade's* attention during most of 1862. The differences between Congressman Ashley and Editor Waggoner over emancipation policy, already noted, had begun a year earlier. Then, on November 26, 1861, Ashley delivered an address in Toledo, entitled "The Rebellion — Its Causes and Consequences," in which he demanded that universal emancipation be made the principal purpose of the war, thus gaining world recognition and approval for the United States. The text of this speech occupied the entire front page and most of page four of the December 17 issue of *The Blade*. An editorial in the same issue rejected Ashley's proposal, suggesting a different policy:

> The rapidly increasing sentiment among Union men everywhere in favor of confiscating the property, Slaves included, of all active rebels — marking as it does a fixed purpose to employ any legitimate means necessary to success — should encourage us to stand firmly by the policy with which we set out as the one most certain to be effective and least likely to work distraction among ourselves. Fidelity to that policy and due confidence in the "logic of events," seems to be all that we need to insure success.

Four days later — on December 21 — Waggoner amplified this

A Steady Voice for the Union 65

argument and concluded: "Let the single purpose of suppressing the rebellion be kept in view and Slave property and all other material interests take their chances in the contest. If Slavery cannot survive this rebellion, let it go down, but the Union maintained." *The Blade* applauded Lincoln when, in March 1862, he sent a message to Congress proposing a system to free the slaves in which the Federal Government would cooperate in every way, including financial, with any state desiring to take such action. This was additional proof of Lincoln's pledge to "use all indispensable means for the suppression of the rebellion." It was still essential, as Waggoner saw it, that the states take the action necessary to free the slaves.

It is not clear exactly when *The Blade* concluded that it must join in an organized effort to unseat James M. Ashley. For some months yet, Waggoner was careful to maintain a respectful—even friendly—tone in any comments on Ashley and his actions. When, as chairman of the House Committee on Territories, Ashley introduced a bill providing that states which had seceded should be reduced to the status of territories and thus be administered by the Federal Government, *The Blade* stated its firm opposition, but at no time accused the Toledo congressman of being vindictive.

Ashley's speeches in the House continued to receive generous amounts of space in *The Blade*. His remarks on "Sea, Lake and River Defenses," urging national improvements of military installations, also promoted Toledo's strategic position and advantages for manufacturing. *The Blade* approved and devoted five columns to the speech in its June 11 issue. Another four columns of space on July 5 contained the text of an earlier speech on separate bills providing for confiscation of property and freeing the slaves of rebels. Ashley declared his intention to vote for both; there was no comment from *The Blade*.

Then, on August 20, *The Blade* announced that it would support the candidacy for Congress of Morrison R. Waite, Toledo attorney, later to be named Chief Justice of the United States Supreme Court by President Grant. Waite was nominated by the official convention of the Union party in the Fifth District, which was dominated by the more conservative element. Ashley was then chosen by more radical Unionists. The issue between them was, of course, whether emancipation should be universal or limited in the way Abraham Lincoln had defined in his proclamation.

Clark Waggoner had no doubt as to the relative merits of the speeches which Ashley and Waite had made in different Toledo locations on August 19. Of Ashley's address he declared that "it bore too much the marks of the partizan *(sic)* and the politician and too little of those of the patriot solicitous for his country's deliverance from the enemies who are struggling to destroy it." He added that "in this particular it was in striking contrast with the utterance of Mr. Waite a short time before."

It had been decided at the Democratic party's convention not to name a candidate for Congress. However, an independent group met to nominate Edward L. Phelps, a Democrat, and the race became a three-man affair. *The Blade* had speculated on that possibility beforehand:

> Many people wonder if the Democrats will enter a third candidate in the Congressional election. We don't know. We do know that Ashley and friends are encouraging Democrats to do so. Then they can say that the District is in danger from the Vallandighamites and Ashley must be elected!

The three-man congressional contest became, in fact, an old-fashioned political brawl, with Ashley and Waggoner as the principal protagonists and the Toledo *Commercial* lending aid and comfort to the incumbent. Waite and Phelps were cast in supporting roles in this melodrama.

The Blade led off on September 11 with a series of letters which had come into Waggoner's hands from an unnamed source. These were purported to have been written by Ashley (as chairman of the House Committee on Territories) to one Frank M. Case, whom the congressman first proposed to appoint as Surveyor General of Utah. Ashley indicated in the first letter that he expected his brother, Eli, to be named Chief Clerk. The gold mines and the Pacific Railroad, he wrote, "will enable a man and his assistant to make a fortune of $50,000 to $100,000 — if he is a good businessman." The locale of the appointment had been changed from Utah to Colorado by the time of the second letter, in which Ashley declared that "if you get it, I want to unite with you as a full partner in all land speculation and town sites." Subsequent letters embroidered these themes, including the statement that "the Pacific Railroad will go through the Territory and it will be a fortune to me if I can get it (the appointment for Case)."

Little more than a week later, Ashley submitted an extended defense against the charges brought by *The Blade* — to which fresh

A Steady Voice for the Union 67

allegations had been added in the meantime. This document occupied two and one-half columns of space in the September 19 issue. In rebuttal, Waggoner declared that Ashley now admitted the letters were his own, disposing of the allegations that they were forgeries. His defense also proved, *The Blade* added, that Ashley's object in getting the appointment for Case was neither the latter's welfare nor the public good, but that the Congressman might make money himself. In conclusion: "Mr. Ashley's allusion to 'libelous comment' of *The Blade* on his acts is entirely gratuitous. We are prepared to vindicate our comments on his course in any way he may select. While we have no desire to wrong him, we have a duty demanding that we speak plainly."

When Ashley filed suit for libel against *The Blade* a week later, asking $25,000 damages, Waggoner captioned his editorial response MR. ASHLEY'S DEFENSE — CHANGE OF VENUE, and declared:

> Driven from the bar of public opinion, to which he first appealed, for the trial of his "official record," and silenced in every attempt to justify before his constituents on the stump or in the press, he now, as a "forlorn hope," resorts to the very cheap expedient of a suit in Court. The trial being placed past the election, he feels safe from the damaging consequences certain to result from it, but hopes it will afford a very little "handful of dust" for his constituents' eyes, while he will be at liberty to withdraw the suit after it has served its purpose.

The Blade kept up its cannonade of editorials attacking Ashley's "Colorado swindle" and his "wholesale office brokerage." From mid-August to mid-October, at least one editorial — more often two or three — attacked Ashley in every issue of *The Blade*. Very occasionally, editorial attention was turned to lauding Morrison Waite's qualifications to serve in Congress. Political editorials in that period continued to be directed primarily *against* a candidate whose defeat was desired, rather than *for* the man whose election was sought. This practice was by no means unique to *The Blade*.

In this instance, the strategy came close to succeeding. Waite carried Toledo and Lucas county by more than 1,200 votes, but Ashley came out on top in the three-man contest, though his total for the district was 4,000 fewer than the combined vote for Waite and Phelps. *The Blade* found the explanation in the fact that, as it had predicted, "the statement that the contest lay between Ashley and Phelps was pressed so incessantly and constantly by the friends of each that it had its effect." Cited as an example was Williams county, where Waite polled only 17 votes to 1,219 for Ashley, 1,218 for Phelps.[17]

The contest was an interesting one — representative of the slam-bang, personal politics of the period, yet casting before it the shadow of what has become a tradition of independent politics with which Toledo and *The Blade* have become identified in the succeeding one hundred and twenty years. That tradition reached its peak during a period from 1897 to 1913, when first Samuel M. Jones, then Brand Whitlock served as independent mayors of Toledo. *The Blade* would find itself opposed to the independent tradition in the Jones-Whitlock era, but would later play an important role in electing Frazier Reams, an Independent Democrat, to Congress for two terms, from 1950 to 1954. Then, in a final ironic development, *The Blade* would endorse and help elect Frazier Reams's Democratic opponent — Thomas Ludlow Ashley, who was a great-grandson of James M. Ashley.

Chapter 6

A Victory and a Great Loss

There were new internal problems and new external developments for newspapers during these years when their readers' attention was occupied almost entirely by what was being reported concerning the war. Exciting things were going on with respect to the telegraph, opening up still further the potential for the transmission of news reports which it had begun to demonstrate fewer than twenty years earlier. THE GREAT TELEGRAPH FEAT was heralded on November 7, 1862:

> The Pacific Telegraph line has been in operation for some months, but dispatches have always been repeated one or more times, according to the state of the atmosphere and the condition of the instruments &c. Direct communication through, without repeating, was never obtained until yesterday afternoon, when dispatches were sent from San Francisco to New York, a distance of three thousand miles! This is unquestionably the greatest telegraph feat performed in the world.

Unfortunately, there was bad news about the telegraph, too, and it was of more direct and immediate concern to *The Blade*'s operations. Notice arrived on November 17 from the Associated Press, source of all telegraph news to newspapers throughout the West, that "on and after December 1st, the charges for such intelligence will be very much higher in all cases, while that for the afternoon report . . . will be absolutely enormous." These terms were "four or five times as high as they have ever been."

There was also the problem of the cost of the paper on which newspapers were printed, which had been going up sharply for the past year. Late in November, *The Blade* discussed with its readers THE PAPER EXCITEMENT:

> The rise in the price of printing stock — especially paper — not only continues but is getting more rapid than ever. We have received notice

from manufacturers of another increase in the rates for flat and letter papers. The aggregate rise . . . now amounts to from 80 to 110 per cent, within 90 days.

Unless some substitute for rags shall come into extensive use or the consumption of paper become less, it is difficult to say what the result of the present state of things will be. — At present it is unsafe to fix one day the price of newspapers or job printing for the next.

Since *The Blade* was not the only newspaper affected by these increased costs, a number of Western newspapers undertook action together. Clark Waggoner was one of a group of more than twenty editors who met in Indianapolis on November 25, 1862. When the group organized itself into the Western Associated Press, the editor of *The Blade* was one of the eight members of its board of directors. The group did not succeed in breaking the monopoly of the Associated Press on the nation's telegraphic news supply, but it did exercise a moderating influence on the New York group which controlled the agency.

Further consequences of mounting costs of producing *The Blade* were made clear in an announcement addressed to its readers on December 21. There were only two alternatives — to reduce the size of the paper or to increase the subscription price. "As we do not believe the subscribers of *The Blade* desire us to reduce its size, we have concluded to increase the price," it was announced. The daily edition, delivered in the city, would henceforth cost $6.00 per year, the Tri-Weekly edition would be $4.00 and the Weekly $1.50.

The Blade was making other kinds of changes, too. That same December 21 issue announcing the subscription price increase contained three columns of NEWS BY TELEGRAPH and COMMERCIAL NEWS on the front page. The long-standing tradition of reserving page one for advertising was giving way to the pressures of war — to some extent because of reader interest in news, to some extent because of the need to conserve space. Once the breakthrough had been made, however, news reports began to appear regularly on the front page, though advertising messages were not yet banished to other pages.

As the nation became ever more deeply involved in war, the relationship between press and Government continued to grow more difficult. *The Blade*, for its part, maintained a consistent position, seeking to combine maximum freedom for the press with the assumption of a greater measure of responsibility on the part of editors. "Dangerous, unjust, pernicious" were the adjectives Clark

A Victory and a Great Loss

Waggoner applied to the rumor-mongering that went on in newspapers from reputedly authentic but unnamed sources — "a person in high authority." He suggested that "President Lincoln's messages and acts form a safer guide to his policy than these reports of private interviews and of incidental remarks dropped without expectation of this use being made of them."

The Blade took the Chicago *Tribune* over the coals a month later, on February 15, for an editorial containing what Waggoner regarded as slanderous implications against Generals Halleck, Grant and McClellan. "A free press is indeed a palladium of liberty," he wrote, "but a freedom to misrepresent and malign individuals, and thus destroy the confidence of the public in them, is not within the province of the press, any more than the freedom of speech gives the right to slander and calumniate."

Clark Waggoner's ambivalent feelings about the imposition of Government restrictions on the distribution of news are made clear, however, in his comment on the tightening of restrictions only two weeks later. In *The Blade* of March 1, he wrote:

> The public are now sadly scrimped in promises, but we have full confidence to believe that the results . . . will be increased by the new order of things. It must be confessed . . . that with the press, the Government's order is not pleasant but grievous. . . . The ordinary labor of the editor has been to divest his correspondence of least interest to his readers; now it is to strike out those most interesting. The difference may be imagined.

The editor of *The Blade* strove mightily to preserve the Union. He worked just as hard at editing a lively, informative newspaper. It was sometimes hard to strike just the right balance between these two concerns that were of almost equal importance to him.

★ ★ ★

There were two groups of his fellow citizens of the Northern states for whom Clark Waggoner had no regard whatever. One of these was the Copperheads, named for a particularly venomous snake, who were openly sympathetic to the Confederate cause. The extent of his contempt is to be found in his comparing them with the Tories and traitors of 1776, suggesting that "the record made for the men of that day will be their record — only made blacker and more indelible by the greater wrong which they now commit." The second group was the Croakers, who were openly critical of the way the war was being conducted and forever urging concessions to the Confederates that might bring an end to the fighting. How Waggoner felt about them is well expressed in an editorial captioned DON'T CROAK, written in the wake of bad news from Gettysburg and Vicksburg in the summer of 1863: "If there is a man in the community whom we feel like going around the block to avoid, it is one of these birds of ill omen."

When, in that same summer, the Copperheads and the Croakers of Ohio gained control of the Democratic party convention in Columbus and nominated Clement L. Vallandigham as their candidate for Governor, the stage was set for one of the most remarkable political contests in the nation's history. *The Blade* lost no time in defining the issue on the day after the nomination: "It is the Union and War, or Disunion and Peace."

In its account of the convention, *The Blade* reported that "a committee of 20 was appointed to wait upon the President and demand permission for his (Vallandigham's) return to the State." For the Democratic candidate for Governor — sometime editor of the Dayton *Empire,* sometime member of Congress from the Dayton district — was not in Ohio, nor even in the United States.

Clement Vallandigham was in Bermuda the day he was chosen as the Democratic candidate for Governor, though he was not there on vacation. A military tribunal at the Union army's Western headquarters in Cincinnati had found him guilty of violating General Ambrose Burnside's General Orders, No. 38, which forbade "publicly expressing . . . sympathy for those in arms against the Government of the United States, declaring disloyal sentiments and opinion, with the object and purpose of weakening the power of the Government in its effort to suppress the unlawful rebellion." All this Vallandigham was alleged to have done in a speech at Mount Vernon, Ohio, on May 4, in which he attacked Lincoln, Burnside, and others.

The military commission which heard the charges found that Vallandigham had indeed violated General Orders, No. 38, and sentenced him to be "placed in close confinement in some fortress of the United States," to be chosen by Burnside. The irascible general chose Fort Warren, in Boston Harbor, as the place of incarceration, but Vallandigham never arrived there. President Lincoln and the members of his cabinet were horrified by the action that had been taken, yet they were loath to embarrass General Burnside by reversing him. Better, they decided, to exile the Ohioan to the Confederacy and he was sent to the camp of General Braxton Bragg. But both Bragg and Jefferson Davis, President of the Confederacy,

A Victory and a Great Loss 73

found his presence embarrassing, so they shipped him off to Bermuda.[18]

Within a week, however, *The Blade* reported that "it is rumored through rebel sources that Vallandigham has run the blockade for Nassau en route for Canada" and that "if successful in this he will soon be in communication with his adherents in this State." It remained to be seen, Waggoner suggested, whether or not the candidate would try to return to Ohio, and declared:

> However this may be, the issue forced upon the people of Ohio by the nomination of this man for Governor, is daily developing itself... As the voters of Ohio shall, by their ballots, choose between Vallandigham and Brough, so they will declare for or against the recognition of the Southern Confederacy, and the disbanding of the Army.

The Democratic candidate was not permitted to return to Ohio to carry on his campaign against the Union party's nominee, John M. Brough, of Marietta. Vallandigham did return in 1864 to campaign for General George B. McClellan against President Lincoln, coming disguised by a beard and a pillow inside his trousers. But he was a candidate-in-exile during the 1863 campaign, meeting with Ohio friends at Niagara and, later, at Windsor.

The Blade bombarded Vallandigham's candidacy unmercifully throughout August and September. Two or three editorials a day were directed against this archetypical Copperhead editor and politician. When the Union party candidate, John Brough, spoke at a meeting in Toledo, Waggoner wrote: "How any man after hearing him can go away and vote for a man like Vallandigham is beyond our comprehension." And when the Democratic candidate said that he felt safe under the British flag in Canada: "Val probably feels something of the same relief that Benedict Arnold did when the 'British flag' protected him from the 'arbitrary measures' of Washington."

There is a certain irony in the fact that the final witness called by *The Blade* against Vallandigham's candidacy was the late Stephen A. Douglas, on whose head it had once heaped vituperation almost as stinging as that with which it now assailed the Democratic gubernatorial candidate. Just five days before the election, it reprinted for the second time within a few weeks a document identified as the LAST POLITICAL WILL AND TESTAMENT OF STEPHEN A. DOUGLAS, dated May 10, 1861. It was identified as "a special legacy to true Democrats and withheld by a portion of the Democratic press" — the obvious reference being to such newspapers as supported Vallandigham. All statements urging readers of Douglas's statement to support the Government in its war effort were italicized.

The Blade signaled John Brough's overwhelming victory over Clement Vallandigham, a sweep by the Union ticket in Ohio and in several other states, with this headline:

JOLLIFICATION TONIGHT!
SPEECHES, MUSIC AND BONFIRES!

It went on to rejoice:

> The first words that every loyal man or lover of liberty should utter in view of yesterday's elections should be a devout thanksgiving to Almighty God that He put it into the hearts of the people of Ohio, Pennsylvania, Indiana and Iowa to vindicate their loyalty to the Union. For all the manifold blessings which this nation has enjoyed at His hands, we regard the great and glorious victory of yesterday as the most important and timely.

Abraham Lincoln put it still more strongly in his wire to John Brough: "Glory to God in the Highest. Ohio has saved the Union."

But the Civil War was not yet over in October, 1863, even though the Union might be saved. The fortunes of war did seem to be turning in favor of the Union, and *The Blade* was heartened by these developments. Little notice was taken of a speech by President Lincoln a month after the Ohio election, though there was a brief report on November 20, under the heading FROM GETTYSBURG: "This famous little town is overflowing with people assembled to witness the dedication of the National Cemetery . . . President Lincoln and distinguished party accompanying him arrived here yesterday . . . The weather being fine, the programme has been carried out successfully."

Next day, Lincoln's Gettysburg Address was reprinted in full on page two, ending with a parenthetical notation that there was "long continued applause." The lack of any comment on what the President had said may have reflected disappointment in the brevity of his address. It had, after all, lasted only about three minutes.

★ ★ ★

Clark Waggoner had no problem deciding whom to support in the 1864 presidential election. Almost a year earlier — on December 4, 1863 — *The Blade* took its stand: "The great consideration is who can best command the confidence and thus combine the strength of

A Victory and a Great Loss

the loyal men of the land?" One man, and only one — Abraham Lincoln — fulfilled that requirement, for these reasons:

1. "Old Abe" is honest.
2. He has stood three years' testing with fidelity and success.
3. The rebels declared that Lincoln should not be President; the integrity of the nation was assailed in him.
4. Choosing him would allay rivalry among Cabinet or other aspirants.

Waggoner was pleased when the Republican party convention nominated Lincoln in June, 1864. Some were unenthusiastic about the choice of Andrew Johnson of Tennessee for second place on the ticket. Not *The Blade*, which described him as "eminently a man of the people, born in obscurity and come to distinction solely through his own unaided efforts and against obstacles . . . no other public man in this country has overcome."

Things did not go well for the Union forces in the field in July, 1864, and there were rumors of another draft call. The Croakers were advised that it was time to croak again: "It is at such times only that the weak and timid can be affected by the forebodings of others," Waggoner wrote. Three months later, however, *The Blade* was exulting in reports of disarray among the Confederate forces, with two-thirds of the troops being absent without leave. "It only remains for the government to press forward with its measures for crushing the rebel army," Waggoner exhorted, "and the people of the North to give it a ready and unflagging support, and Peace will soon come — and come to stay!"

There was great rejoicing in Toledo when, in the following week, Abraham Lincoln was re-elected President of the United States over General George B. McClellan. News of Lincoln's victory was, in fact, delayed several days in reaching readers of *The Blade*, a consequence of damage to the telegraph lines caused by heavy storms.

Joy was unrestrained five months later. RICHMOND HAS FALLEN, the April 3, 1865, issue of *The Blade* proclaimed beneath a picture of the flag and a cannon. When Lee surrendered to Grant at Appomattox, Virginia, on April 9, the next day's front page displayed such headlines as GLORIOUS END . . . THE GREAT CRASH . . . REBELLION COLLAPSED . . . LEE SURRENDERS. Waggoner wrote that "words are inadequate to express the emotions of the loyal heart at a period like this." Citizens of Toledo met the next day at the Board of Trade rooms and made plans for an official observance of the end of the fighting. Rockets were fired. Bonfires were built. *The Blade* described the "wildest delight" with which the city greeted the news.

★ ★ ★

The assassination of President Abraham Lincoln plunged Toledo into mourning only a week later. Details of the death and funeral of the martyred wartime leader were reported lavishly. As the funeral train crossed the nation toward Springfield, Illinois, its progress was followed carefully. So that Toledo residents could view the body, arrangements were made for a special train to Cleveland. *The Blade* memorialized the man who had led the nation through the long, bitter conflict:

> To the Memory of Abraham Lincoln, president of the United States of America, who died a martyr to his country, falling under the hands of a Traitor Assassin, on the night of the 14th day of April, 1865, the Fourth Anniversary of the beginning of the great WAR OF REBELLION, Through which he had led the Nation to a Glorious Triumph, Just completed, when the Dastardly Revenge of Vanquished Treason was wrought in his monstrous murder.
>
> Too sincere in the Simplicity of his Nature to be affected by an elevation, the Proudest among Human Dignities, He stands in the ranks of the Illustrious of all Time as the Purest Exemplar of Democracy. While Goodness is beloved, and great deeds are remembered, the world will never cease to revere the name and memory of Abraham Lincoln.[19]

There was some ambivalence in *The Blade's* attitude toward treatment of the Confederacy and the process of reconstructing a nation torn apart by four years of bitter struggle. In the immediate wake of surrender, Clark Waggoner had urged that the South "continue to be a fellow citizen of a common country." Law and order should be restored as quickly as possible, the damage done by war where it had been fought — almost entirely in the South — repaired. Help and forgiveness did not, however, characterize the editor's attitude toward individuals who had led the rebellion. *The Blade* hoped that the Government's offer of a $100,000 reward for the capture of Jefferson Davis (to whom it had referred throughout the war as "Jeff") and other leaders of the Confederate States would result in the arrest of those "great criminals, and that they may soon be brought, and their tools already on trial, to meet the just reward of their crimes."

The Blade supported specific measures which Abraham Lincoln had proposed and Andrew Johnson now sought to implement. These

A Victory and a Great Loss

were essentially moderate in tone, intended to bring the Confederate states back into the union as soon as possible, while assuring protection of the rights of the blacks who had been freed by the Emancipation Proclamation, or at some other time. One of these latter was the Freedmen's Bureau, established in March, 1865, to deal with offenses against the rights of one-time slaves who had so little means of defending themselves. The Bureau was described as "the most reliable test of a man's Democracy." It would be needed only in the period of transition, after which the freedmen would be able to fend for themselves.

For more than a year, *The Blade* would continue to support Andrew Johnson's reconstruction program. It did not change its position materially with the departure of Clark Waggoner in 1865, when he became owner and editor of the Toledo *Commercial,* with which he had feuded endlessly during the war.

Alonzo D. Pelton now found himself owner and proprietor of *The Blade*. He had been concerned with finding a good financial investment when he became part owner in 1857. Now he began to look for fresh talent and, since his own interests ran to the business side, he was especially concerned to find a man — preferably a young man — who could, in Pelton's own phrase, "add spice" to the columns of his newspaper. It was important, too, that he have potential to take over as editor in the near future.

One possibility was a young man named David Ross Locke, who had operated the weekly *Hancock Jeffersonian* at nearby Findlay since 1861. Some of Locke's satirical sketches, written under the pseudonym of Petroleum Vesuvius Nasby, had come to Pelton's attention and had particularly impressed him. Here was a young man of obvious talent, who had already achieved a considerable following among soldiers in the Civil War — and even in the White House. Pelton decided to send a friend to Findlay to find out more about him. The report came back that Locke was unworthy of confidence, a heavy drinker, and a tough. Pelton's interest cooled. He decided to bring Thomas Hale, a relative of Edward Everett Hale, from Boston to Toledo to take over editorial management of *The Blade*.

PART II
THE LOCKE YEARS
1865-1926

Chapter 7

A New Man in Charge

Fortunately for himself and for *The Blade*, Alonzo Pelton was never quite able to put David Ross Locke out of his mind. The young editor might be a "heavy drinker" and a "tough," but he was surely a wizard with words, and his Nasby Letters were some of the funniest and most effective political commentary being written anywhere in the country. Even after that unfavorable report by the friend Pelton had sent to Findlay, his mind kept coming back to Locke as the man whom he wanted to be his editor.

The owner of *The Blade* had gone so far, in fact, as to write to David Ross Locke to inquire whether he was free and open to an offer. He certainly was, Locke wrote back, but when there was no response from Pelton, he had to look about for another way to earn a living for his wife and three sons. In February, 1865, he joined with J. M. Huber, who had operated the "Old Corner Drug Store" in Findlay for several years. The new firm of Huber and Locke promised to "continue the old style of business." Locke, who had once observed that it is easier to earn a living in the drug business than by operating a newspaper, because "everyone has bowels, while few have brains," seemed about to be lost to journalism.

A. D. Pelton snatched him back from the "Old Corner Drug Store." Early in the fall of 1865, even as he was completing arrangements with Thomas Hale to take charge of *The Blade's* editorial operations, Pelton wrote again to Locke. He told him frankly of the negative report concerning his character and his standing in the Findlay community. Locke responded at once: he was not a drinking man, he attended church, taught a Sunday school class, even preached on occasion. This spirited denial pleased Pelton so much that he wrote to Locke, inquiring what salary he would expect. He didn't care, Locke replied, suggesting that he would be glad to come to Toledo, show what he could do, and let Pelton decide what he was worth.

Pelton invited Locke to come to Toledo and the invitation was accepted promptly. Meantime, Hale had arrived and the two began work on *The Blade* during the same week in mid-October, 1865. Reminiscing some years later, Pelton declared that he never would forget Locke as he first saw him:

> He wore a broad-brimmed cowboy hat, cocked askant on his head, and had on a sack coat about as long as a vest should be, with both hands in his pockets, he sauntered up to where I was at work.
> "Is this Mr. Pelton?" he queried.
> "Yes."
> "I'm Dave Locke."
> "What can you do?" I asked.
> "What can't I do!" responded Locke. "I can do anything and everything around a printing office."
> "What pay do you want?"
> "None till you try me."[1]

Locke began work on *The Blade* at a salary of $2,000 per year, taking charge of the locals department and writing a Nasby letter each week. He did all that and more — writing editorials, even setting type or making up the forms from which the newspaper was printed when a compositor or pressman didn't show up for work. Thomas Hale found the pace of a daily newspaper uncongenial and returned to Boston. Before leaving, he told Pelton: "That man upstairs is a wonderful genius; let him take my place."

That October day in 1865 when the young editor from Findlay had arrived in Toledo and gone to work for Alonzo Pelton was as important as any in the 150-year history of *The Blade*. David Ross Locke in the next quarter of a century would transform the newspaper from a respected local organ into a publication of national reputation. When Locke died in 1888, hundreds of thousands of Americans knew the weekly edition of *The Blade* — most of them referring to it as "Nasby's paper."

When Locke joined *The Blade* at the age of thirty-two, his career had not been particularly distinguished, though he had begun to achieve some reputation as a humorist and satirist beyond the borders of Ohio. Born near Vestal, in Broome County, New York, he was apprenticed at the age of twelve to the Cortland County *Democrat* in Cortland, New York. He had been a tramp printer for

A New Man in Charge

a number of years before buying a weekly newspaper at Plymouth, Ohio, in partnership with James G. Robinson, with whom he had previously worked on the Pittsburgh *Chronicle.* Subsequently he had been involved in operating weekly newspapers at Mansfield, Bucyrus, Findlay and Bellefontaine — always "well down toward the further end of the poverty scale," as he once described it. When Murat Halstead of the Cincinnati *Commercial* paid him twenty dollars a week for some of the Nasby letters, Locke declared: "It was simply boundless prosperity for me. I had never hoped, even in my wildest dream, to possess so much money."

The Blade offered a number of attractions to a young editor whose growing reputation rested on allegiance to the Republican party and unfaltering opposition to human slavery, and whose ideas about newspapers were well ahead of their time. Toledo might not be one of the nation's major cities, but its population of 13,786 in 1860 was far greater than any of the villages in which he had operated weeklies. *The Blade* was a Republican newspaper and the congressional district of which Toledo was a part was represented by James M. Ashley, Abolitionist stalwart. *The Blade* would provide a sympathetic audience for Locke's pro-Republican, anti-slavery views, and this was an attractive prospect.

The new job offered another particular opportunity for David Ross Locke. Already he had begun to conjure up ideas about a weekly publication to be distributed widely, containing something of interest to every member of the family. Locke saw in the *Weekly Blade,* which was circulated locally to about 2,000 readers in 1865, the vehicle that could turn his ideas into reality. It should include, he believed, these ingredients:

> A news department so all-embracing that when the reader was through with it he or she would have a perfect knowledge of what the world had been during the week; this accompanied with editorial comments making clear to the minds of the reader the philosophy of the events; a department for women and girls especially, which would not only be entertaining but instructive; the best literature for the entertainment and elevation of the taste of the people; regular articles on agriculture and mechanical industries; the markets; the politics; and the social movements of the day; and opinion, forcibly put, on all topics of interest, and above all the advocacy of everything calculated to make men and women better.[2]

This prospectus reflects much of the increasing concern in post-Civil War America with the newspapers' role as educators in the broadest sense rather than the political advocates that they had been almost solely over the previous 30 years.

Americans' interests diversified along with their sources of income; newspapers' circulation rose, and so did their advertising revenues.

The *Weekly Blade* was unsurpassed in its appeal to readers in all parts of the United States — especially those in small towns and on farms — who subscribed by the tens of thousands.

★ ★ ★

During its first thirty years, *The Blade's* pattern of operation had — like that of most American newspapers except a very few established early on the eastern seaboard — been unstable. For example, between April, 1837, and October, 1865, it had seven different addresses — some for a period of only a few weeks. Some of these moves provided additional space for new equipment, though in at least one instance the move was "for the accommodation of the postmaster," who had objected to the noise made by a newspaper plant.[3]

The first building erected specifically for *The Blade's* use, at 150 Summit Street, was occupied in 1853, and it was here that David Ross Locke began his association with the newspaper. The increasing stability of newspaper operations is illustrated by the fact that, in the next 120 years, *The Blade* changed locations only three times, despite several fires — some of which did serious damage. The first move was to 150 St. Clair Street in 1874, then to the new building that Locke erected in 1884 at the corner of Superior Street and Jefferson Avenue, and finally in 1927 to the present building at 541 Superior Street.

Just as *The Blade* sought out the best quarters during its first 30 years, so did it try to keep abreast of the best equipment to produce its editions first weekly, then tri-weekly, then daily. The first press, which was hand operated, printed two pages at a time, at a rate of 120 impressions per hour. A new press, purchased in 1838 and used until 1853, was also hand operated, but was capable of turning out 240 impressions per hour.[4]

The Blade's first cylinder press, which could be driven by either steam or handpower, was installed in 1853 when Clark Waggoner took over the operation. Then, in 1860, a drum cylinder press produced by Hoe and Company was installed; it had a capacity of 1,200 impressions per hour. But it was not until 1868, when the

A New Man in Charge

Weekly Blade's circulation had begun to increase dramatically, that David Ross Locke purchased the first double-cylinder press, which could produce 4,000 impressions per hour and could handle an eight-page edition.[5] An enthusiast about any and all kinds of mechanical equipment, Locke took pride in bringing the newest and best to *The Blade*. When a press which made use of stereotyping plates was installed in 1872, he boasted that it would make *The Blade* "the handsomest as it is now the best paper in the United States."[6]

How many people read this handsome publication is hard to say. Newspapers did not generally at this time publish circulation figures; the first available for *The Blade* are in the late 1880s, when the daily figure averaged over 9,000. The phenomenal growth of the *Weekly Blade* is more clearly demonstrable. In 1856, the circulation was 600; by 1862, the total had grown to 2,700; in the 1870s, it reached above the 180,000 mark.

There was even greater reticence about releasing advertising figures until the 1870s, with the first real efforts to attract national advertising. Agencies acting as middlemen between advertisers and newspapers date back to the 1840s, but not until after the Civil War did they begin to play an important part in the newspaper picture. During the decade of the 1870s, these agencies flourished, and David Ross Locke, who was in New York much of that time, was a partner in one of the best known — Bates & Locke. Of his involvement in this venture, one of his associates wrote that Locke "surely was not a safe counselor for an advertiser, after getting beyond advising him to use the Toledo *Blade* — which generally belonged to Nasby as much as half of the time, if not more."[7]

★ ★ ★

David Ross Locke became a partner in the firm of A. D. Pelton & Company, owners of *The Blade*, in 1867. Other partners were Dr. A. P. Miller and John Paul Jones. When Dr. Miller bought Pelton's controlling interest in 1868, the firm of Miller, Locke & Company was formed. Locke and Jones became the owners a few months later, with Locke continuing as editor of *The Blade*.

Trying to keep track of the ownership of *The Blade* during the 1870s was difficult. One of his advertising associates, George P. Rowell, reported that it was said at one time that Locke "made a good living by selling the *Blade* at one season of the year, when someone turned up who thought he could run it better than Locke did, and buying it back a few months later, when the purchaser found that he could not."[8] The transactions of record generally support this impression.

Locke sold *The Blade* to his partner, J. P. Jones, in 1874. When the circulation of the *Weekly Blade* fell from nearly 100,000 to about 25,000, a succession of editors was brought in to stop the loss of readers. More drastic steps were required, and in August, 1876, the Toledo Blade Company was organized with Dr. Miller back again as president and editor, T. P. Brown as vice president, and Frank T. Lane, secretary-treasurer. Later that year, Locke bought the company and became its president. Lane was the operative head of the firm until 1880, when Locke returned to Toledo, and continued as business manager well into the 20th century.

Alexander Reed and Heman D. Walbridge, operating as the Toledo Newspaper Company, bought the daily and tri-weekly editions of *The Blade* in March, 1877. Within a year, however, these properties were again owned by the Toledo Blade Company, which now continued operation of all editions. With David Ross Locke's return from New York came a rebound in circulation of the *Weekly Blade*. By 1883, it had reached a total of 117,000 and the next year (capitalizing on widespread interest in the presidential contest between Grover Cleveland and James G. Blaine) circulation rose as it did in every presidential election year, shooting above the 200,000 mark.

The Blade's physical plant continued to expand with the completion in 1884 of the new five-story building at Superior and Jefferson, at a cost of more than $125,000. Locke hailed it as the finest business building in Toledo. Two Scott web perfecting presses were bought and installed. When David Ross Locke died four years later, not yet 55 years old, the newspaper he had joined less than a quarter of a century earlier had achieved remarkable heights in both influence and affluence.

Chapter 8

The Perils of Reconstruction

Fighting on the battlefields of the Civil War had ceased when David Ross Locke became editor of *The Blade*, but conflict was mounting over what should be done about restoring the Confederate states to the Union and how the former slaves could be assured that the freedoms granted them by the Emancipation Proclamation were to be protected. These problems had been exacerbated by the assassination six months earlier of President Abraham Lincoln, in circumstances clearly suggesting a plot by Confederate sympathizers.

The Blade's new editor was concerned that his Republican party should not lose control of Congress nor of the White House. He feared these things might happen if full suffrage were restored to the South without assurances that qualified Negroes would be permitted to vote. These political considerations did play a part in shaping Locke's position in the struggle over Reconstruction policy. Yet Locke and *The Blade* were not immediately supportive of the Radical Republicans, who wanted to crush and humiliate the Southern states. Indeed, during the first year of Locke's editorship, *The Blade* stood out among Republican newspapers in support of the moderate policies Abraham Lincoln had proposed, which were now urged by Andrew Johnson. Even Petroleum Vesuvius Nasby took a relatively moderate position on Reconstruction policy during the early months of Locke's editorship.

Some historians have distorted Locke's position, basing their judgments, it appears, on a highly selective reading of the Nasby letters during and after the Civil War. Paul Buck sums up a prevalent interpretation:

> If the reporting of Southern affairs was conditioned by habits of

thought that carried over from the war, much the same was true of the great machinery of propaganda that had been used to maintain the popular morale. "The Struggles of Petroleum V. Nasby," for example, had begun in 1861. The letters which serially describe the escapades, principles and ambitions of a burlesqued "Copperhead" settled in Confedrit X Roads, Kentucky, filled the columns of many Northern newspapers, and became in time . . . a major force in winning the war. The picture of President Lincoln reading to his cabinet the latest "Nasby" comment is one of our popular traditions. "Nasby" did not stop writing when Lee surrendered. Nor did he lose his appeal in the Northern taste. Here is no hidden, invidious motivation for the rise of radicalism. "Nasby" was a wartime habit carrying on. He became one of the most powerful as well as vitriolic influences in making conciliation appear ridiculous.[9]

The editorial pages of *The Blade* from November, 1865, to July, 1866, provide a continuing refutation of this over-simplification of Locke's struggles to reconcile his support of the moderate Republican position on Reconstruction policy with the growing confusion created by extremists on both sides of the controversy. On November 24, 1865, for example, *The Blade* offered this clear endorsement of President Johnson's policies:

The same class who doubt Andrew Johnson now, doubted Abraham Lincoln all through the war. Notwithstanding these doubts, President Lincoln saved the country and put down the rebellion, and we have full and complete faith that Andrew Johnson will complete the work his illustrious predecessor began, and leave us the government as it was before the rebellion, purged of its evils, and cured of its weaknesses. So far, he has extended mercy where mercy would assist in bringing about this result — he has hung where hanging would tend to the same end. His course gives us no reason to doubt.

The Blade wrote approvingly on December 5 of Johnson's position on how to restore the Union as outlined in his annual message to Congress: "It is a common sense message. The president desiring above all things the actual restoration of the Union, the healing of the feuds of the past 30 years and perfect harmony between the sections, suggests plainly what measures are necessary to bring it about. He gives not an inch to the prejudices of any class. As anxious as he is to bring about these results, he will not sacrifice one iota of principle, or one single right that the honest citizen of the Republic is entitled to, to accomplish that end."

A *Blade* editorial of December 18 states clearly Locke's position in relation to Andrew Johnson's program: "President Johnson has taken the middle ground between the two extremes. On the one hand

The Perils of Reconstruction 89

he desires the return of the Southern States as soon as possible, and he has been careful to have them so understand it — on the other hand he has been just as careful to have them fully understand that they must stay out until they comply with all the conditions necessary to a peace that shall be lasting."

One of Locke's principal concerns during this crucial period in the nation's history was to bring together the opposing wings of the Union party. When both Democrats and Radical Republicans insisted that President Johnson was being won away from his party, *The Blade* declared:

> Alas! their hopes are blasted. The sun of reality has melted their frostwork of fancy, and they are doomed to tread the downward path in sorrow and gloom.
>
> Very rapidly the difficulties in the way of restoration are subsiding, and now a difference between the leading men of the Union party is almost an impossibility. The fact is, there never was anything to quarrel about. Both wings were laboring to bring about certain results, they differed as to the means to be employed and the manner of using the forces at command. But that difference is being adjusted to the entire satisfaction of all parties except the Copperhead party.

Radical Republican spokesmen continued to assault the President and his policies. When Wendell Phillips, who was one of the most ferocious, declared on New Year's Day that "President Johnson, in attempting to lecture colored citizens, has reached the height of impudence," *The Blade* suggested that "Phillips has become so perfectly crazy on the Negro question that he has really worked himself up to the belief that he is, on the average, several degrees better than the white man." Men like Phillips, Locke concluded, "do some good in acting as pioneers in reform, but it would be a mercy if, when they reached a certain point, they could be deprived of speech. We should be spared a vast amount of nonsense."

The Blade defended Johnson again in February, 1866, when the Chicago *Tribune,* long identified with the Republican party and especially with Abraham Lincoln, berated the President as a pro-slavery man from "habit, education and instinct." It was alleged that "he has been and is playing false to the Republican party, for the purpose of securing the support of the Copperheads of the North and the Rebels of the South." *The Blade* answered back: "When Andrew Johnson betrays the Republican party, or shows any disposition to do so, we will join the *Tribune* in denouncing him, and if it exceeds us it will be because it has more ability in that line. But so far he has done nothing of the kind. He has perhaps disappointed the politicians of the *Tribune* class who imagine themselves the party, and fancy that they make the sentiment of the country. In this, they are grievously mistaken. They are not the party — they are not a majority of the party, nor do they represent it in any sense."

Radical spokesmen in Congress exasperated Locke four days later and he expressed his concern in a strong editorial, entitled "The New Test":

> Messrs. Sumner, Stevens & Co. have established a new test of Republicanism, or loyalty, which are almost synonymous terms. A man may have given the strength of his youth, the vigor of his manhood and the wisdom of his age to the great works of Freedom, he may have sacrificed his property and political prospects, and risked his life for the preservation of his country, or he may have urged the emancipation of the slaves as a war measure, even though by the act he lost the greater part of his worldly possessions — he may have done all this, and yet if he does not go one step further, and acknowledge that the Negroes he has spent a lifetime to free are fit to participate in all the privileges of citizenship, he is to be turned out of the Republican fold, among the Copperheads or rebels . . .
>
> We earnestly hope that wise counsels may yet prevail, and that the danger now threatening the Republic may be averted. We cannot believe that enough of the Union party to jeopardize a single district will follow these disorganizers, and foolishly undo what has cost the country hundreds of thousands of lives, and thousands of millions of money. The Union party carried the country through the Rebellion — it alone can take it through the perils of reconstruction.

When Andrew Johnson vetoed the Freedmen's Bureau Bill on February 19, 1866, *The Blade* was one of a very few Republican newspapers who came to his defense. Horace Greeley's New York *Tribune* said of this action that "the Copperheads at their homes are firing guns in honor of the presidential veto"; the Dubuque *Times,* owned by Gideon T. Stewart, once part owner of *The Blade*, declared that "the message of the President . . . will be read with sorrow by every enlightened and justice-loving citizen."

The Freedmen's Bureau Bill was one of two pieces of legislation (the Civil Rights Bill was the other) introduced in Congress by Abraham Lincoln's long-time friend, Senator Lyman Trumbull of Illinois. Its purpose was to continue and, in some respects expand, the role of the bureau that had been established to protect the interests of the newly freed slaves in the South. Trumbull and other moderates in Congress had discussed the measure with the President

The Perils of Reconstruction 91

and believed it had his approval. Every Republican member of the Senate had voted for its passage.

David Ross Locke had mixed feelings about the veto, and these were reflected in *The Blade's* editorial comment. It suggested that Johnson was wrong to have declared that protection of the freedmen's rights could now be left entirely to the states. Federal assurances were still needed, Locke argued, to protect those rights against "black codes" that were being proposed in some states. But, he conceded, that was an important difference between protecting the freedmen and supporting them, and the President was right to declare that the bill posed a threat to constitutional government by establishing military jurisdiction over all cases involving the immunities and rights of the freedmen. So *The Blade* endorsed the veto, with only minor dissents from Johnson's reasoning. The February 21 editorial concluded: "The present law is imperfect, and amendments are undoubtedly demanded, but the bill under consideration went as much too far as the old one fell short. The amendments should be carefully considered. In our zeal for justice — in our anxiety to make reparation for the injury we have inflicted on the African, we should be careful that we do not inflict injuries on the white, and that we do not add to our already heavy burdens a load we cannot carry."

When spokesmen for the South and for the Northern Copperheads applauded President Johnson's veto and claimed him as their friend and ally, Locke was annoyed. "If the Copperheads infer from his veto . . . that he intends to deliver the blacks over to their late masters they are mistaken grievously," *The Blade* declared on February 22. "Under the present bill he has the power to see that justice, strict and impartial, is done, and that power he will exercise. He vetoed the bill because it contained objectionable features, but he has not nor will he abandon the Freedmen to the mercy of the rebel South."

By the next morning, Locke was less certain of Andrew Johnson's fealty. A group of admirers had come to the White House on the night of February 22 from a mass meeting where speakers had praised the veto of the Freedmen's Bureau Bill. Acknowledging the group's cheers, the President had declared that he was "opposed to the Davises, the Toombs, the Slidells,"[10] but that when he saw "on the other hand men still opposed to the Union . . . I am still for the preservation of these States." Pressed for the names of the men he had in mind, Johnson responded: "I look upon as being opposed to the fundamental principles of the Government and as now laboring to destroy them, Thaddeus Stevens, Charles Sumner, and Wendell Phillips."

Locke was disturbed by the implications of this name-calling, which he saw as disruptive to the Union party. In a *Blade* editorial the next day, he put this conviction forcefully to the President, as he had to the Radicals on several occasions:

> ... That support we shall continue to give him, if, walking in the path he laid out for himself years ago, he holds true to the faith, and carries out in good faith the policy enunciated by his predecessor and repeatedly endorsed by himself. If, on the other hand, under the influence of love for the South, or hatred for the class of extremists at the North, he turns the cold shoulder to the real Union men of the country, and affiliates himself with those who two years ago would have hung him . . . men who have no other idea of Government than one based upon slavery and controlled by those who sought to destroy it; if he does this, we cannot and will not support him.
> We hope for the best.

The Blade's position was further defined in an editorial of March 6, attempting to point out to Johnson the dangers of his own excesses:

> We have urged harmony in the Union ranks, because we believe that the Union party alone can take the Government safely through the perils that beset it. The Stevens and Sumner style of men are dangerous, because they are zealous, because they are intolerant, hasty, and not prudent. We have urged that they cease "hammering" at the President, and in cool blood set to work to solve the great questions which now engross the attention of the people. On the other hand, we beg of the President that he will stop "hammering" at Sumner and Stevens . . . If he could get out of that circle, how much better would he feel in not coming in contact with them, as he must if he continues to sweep around it. The people know Sumner — they don't like him — but the continual telling of them that he is as bad and as wicked as the secessionists is the surest way to give him power.

The President vetoed the second of the measures introduced by Lyman Trumbull — the Civil Rights Bill — late in March and *The Blade* again came to his defense. This bill conferred citizenship on "all persons born in the United States; the right to make and enforce contracts; to sue and give evidence; to inherit, purchase, lease, sell, hold, and convey property; full and equal benefit from all laws and proceedings for the security of persons and property." Johnson took exception to the elaborate bureaucracy that would be established to

The Perils of Reconstruction

carry out these provisions, and David Ross Locke agreed with him. "The Negroes of the South must be protected — they must have all the natural rights the white man enjoys," Locke wrote, "but to give them these rights there is no necessity of overthrowing the whole theory of Government."

Serious deterioration of *The Blade's* support of Andrew Johnson became apparent just a week later — on April 2 — when the President issued a proclamation declaring the war at an end. This meant that all Union forces would be withdrawn from the Southern states. It restored the right of habeas corpus to residents of the states that had adhered to the Confederacy. It declared these residents reinstated and invested with all rights and privileges. Locke thought it was too soon to take these actions, believing that these rights should be withheld and used as pawns to win assurance that the Southern states would acknowledge the basic rights of the freedmen. "The absolute freedom of all men," he wrote, "their freedom from any and all forms of slavery — their absolute equality in everything pertaining to person and property, should be placed above the caprices of the State Legislatures, and until this is done the people of the United States stand guilty before God of a breach of faith as wicked as it is cowardly."

The Blade and its editor did not finally sever all ties with the Johnson Administration until July 3, 1866, when the call was issued for a convention to be held in Philadelphia in August. Democrats and Republicans were invited to launch a bipartisan campaign to elect a Congress that would support the President's Reconstruction program. When the call was taken up enthusiastically by men who had been identified as leaders of the Copperhead cause, the President and his aides were embarrassed, but there was little they could do to dissociate themselves from these self-proclaimed allies. For Locke and *The Blade*, this was the last straw. After listing some who would attend the convention — including Clement Vallandigham — an editorial of July 6 went on to name others who would not be there. These were men (they included Horace Greeley, John Sherman and Ulysses S. Grant) "whose hatred of slavery and whose love for the right is not a garment to be put off and on as convenience or interest may dictate, are not politicians by trade; they love their country more than they do place and position and none will be there."

★ ★ ★

It was at this point that Petroleum Vesuvius Nasby became a

principal weapon in *The Blade's* rapidly escalating war against Andrew Johnson and his Reconstruction policies. Contrary to Paul Buck's assertion, the Nasby letters of Locke's early months in Toledo had little to say about thg President and his program. The Nasby style of satire was not well adapted for use in the kind of conciliatory position *The Blade* had espoused from October, 1865, until now. But it was ideally suited to the slashing frontal attack which *The Blade* now launched.

Nasby had come into existence over a period of years while Locke had been owner and editor of several weekly newspapers in Ohio. He had a flair for humorous and imaginative writing that found expression in many forms. The Nasby letters began to appear regularly in the Hancock *Jeffersonian* at Findlay after Locke had moved there in 1861. It was here, as has been noted, that they first attracted national attention. It was, of course, the Nasby letters that had first stimulated Alonzo Pelton's interest in Locke, resulting in the eventual hiring of the young editor by the owner of *The Blade.*

This Nasby was a thoroughly repulsive character — a shiftless, drunken lout, possessed of all the qualities that any respectable American, living in the Northern states and sympathetic with the Union cause, would find entirely obnoxious. Into the mouth of this reprobate Locke put all the arguments that were typically offered in defense of slavery, in favor of secession by the Confederate states, in support of those Northerners who came to be known as Copperheads. The letters were written in a kind of dialect used by many American humorists at the time. It was represented as backwoods speech. Words were misspelled, and the letters k, q and z — which were presumed to make the reader laugh — were used frequently.

The Nasby letters, read today, are not very funny, and Locke did not, in fact, intend them as humor, but rather as satire. To many of his contemporaries, however, they were side-splitting, and among their most loyal fans was Abraham Lincoln, who is reported to have been reading from a Nasby collection on the afternoon of the day he was assassinated. The letters gained wide circulation and approbation among Union soliders during the war. Indeed, George S. Boutwell, who became Secretary of Treasury in the Grant Administration, declared that "the crushing of the Rebellion can be credited to three forces: the army, the navy, and the Nasby letters." If this was something of an overstatement, it is indicative of the extent of Locke's influence in the guise of Nasby.

The Perils of Reconstruction

Nasby came into his prime in *The Blade* in the late summer of 1866, when Andrew Johnson made a trip. Ostensibly to dedicate the tomb of Stephen A. Douglas in Chicago, it developed into a campaign tour for congressional candidates who might be expected to support the President. Locke accompanied the party and reported its progress, referring to Johnson as "His Accidency," the "Dictator," and the "Mogul." On the party's leaving Toledo, he reported that "the menagerie left this city for Detroit at about 4 P.M." At Cleveland, it was alleged that "the President made another disgraceful exhibition of himself — so disgraceful, indeed, that General Grant, unable to endure it, unwilling to be made the attraction of such a show, pleaded sickness and took a boat to Detroit."

The charge that Johnson was a heavy drinker was made repeatedly in the Nasby letters describing the tour, most bluntly in this account from Louisville: "There wuz a magnificent demonstration here. His Imperial Majesty, who wuz in eggslent condition to make crowds large enough, remarked to me as we wuz ridin through the streets: 'Splent splay! Mor'n ten undered sousand people — mor'n ten million people — mor'n ten undered million people — mor'n ten undered sousand million people — and all uvum sports of my policy. Rah for me!' "

These Nasby letters also capitalized on Johnson's continuing repetition of the same statement in his speeches throughout the tour. Unaware of the changes that a budding communications revolution was imposing on political speakers' techniques, the President made himself an easy target for satire; Locke, in the guise of Nasby, made the most of the opportunity. Several of these letters — along with others Locke wrote later — were published under the title *Swingin Round the Cirkle,* with illustrations by the famous cartoonist, Thomas D. Nast, who became Locke's good friend. Nast also drew a sketch of Nasby that came to be accepted as an authentic portrait.

When the Toledo *Commercial* took Locke to task for having made his own considerable swing around the political circle between March and September, 1866, *The Blade* replied: "We acknowledge our mistake in supporting him (Johnson) at all. We held to him in the belief that he was honest, long after those who knew him better had given up, and therein we erred."

★ ★ ★

The Blade did not at once support proposals to bring impeachment charges against Andrew Johnson when they were first heard in September, 1866. When Thomas Williams, a Pennsylvania congressman, urged in October that charges be filed, *The Blade* observed that "Andrew Johnson has been guilty of high misdemeanors, and with Williams and Butler in Congress, it will be strange if he shall not be made to answer for them," but disclaimed any opinion as to whether impeachment could be sustained.

A resolution was filed in Congress on December 17 to appoint a commission of inquiry into impeachment. Its author was Representative James M. Ashley of Toledo, later to be widely known as "Impeachment" Ashley. *The Blade's* comment was approving but guarded:

> Mr. Ashley, on Monday, introduced a resolution authorizing the appointment of a special committee of seven to inquire if any officer of the Government has rendered himself liable to impeachment. As it was introduced out of order, it could only be got before the House for action by a two-thirds vote suspending the rules. The call resulted yeas 86, nays 49, being within four votes of the requisite two-thirds, and giving a clear majority in a full house for the resolution... The resolution was amended at the President's request and the vote indicates the temper of the House toward His Excellency.

There was another chance to move against Johnson when, on January 9, 1867, he vetoed a bill granting suffrage to Negro residents of the District of Columbia. Ashley now offered a resolution directing the House Judiciary Committee to conduct a thorough examination to determine whether Johnson "has been guilty of acts which are designed or calculated to overthrow, subvert or corrupt the government of the United States."

The Blade approved, declaring that "the matter is now where it should be," though as the investigation continued through the year there was little further comment. Meanwhile, Ashley searched desperately for additional allegations against the President, including a suggestion that Johnson had conspired with John Wilkes Booth and others to assassinate President Lincoln. Asked by the Judiciary Committee for evidence to support this charge, Ashley made such a fool of himself that the impeachment fire went out again after his appearance. *The Blade* put much of the blame for the failure of impeachment at the door of Toledo's own congressman:

> As to Mr. Ashley's share in the business, we have but little to say, and we regret that duty compels us to say anything. His fault was not in moving. Had he held strictly to the charges originally made, he would not

have compromised either himself or his friends. But he did not. He made charges — privately it is true, but coming from one in his position anything done or said has an importance — for which he had not the slightest proof. . . . We censure Mr. Ashley for his imprudence in adopting a course which compromised himself and friends, and which has resulted in making a martyr of the President and giving the enemy a most potent weapon against us . . . Under cover of the failure of this part of the investigation, the President will hide much of the crime he has actually committed.

One final attempt to impeach Andrew Johnson was begun in February, 1868, after the President had removed Edwin A. Stanton from the cabinet in alleged defiance of the Tenure of Office Act, which Congress had passed over his veto. *The Blade* had no doubt this time that the impeachment charges were valid: "As to the justice — the stern necessity of impeachment, there can hardly any longer be doubt in the minds of unprejudiced men. The President deliberately and willfully set himself up as the judge of the constitutionality of the acts of Congress. There was nothing left to Congress but to submit to this one man power or impeach him. The people will sustain Congress in the course it has taken."

Late in April, *The Blade* estimated that "all of this week and part of next will be consumed in finishing the work of ousting a scoundrel and putting in his place an honest man." When the Senate postponed a vote for several days, however, Locke expressed his concern: "The dispatches this morning and this afternoon have a decidedly unhealthy look. We do not give up all hope, but the indications are that there are enough weak brethren in the Senate to acquit the President and continue him in office until the expiration of his time."

The eight Republican senators who were to vote against impeachment — including Ohio's John Sherman — now became *The Blade's* principal targets. "The Republican party is cursed with too many men who have gained their places by buying and selling," Locke wrote, "and it is not to be supposed that they have forgotten the use of such agencies." When the votes on the eleventh article of the impeachment resolution fell one short of the required number, *The Blade* blistered the eight Republicans who "with baseness unparalleled since the time of Judas, deserted their country, and went over to the enemy." Another Ohioan, Chief Justice Salmon P. Chase, was numbered among the traitors. Disappointment at having been passed over as a candidate for the presidency was cited as his motivation for treachery. These Republican "traitors" infuriated the editor of *The Blade* even more than the acts of Andrew Johnson ever had.

The Blade made relatively little use of the Nasby letters as a satirical weapon during the impeachment proceedings. Of the three Locke wrote, the most memorable — "The Impeachment Failure" — appeared on May 21. Chief Justice Chase was here represented receiving congratulatory messages from Franklin Pierce, Clement Vallandigham, and others for his part in the "triumph." Senate Republicans who voted against impeachment drew their share of Nasby's scorn as he discussed prospects for a new party with Postmaster General Randall:

> "Thinkst thou the new programme will result as the President hopes?"
>
> "No, the new party can't succeed no more than our last vencher did. It ain't made up uv the right material. There's more intelleck than sole in it — more bowels than heart. There's Chase, Fessenden, Trumbull, and Grimes. Chase hez ambition, Grimes hate, and Trumbull and Fessenden Dyspepsia, making the engregencies of the new organization half ambition and half Dyspepsia. Never trust a man whose stummick is out of order; take no stock in him whose bowels is unsound. Intelleck is nothin, heart is nothin, onless there's a stummick under 'em on which to build.

Even as the impeachment proceedings drew to a close, however, the Union party was holding its nominating convention in Chicago. The results helped to assuage Locke's unhappiness. He had been a Grant man for many months, making caustic references in his attacks on Johnson to the time when the President would be succeeded by "a real Union man." The Union party chose that man, Ulysses S. Grant, as its presidential candidate on May 20; Schuyler Colfax of Indiana, among the most rabid of Radicals, was the choice for vice-president. *The Blade* exulted: "Grant and Colfax shall lead the Union army to victory now, as surely as the watchful care and patriotism of both earned triumph for the country in the dark days of treason and rebellion. They are the people's choice. Their names are known in every nook and corner of the land as fearless, true and incorruptible champions of loyalty, liberty and human rights."

Grant and Colfax were easy winners in November and *The Blade* looked to the future:

> The new Administration will be under the influence of men who are on principle Republicans. The most important work is lodged with the Congress, — who will not undo just measures enacted over Johnson's

vetoes — and General Grant will faithfully carry out the measures enacted by the men who elected him.

Unless the men of the South change their course, they will make General Grant more radical than he has ever been, or than any Republican now proposes to be. The Southern Democracy has an excellent way of developing Radicals.

Radicals are not made by the speeches of Wendell Phillips and Charles Sumner, but by violent men like Forrest, Hampton and Frank Blair. The Ku Klux lynchers of the South made Radicals by the thousands.

Chapter 9

The Weekly Blade—Nasby's Paper

David Ross Locke dreamed about and worked at ways of improving the weekly edition of *The Blade* almost from the day he arrived in Toledo and went to work for Alonzo Pelton. The *Weekly Blade* was devoted almost entirely to various legal notices from county and city officials. It had, at that point, fewer than three thousand readers — most of them in Lucas County.

More attention should be given to the *Weekly Blade,* Locke urged in conversations with Pelton. More material of general interest began to appear. Within a few months, the *Weekly Blade's* circulation shot up to 12,000, and it continued to grow.

Locke was determined that the *Weekly Blade* should include a wide variety of material that would appeal to all members of the family. A typical edition might include the following:

*On the first page, a column of poetry — most of which seems to have been contributed — usually sentimental and melodramatic.

*A feature entitled "Wit and Wisdom."

*Several columns of short stories. Sample titles: "The Engineer," "Wild Bill's Story," "Inch by Inch," and "The Story of a Purse."

*An "Agricultural News" column. Typical items: "How to Find a Horse's Age," "Milk for a Pound of Butter," and "Leached Ashes."

*"Religious Reading," which included "Heavenly Certainties," "Sacred Earth," "The Eclipse of the Soul."

*A department of "Reading for Little Folks," with such titles as "Giant Despair" and "Practical Jokes."

Editorial opinion, including the Nasby letter of the week, was on the second page. Most of the *Weekly Blade's* editorials had appeared first in the daily editions, although a few were written especially for its different audience.

Summaries of news received by telegraph during the week occupied the third page, with a remarkably complete report of Congress' activities during the week. There was also a column of financial news and some advertising messages.

The bulk of the advertising appeared on the back page, along with correspondence (letters from readers and others), pieced out with a miscellany of items, including lurid accounts of murders and assorted other atrocities.

The *Weekly Blade's* first eight-page edition appeared on November 5, 1868, becoming increasingly similar to a magazine in both appearance and content. Its front page was devoted almost entirely to serialized features. An installment of a story such as Willkie Collins' "The Yellow Mask" or Ernest Warren's "Throne and Scaffold" appeared in each issue.

Locke took particular pride in a new department called "Answers to Correspondence." Of this service, it was boasted:

> One man is paid a very high salary to answer correspondents, and aside from the fact that he is a walking dictionary . . . he has at his command one of the most perfect reference libraries in the world. It will be found difficult to ask any question that the *Blade* cannot correctly answer. To show something of the pains taken in this department we will say that in 1868 it cost the *Blade* $765 to answer one question. That is what the *Blade* paid one of the best lawyers in the United States to go to Washington and investigate one inquiry as to Bounty and Back Pay, which settled the question forever for thousands upon thousands of soldiers.

The "Household Department" and "Our Young Folks" occupied most of another page. In 1886, the *Weekly Blade* inaugurated a "Medical Bureau." Inquiries were invited, and they poured in. Responses often included specific instructions for druggists' prescriptions — among them remedies for "sexual failing" and other intimate problems.

No record exists of how much of the *Weekly Blade's* fiction — short stories and serialized novels — was written by David Ross Locke. His literary work appeared throughout his life in various publications, sometimes under pseudonyms. The *Weekly Blade* did publish two works of some significance under his own name. These were "Jethro Throop's Night Thoughts" and "Confessions of a Drunkard" — both about the effects of liquor — one of Locke's principal concerns in his later years.

Locke expanded the editorial staff, too. One of the men he

brought to Toledo to help improve the *Weekly Blade* was Robert McCune, who had been editor of the *Christian Statesman*. He became managing editor, then accepted the ministry of a Toledo church and was in charge of Locke's funeral services in 1888.

Other means were used to build circulation. Readers who secured "clubs" of new subscribers received a free subscription as a reward. Many kinds of premiums were offered — among the most popular a Waterbury "Nasby" watch, combined with a year's subscription at a cost of only $3.50. A combination price of $18 was offered later with a Jewel sewing machine — produced in the Toledo plant of the Jewel Manufacturing Company, of which Locke was president. The company was incorporated with a capital stock of $300,000 to produce sewing machines and other specialties.[11]

The best means of building circulation was, however, a rousing presidential election contest, and the numbers of subscribers rose and fell with the political tides. The Grant-Greeley campaign in 1872 provided the first significant leap in circulation — to 120,000. Circulation climbed over 200,000 in several subsequent national election years, then fell back once the campaign excitement was over. These fluctuations created problems and Locke discussed some of them in the issue of September 3, 1868:

> For the past two or three weeks many of our subscribers have had just cause for complaint, on account of not receiving their papers as promptly as they should have had them, and a word of explanation is due them . . .
> In the first place, the unprecedented increase in our circulation three times completely exhausted our edition, leaving for each of these three weeks from three to five thousand of our new subscribers unsupplied with the first number of the paper issued after the receipt of their subscriptions. This, too, after we thought we had printed a surplus of two thousand copies above any demand likely to be made. Thus, in some cases, it happened that subscribers who expected to receive their papers by return mail were delayed so long that we don't wonder some of them found their stock of patience well nigh exhausted.
> In the second place, we soon found that our steam power would be entirely inadequate to run our press at a speed necessary to get off our enormously increased edition in time for all the mails. We immediately purchased a new engine and boiler, of more than four times the power of our old ones; but everybody knows that such a piece of machinery requires a time to get it set and running; and although we pushed the work with all the energy possible, we have but just completed the work, and we feel happy this new engine is now running beautifully, and will furnish us power sufficient to print an edition of half a million . . .
> And now a word as to the future. One of our firm is now in New York

for the purpose of purchasing a new press upon which to print the enlarged *Blade* which we expect to send out to our readers not later than the first of November, and just as much earlier as the manufacturers can build the new press. The *Blade* will then be one of the largest and the *very best* family newspapers in the United States.

The press was a double-cylinder unit, with an attached folding machine capable of turning out 6,000 copies an hour. When it was installed, the format of the *Weekly Blade* was changed — from a folio, nine columns to the page, to a quarto with pages of seven columns each. Now the *Weekly Blade,* by the subsequent account of its own editor, "began to be something what its projector desired it to be."[12]

★ ★ ★

Petroleum Vesuvius Nasby was the *Weekly Blade's* star attraction, and one of his letters appeared in almost every edition. Nasby was a natural as the top attraction for the audience of "the better class of farmers and mechanics, outside the great cities," toward whom the publication was now directed. The *Weekly Blade* quickly became known as "Nasby's Paper," and to many of its readers Nasby was a flesh and blood individual. The Nasby letters were eagerly anticipated and voraciously read.

It was as Nasby that Locke's fame continued to spread. Beginning in 1867, he became involved in more and more activities that diverted his attention away from *The Blade*. His lectures around the United States made him a national figure. He spent much of the decade of the 1870s in New York, where he became involved in a variety of enterprises.

Locke's career as a lecturer on the Lyceum circuit testifies eloquently to the extent to which he became identified in the public mind with the character he had created as the agent of his satire. He had almost no talent for public speaking, yet he became one of the Lyceum's star attractions, drawing audiences of thousands and receiving fees comparable to those paid Mark Twain, who became his good friend. He was always presented as Nasby and was always received with enthusiasm.[13]

On these lecture tours, Locke remained active in writing for *The Blade*, observing conditions in the places he visited and reporting what he saw in letters that appeared regularly. A series of letters from and about several towns in Iowa appeared in *The Blade* immediately preceding an announcement of his return from his latest tour. The advantageous location of an unidentified Illinois town, "close to the

Wisconsin line," in attracting new industry was discussed later. Locke was obviously using what he saw on his travels to buttress his arguments for Toledo's growth and improvement — a topic which continued to occupy considerable space in *The Blade's* editorial columns.

The Nasby letters also appeared regularly while Locke was on the lecture circuit, though he was sometimes hard-pressed to find a subject. He decided to create a situation worthy of his talents on one occasion. John B. Gough, a noted temperance lecturer, was registered at the same hotel in St. Paul where Locke was staying. He ordered two whiskey cocktails sent to Gough's room. Then, he declared, "I wrote my letter on what I saw."

David Ross Locke made his last grand-scale tour of the Lyceum circuit in February, 1871. He had risen in five years from poverty and relative obscurity to a position of substance. Several metropolitan newspapers had sought his services as editor. He had become the friend and associate of many influential journalists, politicians, and others.

Now, in the years between 1871 and 1879, Locke embarked on a series of new adventures in New York. He was editor and business manager of a newspaper, partner in an advertising agency, sales representative for a new-fangled invention called the "type machine." He also tried his hand at many kinds of writing, including novels, plays and essays. And he managed to keep a hand in the affairs of *The Blade*, even at a distance.

Chapter 10

Years Of Locke's Absence

During his years on the lecture tour in the late 1860s, David Ross Locke had come to rely more and more on the managerial skills of Frank T. Lane. In the following decade, as his various New York enterprises kept him away from Toledo, Locke put *The Blade* in the hands of Lane and John Paul Jones, with whom he had also been previously associated. Locke continued to write the Nasby letters, especially for the devoted audience on the *Weekly Blade,* though they appeared less and less frequently as the years passed.

Locke continued to give his attention to major decisions concerning business and editorial policies. He anticipated that his son, Robinson, would soon take an active part in the business. In 1871, Rob Locke was a handsome, brilliant youth who already had shown an interest in the newspaper, had tried his hand at reporting, and had learned the printing trade. He would join *The Blade* staff when he was graduated from Toledo Central High School in two years. And should Locke's successes in his new ventures keep him elsewhere, his son would be prepared to assume the responsibilities in Toledo.

Changes in ownership and editorship of *The Blade* during the 1870s were — as has already been noted — frequent and sometimes difficult to follow. The firm's name was changed in 1872 to Locke and Jones, with the former as editor, the latter business manager. The plant was valued at $170,000 at that time. By 1874, when Jones became sole owner, with E. A. Higgins as editor, it had increased to $250,000. The Blade Printing and Paper Company was organized in December, 1873, with Locke as president, Jones as vice-president, and George D. Chaflin as secretary-treasurer. The company was engaged in general printing, manufacturing of blank books and boxes, selling paper and stationery.

Jones was listed as publisher and owner of *The Blade* in 1875, with Locke as editor. The Toledo Blade Company was incorporated in 1876 and Jones left the newspaper in May of that year. Later in 1876, Locke became president of the company, with A. W. Gleason as vice-president. The firm now published daily, tri-weekly and weekly editions of *The Blade, Locke's National Monthly* and the *American Farm Journal*. The *Journal* was established in September, 1871, the *Monthly* in December, 1872. Several of Locke's stories appeared in these publications before both were suspended in 1878.

★ ★ ★

Locke continued to find time to address himself to problems of concern to readers of both the daily and weekly editions of *The Blade*. Early in 1870, for example, some Toledo residents objected when Negro children were admitted to schools that had been all-white. *The Blade's* position was forthright and predictable: "The law should not allow the question of color, race, or creed to enter into its provision in regard to schools . . . colored children should be given equal opportunity for education." A month later, Locke expressed his belief that Negroes would prefer schools of their own, but where these were not available, they should be permitted to attend the school nearest their home. "Men have hearts," he added, "and whatever prejudices we may have, few of us care to indulge them in such degree as to set both justice and humanity at defiance."

The Blade expressed its approval of the Fifteenth Amendment in April, 1870, by way of a Nasby letter that purported to have been written from the "Harp uv Erin S'loon" in New York City. Nasby, who had moved there after losing his postmastership in Kentucky when the Grant Administration came to power, now joined with his Irish friends to submit the following resolutions:

> Resolved, That the Dimocrisy uv New York, considerin and beleevin the nigger to be a beast, a burlesk on hoomanity, and incapable uv dischargin any uv the dooties uv citizenship, do hereby protest agin his bein given the ballot on an ekality with white men.
>
> Resolved, The Dimocrisy uv New York, ruther than submit to this degradashen, pledges itself to the exterminashen uv the accusid race.

Locke's faith in the Grant Administration was shaken momentarily by the series of scandals that developed. He thought in December, 1871, that "the time has come for members of the

Republican party to speak with each other with the utmost plainness and candor." He deplored the "mistaken policy of the friends of the President in removing Senator Sumner from the chairmanship of the Senate Committee on Foreign Relations." He conceded that the President "has made appointments and removals which we regretted," adding "nor can we close our eyes to the evil consequences of some of these errors." Even so, Locke defended Grant for having "kept the United States at peace with England" and for treating the Indians with a greater degree of humanity. Finally, whatever the President's errors, they paled by comparison with those of Buchanan or Johnson.[14]

When a one-term limitation was discussed, *The Blade* approved the idea. "If the Presidency be bestowed as an acknowledgment of distinguished merit or service, as in the case of General Grant," an editorial declared, "one election, and one term of useful service answers that end, and connects the name of the individual with the history of the nation forever."[15]

The Blade had no problems, however, in supporting Grant for re-election in 1872. None of the reservations expressed earlier concerning the scandals or the less than satisfactory appointments and removals was of any significance now. History had already written Grant down as the foremost of American soldiers, *The Blade* insisted, and his administration was the most successful on record. "Peace has been maintained; the law made supreme; taxation and the debt reduced by millions . . . and the rights of all citizens, of every grade and color, have been maintained." So read a paean of praise to the Grant Administration on June 6, 1872.

When Horace Greeley was nominated by both the Democrats and the Liberal Republicans — a reform group, including many newspaper editors — *The Blade* was not in the least tempted to join in support of the editor of the New York *Tribune*. The editor could see no future for the Liberal Republicans and called the party a "heterogeneous hodge-podge." As for Greeley, *The Blade* insisted that he could not be a Republican, having left the party with bitterness in his heart and with expressed contempt for its time-honored policy. "He is not a Democrat," it was further contended, "because in the dissolution or demoralization of the Democratic party is his only hope as a Greeley man."

As had been true in earlier elections, *The Blade* did not so much support the candidate of its choice as it opposed the man running against him. Little was said in favor of Ulysses S. Grant, but there were daily blasts against Horace Greeley. The Toledo *Commercial,* now owned and edited by Clark Waggoner, the Civil War editor of *The Blade,* alleged that there had been secret negotiations between Greeley partisans in Toledo and the owners of *The Blade,* "whereby, for so much money, to be paid by the Greeley men, that paper was to abandon the support of Grant and the Republican party, and support Greeley and his party." *The Blade* responded that this was "a lie manufactured out of whole cloth, and as malicious a lie as Clark Waggoner, editor of the *Commercial,* is capable of inventing, which is saying a great deal for the quality thereof." When Grant defeated Greeley by a margin of fewer than 200,000 votes out of just under six million, *The Blade* reported that "it is difficult now to find a Democrat who did not know that Greeley would be about the worst whipped man ever nominated for the Presidency." When Greeley died, three weeks after the election, *The Blade* offered no more than faint praise: "At one time there were few men in the nation who had a stronger hold upon the sympathies of the intelligent people of the Northern states than Greeley . . . that he made some mistakes, none will deny."

Neither the Panic of 1873, which resulted in mass unemployment, widespread hunger, and a decline in the immigration rate, nor the continuing smell of scandal about the Grant Administration in its second term shook *The Blade's* loyalty to the Republican party. Republicans dominated both state and local politics throughout this post-war period and received the consistent support of *The Blade,* which occasionally resorted to "waving the bloody shirt" in attacking a Democratic candidate. Thus, when Frank H. Hurd was nominated for Congress in 1872, he was characterized as having "the odium of his immediate anti-war action hanging about him" as a result of his close association with Clement L. Vallandigham. *The Blade* supported Isaac R. Sherwood, a Republican and Civil War hero, for Congress in 1872. But two years later, it found his Populist tendencies unattractive and turned against him to help win the nomination for A. M. Pratt, who was in turn beaten by Hurd in the general election.[16]

The Blade had little trouble deciding which candidate to support in the 1876 presidential election. Rutherford B. Hayes, who bore the Republican standard, had been three times elected governor of Ohio, and each time *The Blade* had supported his candidacy. Hayes, who

Years of Locke's Absence 109

had grown up and practiced law at nearby Fremont, was a competent if unexciting governor. When he was nominated by the Republican convention at Cincinnati in June, 1876, it was generally agreed that he had won because he had avoided antagonizing anybody. *The Blade*, approving the party's platform, observed that the strength of the candidate was more important than any framework of words.

The Democrats nominated Samuel J. Tilden, and the contest that followed was one of the most remarkable in the nation's history, with Hayes eventually being declared the winner by a single electoral vote, 185 to 184. *The Blade* campaigned intensively on Hayes' behalf although — as had so often been true in the past — its support consisted of a steady barrage of reasons why Tilden should not be elected rather than reasons to prefer Hayes. Voters should not cast their ballots for Tilden because: he is a fraud and a sham; he stands as the representative of the worst elements of state and society; he has not the respect even of his own party.[17]

The winner of the election was not confirmed until two days before the inauguration, when contested votes from Florida, Louisiana, South Carolina, and Oregon were finally decided in Hayes' favor. Tales of deals by which the election was bought for the Republican candidate persisted, and Hayes himself believed there was a strong possibility that the outcome would be contested. *The Blade* described Hayes' inaugural address as "calm, manly, dignified, and easy of comprehension to all," adding that "it is not the language of a usurper, but that of the legally constituted President of forty millions of people." Not everyone agreed. Some newspapers referred to Hayes as the "Fraudulent President" and, in 1891, the Cleveland *Plain Dealer* spoke of the election as "The Crime of 1876."

The Blade feuded at frequent intervals with the Toledo *Commercial*. Both papers professed to be loyal to the Republican party, but they had managed to find little in common from the day Clark Waggoner had sold his interest in *The Blade* and become owner of the *Commercial* in 1865. It was *The Blade's* contention that Democrats and supporters of Andrew Johnson had advanced $3,000 toward Waggoner's purchase of the *Commercial* for the purpose of having a newspaper that would oppose Congressman James M. Ashley. Waggoner had, indeed, attempted to bring about Ashley's defeat in 1864, while still editor of *The Blade*. Then, in 1866, the *Commercial* did support the Democratic candidate, General Henry

S. Commager, whom Ashley defeated. No evidence was ever produced to support the charge that Waggoner had accepted financial aid from the Democrats; nor was the allegation specifically disproved.

★ ★ ★

David Ross Locke's Toledo operations continued to prosper, despite his frequent absences, during the first half of the 1870s. A detailed picture of his financial investments and holdings as of April 15, 1875, is contained in a "statement of my affairs this date, starting for California."[18] These included a farm on which a brother, Henry Locke, lived near Toledo and notes totaling over $150,000, including one for about $125,00 from John Paul Jones, to whom he had recently sold *The Blade*.

Young Robinson Locke, having completed high school, was taking a more active part in the operation of *The Blade*. But he was restless, and had other ideas about his future. In 1874, he tried to persuade his father that he should come to New York to join him. David Locke discouraged this notion, writing to his son in the whimsical style of *Abou ben Adhem*:[19] "Bethink you of the public. While you were disporting yourself in the great city they would be mourning for that daily pabulum of which you are dispenser."

Rob Locke received copious advice from his father as to what he should do to prepare himself for a more important role in the management of *The Blade*. A letter from New York late in 1876 is typical:

> I want you to get into the inside of the business of the Blade Office. Talk with Lane . . . about the business, get posted as to the rates, and both daily and weekly, learn every day how subscription and advertising is coming in, make suggestions when they occur to you and slosh about, modestly, as though you had what you will have in a year or two, an actual money interest in it. Get up and interest yourself in the business part of it, and train yourself to do something in that as well as your own immediate department. And talk with the editors, and get their notions and make such suggestions to them as seem good to you — always doing it with modesty and discretion as befits a young man, and more with the view of getting information than giving it. All the same I believe you could teach some of them. I want you to know something of the money end of the concern which you will, in time, take from me. It is excellent knowledge to have.

A year later, after the daily and tri-weekly editions of *The Blade* had been sold, Robinson Locke began to explore the possibility of starting a new Sunday newspaper. It was a good idea, his father thought, and wrote to make several suggestions:

Agree with McElroy[20] as to terms. You must insist upon being the business man and having control of the books and finances. That is, you receive and pay out everything, and keep the books. This is a point of advantage — not holding it has cost me many a thousand. I know I am honest and will not defraud a partner — I am never so sure of others.

Decide on the name and style. It ought to be a society, personal, Toledo paper — full of local news done in good style. Ignore politics and devote it to Toledo and its interests. Make it a bitter fighter for the trade and growth of the city.

When arrangements with McElroy fell through, Rob Locke proposed entering into partnership with a cousin, James Parker Locke.[21] His father disapproved:

I don't want you and Jim together in business. It makes too much young man and won't do. There must be an older head connected with you . . . I don't want Jim to know that I said this, for it is no disrespect to him, but it wouldn't answer to have two young men together. Possibly I may underrate your capacity — I certainly do not wish to, but I don't want to put money into a failure.

You want a first-rate Sunday paper in Toledo, till such time as you can get hold of one of the dailies, at a time when dailies can be made to pay. That is not now — while a Sunday paper will. I can help you here in advertising and editorial work, and can be of assistance to you in many ways.

David Ross Locke had written to his son in December, 1877: "I am editing and publishing the *Mail* at a salary of $150 per week. Don't say anything about the salary I am getting to anybody." Next day he wrote again: "I shall be kept here, I suppose. I am editing and publishing the *Mail* and making a success of it. It may be that I shall have to make this a permanency."

Editing and publishing the *Mail* proved, however, to be no permanency for Locke. Early in 1878, he became involved in a conflict between its owners, Clark Bell and William Hansford White. Bell, who was the active partner, had fired Major James M. Bundy as editor to make a place for Locke, with explosive consequences. White sued Bell and the *Mail's* situation so deteriorated that it suspended publication between May 15 and July 3. When publication finally was resumed (after a premature obituary for the *Mail* in the New York *Times*) White announced that he had bought Bell's interest. Locke departed with his sponsor, Bell, and Bundy was reinstated as editor.

Chapter 11

Busted Bankers and the Rum Power

George Santayana wrote of the decade of the 1880s that "there was no other time when men knew so many facts and had so few principles." In that decade *The Blade* reached the peak of the influence and prosperity it achieved during the period of almost sixty years of Locke family ownership. David Ross Locke's health began to fail in 1885, but he drove himself and those about him toward the achievement of ever higher goals.

The Toledo to which Locke returned from New York was almost four times as large it had been when he had arrived fifteen years earlier. Its population was listed in the 1880 census as 50,137 and it seemed likely to continue to grow and expand. Toledo's location at the point where the flat, fertile expanse of the Western Reserve bends around the westernmost tip of Lake Erie made it a natural division point on many of the booming new railroads. Products of the West and South were transshipped to Great Lakes freighters, and branch railroad lines made connections with the New York Central, the Pennsylvania, and other railroads.

Toledo had advanced on other fronts in the years of Locke's absence. Jesup W. Scott, former editor of *The Blade*, and his wife had donated land for the Toledo University of Arts and Trades in 1872. In 1878, the city's first telephone linked its finest hotel, the Boody House, with the Western Union office. President Hayes approved an act of Congress in 1872 establishing a United States district court in Toledo. The Lake Erie Islands, east of Toledo, were being developed as a recreational and resort area.

David Ross Locke's Toledo interests had been maintained while he was absent. His son, Robinson, now twenty-five years old, had become increasingly involved in the operation of *The Blade*, and a

Busted Bankers and the Rum Power 113

dependable and competent staff of some one hundred people had been assembled. Frank T. Lane, business manager, and Emily S. Bouton, literary and household editor, were long-time associates of Locke. Both were loyal and devoted friends of the entire Locke family. Another valuable addition to the staff was Samuel S. Knabenshue, who became managing editor in 1883 and continued in that capacity until 1904, when he received a diplomatic appointment. Knabenshue's contemporaries regarded him as a brilliant man and an able editor, though he probably became best known as the father of A. Roy Knabenshue, who flew the first successful dirigible flight in the United States on October 25, 1904, at the St. Louis World's Fair.

The *Weekly Blade* had languished in Locke's absence, and on his return to Toledo he lavished most of his attention on its improvement and expansion. Capitalizing on the 1880 presidential election, he gave enthusiastic support to a fellow Ohioan, James A. Garfield appealing to Republicans throughout the country to subscribe to the *Weekly Blade* as a means of advancing the party's cause. Petroleum Vesuvius Nasby lent a hand to Locke's efforts on behalf of Garfield, and campaign booklets of Nasby's comments on inflation, as well as other issues and events, were widely distributed in this and subsequent elections.

Another principal attraction of the *Weekly Blade* at this time was a series of articles by John McElroy, who had been Locke's first choice as a partner in his son's Sunday newspaper venture. The series, based on the author's experiences in Confederate prisons during the Civil War, was received so enthusiastically that it was published in book form under the title of *Andersonville*. McElroy wrote in a preface to the book that "we only desire that the Nation shall recognize and remember the grand fidelity of our dead comrades, and take abundant care that they shall not have died in vain." The predictable effect of these stories was to stir up old hatreds against the South, in keeping with the practice of "waving the bloody shirt," which had become a staple of many northern politicians in the years after the war. Whatever the reasons for publishing them, the *Andersonville* stories helped rebuild the appeal and circulation of the *Weekly Blade*.

Yet another popular feature of both the daily and weekly editions of *The Blade* at this time was a series of travel accounts written from Europe by David Locke and describing the trip which he and his son,

Robinson, took in 1881. They were gone for almost six months and Locke left instructions that, in his absence, management of *The Blade* should be in the hands of Frank T. Lane, "by which I wish it understood that he shall dictate its course, editorially as well as in business, and in case of any difference of opinion his decision shall be final and without appeal."

The Lockes took the Grand Tour, visiting London, Paris, Geneva and several other cities, before making an extended visit to Ireland. The letters were published in book form a year later by the Blade Printing & Publishing Company under the title *Nasby in Exile*. Robinson Locke made a contribution to the letters, writing many of the descriptive passages.

These letters, while they reflect some of the prejudices of a typical American who has not previously traveled outside the United States, also demonstrate that their author was a keen observer who was not afraid to change his attitudes. Bitterly anti-Irish when he arrived in Dublin, he was converted to strong support of the Irish Republican movement after a tour of the countryside with James Redpath, a partner in the Lyceum bureau for which he had been a star attraction as a lecturer. "Legal brigandage" and "an organized hell" were terms Locke now applied to the British system of landlordism in Ireland.

David and Robinson Locke returned to Toledo in October, 1881. Within a month, the son went back to Europe to improve his knowledge of the continent — particularly of its languages. Rob Locke was ambitious for a career in the foreign service, and his father encouraged this interest, even though he hoped and expected the young man eventually to take over as editor and publisher of *The Blade*. Besides, he wanted his oldest son to have the opportunities of education and cultural refinement that had been denied him.

David Ross Locke rejoined his son in Europe in July, 1882, and remained overseas until May, 1883. There is some indication that both of these trips were made in the hope that Locke might thus be helped in getting some measure of control over the addiction to alcohol that had become increasingly a problem during the years he spent in New York. On this second trip, Rob Locke wrote to his mother in Toledo: "Pater is doing bully! He can have the whole bakery now whenever he wants it. He deserves it, and make no mistake." Was this cryptic reference intended to suggest that David Locke had managed to curb his compulsive appetite for liquor? It is a logical explanation in the circumstances, especially since the elder Locke told friends in 1888, not long before his death, that he had managed to give up drinking about five years earlier.

When the senior Locke returned from his second trip to Europe, he left his son to continue his studies for two more months. He arrived just in time to embark on an editorial campaign of the kind he enjoyed most and at which he was particularly effective.

On April 2, while Locke was in Paris with his son, *The Blade* had reported:

> A rumor took to itself wings this afternoon to the effect that the Commercial Bank, better known to the public as the banking house of C. H. Coy & Co., had been forced to the wall — in other words had failed . . .
> It is understood that the deposits amount to about $80,000, which is the extent of the liabilities. The failure is understood to be due to the failure to negotiate the bonds of the new T. & I. Railway, of which Mr. Coy is Treasurer. Mr. Coy has advanced money for the construction of the road, and has been the main source of revenue.

Next day *The Blade* reported that the failure had caused some excitement in New York banking circles, especially when it became known that Coy & Co. had closed after the Chase National Bank's refusal to honor Coy & Co. drafts. It was not judicious "for a banking house to have a railroad telescoped with it," the president of Chase National declared. To reassure local residents, *The Blade* reported that bank officials insisted that depositors would be paid in full and that no other Toledo bank was involved.

Frank Lane's assessment of the nature and magnitude of the failure was soon changed. "Truth compels the admission that every day gives an uglier aspect to the situation," *The Blade* asserted on April 7, asking why there was such an "astonishing discrepancy between the assets and liabilities of the Toledo and Indianapolis Railway Co., now revealed to be $300,000. The bank, it now appeared, would be able to pay only about ten cents on the dollar to its depositors, one of whom — in the amount of some $1,400 — was D. R. Locke.

Further developments showed that Coy had transferred his residence to a brother-in-law and had handed over $20,000 to an unidentified "leading banker." It also became known that relatives of Cyrus Coy had withdrawn their deposits not long before the failure, and that $40,000 which the banker had received from the sale of a business block had disappeared.

The Blade roundly condemned Coy the next week and demanded a "radical change of our banking laws, and our methods toward bankers who abuse trusts." In later issues, Lane deplored the fact that Coy was reported hiding in his home and there was repeated emphasis of the banker's having victimized the poor and the weak. The assignee of the bank filed a report of assets and liabilities with the Probate Court on April 20. *The Blade* reported these figures — total liabilities of almost $300,000, assets of $158,000.

For the next six weeks, nothing more appeared in *The Blade* concerning the Coy failure, or about any legal proceedings. Then, on June 5 — a few days after David Ross Locke had returned to Toledo — it was proposed that "Mr. Cyrus H. Coy should immediately make a showing of his affairs" and that "delay is very dangerous in this case." Next day, Locke probed deeper:

> When Mr. Cyrus H. Coy has stripped himself of all his property, and reduced himself to the condition financially of the poorest washerwoman who entrusted him with the keeping of her little all, and the proceeds thereof have been divided among his cruelly outraged depositors, the people will admit that he was an honest though very incompetent banker . . . If there is any money to be lost it must be *his* money, not that of poor workingmen and women and widows and orphans. And if Mr. Coy wishes to preserve a shred of an exceedingly damaged reputation, he will do this without delay.

Locke promised that the Coy failure "shall be kept very fresh in the minds of the outraged people," and he more than made good on his promise. He was ready to roll out the big guns in his attack, and during the following weeks and months, he fired at will. His assault on Coy was mounted on three principal themes:

1. Sympathy for specific individuals who had lost their savings.

2. Imaginative satire in which a wide variety of methods used in other countries to deal with "busted bankers" was represented.

3. Direct attacks on Coy, his motives, his business practices, and, particularly, his continuing to live comfortably beyond the reach of the law.

Locke first created a cast of characters among depositors of the bank, thus providing specific, individual victims with whom readers might easily empathize. Some were identified by name, others were anonymous. On June 14, the Forsyths — a mother and two daughters — were introduced to readers of *The Blade*:

> When the red hand of treason struck at the national life, a young man named Forsyth, born and bred in the Maumee Valley, was among the first

to volunteer in defense of the good old flag. He was a thorough patriot, a young man of excellent parts, and because of merit was promoted till he reached the position of Captain. He was taken prisoner and confined to Libby Prison. One day, while looking out a window, a guard, in sheer wantonness, shot him. It was a cruel, brutal and inexcusable murder. That shot deprived a widowed mother of a stay for her declining years and two sisters of help and protection.

Severe as was the blow, the mother and sisters did not permit it to crush them. The same blood that impelled the young man to give his life to his country gave to the widowed mother and bereaved sisters strength to battle with the world. The sisters taught school in a modest way, and not only managed by this hard labor to maintain themselves respectably, but to save something against that rainy day which comes to everybody in this imperfect and incomprehensible world. They labored hard, they lived economically, and thereby accumulated not much, but something.

For safe-keeping, they deposited their little savings in a bank. By some inscrutable law which will be made plain in another and better world, but which is not to be understood in this, such people always get their money in the wrong bank . . . Need we say that in the list of depositors of Mr. Cyrus H. Coy's bank the following appears:

Mrs. C. S. Forsyth...$140.00
Miss C. S. Forsyth.. 300.00
Miss M. A. Forsyth.. 250.00

These three Forsyths are the mother and sisters of the gallant young soldier who was murdered in Libby prison. The principal post of the Grand Army of the Republic in Northern Ohio was named for him.

Six hundred and ninety dollars that these noble women had accumulated by the hardest kind of work, and the most rigid economy, that they might live respectably and decently in the world, Mr. Cyrus H. Coy took them for safe-keeping and it is today in his hands. Will they ever see it again? How much does Mr. Coy propose to pay them? Where is it? What did he do with it? Where has it gone?

We ask this question who should not. The comrades of poor Forsyth ought, for the protection of the mother and sisters of the dead hero, ask it of Mr. Coy with great emphasis.

The Forsyth family and various other members of the cast of characters Locke had assembled from among the victims of the Coy bank failure appeared in the editorial columns of *The Blade* many times in the following weeks. Their sad plight was contrasted each time with the affluence in which Cyrus H. Coy continued to live. Usually it was promised that "we shall make further examination of the list of Mr. Coy's depositors."

But melodrama was not Locke's only weapon. Another was satire, with which he was even more effective. He worked now in the tradition of Nasby and, even more directly, in that of Abou ben Adhem, who made an occasional brief appearance in this aspect of the assault on Coy. On June 14 — the same day that the plight of the Forsyth ladies was brought to the attention of *Blade* readers, Locke began to create a series of imaginary situations in which he discovered how the "busted banker" was dealt with in many different countries of the world:

> The more we think of it the more we are compelled to approve of the Chinese method of dealing with exploded bankers. There is something so simple, so direct, in taking a banker who has failed out into a square and chopping his head off with a very dull cleaver, that we wonder other nations have not adopted it. Many things, this especially, in the languid East are far in advance of the vigorous West.

Locke embroidered this notion in a rich and extended manner. Through the character of Hing Foo (described as a Mandarin of Two Tails and Three Swords, and "analagous to our Police Judge") he arrived at this conclusion:

> It is not necessary to add that bankers do not fail in China any more. Hing Foo, to keep them in mind of the necessity of absolute integrity and level-headedness in their business, had the Government send a dull cleaver to all new bankers, with positive instructions to keep it suspended immediately over the President's head.
>
> There is something so fascinating in the investigation of Chinese banking that we shall pursue the subject farther.

Two more extended tales of Hing Foo's dealings with "busted bankers" were devoted to continuing the pursuit. But the Chinese method of dealing with men of this class was by no means the only one Locke explored. He found much to admire in the way such things were done in many other lands — India, Persia, the Philippines, the Sandwich Islands. Each tale sought to outdo the last in graphic description of the treatment accorded to "busted bankers" in these far-off places, invariably putting an end to such failures forever.

The direct attacks on Cyrus Coy which represented the third variation in *The Blade's* campaign also made use of imaginative situations and satiric devices of many kinds. Much was made of the many days the banker spent on the steamship *Waite*, which operated on Lake Erie. It was suggested in one of these that "he does not go upon the steamer, as might be supposed, because of the facilities it affords for suicides . . . Men of the happy mind of Mr. Coy never jump off the decks of steamers or put a pistol to their heads, no matter how bad the bust." The banker was contrasted with another passenger — "a poor woman, shabbily dressed and with a pinched, hollow face that showed that her meals were not regular and that she was managing to live without sufficient nourishment." The woman had with her "a poor, sick child, whom she was taking down the Bay for the sake of the air." She was, it proved, "one of those who deposited their money with Mr. Coy."

Not until the following year — in February, 1884 — were the depositors of the Coy bank provided the kind of statement Locke had repeatedly demanded, and then it was signed by Coy's assignee, Lysander K. Parks. The banker was revealed by this statement to have been insolvent for eight years before finally closing down. Coy had continued during that time to speculate in grain and to use his depositors' money in other personal financial ventures, notably the Toledo and Indianapolis Railway. *The Blade* declared:

> Society can guard itself against the common thief, but what is it going to do with the man who writes "Banker" under his name, solicits deposits from poor people, and uses their money in grain and railroad speculations? The common thief wears stripes in Columbus — the banker explodes and buys a heavier coat for the winter ...
>
> Our Legislature can do no better thing than to enact a law applicable to these cases, and [some of those victimized by Coy] would like very much to have it retroactive.

Locke's campaign against the "busted banker" was a classic example of the editorial techniques of which he was a master and of a style of personal journalism that was even then beginning to wane in American newspapers. *The Blade* helped to create a public demand that bankers and financiers be held accountable for funds entrusted to them. States began to enact more stringent banking laws, but the Ohio Legislature waited until 1908 to enact new banking legislation.

★ ★ ★

David Ross Locke began an editorial campaign — buttressed by some early examples of investigative reporting — in the *Weekly Blade* that year which was to enhance the national reputation of the newspaper and its editor. This campaign summoned Americans to "Pulverize the Rum Power!" and it became almost as popular as the Nasby letters. Among an entire generation of Americans growing up on farms and in small towns, Locke's name became most firmly associated with the fight against the liquor interests.

These editorials, which began in October, 1883, continued until shortly before Locke's death in March, 1888. They usually appeared in both the daily and weekly editions of *The Blade*, but they were received with particular enthusiasm by the *Weekly Blade's* readers

— many of whom already regarded it as almost a second Bible. In the homes of many of those readers, the Demon Rum was a long-acknowledged enemy. Boys and girls took the pledge that liquor should never touch their lips and wore the white ribbon of Temperance before they understood its meaning. David Ross Locke's editorials slaked these families' thirst for authoritative support of prohibition, and he became their hero.

Much has been made of the seeming incongruity of attacks on liquor by a man who had consumed large quantities of it over a forty-year period, but the accusation of hypocrisy cannot be sustained. Locke had acknowledged long since that he drank compulsively and had several times made a serious effort to cure his addiction — apparently with some success just before he began the series of editorials. He was, in any case, the very man who might most logically have been a leader in this fight, having become convinced that the only way to deal effectively with the problem was to keep liquor out of reach.

It has also been charged that Locke's motives in the "Pulverize the Rum Power!" campaign were wholly political. The assault undoubtedly was triggered by his deep involvement in politics — specifically the 1883 state elections. Locke was disappointed when the Republicans failed to nominate as their candidate for governor Murat Halstead, the Cincinnati editor who had been the first to recognize the appeal of the Nasby letters, more than twenty years earlier. *The Blade* had endorsed Halstead in February, 1883, as "a man of national reputation, and one whom every voter of Ohio knows and respects for his ability, whatever he may think of his politics."

The Republicans nominated Joseph B. Foraker, and Locke accepted the choice, but with little enthusiasm.

The Democrats nominated Judge George R. Hoadley, who had been an attorney for the liquor interests. Locke needed no more excuse to launch an attack on the liquor men. The assault was two-pronged, and the July 5 issue of *The Blade* included both an extremely blunt editorial and a report from Nasby on "More Trouble in the Corners Growing Out of the Liquor Question," which includes startling developments when a tax on liquor is proposed:

> That feend Joe Bigler, and his aider and abettor Pollock, the Illinoy store-keeper, hev bin workin at Issaker Gavitt, and hev finally got him. They hev succeeded in reversin the regler things by convinsin Issaker that Bascom is under obligation to him and not he to Bascom, and they hev

Busted Bankers and the Rum Power

worked the poor imbesil up to sich a pitch uv loonasy that Issaker hez organized a rebellion in the Corners, and is actilly movin to hev a tax put upon Bascom's biznus.

When it was fust perposed Bascom gasped with astonishment, and staggered and wood hev fell prostrate on the floor ef it hadn't bin for the bar which pervented it.

"Tax me!" he gasped, "tax me — tax the likker biznis? Wat becomes uv yer persnel liberty?"

And then Joe Bigler struck in.

"Yes, Bascom, we hev made up our minds to tax you. Issaker hez bin pourin a flood of lite into my mind for several nites, and Mrs. Gavitt hez been in the lite biznis herself.

"Mrs. Gavitt demands in thunder tones why it is the wives uv likker sellers wich hev silk dresses, shoes that button and red silk stockins, and not the wives uv likker drinkers? And then Issaker bethawt himself uv the Dimekratic Convenshen that was held last fall and the procession in the afternoon, and he wuz just sober enuff to notis that the s'loon keepers uv the county in that splendid procession all rode in kerridges, while the likker drinkers hooft it along thro the dust on foot . . ."

Nasby lauded the alliance with the liquor interests as politically expedient for his party, the Democrats. As a Republican, Locke summed up the case against the Democrats and their allies in an adjoining column:

For the first time in the history of the State of Ohio, the liquor interest has declared itself as the ally of one political party and has assumed the control of the policy. It was the liquor interest that dictated the nomination of Judge Hoadly for Governor, the liquor interest has controlled the nomination of Democratic candidates for the Legislature all over the state . . . The liquor dealers have subscribed and paid the sum of $75,000 to the Democratic State Central Committee, the amount having been made up by assessments on saloons of the State in proportion to the business done by each, and on that money the Democrats are running their campaign.

There is no trouble accounting for this action on the part of the Liquor Dealers. The Scott Law taxes them somewhere in the neighborhood of $2,000,000 per annum and to get rid of that tax by a contribution of $75,000 is a very sound business transaction . . .

The party that bargains with an interest so dangerous will find it will have that interest alone to depend upon . . . In espousing the cause of the liquor dealers, the Democracy has erected its own tombstone.

The Blade's obituary for the Democrats proved premature. Hoadly defeated Foraker by 12,000 votes in the fall election, the Democrats won a majority of seats in the legislature and elected their entire state ticket. Two constitutional amendments were defeated —

one establishing a licensing system for the sale of liquor, the other prohibiting its manufacture and sale.

Victory for the "liquor power" was deplored by *The Blade*, which proclaimed it "as bitter and relentless as ever the Slave Power was in its hostility to its opponents." Then came a call to battle: "It is now the question addressed to every man whether he will rouse himself to join in the desperate battle for the overthrow of this towering despotism. He must either do so or yield his neck abjectly to its yoke. There is no longer any half-way place. Men must either fight the Liquor Power or become its servile myrmidons."

Thus began the editorial campaign with which Locke and *The Blade* were to become so widely associated. To this campaign, as to many others, Locke brought a determination to explore every aspect of the problem with which he dealt. He dug deep and ranged widely for material supporting his position.

The Blade first sounded the call to "Pulverize the Rum Power!" in an editorial late in October, 1883. Locke experimented with variations in succeeding weeks, urging readers to "Pulverize the Whiskey Power!" or to "Pulverize the Liquor Power!" But his ear for words quickly told him that his first inspiration had been the best. From then on, it was always the "rum power" that was to be destroyed.

It was not true, as Locke's political opponents sometimes alleged, that his attacks on liquor were confined to the *Weekly Blade*. Nearly all of the "Pulverize the Rum Power!" editorials appeared first, in fact, in the daily edition. Locke did recognize that this campaign would have particular appeal among the *Weekly Blade's* rural and small town readers, and circulation figures soon substantiated his judgment. Readers increased from 113,000 in September, 1883, to 187,000 four years later.

Some aspects of the campaign did appear exclusively in the *Weekly Blade*. One of these was introduced on November 29, 1883:

THE LIQUOR TRAFFIC
Does Prohibition Prohibit?
Important Announcement

Whether Prohibition lessens the sale of intoxicating liquor is a question that has been more discussed than almost any one in which the public has taken an interest.

To the end of determining this question, Mr. D. R. Locke, the editor of the Blade, will make a thorough tour of Maine and Vermont, where the sale of intoxicants has been prohibited by law for 30 years.

This investigation will be thorough and will include—

The condition of the liquor trade in the commercial, manufacturing and agricultural sections, prior to Prohibition and since.

The effect of Prohibition upon the youth of the State.

The amount of liquor consumed in various localities.

How and where drinking is done, and whether the legal impediments in the way have lessened the consumption.

The effect of Prohibition on the morals of the State, as determined by the Court records, statistics on pauperism and crime, and other sources of information.

All these statements will be comparative. In short, the object is to determine the question: "Does Prohibition prohibit?"

The articles Locke wrote, based on his findings in the two states, appeared in four issues of the *Weekly Blade* — December 20 and 27, 1883, January 3 and 10, 1884. They are of special interest as early examples of what is today called investigative reporting or reporting in depth; they provided a detailed comparison of conditions before and after enactment of laws prohibiting the sale of liquor. The wealth of detail and its indication of extensive interviews testify to the thoroughness of Locke's study, though it is also clear that he tended to rely on material supporting his pre-conceived belief in prohibitory laws.

The Blade found many occasions to attack the Rum Power at home, too. Locke blamed the city's brewers for Toledo voters' rejection in 1884 of expanding and improving the city's public parks, despite *The Blade's* enthusiastic support for the plan: "For were there parks in the various wards fitted up and easy of access, where air and shade and pleasant surroundings could be secured without beer, they would go there instead of thronging the beer gardens."

The "Pulverize the Rum Power!" campaign climaxed in May, 1887, when Locke published in both daily and weekly editions of *The Blade* a four-column-long, front-page article summing up his convictions on the need to enact prohibition laws. It appeared under his by-line, and this was the heart of his argument:

There is but one evil thing in the United States that is above the law — one evil that is sacred — one evil that the leading politicians are afraid to touch, and that one evil is liquor, the greatest curse that afflicts humanity, the one curse that includes all others. Law makers are not at all tender upon Mormonism, nor do they hesitate at all to attack other sins of omission and commission. Congress dares to reach out its restraining hand against railroad oppression, and legislatures pass all sorts of laws protecting the people against all sorts of evil, that worry or even threaten them, but this curse, Rum, alone is sacred . . .

I have simply skimmed the surface of this question, the most important one now before the American people. The vice of Intemperance is the standing menace to the church, the school, and the community at large. It is a wide stream with soft loam banks into which the current is eating with frightful rapidity and still more frightful persistence. It threatens the existence of everything that is good and the dominance of everything that is bad. Let it go on as it is now going, and in twenty years it will control everything. The American people are in danger of becoming a race of drunkards.

It is time there should be an awakening on this subject, a thorough and complete awakening. Wherever prohibition has been tried it has proved a great and incalculable good. It has saved Maine, and in Iowa, Kansas and Georgia, it is doing an equally beneficent work. There is not a state in the nation that has not a majority in favor of Prohibition could it only be gotten together. It is high time that this union for Prohibition be made.

Reader, what will you do toward it!

There is no way to measure the extent of the influence of the "Pulverize the Rum Power!" campaign in the effort that did culminate thirty years later in the Eighteenth Amendment and the Volstead Act. It can be said that these editorials and other materials which Locke used in the campaign were highly esteemed by other Prohibitionists. Their wide circulation in the *Weekly Blade* undoubtedly stimulated enthusiasm for the cause throughout the country. It would remain for another publisher and owner of *The Blade*, Paul Block, to play a leading part in the repeal of Prohibition half a century after David Ross Locke had begun the fight for its enactment.

Chapter 12

David Ross Locke's Last Years

"Busted bankers" and "rum power" were David Ross Locke's pre-eminent concerns after his return to Toledo in the early summer of 1883. But having been away from his home and his business for nearly two years, he found other issues of importance in the five years of life that remained to him.

The railroads had made further gains and were to be praised. James M. Ashley was in charge of building the Ann Arbor Railroad, and he was "making progress every hour that can be seen and measured," *The Blade* reported, adding that "this is a work that Toledo people should take a lively interest in, as every step in its development is a direct lift in our business prosperity."

The Blade expressed its concern when, in October, 1883, the Supreme Court invalidated the Civil Rights Law enacted in 1875. Locke feared that a result of the decision might be "to reopen the contention in regard to the races, and arouse once more the prejudices and passions that seemed in a fair way to be laid finally to rest." There was danger in the possibility that "Negroes aroused by the decision which they will understand takes away some of their newly acquired rights, may be disposed to push their privileges where they are allowed."

Locke wrote a few days later that it was unlikely the decision would much change the status of Negroes: "It will not in their social status, since that is something outside the law, and determined by influences and causes over which legislation and the courts have no control. As far as their legal status is concerned . . . the Negroes are citizens of the United States, and clothed in all their rights, privileges and protection of that citizenship." Locke was correct in this conclusion, though he failed to see that the legal and constitutional rights of black Americans would be widely ignored.

Robinson Locke came home from Europe in October, 1883, to take his place on the staff of *The Blade*, but again it was for only a brief time. In December, President Chester A. Arthur named him United States consul at Newcastle upon Tyne. The appointment fulfilled his ambition for a career in the diplomatic service, an ambition his father shared, even though the elder Locke wished to have Rob with him on *The Blade*.

Soon after his son's departure, David Locke also resumed traveling. He went south with his publisher and friend, Charles A. B. Shepard of Boston, early in 1884. He took along with him many of the convictions and prejudices he had accumulated over more than three decades, and these were sometimes reflected in a series of letters published in both the daily and weekly editions of *The Blade* during the next three months, under the title "Nasby in the South." On the whole, however, Locke proved to be an objective reporter. He was not won over to the South, as he had been earlier to the Irish, but his dispatches were neither bitter nor vindictive; they seem to have reflected what he observed.

Locke returned to Toledo in May, 1884, and almost immediately *The Blade* became embroiled in a rousing newspaper fight. The adversary on this occasion was the Toledo *Telegram* (formerly the *Commercial*), which had been acquired a few years earlier by a group of Republicans who resented Locke's influence in party affairs. Front man in this operation was J. B. Battelle, who had been one of Locke's associates on *The Blade* for many years. Battelle had then disposed of the *Telegram* to Brigadier General James M. Comly, lately recalled by President Arthur from the post of United States minister to the Sandwich Islands (Hawaii). Comly was a newspaper man of some experience, having been editor of the Ohio State *Journal* in Columbus.

The fight began when the *Telegram* attacked President Arthur for his adamant support of civil service reform, and *The Blade* came to Arthur's defense. The *Telegram* suggested that these tender feelings toward the President might be explained by Robinson Locke's holding a consulate under the Arthur Administration. David Locke responded: "We might remark, as well, that if Pres. Arthur had not unceremoniously and peremptorily recalled the editor of the *Telegram* from Honolulu, the said editor might be, what the *Blade* is not, an ardent supporter of Pres. Arthur for the succession. The modest and un-egotistic General — by brevet — who controls a newspaper — by brevet — has grievances."

Soon the battle shifted to old differences over local politics. *The Blade* insisted that "there are men in Toledo who have been in the ranks quite as long as Gen. Comly, who have a right to a proper expression of their preferences," and concluded with this salvo:

> We regret that the *Telegram* does not like the style of the *Blade*, because something gives the *Daily Blade* a vastly larger circulation than the *Telegram* has now, or even had when Mr. J. B. Battelle, with all his experience on the *Blade*, gave it up as utterly hopeless and unloaded it gaily upon Brigadier General Comly. The *Weekly Blade* somehow finds favor in the eyes of 112,000 families. It sheds its pure light at over 22,000 postoffices in the United States and goes into every State and Territory. Everybody seems to like the *Blade* but Brigadier General Comly. As he receives his copy free (of course we exchange, but that gives him the *Blade* for nothing) that doesn't worry us, being a mere stooper for money. There are many thousands of people who do like it to the extent of paying for it, and we must be content to grub along with them.

The Blade had other interests and concerns. It played a leading part in promoting Toledo's first major art exhibition. A reporter was assigned to devote full time to this event, and the first of a series of "art receptions," held June 2, 1884, was commended:

> The Art Reception at the Draconian Club today is an event of very considerable importance to the City. When the Club proposed to give a loan art reception it was supposed that to make even a respectable exhibit it would be necessary to draw upon the resources of art dealers in other Cities, but to the surprise of those active in the movement, it was found that our own citizens had upon their walls excellent pictures in sufficient numbers not only to occupy all the space that could be assigned, but to afford material for a succession of exhibits . . .
>
> The effect of this exhibition upon the taste of the City will be marked. The bringing together of so many fine pictures will stimulate the rapidly growing love of art in Toledo, and will be the means of bringing to the city not only more pictures, but a better class of them.
>
> It was an experiment, and a rather ambitious one, but its success has been so marked that these delightful receptions will be repeated monthly during the coming season.[22]

Ever since his return to Toledo from New York, David Ross Locke had been planning the new building to house *The Blade*. He had bought the lot at the corner of Superior and Jefferson, in the heart of Toledo's expanding downtown district, for the price of $21,000. Late in September, 1884, the new building was completed and occupied. It included all the latest equipment. Locke wrote to his son in England: "We have a new Scott press running, and it is a very fine one. We need two now, as our weekly is very near 200,000 — it will be next week. There is nothing like it on earth."

David Locke's health had already begun to fail. He was concerned about the future of his family and his newspapers. In another letter to Robinson Locke at about this time, he expressed these concerns:

> I want next year, unless something very big turns up on the other side, for you to come home, sit down in Lane's office and learn his business thoroughly. He isn't going to last always and the time is coming when I want to be relieved. The weekly is to-day the best newspaper property in this country, and has got to the point where it is standard. Renewals come without work, and steadily. It is established on a very firm basis, and I want you and your children to run it forever . . . However, there is time enough for that after you have served abroad a year or two longer.

The 1884 presidential election settled the problem of how long Robinson Locke should remain abroad. David Ross Locke had been sure James G. Blaine would win, and when the Republicans carried Maine in September, he wrote to Rob that "there will be no trouble in getting a promotion for you, to a second-class mission . . . or at least a consul-generalship." But "Rum, Romanism and Rebellion" intervened, and Grover Cleveland was the winner in November, not Blaine.

"They will give you a chance to resign in July," Locke wrote to his son in May, 1885. Robinson Locke did resign and returned to the United States. When he arrived in Toledo, he was placed in charge of the family's newspaper operations.

David Locke remained active in the affairs of *The Blade*, concentrating on writing for the *Weekly Blade*. When he was in Toledo, he went regularly to his office until the last few weeks of his life. A surviving relative recounts that on one of these occasions he observed a new reporter in the newsroom and, having looked the new man over carefully, went to the office of his nephew, Charles Locke Curtis, who was managing editor of *The Blade*.

"I see we have a new reporter," Locke observed.

"Oh, yes," Curtis replied, "he's a very good man. Just came from New York. We are very lucky to get him. He's very good."

"Fire him immediately," Locke barked. "He's wearing a Norfolk jacket and I won't have any damn fool working for us who doesn't have sense enough not to wear a thing like that in Toledo."

★ ★ ★

The Citizens Natural Gas Company was established in the spring of 1886, with Locke among its organizers, to drill for gas and install pipelines throughout the city. *The Blade* became involved almost immediately in what came to be known as the "Natural Gas Pipe-Line Controversy," which was to continue for many years after David Locke's death in 1888 and to become a dominant issue in Toledo politics.[23]

Huge natural gas reserves had been discovered in the oil fields at nearby Findlay in 1884, and by 1887 the Findlay gas wells had produced as much as 15,000,000 cubic feet. Real estate promoters saw free gas, or at least prices below those in eastern cities, as the means of attracting new industries. Whether private monopolies or municipally-owned companies should control the gas supplies soon became a principal point of contention.

Two companies were organized in Toledo, and the Standard Oil Company became involved in both. Standard had provided early financial backing for the Northwestern Ohio Natural Gas Company, and Standard soon secured an interest in Citizens Natural Gas Company, which Locke had helped to organize. Both firms received franchises from the city in September, 1886. That the city got no payment for these rights became an important consideration in later franchise disputes. The city could always get into the gas business later if it seemed advisable, citizens were told, since these were not exclusive grants.[24]

The Blade, sounding a bit as it had under the editorship of Jesup Scott, hailed completion of the lines and the turning on of gas in Toledo in September, 1887: "With her unrivaled system of transportation, and with natural gas as a fuel, our city should become the greatest manufacturing city of the West." Both companies charged rates somewhat lower than those asked in eastern cities, but a bit above other cities with municipally owned facilities. Even before the gas was turned on, however, opposition had developed, and there was considerable support for construction of a municipally owned natural gas plant to assure special inducements that were necessary to attract new industries.

The Blade supported a municipal plant when it was first proposed; Locke believed there was "but one sentiment among the people concerning the proposition, and that one favorable to the plan." He painted a bright picture of the future: "Toledo would at once enter upon a growth so rapid, so enduring, that the past dreams of her greatness will not only be realized but surpassed in the enormous extension of her industries. She will become a mighty hive of industrial workers, a city of wealth and power, and the great industrial metropolis of the West."

Within a few months, however, *The Blade* had become disenchanted with the notion. When Toledo's Representative Charles P. Griffin introduced a bill in the Ohio Legislature in January, 1888, authorizing the city to issue bonds to erect a gas pipeline, *The Blade* opposed it. Siding with Mayor J. K. Hamilton, local business leaders, and the Standard Oil Company, *The Blade* regretted its passage by the House of Representatives, 56 to 8, and applauded a month later when "Mr. Griffin's gas bill to bond Toledo for $750,000 was gloriously and indefinitely postponed in the Senate on motion of Senator Carlin."

After the Toledo Natural Gas Trust was organized in August, 1888, "to furnish free gas to manufacturers," *The Blade* once more reversed its position on municipal ownership.[25] One of the Trust's directors was Edward Drummond Libbey, who had moved his glass factory to Toledo from Cambridge, Massachusetts, on the strength of the availability of natural gas. Libbey and his fellow directors represented, *The Blade* declared, "Toledo's most wealthy and influential citizens, and the manner in which they take hold of the work shows that if such a thing as free gas is possible it will be had, and that very soon."

Continuing support of the municipal project was provided in a December editorial: "We shall labor to have the city pipe line project go through, and at the same time endeavor to show up every scheme of personal advantage, if any be developed, which is attempted to be worked in this connection."

Again in January, 1889, *The Blade* urged a municipal gas system to attract new industries. Yet, only two months later, after the Griffin Bill had been revived and an election on a proposal to issue bonds for construction of a gas line had been set for April 1, *The Blade's* editor had another change of heart. "Can we afford it?" was the question asked repeatedly in a series of editorials examining the feasibility of the municipal project. Rumors circulated that *The*

Blade had allied itself with the Standard Oil Company in opposing municipal ownership. These were denied:

> The *Blade* is not purchasable, and all intelligent men, familiar with the paper and its consistent course as an advocate of the best interests of Toledo and its citizens, know this. The *Blade* is not in the service of the Standard Oil Company, nor of either of the natural gas companies, or of anybody else . . . The Standard Oil Company is not wealthy enough to buy an editorial utterance.

The Blade also sent a reporter to several cities to explore municipal gas operations. These included four in Ohio — Bowling Green, East Liverpool, Youngstown and Findlay — as well as Jamestown, New York; Wheeling, West Virginia; Indianapolis and Pittsburgh. These reports cited a number of factors likely to discourage Toledoans from supporting municipal ownership, including early exhaustion of gas wells, rate increases, failure to maintain a supply of free gas. The motives of those supporting the plan were questioned, and the articles cited court records in Hancock and Wood counties to show that the pipeline advocates had holdings that they expected to sell to Toledo if the bond issue were approved.

Despite these efforts, the proposal was carried with the approval of sixty-two per cent of the voters. *The Blade* would not oppose the decision, it declared, while claiming that Republican votes were "openly traded to secure votes for the pipeline."[26]

More than ten years later, and after the whole natural gas undertaking had deteriorated into a fiasco, *The Blade* would summarize its part in the continuing fight over municipal ownership in an editorial of April 17, 1897:

> Perhaps the hardest fight the *Blade* ever undertook was that in opposition to the natural gas project. The whole subject was carefully considered from the start. The *Blade* believed then what everyone now knows to be true — that the natural gas was simply a supply stored in the rock, and which would be exhausted in a few years — but which few then believed. It felt that the enormous expenditure which would be incurred could not be paid off before the gas supply would be exhausted, and that the taxpayers would eventually have to meet the cost.
> It took up the fight fearlessly to prevent, if possible, the saddling of a million and a half of bonded debt upon Toledo. It pointed out that the scheme was fathered by men who had axes to grind and who were wheedling the people into turning the grindstone. The bill authorizing the bond issue contained a section requiring an affirmative vote of the people. The campaign on this issue was one of the hottest Toledo ever had, as many will remember.

It is supremely ridiculous now to recall the pleas that were made to induce people to vote for the scheme. "Free gas" was the cry, and hundreds of the less intelligent voters supported the project at the polls because they really believed they would get free gas. The *Blade* was the target of all kinds of abuse. Men who knew better denounced it in public speeches as being "purchased by the Standard Oil Company," and hundreds of gullible people actually believed the charge. The vote in favor of the bonding of the city was carried by an immense majority, the bonds were sold, the gas territory secured, the pipeline built.

Well, looking over these few years, who was right? The *Blade* or the men who voted for bonding the city? The question answers itself. The interest on these bonds is met today out of city taxes. The principal must be paid by taxation. An enormous burden was laid upon Toledo, and nobody benefitted in the least — except the men who originated the scheme, who made snug little "rake-offs." The people of Toledo will have to pay some three million dollars, principal and interest, from not following the course advised by the *Blade*.

Toledo's natural gas controversy attracted considerable attention throughout the country, becoming a kind of classic case of its kind. Henry Demarest Lloyd made it one of the principal concerns of his *Wealth Against Commonwealth,* a widely read contribution to the reform literature of the period. *The Blade* had an important part in the controversy, if perhaps not quite so omniscient as this "looking backward" editorial suggested.

★ ★ ★

David Locke carried on a variety of battles of his own on behalf of reform causes during his last few years as editor of *The Blade*. His newspaper's reputation as a rock-ribbed Republican organ was accurate only to the extent that *The Blade* finally did support the party's candidate at election time, after carrying on a running battle with Republican leaders in the intervening years.

Women's rights and labor's right to organize and bargain were among the causes of which Locke was an early advocate. He continued to insist upon protection of the rights of blacks, and he was increasingly disturbed by accumulating evidence that these rights were being widely denied — especially in the South.

Some of the positions taken by *The Blade* under Locke's editorship foreshadow those with which it has come to be identified more recently under the ownership of the Block family. Thus, in the matter of reporting crimes, *The Blade* in 1886 responded to a letter from a reader who complained because some details of a crime had been omitted from the newspaper's account:

> Criminal items are the least worthy that enter a newspaper's columns. They subserve no good purpose. The *Blade's* rule is, to give the mention . . . but to omit all details . . . We have no desire to rival the Police Gazette and papers which follow the same general lines . . . We are sure that if our correspondent complaining about crime stories not printed will consider the matter in all its bearing, he will agree that it is the only proper way to run a responsible newspaper.

The Blade's concern almost a century ago was with matters other than protecting the pre-trial rights of accused persons, which has been the basis of more recent actions having to do with the reporting of crimes. But the parallel is interesting, suggesting a continuing tradition in newspaper policy.

David Locke became ill with tuberculosis (then usually called consumption) in 1885. He spent some time during the winter of 1886 at Hot Springs, Arkansas, in search of a cure, and he went to Star Island, off the coast of New Hampshire, in the summer of 1886. Despite his illness, he continued to be active in *The Blade's* affairs until November, 1887, when he was confined to his home for most of the remaining three months of his life. More and more of the responsibilities of the newspaper operations were turned over to his son, Robinson, who had returned to Toledo in 1885.

Illness did not, however, lessen David Locke's interest in political affairs. He had often admonished editors to refrain from seeking office for themselves and, until 1886, he had adhered to that policy. When he decided in that year to become the Republican candidate for alderman from Toledo's third ward, friends warned him against permitting his name to be placed on the ballot. His strong stand against liquor, they reminded him, had incurred the enmity of its local representatives, who would make every effort to defeat him. Locke was not discouraged.

Municipal election campaigns at that time were whirlwind affairs. Parties nominated their candidates on March 31; the election was held just five days later, April 5. As Locke had been warned, Toledo liquor dealers held a meeting the day after his nomination and decided to wage an all-out campaign to defeat him. *The Blade* commented:

> Mr. D. R. Locke is the Republican candidate for Alderman in the Third Ward. On yesterday . . . the Liquor Dealers' Protective Association (we believe that is the name) held a meeting and decided that all possible efforts should be made to defeat Mr. Locke, because of his belief in Prohibition.

Mr. Locke was not nominated on the Prohibition issue, nor has the issue entered into the city campaign. He was nominated in the interests of good government, in the interests of the growth and improvement of the city, and the development of her industries.

These persons have seen fit to inject another issue into the canvass in the Third Ward, viz: whether the people who desire to facilitate the growth and material prosperity shall govern the city, or whether it shall be ruled by the "bummer" element, under the direction of the Rum Power. This is now the question which the voters of the Third Ward will have to answer by their ballots at the polls next Monday . . .

For the enlightenment of the voters who may not be acquainted with the facts in the case, it is proper that the *Blade* should give them some of the facts as to the usefulness of Mr. Locke in the community. Within the past two and one-half years, he has erected buildings for manufacturing, business, and other purposes whose total cost foots up to $286,000 . . . His time, his talents and his capital are devoted to the building up of Toledo, increasing her manufacturing facilities, and thus to aiding her working population to obtain permanent and paying work . . .

But the Liquor Dealers Association has chosen to declare that he shall be defeated if their efforts and their money can compass such result. They have declared that Mr. Locke must be "pulverized."

When Locke was elected, receiving 706 votes to 443 for his Democratic opponent and carrying all three precincts in the Third Ward, *The Blade* confined its comment to a single paragraph, captioned "Business Beats Beer": "The 'side issue' injected into the contest for alderman in the Third ward of this city by the Liquor Dealers Protective Assoc. did not eventuate as its projectors intended. A resolution was adopted to defeat Mr. D. R. Locke, the Republican candidate, because of his pronounced Prohibition views . . . The result of the struggle was the election of Mr. Locke by a majority of 263. It was a contest between Beer and Business."

David Ross Locke believed firmly in the two-party system, and *The Blade* had little sympathy for attempts to accomplish reforms through third parties, even those formed to advance causes which had Locke's support. When the fledgling Prohibition party failed to do well at the polls, *The Blade* took an "I told you so" attitude. For those parties identified with coalitions of farmers and laborers — the Greenbackers, the Nationalists, the Populists, and others — Locke had nothing but contempt. He conceded such groups' right to organize and to place those from their own ranks in the lists of candidates, but argued that history had proved such efforts produce nothing of value. "It is the unbroken experience of the labor movement in this country," *The Blade* declared, "that in the contest for nomination a broken down political hack, whose utter worthlessness or worse is a patent fact in his own party.... stands several chances of success where the leading laboring man stands none."

★ ★ ★

David Locke's final involvement in presidential politics had to do with the 1888 election, although he did not live to see the Republican party choose Senator Benjamin Harrison of Indiana as its candidate against President Grover Cleveland in that contest. Leading contenders for the nomination a year before the Republican convention appeared to be Senator John Sherman of Ohio and James G. Blaine, who had lost to Cleveland four years earlier. Locke, who had little enthusiasm for either man, was looking for another candidate.

The *Weekly Blade,* declaring that "no newspaper in the Union was more influential in the campaign of 1884" than it had been, inaugurated a nationwide poll among its readers in May, 1887, as to their preferences. Each reader who participated was asked to answer three questions:

1. Who is your first choice for the Republican candidate in 1888?
2. Who is your second choice?
3. Who is your choice for vice president?

Results of the poll were announced on July 14. Leading choices for president were Blaine and Sherman in that order; Robert T. Lincoln, Abraham's son, was a substantial third. For vice president, Lincoln received a clear majority of all votes cast. The *Weekly Blade* commented:

> The most surprising thing revealed in the vote is the quiet strength revealed for Robert T. Lincoln. There has been no Lincoln "boom"; the papers have not been full of speculation concerning him, but he stands third for first choice for President; third for second choice, and first for the Vice-Presidency ...

Since he had little enthusiasm for either Blaine or Sherman, Locke was impelled to do what he could to promote Robert Lincoln as a presidential candidate. He went to Chicago in August, 1887, to talk with Republican leaders and, while there, he interviewed Robert Lincoln. An account of this interview occupied two columns in the *Weekly Blade* of September 1, with this editorial comment:

> Mr. Lincoln talked frankly ... and what he said is open to no misconstruction. He is not an aspirant for the office; he would prefer to remain where he is. But he would yield his personal preference were he called by the people to accept the highest office within their gift.

> How is it regarding Lincoln? He believes in civil service reform. He could rally the mugwump strength in New York — and in fact all over the country. It may be interesting just here to relate a fact which has never before gotten into the newspapers. Roscoe Conkling was in Chicago several weeks ago. In conversation with a prominent Republican on political matters, he said: "Why don't you Republicans in the West insist on nominating somebody who can win? You have here in Chicago a man who can sweep New York by a heavy majority — and the Republicans must have New York to win. Who is he? Why, Bob Lincoln, of course."
>
> These are things to be pondered by the Republicans. The party must win the Presidential contest, or remain in the minority for an indefinite period in the future. It is too early to pin one's faith upon any one candidate; but it is not too early to consider the availability of any and all of them. The *Blade* has no desire to boom any candidate; but it has a lively interest in seeing that the possibility of success for the party is not frittered away by the blind following of any one man's lead . . . Let us name a strong man; a man whose record is unassailable; a man who can unite all Republicans and all friends of progress under his banner. If Lincoln be that one, let us take Lincoln; if there be a better man, let us take him.

The fight over the presidential nomination raged openly among Ohio Republicans throughout the months that followed. When the party held its state convention in Toledo in July, 1887, those who supported Sherman introduced a resolution pledging Ohio's support for him in the convention to nominate a presidential candidate the next year. Locke and his friends opposed the resolution. *The Blade* stated their position:

> The opinion of the *Blade* that the injection of the Presidential issue into the state campaign in Ohio this year is "bad politics" is shared by a large majority of the delegates to the state convention assembled in this city. There are very many of these, however, who are willing to vote for the resolution because Senator Sherman desires it . . .
> There are a number of delegates, however, who are strongly opposed to the resolution, and who have expressed their intention of fighting it in the convention. Tremendous pressure has been brought to bear upon them ever since the arrival of Senator Sherman last night, to avoid an open opposition to it in the convention. The resolution itself has been worded as smoothly as to render it as unobjectionable as possible, but the kernel still remains — an endorsement for the Presidency . . .
> The cold fact still remains, however, that the resolution does not represent the sentiment of all Ohio Republicans. Today John Sherman could not secure a two-thirds delegation from Ohio. Whether he can next year remains to be seen . . . But he can never get it through machine methods.

The convention approved the resolution endorsing Sherman, but the fight had left lasting scars. After Locke's death, the charge was made that he had been Sherman's "most relentless enemy, and took every opportunity to 'dig him under the fifth rib.' " *The Blade* vigorously denied the allegation; so did Senator Sherman, who wrote to Robinson Locke, lauding David Ross Locke for "his ability and for his great usefulness as a Republican journalist."

The Blade further explained that Locke had no personal feeling against Sherman, but that "he doubted the Senator's availability as a Presidential candidate, becuase he is not a man who can arouse enthusiasm among the people, nor one who excites strong friendships; while like many others who have been long in public life, he has excited antagonisms which would, in certain sections, be sources of weakness."

Those who had been readers of *The Blade* twenty years earlier, when John Sherman joined seven other Senate Republicans in opposing impeachment of President Andrew Johnson, may have recalled the intensity of David Locke's anger at that time. They might logically have suspected that he never actually forgave what he regarded as Sherman's apostasy.

Chapter 13

A New Generation Takes Over

David Ross Locke was not yet fifty-five years old when he died on February 15, 1888. The great and near great paid him tribute. Subscribers to his newspapers — especially readers of the *Weekly Blade* — wrote to express their feeling of personal loss. It was hard for them to believe that their beloved Nasby was dead. Rutherford B. Hayes, former President of the United States, dispatched this message from Spiegel Grove, his home in nearby Fremont:

> I am at this moment in receipt of the announcement of the death of D. R. Locke. I beg you to convey to his family my sincere sympathy with them in their bereavement. With his pen Mr. Locke gained for himself a conspicuous and honorable place among those who fought the good fight in the critical years of the anti-slavery conflict before the war. During the war and after it, he was surpassed by no writer in the extent and value of his influence in the march of events until its great results were substantially secured. He had the satisfaction of receiving from Mr. Lincoln himself the first meed of praise for his matchless service in the hour of his country's trial.

Emily S. Bouton wrote *The Blade's* obituary of Locke. A member of its staff for eleven years, she had become literary and household editor, and later edited the society section. This remarkable woman, who had taught in the Toledo public schools before joining *The Blade*, had won David Ross Locke's affection and respect. Now, praising him as writer and editor, she also provided perceptive personal insights:

> There were two sides of his personality. His vein of quaint humor and of satire, sometimes biting, sometimes kindly, which is exemplified in the Nasby letters, was given full play in ordinary conversation, when amid congenial society . . . To this deeper part of his nature may be ascribed his intense hatred of shams, political or social, and the fact that the whole

A New Generation Takes Over 139

influence of his potent pen was thrown invariably for the eternal Right, in whatever field the battle was cast.

During most of the last three months of his life, Locke was confined to his home and, increasingly, had been unable to leave his bed. Otis Locke, a half-brother, made the trip daily from Tiffin to Toledo by train to be at his side. According to a niece, Mary Locke Hurin, he was frequently delirious during these last weeks.

Locke was, according to another account, "full of fun up to the last. He joked just the same after he knew he was bound to die, and his doctor tells many stories of his wit during his last hours. At one time, when calling on him for a consultation, Nasby, who was lying down and was suffering great pain, asked: 'Well, Doctor, you say there is no chance for me? I would like to know why.'

" 'Your digestive powers are exhausted,' was the physician's reply, 'and your stomach has been tampered with by indigestion until it is now entirely burnt away.'

" 'Well,' replied Nasby, 'in that case I am mighty glad I have a vest to cover it.' "[27]

Few men have had greater impact on a newspaper than David Ross Locke had on *The Blade*. Although his importance has been generally overlooked by historians of journalism, he was one of the truly innovative owners and editors of the latter half of the 19th century — a man who helped initiate and carry out significant changes in the role of the newspaper in American life. He was associated with *The Blade* for just over two decades, and in that period he helped to lead the way in the transformation of newspapers from party organs to agencies of information and education.

His achievements have, for understandable reasons, been associated almost exclusively with the *Weekly Blade,* which he built into a journal of national reputation and influence. In doing so, he demonstrated that a newspaper can be more influential among its readers when its appeal is based on editorial material than it had been as a blatantly and exclusively political organ.

What is not generally appreciated is that, at the time the *Weekly Blade* was achieving a national readership and reputation, the daily edition was undergoing the same kinds of changes, and with similar consequences. *The Blade* was, at David Ross Locke's death, a newspaper much improved over the one with which he had become associated two decades earlier.

Practice of the principles Locke had espoused for the improvement of newspapers generally was largely responsible for bringing about these changes. There were other contributing factors, of course. The Civil War had greatly stimulated interest in news and readership of newspapers. The press associations which provided reports to newspapers by telegraph greatly expanded their facilities in the postwar years. The technology of newspaper production moved forward on many fronts.

This was also the period in which there was a dramatic increase in the volume of newspaper advertising — especially of products on a national scale. One consequence of the growth of advertising was a basic change in the financing of newspaper publication. This freed most newspapers from their reliance on political subsidies and shifted the source of income from the reader to the advertiser.

★ ★ ★

Robinson Locke, not yet twenty-nine years old, assumed editorship of *The Blade* at his father's death. Robinson's ten years of grooming for the position had included his travel and study in Europe and his consular service at Newcastle upon Tyne. David Locke had been determined that this favorite among his three sons — the only one who had shown any interest in the family's newspaper holdings — should have the advantages of foreign travel and education which he had been denied. He wanted Rob to be able to speak and write other languages than English, to cultivate interest in and knowledge of music, the theatre, and the other arts.

He had also seen to it that his son became familiar with all aspects of the newspaper business. Robinson Locke had been a reporter on *The Blade*. He had served a kind of apprenticeship with Frank Lane, the business manager on whom David Locke had relied so heavily. He had collaborated with his father in writing the *Nasby in Exile* articles and was acknowledged, in David Locke's preface, as the author of the descriptive passages when the articles were published in book form.

The property which David Ross Locke passed along to Robinson was valuable, although evidence suggests that it probably was worth not more than $200,000 in 1888. Locke had placed heavy mortgages on *The Blade* to support his extensive investments in real estate — business buildings, houses, and the new building constructed four years earlier to house the growing operations of *The Blade*. It is a considerable tribute to Robinson Locke's business acumen that, by

A New Generation Takes Over

1895, the value of *The Blade* was estimated at $1,000,000, with an annual profit of about $100,000.[28]

One of Robinson Locke's first considerations as editor of *The Blade* was to further elevate the status of the daily edition. Under his father's guidance, the *Weekly Blade* had become a national institution. Its daily counterpart was prosperous and wielded a strong influence in the Toledo area, but it had been obvious that the interests of the weekly edition came first. A typical edition of *The Blade* at this time was still only four pages, and it had changed but little in size and general layout in the last twenty years. One change was that the front page was now largely devoted to news — most of it state and national — along with market and weather reports, and some advertising. Editorials, local news and advertising continued to dominate the second page, and page three was given over to more local news and advertising. The back page was almost entirely occupied by advertisements, which were increasing in keeping with a national trend. More news and more advertising provided readers with additional information.

The Blade was proud of its news coverage. In a variety of ways, it was emphasizing this fact, along with the decline of partisanship, except in its editorials. Boxes on the front page of the June 7, 1888, edition proclaimed:

> REPUBLICANS will, of course, look to the *Blade* to furnish them all the news incident to the great St. Louis convention, and of course the *Blade* will do it in good style.
>
> DEMOCRATS realize that the *Blade* is giving them the best reports of their National Convention, and they will read its columns with avidity. The *Blade* prints all the news.

Circulation figures were published on the second page of *The Blade* each day. Those of its competitors were also published — when they could be obtained. Rowell's *American Newspaper Directory* listed the circulation of *The Blade* in 1890 as being in excess of 10,000; its closest rival, the *Bee,* had 7,500 subscribers. The *Weekly Blade* was one of fifty-five newspapers in the country with a circulation of more than 100,000. Contests were sponsored to help build circulation. One of these, in 1890, involved predicting what Toledo's official population would be when the decennial census report was issued that year.

The Blade averaged eight pages for each edition by late 1890, continuing to expand in size. A considerable part of this growth was due to development of *The Blade's* Saturday edition, which began to include many of the features of the Sunday editions which some newspapers were beginning to inaugurate.[29] The Saturday *Blade* typically had twelve pages; Monday editions were four pages; Tuesday through Friday editions were usually eight pages. Carriers distributed about half of each day's papers to readers in the city, and the remainder were sent outside Toledo by mail.

Young and relatively inexperienced as he was, the new editor of *The Blade* was fortunate to have the help of a staff that included such experienced and loyal individuals as S. S. Knabenshue, Emily S. Bouton and Frank Lane. They provided a measure of continuity and stability that was sorely needed by anyone taking over the editorship from David Locke — even his own son. But Robinson Locke had ideas of his own about how to strengthen and improve *The Blade*, and he wasted little time in setting about to infuse his staff with new talent and new ideas.

Dr. Franklin T. Howe, who had been with *The Blade's* Washington bureau, was moved to Toledo to bring a national viewpoint to the editorial operations. Several new columns were added, although their authors' names were not published. Two of these, appearing in 1890, were "Here in Toledo" and "The Man on the Corner." As their names suggest, they were made up of local items of a personal nature.

The American newspaper reporter, who had been almost entirely anonymous, began to be identified late in the 19th century, when the use of bylines was introduced. First to receive this recognition in *The Blade* — in the edition of November 19, 1900 — was O. K. Schimansky, a member of the Washington bureau. Feature stories by Emily S. Bouton had been signed for several years, but Schimansky's were the first news stories so treated.[30]

★ ★ ★

Robinson Locke's most important influence on *The Blade*, however, may well have been the reflection of his own intense interest in music, art and, especially, the theatre. Under his editorship, *The Blade* achieved a reputation for criticism of the arts that was acclaimed throughout the United States, as the following excerpt from *Musical America* in November, 1910, attests:

> Thanks to Mr. Locke, the dramatic and musical departments of *The Blade* have long since been looked upon as the very finest in that section of the country, and those artists are few who do not ardently aspire to its good graces. Mr. Locke is a critic who has no fear of attacking the unworthy in music or drama in a most scathing manner. Being asked once

A New Generation Takes Over 143

whether he was as severe in his musical as in his dramatic criticism, he replied epigrammatically, "There is not as much bad music as there is bad drama."

Robinson Locke wrote dramatic criticism under the name of Rodney Lee. He had studied ancient and modern drama and he wrote knowledgeably and authoritatively about the American theatre for twenty-five years. He became a close friend of Charles Frohman, the New York producer, and scores of actors and others affiliated with the theatre were among his friends. Both the Lambs Club and the Friars in New York elected him to membership.

In Toledo, Locke had enormous influence in expanding and improving the quality of offerings by road shows. Among the leading performers of the turn of the century period who appeared in Toledo were Mrs. Patrick Campbell (in "The Sorceress"); Sarah Bernhardt (in "La Dame aux Camelias"); Lillian Russell (in a musical, "Lady Teazle," loosely based on Sheridan's "School for Scandal"). Another was Minnie Maddern Fiske, whom Locke admired, and he worked at getting a Toledo theatre to book her company. On February 4, 1905, *The Blade* devoted a half page, with pictures, touting Mrs. Fiske's "Leah Kleschna," with a cast that included a young actor named George Arliss.

Robinson Locke's interest in the theatre is memorialized in a collection of newspaper articles, programs and other memorabilia that he began to assemble on December 25, 1895, when Joseph Jefferson made his first appearance at the Valentine Theatre in Toledo (a building recently saved from the wreckers' ball by a campaign led by *The Blade*). This collection, which was presented to the New York Public Library in 1924-1925, is contained in nearly 500 bound scrapbooks and 4,700 portfolios of unmounted items. Valued at several hundred thousand dollars, the collection is widely used — especially by theatre people — as a reference.[31]

The important part Locke played in establishment of the Toledo Museum of Art has been little publicized. It is attested to in a letter of June 22, 1908, from Edward Drummond Libbey, expressing his thanks for having been Locke's guest of honor at a dinner party the previous night at the Toledo Country Club. "I shall feel not only more than doubly interested in the work of our Art Museum, but be under further obligations by the universal compliments I've received," wrote the man who had already donated money and land valued at more than $125,000 for the museum. Libbey also thanked

Locke for the "very dignified and satisfactory articles" *The Blade* had published about the museum, especially since a campaign had been started in April, 1908, to match the $50,000 gift that Libbey already had offered (he subsequently more than doubled that amount in June). When the Toledo Museum of Art was incorporated April 18, 1909, Edward Drummond Libbey and Robinson Locke were among its incorporators. Libbey was its first president, Locke its first vice-president.

The breadth of Robinson Locke's interests is reflected in the variety of organizations of which he was a member and officer. He was president of the Toledo Symphony Orchestra League in 1897; president of the Toledo Art Loan Association, 1898; president of the Ohio Library Association, 1899. He played an important part in founding the Toledo Medical College, receiving the official thanks of the secretary of the college for the "excellent articles . . . complimentary to our college." He was a charter member of the Northwestern Ohio Historical Society.

Locke had a reputation for maintaining high literary standards, too, and evidence to that effect is amusingly provided in an exchange of notes with Miss Sadie Beatty, of Fostoria, in November, 1893. Miss Beatty, having submitted samples of her work, inquired whether she was "capable of writing for remuneration," to which the editor replied: "We beg to say that you may be, but you will require a long course of study, and you will need to give a great deal more care to your compositions than has evidently been bestowed upon the enclosed. If the best newspapers always accept your poems for publication, they will doubtless be glad to pay you for them." Back from Fostoria came the following response: "I herewith return your slap in the face you gave me. You may need it as a form to follow to insult someone else . . . I could say I am not entirely crushed and there are leading newspapers besides the Toledo *Blade*."

There are numerous stories of Locke's affinity for young writers of promise; some are true, others fictional. One of the latter is to the effect that Theodore Dreiser was employed as a reporter on *The Blade* in the 1890s and that, with Locke's encouragement, he wrote *Sister Carrie* while living in Toledo. The tale has an element of truth, but Dreiser did not work for *The Blade*, and his benefactor was not Locke but Arthur Henry, a writer of some reputation, who was city editor of *The Blade* in 1892-1893. Henry was hired on the recommendation of Brand Whitlock, with whom he had worked in

A New Generation Takes Over

Chicago. Soon after his arrival in Toledo, the new city editor was married to Maude Wood of Maumee, and they bought property on the River Road known as "The House of the Four Pillars," which became a rendezvous for Toledoans with literary interests. Henry, who had become acquainted with Dreiser in New York, brought the author and his wife to Toledo. The Dreisers spent the summer of 1893 in the Henry home and it was in the basement of their landmark house that much of the manuscript of *Sister Carrie* was written.

★ ★ ★

The Blade continued to support the Republican party and its candidates under the editorship of Robinson Locke, who maintained, however, some of the same independence that David Locke had always demonstrated. "The newspapers of this country which have been notably successful," he wrote in 1892, "are those which have refused to follow the beck and call of party leaders at every turn, but exercised a salutary independence when the latter were judged to be in the wrong." The young editor kept a close watch on political developments — in Washington and Columbus as well as in Toledo. He covered Congress for *The Blade* in 1897.

Despite its professed independence, however, *The Blade* seldom failed to support Republican candidates in local, state and national elections during the next seven years. Benjamin Harrison was endorsed for President in 1888, when he defeated Grover Cleveland, and again in 1892, when he lost to the same opponent. Locke's choice as the party's candidate in 1892 was James G. Blaine, and *The Blade* expressed surprise and disappointment when the Plumed Knight declined to be considered for the nomination that many believed was his for the asking.

The Blade supported Governor Joseph B. Foraker for re-election in 1889 and regretted his loss to the Democratic candidate, James E. Campbell. The new governor's proposal, in his inaugural address, to adopt the Australian ballot was endorsed by Locke, who was a firm believer in electoral reforms, including substitution of primary elections for conventions in making party nominations. *The Blade* rejected Campbell's other recommendations, however, as "shopworn goods . . . a mediocre effort of a mediocre man."

A bill to create a Board of Public Affairs in Toledo was introduced into the state legislature in March, 1890. It proposed to abolish the board of water works trustees, the fire commission, and the police board. *The Blade* urged that "every decent citizen, irrespective of politics, should enter his protest against the scheme and the party which has to resort to it to obtain a control denied them by a majority of Toledo voters." The Ohio senate approved the bill, but it lost by a 51-48 margin in the lower house of the legislature.

When William McKinley defeated Governor Campbell in the 1891 gubernatorial contest, *The Blade* headlined its election story OHIO IS REDEEMED. An editorial suggested that Ohio had fired the opening gun in the 1892 presidential campaign.

Locke and *The Blade* kept a close watch on municipal affairs, too. When seven members of council were accused in 1892 of accepting bribes to support legislation favorable to local utilities, *The Blade* urged immediate trials and was satisfied only when the men had been convicted. An earlier *Blade* campaign had succeeded in removing the chief of police for failure to perform his duties.

Toledo was hard hit by the Panic of 1893. Many of the city's industries shut down or drastically curtailed their operations, and the unemployed were to be seen increasingly on the streets. *The Blade* was concerned, but was inclined to put the blame on the Democratic administration of President Cleveland. For the efforts of a fellow Ohioan — Jacob Coxey, a Massillon quarry owner — to deal with the problems confronting the nation, it had no use at all. Coxey's Army, which was made up of the unemployed, marched on Washington in 1893-1894, and when a group of its members visited Toledo in August, 1894, *The Blade* described them thus: "Bandana hats, red umbrellas and white linen dusters worn by the most extraordinary company that ever passed along the roads of Lucas County."

For Coxey's programs and procedures, Robinson Locke had even greater contempt. Reflecting the disdain his father had always shown toward attempts to solve problems outside the framework of established government procedures and the two-party system, Locke wrote that the "central fallacy of Coxeyism and the whole book of socialistic and communistic crank ideas which are voiced here and there by fools and demagogues, consists in looking upon our government as an entity apart and separate from the people and in many ways antagonistic to them."

Chapter 14

The Coming of 'Golden Rule' Jones

The Republican who finally made it impossible for Robinson Locke to remain loyal to the party's candidates was Guy C. Major, first elected mayor of Toledo in 1893. Major's rise to power corresponded with that of the American Protective Association, an anti-Catholic secret society organized in 1887. The A. P. A. grew slowly until it was given impetus by the Panic of 1893. The appearance in the same year of the spurious encyclical attributed to Pope Leo XIII provided further stimulation. This forged document called for a rising of "the faithful to exterminate all heretics found within the jurisdiction of the United States of America." Mayor Major was reported to have had national guardsmen on duty during the Labor Day weekend, 1893, and a deputy sheriff inspected a local Catholic church in search of a cache of arms reported to be hidden there.

At its height, the A. P. A. claimed a million members and was supposed to have had seven thousand Toledo voters on its rolls. These figures may have been exaggerated, but the importance of any sizable block of voters becomes apparent when it is realized that Major polled fewer than 7,500 votes to win election as mayor in 1893, and then by a margin of only 160 votes. This was two thousand fewer than the Republican plurality had been two years earlier.

The Blade endorsed Major's candidacy in 1893, attacking the previous Democratic administration as "dirty in every way." Locke expressed his approval when the Republicans swept the election, carrying every city office but one. *The Blade* also commended the city council three months later when it enacted a wheel tax, believing it would provide additional revenue to keep Toledo's streets in repair. Charges include $2 a year for each sulky, $4 for a one-horse cab or hack, and $15 for an ice wagon or a beer truck.

Allegations of corruption and lax law enforcement began to circulate early in the Major administration. A Civic Federation group was formed before the 1895 election. Many of the city's leading citizens, and especially its ministers, were among its members. This group's first target was the city's saloon keepers who, it was complained, sold drinks on Sunday, in addition to selling liquor to minors. Next on the Civic Federation's list were gamblers. There was criticism, too, of the city's bookkeeping system, although *The Blade* dismissed this as only an effort by petty thieves to restore the system to its original form so they could receive some of the funds. Municipal reform, *The Blade* noted, was the watchword in a thousand cities at this time.[32]

The Republican city convention renominated Guy Major in 1895, and *The Blade* refused to go along with the party's action. The Democratic candidate who then became the first of his party to receive Rob Locke's endorsement for mayor was Parks Hone. "Down with the gang!" was *The Blade*'s war cry. Major and his friends were alleged to be making a good thing of the city's revenues and doing nothing to reduce taxes. Locke's endorsement of the Democratic candidate was back-handed, it's true: "Mr. Hone will make a good one-term mayor" and "while not brilliant, we believe him safe." Mayor Major was, nonetheless, re-elected, squeaking through by a margin of only sixty votes.

After two more years of Major, *The Blade* began early in 1897 to prepare for another attempt to defeat him. An editorial appeared on January 21, 1897, outlining the characteristics that the next mayor of Toledo must possess:

> The man to be elected by the Republicans for mayor should not be a politician . . . He should not be a member of any ring . . . He should be a man who has been successful in business, whose interests are in Toledo, who has shown himself to be interested in the city's welfare, and whose integrity is not a matter of doubt. He should be a man who has force of character . . . He should be a man who understands the city's needs, who has the ideas and the strength of purpose to carry them into execution, and who will fearlessly wield the ax in cutting down expenditures.

The man *The Blade* had in mind who measured up to these specifications was John Craig, a leading builder of shipping vessels in Toledo, who had indicated his willingness to run for a single term as mayor, after which he would return to his profitable business.

The Coming of 'Golden Rule' Jones

Craig announced his candidacy immediately, but in the Republican nominating convention a month later, he proved to be a weak candidate — particularly lacking appeal to the labor forces that were prominent in the party.

At least three different groups were involved in the complicated and confusing contest for the nomination. One factor was the long-running feud for Republican state leadership between Mark Hanna and Joseph B. Foraker. Each faction had its candidate. The Hanna forces backed James Melvin, a 70-year-old clothier; the Foraker men supported Charles P. Griffin, frequent office seeker and widely known as "the bald eagle of the Maumee." James M. Ashley, Jr., son of the congressman from the Toledo district who had been known as "Impeachment" Ashley, was the choice of a group of businessmen, including many who had first backed Craig. That Melvin was clearly Mayor Major's man in the contest provided a further complication, since it meant that all of the various reform elements bitterly opposed him.

Even so, Melvin appeared likely to win the nomination as things developed in the early balloting at the city convention. Robinson Locke, Jim Ashley and other anti-Major Republicans now began looking for a dark horse candidate who would head off this threat. After five ballots, during which Melvin's total grew closer to the number required to nominate, agreement was reached on a candidate who might be able to turn the tide against the combination of Hanna and Major forces. Some had preferred George B. Ketcham, wealthy Toledo theatre owner and horse racing enthusiast. The choice for dark horse, however, was Samuel M. Jones, who had moved to Toledo only five years earlier from Lima, Ohio, and had established the Acme Sucker Rod Company, manufacturers of oil drilling equipment on which he had perfected an improvement. Sam Jones was so little known at the time that, when Jim Ashley rose to withdraw his own name and to present that of the man who had been agreed on, one delegate stood up and asked: "Who in hell is Jones?" No matter, for Sam Jones was nominated on the sixth ballot, and his candidacy was widely acclaimed. Some Republicans thought it distinctly odd that even Negley Cochran of the *News-Bee* seemed well disposed toward the new man on the political scene in Toledo, but little attention was paid to their suspicions.

Robinson Locke found much to admire in the man who would become nationally known as "Golden Rule" Jones — an immigrant from Wales at the age of three, with little formal education, a worker in the Pennsylvania oil fields as a young man, who had got together enough money to move to the new fields near Lima, where he had brought in the first major well in the area. Jones's first wife had died in Pennsylvania, and in 1892 in Lima, he married Helen Beach, who had taught music in Lima and was a member of a prominent Toledo family. They moved to Toledo soon after their wedding and Sam Jones opened the sucker-rod plant in 1894. Everything about him that was visible on the surface suggested that he could be counted on to represent what most Republicans regarded as the better interests of Toledo — including, naturally, the Republican party.

Sam Jones, *The Blade* proclaimed, was an "unflinching Republican" and the "colors of the party are in safe hands." The one issue in the election, Locke insisted, was "whether we shall have good government for the city of Toledo," and he was sure Jones would clean up the ring of corrupt politicians, gamblers, saloon keepers, and other reprehensible elements. Parks Hone, whom *The Blade* had supported against Mayor Major two years earlier, was again the Democratic candidate. Despite Locke's prediction that the election would be a Republican landslide, Jones defeated Hone by just over 500 votes. This victory was hailed in an editorial captioned THE BUM ELEMENT DEFEATED, which contended that the real threat to Jones had come from the liquor interests.

The Blade continued to support Jones during his first year in office, if not always with great enthusiasm. Locke entered a mild dissent when the new mayor resisted local ministers' demands that Toledo's saloons be closed on Sunday. He wrote: "It is presumed that this law will be enforced not only in Toledo, but throughout the state." Jones observed at the next meeting of council that *The Blade* had been right.

Disenchantment came on gradually. Locke was suspicious of some of the speakers Jones helped bring to Toledo in the interest of exposing local residents to some of the social, political and economic ideas that were being developed at the time. When, in February, 1898, Professor George D. Herron of Iowa College (now Grinnell) expounded the doctrine of Christian Socialism and criticized some policies of the United States government, *The Blade* suggested that if he "does not like the government of the United States," Herron should "collect his things and move out," adding, "the fewer of such men the better."

The Coming of 'Golden Rule' Jones

Some doubts as to Sam Jones's unflinching Republicanism were expressed by *The Blade* as early as July, 1898, when it declared: "Of course Jones was elected mayor as a Republican, but party never worried him and he is frank enough to admit that he is not certain where he belongs." When Jones delivered his second annual message to council in October, Locke's mixed feelings about him were again evident. *The Blade* expressed reservations about his "socialistic" proposals — most of which were concerned with municipal ownership of public utilities. Suggestions for improvement of the police force, the need for money to pave streets, and other civic projects were, however, "heartily approved."

In truth, "Golden Rule" Jones and Robinson Locke never were close in political philosophy. Jones was profoundly disturbed by conditions he observed among unemployed workers at the time he was establishing the Acme Sucker Rod Company in Toledo, at the depth of the 1893-1894 depression. These observations led him toward socialistic concepts and, although he was not by temperament attuned to doctrinaire socialism, he believed the answers to many of what he regarded as the industrial abuses of the day were to be found in the eight-hour day, profit-sharing plans, and other practices that most employers still regarded with hostility. His identification with the Golden Rule began when he posted it in the Acme Sucker Rod factory instead of the kind of code of rules that was common in most industrial plants at the time.

As mayor, Sam Jones took clubs and firearms away from the police and replaced them with canes. And he horrified many Toledoans when he seemed to suggest that the only real solutions to problems of crime and lawlessness lay in the responsibility to forgive and lend a helping hand to those who had transgressed the prevailing legal and moral codes.

Perhaps the classic tale which illustrates why Sam Jones's critics — including Robinson Locke — found it so difficult to understand him has to do with his response to a delegation of ministers who came to his office to protest his failure to keep the city's streets free of prostitutes. Jones agreed that this would be a desirable state of affairs, but first he expressed doubt as to how it could be accomplished.

"Where would you have me send them?" he asked. "To Detroit? To Cleveland? Out in the country somewhere?" Then he offered a proposal:

"If you and other ministers of the gospel of Jesus Christ will each take one of these erring women into your own home, and give her the opportunity to live a decent and even devout life, Mrs. Jones and I will do the same thing for two of them in our home."

The ministerial delegation is reported to have left without a further word.

Sam Jones had been elected mayor with the support of the ministerial association and the Civic Federation reformers. What they had expected from him was traditional reforms, especially stricter law enforcement — closing saloons, clamping down on gambling, prostitution, and other practices they regarded as major social evils. They felt doubly betrayed when their mayor turned out to be a different kind of reformer from most of them: a kind of Tolstoyan philosophical anarchist.

It was a group of Republican businessmen, however, who took it upon themselves to attempt to toss Sam Jones out of the mayor's office in 1899. "Big Jim" Ashley and others decided they had had enough of Jones. They met in January and decided to back Charles E. Russell, a Toledo insurance man, for mayor. The Republican convention in March was a wild one, finally nominating Russell over Jones by a narrow margin.

When Jones immediately declared his candidacy as an independent, *The Blade* observed that "any man who appeals to a party for a place on its ticket, and enters upon a pre-convention canvass, should consider himself honor bound to abide by the result." The knife was given a further twist with the comment that "it is a plain application of the Golden Rule to political matters."

In supporting Russell, *The Blade*'s principal criticism of Jones was concentrated on his advocacy of municipal ownership of public utilities, calling on the mayor for a direct statement of his intentions:

> Will Mayor Jones come down to facts and state his plan for what he calls "public utilities" under the ownership of the city? Does he expect to confiscate those already existing? If so, what method does he propose? Does he expect to buy them, or to construct new plants? In either case, where is the money to come from to buy or build? Is there any way to get it except by the issue of more bonds, with a consequent increase of the annual interest burden? Is the experience of the city with the "public utilities" it already owns such as to render it a good business proposition to go in deeper?

The Blade warned that the experiments with municipal ownership which Jones planned to undertake would be costly, resulting in the flight of business to cities where taxes were lower and, "in the end, grass will grow in our streets." When over-enthusiastic supporters of the mayor invaded Republican and Democratic meetings and abused the speakers on several occasions, *The Blade* commented caustically that Jones's "beautiful theory of the brotherhood of man is interpreted by them to mean that they have the right to deny the right of free speech to those who do not agree with them . . . Probably the mayor does not realize it, but his speeches directly inflame his hearers against all men who are prosperous. The majority of them cannot understand his fine-spun theories, except this far: they are told by the mayor that somebody is making money which ought to be theirs."

A number of cartoons appeared in *The Blade* attacking Jones, with references to him as "Samuel of Wales," "Millionaire Jones," the "Golden Sucker Man," and "Sucker Sam." It was alleged that he was supported by members of the group that had backed the municipal pipeline and that everyone active in the Jones campaign was tainted by fraud. Robinson Locke joined the clergy in demanding the election of a mayor "who will execute the laws, and not only like Mayor Jones, who boldly proclaims that he will enforce only such laws as he sees fit."

Jones was overwhelmingly re-elected, polling almost seventy per cent of the total vote to achieve what his enthusiastic backers subsequently referred to as "the glorious victory." *The Blade* found "no political significance whatsoever" in the outcome; the chief factor in the result had been the mayor's "extreme popularity because of his benevolence and philanthropy." From that day forward, *The Blade* opposed the Golden Rule mayor of Toledo on almost every issue. Robinson Locke had become almost entirely disillusioned with the man he had helped nominate as the Republican candidate for mayor in 1897. In April, 1900, *The Blade* asked: "What is the distinctive policy of Toledo's Mayor Jones?" Locke answered his own question:

> It has been to make Toledo not only a "wide open" town, but to make the opening the widest . . . in the United States. Gambling goes on without the slightest restriction . . . The city is the resort of all the great fraternity who make their living off the frailties and follies of their fellow men . . . Tramps and bums drift to this city, attracted by the mayor's public pratings on the "brotherhood of man."
>
> He has not enforced the laws. He goes on speech-making tours over

the country preaching his socialistic theories, but neglecting the duties of the office to which he was elected.

Sam Jones, the editorial concluded, was "generous, philanthropic and great-hearted." However, "like many another good man, he is blinded by the glamour of rainbow theories, and wastes his energies in their advocacy."

Locke was even less kind toward Jones when, two months later, he told an interviewer for the Minneapolis *Journal,* while he was visiting in the Minnesota city, that the mayor of Toledo was "a demagogue pure and simple." Jones was, at the time, being urged to declare himself as an independent candidate for Congress. "If he does," Locke said, "we will bury him so deep he can never be excavated." To which Sam Jones responded that "if we may judge the future by the past, a prediction by Mr. Locke of defeat would be the best kind of a guarantee for overwhelming success."

The Blade again opposed Jones when he sought re-election in 1901. One of Locke's editorials declared that the mayor's campaign talks "have about as much to do with municipal affairs as the report of the minister to Dahomey." Jones, running as an independent, was also endorsed by the Democratic party convention, which nominated no candidate of its own. The mayor easily defeated the Republican candidate, General William V. McMaken, a Civil War hero. His margin was, however, considerably reduced from his "glorious victory" two years earlier. Jones's victory, along with those of two Democratic candidates for mayor — Tom Johnson in Cleveland and John N. Hinkle in Columbus — drew this terse comment from *The Blade*: "Jones, Johnson and Hinkle! Are the voters of Ohio becoming daffy?"

The closest Locke came to agreement with Jones during the latter two terms of the Golden Rule mayor was on a new charter for Toledo. The mayor vigorously supported this document, which he had played a considerable part in shaping. *The Blade* took no position on the charter, which proposed extensive streamlining of the city's administrative machinery, putting additional power into the hands of the mayor, but Locke's editorials were sympathetic to the need for change. "The great problem at the opening of the twentieth century," *The Blade* declared, "is the management of our great centers of population. Those who vote for or against the new charter tomorrow will vote for or against an experiment." Toledoans turned

The Coming of 'Golden Rule' Jones 155

down the new charter, but by a much narrower margin than had been anticipated.

Not even this momentary abatement of continuing differences could stem the mounting tide of *The Blade's* dislike of Jones, however. In May, 1902, during a fight between the mayor and Republican leaders over who should name members of the Toledo police board, bitter words were heaped on Jones: "The absurd inconsistency of the notoriety-loving individual who poses as the Golden Rule Mayor of Toledo has never been so forcibly shown as it is in this unseemly police board squabble. Here is a self-advertising, self-admiring, self-laudatory person stultifying himself to gain cheap notoriety." Jones replied: "The man who wrote that must have been very unhappy. I suppose it was Bob Locke. I feel very sorry for him."

Sam Jones declared himself a nonpartisan candidate for a fourth term as mayor in 1903, insisting that the day was not far distant when all political parties would cease to exist. *The Blade* adopted a policy in this election of ignoring Jones altogether — in the news columns as well as on the editorial page. The mayor made much of *The Blade's* refusal to publish his statements or accounts of his meetings and called on voters to demonstrate that no newspaper controlled Toledo's affairs. The Republicans offered a particularly strong candidate for the 1903 election — Charles M. Dowd, who had been superintendent of the city's schools and was highly regarded across party lines. But Jones was again the winner, though for the first time he was the choice of a minority of the voters. He polled 10,350 votes to just over 12,000 for his three opponents. *The Blade* lamented that a majority was opposed to Jones but had been unable to agree on which of the others should be his successor.

When Samuel Milton Jones died in July, 1904, *The Blade* pointed to the spectacular career that an impoverished immigrant boy had achieved and noted that the poor would always respect and revere Jones's memory. But there were some things Robinson Locke could not forgive Jones for, even in death. The mayor of Toledo was undoubtedly sincere in his "preachments on the brotherhood of man," *The Blade* declared, "but he would at once change the characteristics of humanity and make everybody instantly conform in theory and practice to the idea he himself had set up." Locke believed that "instead of fostering and augmenting discontent in the ranks of the people he wanted to help," Jones should have shown them "how to make the best of their present conditions" and helped them to "gradually better these conditions."

Sam Jones was wanting in formal education and intellectual discipline, Rob Locke contended, with the result that many of his concepts which were intended to improve the lot of the people were not thoroughly thought out. Jones and Locke agreed on the need to strengthen and streamline municipal government and to invest in capital improvements that would make Toledo a pleasanter and more convenient place to live. They parted company at the point where the Golden Rule mayor urged municipal ownership of all public utilities; they were poles apart in relation to law enforcement, the judicial delivery system, and the philosophical anarchism that was at the root of much of what Jones believed and tried to implement. The outcome of their rivalry is probably best characterized as a draw. Jones won the elections and his position as mayor provided a forum that carried his message to a national audience; Locke was on the winning side in most contests over specific issues in the city both men loved and sought to improve.

Chapter 15

A New Mayor, A New Editor

The movers and shakers in Toledo's Republican and Democratic parties had assumed that the death of Sam Jones marked the end of mavericks bent on political independence, nonpartisanship, unorthodoxy, and radical reform. Vice Mayor Robert H. Finch, a more or less regular Republican, took over as mayor. There was nothing startling in his annual message to council in January, 1905 — a new city hall, a popular election on a proposed 25-year street railway franchise, employment of additional firemen, hiring a purchasing agent for city supplies, and postponing purchase of a fire tug. *The Blade* approved of all of these proposals, with the exception of the delay in buying a fire tug. Locke repeatedly urged the purchase of more tugs for use on the Toledo waterfront.[33]

Toledo Republicans nominated Finch as their candidate for a first full term in 1905. After the defeat of their candidate for a third straight time in the 1903 election, party leaders had begun to worry. Robinson Locke was one of twenty-three members of an advisory committee that recommended that party leaders should not favor or oppose the nomination of any particular candidate. *The Blade* had recommended that the suggestions of the advisory committee concerning the free nomination of candidates should be adopted.

But, although "Golden Rule" Jones was dead, the spirit of the man and the things in which he believed had survived him. So did a group of men who had been close to him during most of the period of more than seven years that he had been mayor — including Negley D. Cochran, editor of the *News-Bee,* and Hiram P. Crouse, general manager of the *Times.* These men took the lead in organizing the Independent party to carry on in the Jones tradition. Their approach to the practice of politics was, however, considerably different from that of Jones. This was a genuine political party, concerned not just with electing a popular figure as mayor, but with winning control of council, whose members could give the mayor-elect the support Sam Jones had never had in affairs of municipal government. The new party also entered candidates for county offices and for the state legislature.

The Independents presented a complete ticket in the 1905 election, and *The Blade* described it as a full-fledged party, which could no longer claim votes from the Republicans and Democrats. "Instead of being citizens of immaculate purity, above officeholding and proof against the seduction of partisanship," Locke observed sarcastically, "they are just common everyday mortals, made of the same clay as other people, affected by the same desires, and moved by the same sordid purposes."

The man around whom the Independent party united and who became its first candidate for mayor was Brand Whitlock, who was to serve as mayor of Toledo for the next eight years. A native of Urbana, Ohio, he had worked as a reporter on *The Blade* from 1887 to 1890, becoming acquainted with the city and with Robinson Locke. He moved to Chicago in 1891 and, for the next three years, worked as a reporter on the *Herald,* a Democratic newspaper. He became interested in Illinois politics and met John P. Altgeld, who became his hero. When Altgeld was elected governor, Whitlock got a state job in Springfield, where he studied law and was admitted to the bar. Whitlock moved back to Toledo and opened a law office in 1897, the year "Golden Rule" Jones was first elected mayor. Eventually he became a close associate of the mayor, campaigning with him, serving as police judge when designated by Jones for that duty in the incumbent's absence. The two men waged a continuing battle on behalf of equal treatment in the courts of the poor and underprivileged.

Whitlock showed considerable promise as a novelist and was ambitious for a career in literature.[34] He had resisted repeated efforts during the years of Jones's mayoralty to lure him into becoming a candidate for office, insisting that he wanted to have more time to write.[34] Now, however — perhaps because he felt he owed something to the memory of Sam Jones — Whitlock became deeply involved in the Independent party. His feelings about it are described in his autobiographical memoir, *Forty Years of It:*

A New Mayor, A New Editor 159

We put forth our belief that local affairs should be separate from, and independent of, party politics, and that public officers should be selected on account of their honesty and efficiency, regardless of political affiliations; that the people should be more active in selecting their officials and should not allow an office seeker to bring about his own nomination; that the prices charged by public service corporations should first be submitted to a vote of the people; that the city should possess the legal right to acquire and maintain any public utility, when authorized to do so by direct vote of its people; that every franchise granted to public service corporations should contain an agreement that the city might purchase and take over its property at a fair price, whenever so voted by the people, and that no street railway franchise should be extended or granted, permitting more than three-cent fares . . . and we demanded from the legislature home rule, the initiative and referendum and recall.[35]

These were sentiments not likely to win the support of *The Blade,* which continued to regard municipal ownership of utilities as a "beautiful theory, easy to talk about, and attractive to the average voter because in almost every instance the promise is held out that the poor man will reap a benefit." Not surprisingly, Locke urged the re-election of Robert H. Finch as mayor in 1905. He believed Toledo gamblers were backing Whitlock, while Finch would see that they were put out of business. *The Blade* urged Whitlock to express his positions on such issues as the street rail franchise, gambling, closing of wine rooms, Sunday closing, municipal ownership of the electric lighting plant, and others, but he did not answer such questions directly. "No one has a right to ask these questions until his own skirts are clear," was Whitlock's response when they were put to him.

The Blade predicted that Whitlock would be low man among the four candidates on election day. But the next day's headline was INDEPENDENT CANDIDATES WERE THE WHOLE THING. Whitlock had done better than Jones had done in 1903, winning by a clear majority. He received 15,148 votes to 9,946 for Finch, while the Democratic and Socialist candidates had a combined total of just over 2,000. The *News-Bee* called it the most complete and effective housecleaning that had been experienced in any American city. *The Blade* took a non-committal position. Locke observed that the new mayor had had little practical experience in administering a city, but had been exposed to Toledo's problems through the long association with the administration of Mayor Jones. Whitlock declined to see reporters when he took office on January 6, announcing that when he had something to say he would say it. Locke approved and concluded that Toledoans should be gratified "to know that they are to have something besides a machine-type administration."

When Mayor Whitlock announced early in his first term that he intended to "put the lid" on Toledo, *The Blade* gave him enthusiastic support. All saloons were to be closed at midnight. Wine rooms would be shut down later, saloons were not to open on Sunday, there might even be no Sunday theatre and baseball. But the duration of Robinson Locke's enthusiasm and support for the new mayor was brief. On April 2 — just three months after Whitlock had taken office — *The Blade* proposed that he be impeached for failure to enforce city ordinances — especially those related to Sunday closing. When Whitlock said two weeks later that he would not move against Sunday baseball games because the people wanted them (an argument that had been used often by his friend, Sam Jones) *The Blade* concluded that he might as well "pack up his golf outfit and fishing tackle and take himself to the wilds of Michigan" as far as anything he had yet done was concerned.

Locke was further riled when, in October, 1906, Whitlock refused to provide the kind of police support to which the owners of the Pope Automobile Company believed they were entitled after their workers had called a strike. It was alleged that the police had failed to maintain order at the Pope plant, and *The Blade* complained that "the industrial welfare of Toledo cannot and should not be sacrificed to the whim of its mayor." *The Blade* did praise Whitlock, however, when he played an important part in settling the strike in March, 1907.

Like Sam Jones before him, Brand Whitlock clashed often with the city's ministers. After an East Side pastor had criticized the mayor for neglect of the city, *The Blade* asked: "Do the people want their city known as a wide-open town? Is there a general disregard for law? Is Mayor Whitlock right? Is there no desire for decency and respectability? These are some of the questions the voters must answer next November." Robinson Locke was sure that a majority of the residents of Toledo agreed with *The Blade*, and with the local ministers. The reputation as a wide-open town that was increasingly attached to Toledo disturbed them.

The Republicans nominated Rudolph A. Bartley, a wealthy and respected businessman, as their candidate for mayor in the fall of 1907. They worked hard to defeat Brand Whitlock and the Independents, with enthusiastic support from the clergymen and from *The Blade*. Bartley would make Toledo a "decent city for

A New Mayor, A New Editor

decent people," Locke declared in urging the defeat of Whitlock. The Good Government League brought in Wayne B. Wheeler, superintendent of the Ohio Anti-Saloon League, to make a series of speeches against Whitlock. And Percy C. Jones, oldest son of Sam Jones, was quoted by *The Blade* as saying that his father, if he were alive, would refuse to vote the straight Independent ticket. He expressed hope that the "Independent machine will receive a knockout blow . . . in order that REAL independence may continue and that the voters of Toledo will not vote the ticket straight."

All this effort to unhorse Whitlock and the Independent ticket was to no avail. When the votes were counted, the mayor had a margin of almost 7,000 over his Republican opponent, and the Independents had elected ten members of council to six for the Republicans. The *News-Bee* proclaimed it a victory for the people. *The Blade* saw it differently, insisting that Whitlock had won because he had the backing of the brewers and all their immoral associates.

★ ★ ★

Some subtle change in *The Blade*'s relationship with Brand Whitlock began to make itself evident in the next year — 1908 — for the very good reason that there was a change in editors. Robinson Locke had been editor for twenty years, since the death in 1888 of his father, David Ross Locke. He now decided that he wanted to be relieved of these responsibilities. More and more, he had become interested in the theatre — both as critic and historian. His concern with all of the arts, with his growing collections of paintings and rare books, occupied increasing amounts of his time and energy. His collection of theatre articles and memorabilia alone was a major undertaking. He now employed a staff full time to gather materials for these scrapbooks. For all that Robinson Locke had done to improve the quality of the arts in Toledo — the new art museum, better offerings in the theatres by traveling companies — he was increasingly drawn to New York and other major art centers. It was in New York that he met Mabel Dixey Dunham, the actress to whom he was married in 1909 — the year after his retirement as editor.[36]

An announcement on the editorial page of *The Blade* on June 30, 1908, reported that "Mr. Nathaniel C. Wright and Mr. Harry S. Thalheimer[37] of the Cleveland *Leader* assume newly created positions of Editorial Manager and Business Manager of *The Blade*, respectively." There were the usual assurances that no changes in the policy or staff of *The Blade* would be made. Neither representation was, in fact, quite accurate. The Cleveland newspapermen were more than employees occupying newly-created positions. They had arranged to lease *The Blade* from the trustees of the David Ross Locke estate, who included Robinson Locke. Barton C. Smith, a Toledo lawyer who was attorney for the Locke estate, played an important part in making the arrangements. The lessees were in complete charge of *The Blade*'s operations, while continuing to edit and publish the Cleveland *Leader*.

It was announced on July 16 — little more than two weeks after the change in management — that F. L. Dustman, managing editor, and C. Locke Curtis, editorial writer, would leave *The Blade* to manage a new insurance firm in Toledo — the Aetna Life Insurance Company. Both were praised for their many contributions — Dustman "for twenty years as one of the best political writers in the state," Curtis as "a graceful and convincing writer," whose editorials had been reprinted all over Ohio. Whether the two men left as a result of the change in management is unclear. Curtis, who was a cousin of Robinson Locke, had been particularly close to him and was regarded by some members of the Locke family as having carried much of the responsibility for *The Blade*'s editorial operations in recent years.

The Blade had continued to grow and to improve. For the week ending January 31, 1908, its average daily circulation was 25,333; the Saturday edition had about 27,000 readers. Special features of the Saturday edition included a full page devoted to "The Stage" on which "Mac's Gossip of the Stage," signed by Idah M'Glone Gibson, of Chicago, occupied several columns. There was also a page of "Sports of All Sorts" and one of "Accurate Market Reports."

E. B. Johns was head of the Washington bureau in 1908, and L. J. (Luke) Beecher — one of the most gifted reporter-editors in *The Blade's* history — was in charge of the Columbus bureau. These two played key roles in a campaign *The Blade* waged in the spring of 1908, which Beecher kicked off in a dispatch from Columbus declaring that "if the Republican ticket that was nominated at the Memorial Hall convention (in Columbus) last week is elected in November, Walter F. Brown, of Toledo, and W. D. Guilbert, auditor of state, will assume control of the most thoroughly assembled, delicately adjusted and perfectly oiled political machine ever built in Ohio." The names of George B. Cox, long-time Republican boss of

A New Mayor, A New Editor

Cincinnati, and State Treasurer W. D. McKinnon, of Ashtabula, were added to the "organization that Chairman Brown has completed," which was described as being "well calculated to be self-perpetuating if it succeeds at the polls next fall."

There were further reports: From Beecher that "among state office-holders, candidates, politicians and members of the general assembly, the demand for copies of the *Toledo Blade* . . . containing the expose of the Brown-Cox-Guilbert manipulation of the Republican state convention was almost frantic." And from Johns, in Washington, that "President Roosevelt has decided to demand a new deal in Ohio" as a protest against the boss-managed Republican convention. Editorially, *The Blade* declared its intention "to acquaint the voters of Ohio with the situation as it exists . . . *The Blade* is fighting for the right and is confident of its ultimate vindication at the hands of the people."

This campaign continued into August and September, despite the change in management. *The Blade* demanded in March that the Republican candidate for treasurer of state, Charles C. Green, be removed from the ticket. Green was still on the ticket in July, when *The Blade* insisted that he and two other Republican candidates for state offices must be defeated. "THE BOSSES WON'T WIN," Wright thundered, adding that "next November is the time to do the housecleaning." Walter Brown, the new Republican state chairman, was singled out for attack in August. "He has wrecked the Republican party in his own county and his own city," *The Blade* charged, with the result that normally solid Republican Toledo was now being run by a "dreamy, impracticable, inept, Independent party."

Then, suddenly — on September 21 — *The Blade* switched its attack from the Republican state ticket to the party's candidates for the Ohio legislature from Lucas County:

> It is being openly charged by men of high standing in the community that the entire Republican legislative ticket in this county were named by the liquor interests . . .
>
> This newspaper is conducting a searching investigation of the manner in which the Republican legislative ticket was nominated. It will give the result of that investigation to the public, fully and frankly . . .
>
> If the Republican party in Lucas County has sold its birthright, if it has bent its neck to the brewery corporation collar, then it is time for the purging . . . And if the truth shall crush Republican chances in Lucas County, the Republicans of the state will place the blame not on the

people who refused to countenance an outrage, but on the hands of that distinguished Cox imitator, Walter Brown, chief counsel of record for the Toledo Brewery Merger, and the group of corporations which make his existence possible.

Walter Brown remained the principal target of *The Blade's* attack, whether the individual volleys were fired at the state ticket or the Lucas County legislative nominees. As chief counsel for the Huebner-Toledo Breweries Company, it was now alleged, Brown had dictated not only the Republican party's legislative ticket, but those of the Democratic and Independent parties as well. There was but one alternative — a Non-Partisan legislative ticket, headed by incumbent Senator Sylvester Lamb — and *The Blade* now marshaled all the weapons at its disposal to defeat Brown and the breweries.

The cartoon was a favorite device for attack, and a typical one — by a cartoonist named Bischoff — depicted a figure identified as Liquor Corporation Interests lording it over the three political party machines, along with a fourth character identified as Evening Organ — the *News-Bee,* of course. It was captioned SHALL HE BE *YOUR* MASTER, TOO? — the reference being to the Liquor Corporation Interests.

A series of front-page editorials also figured in the assault on Brown and the breweries. Typical captions included:

> SHALL A GREEDY CORPORATION RULE OHIO?
> WHAT ARE *YOU* GOING TO DO ABOUT IT?
> YOUR HOME OR THE TRUST — WHICH?

The last of these three was a real tear-jerker, indicating that the melodrama that had characterized some of David Ross Locke's editorials several decades earlier was not yet entirely out of fashion:

> Perhaps you own a little home, Mr. Voter. Perhaps you rent a little place now in the hope of owning your own roof-tree in the days to come. Whatever it is, that home is your haven and your kingdom. A little woman sits enthroned there — a little woman, God bless her, who cares more for you and your interests than all the trusts and all the money and all the parties in the universe. SHE'LL be loyal to you, no matter what you do. SHE'LL not distrust you, no matter how you vote. All the corporate wealth of all the world can't move her an inch in her faith in you.
>
> What are you going to say to HER tomorrow night when she asks you if you voted for Lamb? How are you going to explain to her that party loyalty looked bigger to you, in the voting booth, than loyalty to her and your home?

A New Mayor, A New Editor 165

Most Republicans obviously failed to heed *The Blade*'s impassioned pleas and remained loyal to their party. Three of Walter Brown's candidates (one of whom was John Paul Jones, long associated with David Ross Locke and *The Blade*) were elected, along with a single Democratic-Independent — Cornell Schreiber, who was later to be elected mayor of Toledo on the Independent ticket. Levi Lamb and the other Non-Partisan candidates backed by *The Blade* were snowed under.

N. C. Wright attributed the result to the "wave of Republican sentiment which swept county-wide, and the fear of thousands of voters of mismarking the blanket ballot." Not a word was said about the election of the three Republican candidates for state office, so bitterly attacked by Robinson Locke earlier in the year. There was reason enough for rejoicing about the vote for the presidency: William Howard Taft, whom *The Blade* had supported enthusiastically, was an easy winner over William Jennings Bryan.

The Blade did not abandon its fight against bossism. When the Ohio legislature convened in January, 1909, with a Republican majority, George B. Cox, the Cincinnati boss, managed to exert influence on a number of Democratic legislators to support his choice for chairman of the Senate finance committee, who thus defeated the candidate of the party leadership. Under the caption THE MENACE OF COXISM, Wright declared:

> He isn't saying a word. But he has, nevertheless, a message for Ohioans. It runs like this:
> To the People of Ohio:
> I am boss of your state legislature. I intend to be boss of your state. I own the Republican machine in Hamilton county. I own the Democratic state machine. I own some of the most unscrupulous politicians in both parties. And I have, so far, done exactly as I please with the assembly.
> I have named the senate finance committee chairman. I can throttle investigations. I can choke to death unfriendly bills. I can dictate legislation.
> What are you going to do about it?

A list of Republican and Democratic senators allegedly controlled by Cox was published, along with this statement: "Watch their every move. Their steps will be guided by Cox."

Three months later — after Taft's inauguration as President — *The Blade* was pleased to note specific evidence that the new man in the White House would not bow down to "bossism." Walter Brown had worked actively to be appointed Collector of Customs for the

Port of Toledo, but Taft chose G. W. Huntley instead. A *Blade* editorial on April 17 approved the appointment of Huntley, and added: "Furthermore, most happily he can be in no sense regarded as a part of the Brown-Guilbert machine and his appointment cannot be credited to the Brown influence."

★ ★ ★

Now, however, political interest in Toledo was beginning to swing back toward municipal considerations, with the Republicans primed to make another attempt to unseat Brand Whitlock as mayor and to wrest control of council from the Independent party. There had been some indications early in 1908 that *The Blade* might be less critical of the mayor after it had supported his suggestions for a number of capital improvements. These were, however, the kinds of proposals Rob Locke had approved in the past. As the 1909 election approached, the new editor, N. C. Wright, was deploring the inefficiency and machine tactics of the Independents. A front-page editorial, captioned THE SIGN AT THE CROSSING, urged Toledoans on May 27 to stop, look and listen:

Is it difficult for you, Mr. Citizen, to find the fundamental evil in the conditions which threaten YOUR future? Is it a difficult task for you to hark back, in memory, to the days before the little coterie that now rules Toledo grabbed the municipal reins? Do you remember the oratorical outbursts, the sounding, rounded phrases, the broad, sweeping promises, the glittering rhetoric and the glad hand that were meted out to you then, when these men sought prestige and power? Do you remember their clamor about "the rights of the people," and their clatter over "the brotherhood of man?"

They told you then that all you needed was them . . . Well, you believed them . . . They have had it for years. WHAT HAVE YOU HAD?

. . . The annual dues in the brotherhood of man are too high in Toledo. There are too many pavement holes and painted harlots in the streets of Toledo and not enough of the whirr of wheels and the smoke of chimneys in the air of Toledo. There is too much vote-grafting talk about the rights of the people and not enough honest protection of those rights . . .

The California multi-millionaire who owns the Scripps-McRae league of newspapers boasts that his Toledo paper, the coterie's organ, has increased its earnings by sixty thousand dollars a year within the last five years. But have YOU had any of the sixty thousand? The mayor, the coterie's head beneficiary, has been a much better commercial proposition in the magazine field since you elected him. But have YOU had any of that magazine money?

The Blade praised the Republican candidate for mayor in 1909, David T. Davies, for conducting his campaign with self-restraint and dignity, but he lost to Whitlock by more than 5,000 votes and the Independents tightened their hold on city hall. "His closest friends have admitted that Mr. Whitlock has been indifferent to the needs and interests and ambitions of Toledo," *The Blade* lamented. "His four years in office have been marked by no material achievement. They are wanting even in moral gains." Wright did conclude on a conciliatory note. The city was proud, he declared, of the mayor's attainments in the literary world and "if he will alter the potential energy which is his to dynamic energy, there is no honor within the power of Toledo to give which will not be his."

Mayor Whitlock incurred *The Blade's* displeasure again soon thereafter for his alleged laxness in enforcing the laws of city and state. When one of his associates, Police Judge James Austin, Jr., proposed to establish a new kind of workhouse on the outskirts of Toledo, Wright was as withering as Locke had ever been in criticizing the mayor and the Independent administration, though *The Blade* had given enthusiastic endorsement to Austin for the police judgeship. His proposal for a large farm where prisoners would work and receive fair wages brought this derisive commentary:

> By all means let Toledo hasten to found James Austin's country place for law-breakers. To lock men up is a sin and shame, to lock them up in a city, especially when the robins begin to yank worms from the brightening sod, is more sinful and more shameful still. It borders, in fact, upon insolence . . . With the grant of proper allowances for tobacco, for alimony if need be, pins, papers and messengers, the city would be somewhere near doing its duty. Above all things, do not call it a farm. The word is vulgarly suggestive of early hours, overalls, and the place where the good things come from — not to. We propose resort. It has a more pleasant sound upon the ear. Besides, it will keep most of the residents from feeling homesick.

One subject on which Brand Whitlock and *The Blade* did agree was the need for reforms that would make it possible for municipal government to function effectively and efficiently in Toledo. N. C. Wright was interested in the commission form of city government, and he sent Calvin Goodrich, an associate editor, to study the government organizations with which such cities as Galveston, Texas, and Des Moines, Iowa, were experimenting. Whitlock urged extensive changes in the state constitution, which would include initiative and referendum, absolute home rule for cities, tax reforms, increased assessment of all franchise values and unearned increment of every kind, the short ballot, voters' right to recall officials, and many others.

★ ★ ★

One of the most protracted fights over a street railway company franchise in any American city took place in Toledo, beginning in 1904—Golden Rule Jones's final year as mayor—and continuing for more than fifteen years. The *News-Bee* took a much more active part in the almost continuous fighting over the issue than did *The Blade*, which seemed willing to let the city council and the Rail Light Company settle the issue. This relatively moderate position resulted, in 1909, in allegations that *The Blade* had a selfish interest in a franchise favorable to the Rail Light Company, whose general counsel, Barton Smith, was attorney for the Locke estate, which still owned *The Blade*. N. C. Wright hotly denied these charges in a front-page editorial on June 7:

> *The Blade* DOES intend to maintain a most personal and vital interest in future traction franchises. BUT THAT INTEREST IS AND WILL BE PURELY THE INTEREST OF THE PEOPLE. So far as its ambitions go and so far as its influence reaches, *The Blade* intends to see that any grant of the people's rights, that any franchise to any public service corporation of whatever nature, shall be a grant of franchise FOR and BY the people, as well as FROM them. It intends to protect the citizens of this town to the limit of its abilities in such matters, for *The Blade* feels itself to be a PART of Toledo — it feels the PEOPLE'S interests to be ITS interests.

Ten days later, *The Blade* declared that it didn't really care what corporation got the franchise: "If Rail Light, with its many local stockholders, can make acceptable terms, well and good. If it can't, then some other corporation must." For that matter, Wright added, "there is no immediate necessity for the granting of a new franchise. There is plenty of time to witness and profit by the results of experiments in other cities."

The franchise issue still had not been settled, however, when the 1911 mayoral election rolled around. It was generally conceded that Whitlock was a sure winner and *The Blade* thought it might be a good idea, since he would hold office until the franchise matter was settled. In his campaign, the mayor urged lower streetcar fares, cheaper light and water rates, a square deal for labor and for honest capital, moral uplift, a healthier city and business growth. Carl Keller, who had been elected to the Ohio senate over *The Blade's* opposition in 1909, was the Republican candidate. Whitlock de-

A New Mayor, A New Editor

feated Keller, though his margin was cut to 3,000 votes. The Independents elected ten of eighteen members of city council.

Most of Whitlock's attention during this, his final term as mayor, was occupied with efforts to settle the questions of transit franchise and rates. *The Blade* concluded in the second year of Whitlock's term that the situation had become deadlocked. On January 10, 1911, Wright noted these competing interests:

> First: The street railway company, which wants to get as much as it can and get out of it with as much as it can get out of it.
>
> Second: The Standard Oil Company which, supported by the "Independent" party bosses and organ, wants to get hold of the . . . artificial gas franchise, combine it with its natural gas holdings and squeeze Toledo as it has been squeezing Cleveland.
>
> Third: Mayor Whitlock who, recognizing the damage to Toledo and its people resulting from present conditions, is striving honestly and earnestly to bring about an equitable settlement.
>
> Fourth: The "Independent" bosses and the councilmen who want continued power and the "Independent" newspaper organ, which wants to hold its position as political dictator, all of whom oppose a settlement in the hope of holding the question open as another campaign issue.
>
> Fifth: The people.

Mayor Whitlock and A.E. Lang, the president of the Toledo Railway and Light Company, tried without success to resolve the differences. The city demanded a three-cent fare, a true valuation of the Rail-Light property, and a $250 daily rental fee from the company. Frank B. Coates of Chicago succeeded Lang as Rail-Light president in December, and he proposed a sliding scale for fares starting at six for twenty-five cents, with universal transfers. The company asked in return a twenty-five year franchise and valuation of its property at $8,000,000, with an eight per cent yearly return on the investment. A ninety-day agreement was reached in January, 1912, setting fares at three cents during rush hours and six for twenty-five cents at other times. A majority of Toledoans now endorsed Whitlock's demand for "no renewal of franchises at a rate of fare higher than three cents," which he had supported since his first election.

The H. L. Doherty interests bought the Rail-Light Company in 1912 and took control the following February. To give the new officials a chance to get acquainted with the situation, a year's postponement of proceedings for a new rate and a new franchise was asked and granted. This put an end to Whitlock's efforts to resolve the traction problems, which dragged on until 1921 through a series of developments both tragic and hilarious. Voters approved a plan in November, 1920, for the city to purchase the company. Municipal operation as the Community Traction Company began February 1, 1921.

★ ★ ★

Soon after his election to a fourth term as mayor, Brand Whitlock announced that he would never again be a candidate for that office. *The Blade* believed the Independent party had outlived its usefulness: "It is a political anachronism. It is a toothless and hungry wanderer in dreams of days gone by. And it is getting tiresome." Wright admitted that the party was born of a civic need (Robinson Locke might not have made that concession) and that it had done great good. But, *The Blade* editor believed, the city had since outgrown the need for such an organization.[38]

On December 31, 1913, Brand Whitlock's last day as mayor of Toledo, *The Blade* summed up his eight years in office in a two-column paean of praise, suggesting the high regard in which N. C. Wright held him despite the differences between Whitlock and *The Blade* that had carried over into Wright's editorship:

> For definite and tangible material betterments brought about in the four terms of Mr. Whitlock may be recited: The transformation of the water works system, the reorganization of the police department, the spurring of the fire department to better service, the establishment of traffic regulations, practical work toward the elimination of the smoke nuisance, the encouragement of more sanitary practices in the manufacture and distribution of food, the planning of a civic center, the reconstruction of the Cherry Street bridge and the placing of a new bridge connecting the northern sections of the city.
>
> The police department has grown from 135 men in 1905 to 192. There has also been an increase in the fire department personnel and equipment, and work has been accomplished in the health department and on the city streets.
>
> The subtler influence of Mr. Whitlock upon his home city may be noted in his effort for children's playgrounds, the finding of work for the unemployed in time of hard weather and unemployment, the suggestion for a city emblem in keeping with an honorable history and the removal of the old marks of shame visited upon the workhouse prisoners . . . Not until we shall be allowed to wash away the stains of labor can account be taken of each separate labor finished. Not until then may we give the fullest due to Mayor Whitlock.

The Blade was, of course, never so hard on Brand Whitlock as it had been on Sam Jones. Even Robinson Locke, who did not share many of Whitlock's political and social convictions, was much more at home with this polished, well-educated man, who shared many of his tastes and interests, than he had been with Jones. The considerable reputation Whitlock had already achieved as a novelist impressed both Locke and Wright. And it was no real problem for N. C. Wright, who had put *The Blade* on record as supporting the Bull Moose candidacy of Theodore Roosevelt for the presidency in 1912, to express his admiration for the man who would become United States ambassador to Belgium in the Woodrow Wilson presidency.

Chapter 16

Grove Patterson Joins The Blade

The early years of the twentieth century were not the best of times for *The Blade*. The building at the corner of Jefferson Avenue and Superior Street, which David Locke had boasted was the finest in Toledo when it was completed in 1885, was damaged by fire in 1902 and again in 1911. The latter was the more serious, destroying most of David Ross Locke's letters and papers. Robinson Locke's collection of theatrical materials escaped damage, even though it was only a few feet from the fire's origin and where the flames were fiercest. A new press was a casualty, but the plant was moved to an adjoining building while damage was repaired and the press capacity was further enlarged.

Changes outside *The Blade* had their effect, too. In 1903, the Scripps-McRae League (forerunner of the Scripps-Howard organization) bought three Toledo dailies — the *Bee*, the *Times,* and the *News*. The two evening papers were combined into the *News-Bee,* while the *Times* continued as the morning paper. "The biggest newspaper coup of my career" was the way Milton A. McRae described these acquisitions, and they made a profound difference in the city's newspaper operations. The *Bee,* edited by the able and colorful Negley Cochran, had always provided stiff competition for *The Blade* in the afternoon. Now Cochran continued as editor of the *News-Bee* and, with the support of strong ownership, improved the paper in many ways. For the next 35 years, *The Blade* and the *News-Bee* competed head to head for dominance, with the political affiliation of the reader continuing to play an important part in his choice between them.

Robinson Locke's decision to retire as editor of *The Blade* five years after the Scripps-McRae merger was momentarily hurtful, too.

It brought to an end a period of forty years in which editorial control had rested in the hands of the Locke family. The departure of F. L. Dustman and C. Locke Curtis within a month after Robinson Locke's retirement was a considerable loss. So, although N. C. Wright and Harry S. Talmadge proved to be competent newspapermen, this was a time of uncertainty in the operation of *The Blade*.

Some interesting additions were being made to the content of *The Blade* — especially its Saturday edition — during the months immediately after Wright and Talmadge leased it. The first Saturday Evening Feature Section appeared on August 29, 1908, its entire front page occupied by a comic cartoon entitled "Sambo and His Funny Noises." Two other comics — "Mary and Her Little Lamb" and "Simon and Mose's New Dawg" — were also included. The remaining contents of this section were largely concerned with women's fashions and miscellaneous feature material intended to entertain.

Several months later — in February, 1909 — the Saturday edition began to include on its front page the popular "Mr. Dooley" letters of Finlay Peter Dunne, former Chicago newspaperman who had become one of the editors of the *American* magazine. The Dooley letters, which were now being syndicated widely, were concerned early in 1909 with Theodore Roosevelt's imminent departure from the White House, and the scheduled inauguration of William Howard Taft as his successor. Typical of these letters, which enjoyed an enormous popularity, is the one appearing on February 27, captioned "ME FRIND TAFT WILL SOON BEGIN HIS VACATION," SAYS DOOLEY:

"Well, sir," said Mr. Dooley, "in a few days me frind, William Taft, will begin his vacation and I must say 'tis well-deserved. I can see him goin' back to the White House on the Fourth iv March, lockin' the dure, crawlin' into bed, an' sayin': 'Don't wake me up till iliven o'clock nineteen hundherd an' thirteen'. . .."

Special inducements to enjoy many of the comforts and luxuries that were increasingly within reach of the average American were offered by *The Blade* to its readers. The advertising staff took care of that, planning supplements devoted to a variety of merchandise. Thus, during the week of March 20, 1909, such supplements dealing simultaneously with Paris and American Fashions for Spring and Summer and the Toledo Auto Show introduced readers to the latest models in both clothing and cars. Enterprise of this sort enabled *The*

Blade to boast in June of having "carried a total of 448,544½ inches of display advertising" in the first five months of 1909, and to add that "this is 11,502½ inches more than any other Toledo newspaper."

Newspapers of the time — before the coming of radio — made much of on-the-spot coverage of news. A variety of ingenious devices helped give Toledo newspaper readers the impression that they were present — or as near as can be imagined — for such major events as baseball games and elections.

For the 1908 presidential election, for example, everyone was "invited to come to *The Blade* corner tomorrow evening and receive the . . . returns." This year, it was explained:

> . . . *The Blade* will offer two attractions. First, on a big screen on the Lasalle & Koch building . . . will be flashed the results of the election in the county, district, state and country over. Moving pictures, the latest and most expensive, will intersperse the returns, and cartoons by "Brink" will help to make the crowds happy and keep them joyous.
>
> The master stroke in newspaper enterprise will be seen on a big screen on the Secor Hotel. . . . There the wonderful telauthorgraph — writing telegraph pencil — will write on the screen the bulletins just as they come to *The Blade* office from all parts of the United States.
>
> The mysterious hand will write the news, figure or letter, with perfect human movement. Nothing like this has ever been seen in Toledo.

N. C. Wright worked hard to establish himself with *Blade* readers as being interested in the welfare of Toledo. Once the 1908 election was out of the way, he turned his attention to a series of editorials under the general title of THE GREATER TOLEDO. Eleven of these appeared in the next thirty days, dealing with a broad spectrum of Toledo's problems at the time. Among the topics discussed were:

Civic Improvements (November 30).
The City As Industrial Center (December 2).
The Financial Outlook (December 4).
Railroads and Other Land Transportation (December 7).
The Lake Trade (December 9).
Ohio's Youngest Big City (December 16).
The Advantage of Conventions (December 21).

A skillful editorial writer, who was a good deal more terse than most of his contemporaries, Wright attacked a variety of issues. In March, 1909, he embarked on a series directed against what he referred to as "Joecannonism," which he was able to terminate when

Grove Patterson Joins The Blade

the House of Representatives in Washington took action to curb the worst excesses of its presiding officer.

When, in May, 1909, Great Britain embarked on daylight-saving time, *The Blade* thought it a good idea, suggesting that "a little toying with clocks and watches might prove welcome to the breadwinners in America. Here is a crusade for the unions — fix it so that the factories will close as the ball game begins." And when Dayton staged a big homecoming for the Wright brothers, N. C. Wright (not a relative) observed of what many Americans still regarded as some sort of "damned fool contraption" that "although unfitted for transportation of heavy freight, there is no reason to believe it will not be used for the carriage of express mail."

The Blade used every weapon it could find in its circulation war against the *News-Bee* in this critical period, and it was handed a particularly effective cudgel in April, 1909. NEWS-BEE DRIVEN OUT OF THE ASSOCIATED PRESS was the front-page banner headline in the April 21 edition of *The Blade*. This was the first time in fifteen years that the board of directors of the AP had forced a newspaper to give up its membership. The action grew out of charges that the *News-Bee* had given news to the United Press, owned by E. W. Scripps, who was identified as "the California multi-millionaire." The *News-Bee* was, of course, a part of the Scripps organization.

Three days later a boxed notice at the head of the editorial column proclaimed that *"The Blade* Is the Only English Evening Newspaper in Toledo Receiving the Associate Press Dispatches." It was a major victory for *The Blade*.

★ ★ ★

A young man named Grove Patterson went to work for *The Blade* on June 20, 1910. This was the beginning of a relationship that lasted almost fifty years, and it brought to *The Blade* one of the great American editors of the twentieth century. Until his death in 1957, Grove Patterson became increasingly the man with whom *The Blade* was identified and who brought growing recognition, both in the United States and abroad, to *The Blade*.

Grove Patterson was born November 5, 1881, in Rochester, Minnesota, but he returned at the age of three with his parents to Lorain County, Ohio, where they had lived before moving to Minnesota. When he was eleven years old, the family moved again — this time to Carlyle, Illinois, forty-eight miles east of St. Louis. He grew up and attended high school in the small town on the Kaskaskia

River, of which he later wrote that it "is now and ever will be my home town."

Patterson, who always said that he had little affinity for study, did not distinguish himself as a scholar in the three years he attended high school in Carlyle. His parents decided that he needed a stiffer challenge and they sent him back to Ohio for his final year — at Oberlin Academy, a preparatory school for Oberlin College. This was an enjoyable year for young Patterson. Among other important experiences, he got his first taste of writing for newspapers, on the local *Herald,* though he had been a printer's helper on a weekly paper in Carlyle.

Because a brother was a member of the faculty of Syracuse University, Grove enrolled as a freshman there instead of staying on at Oberlin.

Patterson returned the next September to Oberlin, where he earned a degree even though, as he insisted, he was "a forerunner of that lackadaisical type of young man who is sent to college to get a sheepskin and settles for a raccoon coat." He did excel as a debater, public speaker, and editor of the student newspaper, becoming a considerable campus hero in these roles.

After his graduation from Oberlin (which, he would later say, was made possible only by the nine hours of credit he received for his extracurricular activities on the debating platform and the newspaper), Patterson turned down a job as booking agent for the Redpath Bureau, which had scheduled the lectures of David Ross Locke forty years earlier. Instead, he went to work as a reporter on the Lorain *Times-Herald.* From Lorain, he moved to Cleveland, where he got a job with the *Plain Dealer.* After a year and a half there, he wrote in his autobiography, *I Like People,* he "got on a horse which was much too big for me and rode away. I moved to Toledo. It was a fateful day — and there were times shortly thereafter when I thought the right word was fatal."[39]

The job Grove Patterson took in Toledo in May, 1909, was that of managing editor of the *Times.* He was not, he insisted, qualified for the job, having had no managerial experience. Besides, he was assuming responsibility for a newspaper that was badly understaffed and in dire financial straits. When the hard-pressed publisher of the *Times,* George C. Dun, fired Patterson a year later, he thought he deserved it and held no grudge against Dun.

But he had to have a job and, in June, 1910, he applied to N. C.

Wright, editor of *The Blade*. Grove was somewhat surprised when Wright complimented him on the job he had done on the *Times*, insisting that when account was taken of the small staff and the lack of funds, the young editor had done very well. What was more important at the moment, Wright offered him a job on *The Blade* — as news editor. His duties, he was told, were to act as a kind of liaison between the managing editor, above him, and the telegraph editor and city editor, below him. Unfortunately, the occupants of the two latter positions saw no reason whatever for a "news editor." So, Patterson wrote later, "when I joined the *Blade* family I heard no welcoming bells and caught no slighest glimpse of a red carpet."

Blacque Wilson, managing editor of *The Blade* in 1910, has been described by Patterson as "the thinnest man I ever saw" (he weighed ninety pounds). Wilson, who became a legendary figure, took a liking to the young man who had no real job and made a place for him as a kind of glorified copyreader. When Blacque Wilson's health forced him to take a long leave of absence in Arizona in 1913, Patterson was named acting managing editor. Wilson returned to assume a less demanding job on the *Weekly Blade*, but his successor was not made managing editor in his own right until 1917, since it apparently had been assumed that Wilson would be sufficiently recovered to be able to resume that position.

It was during this period that Grove Patterson first became associated with Paul Block, who was to become owner and publisher of *The Blade* in the next decade. With Clarence Vernam of New York, N. C. Wright and H. S. Talmadge, Block bought the Detroit *Journal* in 1916. The new owners asked Patterson to help them operate the *Journal*. For six years, he commuted between Toledo and Detroit, designated as editorial manager of both *The Blade* and the *Journal*. When Paul Block — along with Talmadge, Wright and Vernam — also bought the Newark *Star-Eagle*, they asked Grove Patterson to supervise its news department, so that he stretched himself over three such jobs for a period of years.

More and more, however, Patterson devoted his time exclusively to *The Blade*, which was engaged in a bitter contest for the afternoon field in Toledo with the *News-Bee*. The Scripps paper had gained a considerable advantage over *The Blade* in circulation during the first decade of the new century. When Grove Patterson became managing editor of the *Times* in 1909, the *News-Bee*, which sold for a penny, had 86,000 subscribers — more than twice *The Blade's*

40,000 at two cents per copy. It would be some years before this ratio changed substantially. Negley Cochran, the *News-Bee's* editor, and his newspaper had a firm hold on a large audience of Toledoans. It became Grove Patterson's job to try to change that situation.

Chapter 17

Battling for the Lord

Theodore Roosevelt was a particular favorite of *The Blade*, and of the people of Toledo, from the time he first appeared on the national political scene until his death — a period of more than twenty years. That his decision in 1912 to "stand at Armageddon" should have been the occasion for *The Blade's* first break with a long tradition of supporting Republican party candidates for the presidency cannot too much have surprised anyone who had read the newspaper during the previous decade. Both Robinson Locke and Nathaniel C. Wright were strong for Roosevelt.

Locke had been, of course, an admirer of William McKinley — another in the long line of Ohio presidents between 1876 and 1923. When, in June, 1901, McKinley declared that he would not seek a third term, *The Blade* approved and declared that he "has placed himself higher than ever in the esteem of his fellow countrymen." In September, President McKinley was fatally wounded while attending the Pan-American Exposition in Buffalo. When he died, eight days later, Theodore Roosevelt was inaugurated as his successor.

The Blade was alarmed that Leon Czolgosz, who shot McKinley, was a self-admitted anarchist. A series of articles demanded an all-out campaign to suppress anarchy, concluding that "the Republic is secure, but a radical remedy needs to be adopted to rid it of every specie of anarchy." Some members of the Republican party's hierarchy, of course, regarded the man who was about to succeed McKinley as the next thing to an anarchist. Hadn't it been rumored that the vice presidential nomination had been bestowed on him in 1900 in the hope that he would be lost and forgotten in that familiar graveyard of political ambitions?

No such reservations troubled Robinson Locke. He hailed the

new president as a worthy successor to McKinley and began early in 1903 to boost the drive for TR's nomination to his first full term. Ohio's Senator Joseph B. Foraker, one of the leaders in the campaign for Roosevelt's nomination, wrote to Locke in January, 1904, to "thank you and assure you of the proper appreciation of the President, as well as myself, for the very effective work the *Blade* has been doing in meeting and countering the hostility to the nomination of the President." Foraker mentioned in his letter that there was opposition to a Roosevelt nomination among the more reactionary elements of the New York business community, but it was not shared by readers of the *Weekly Blade*. Never before had its presidential preference poll produced such a unanimity of choice. The totals, announced in March, 1904, were: 138,169 for Roosevelt; 1,119 for Mark Hanna; 197 for assorted others.

The Republicans did nominate Roosevelt at their Chicago convention, despite the grumblings of the Old Guard, and he scored a landslide victory over the Democratic candidate, Judge Alton B. Parker. *The Blade* continued to give solid support to TR, who carried Toledo by 12,000 votes in November and helped elect twenty of the twenty-one Republican candidates to Congress from Ohio.

The Blade applauded the series of progressive measures enacted by Congress under the president's prodding. These included the Dolliver-Hepburn bill regulating railroads, an employers' liability act, a safety appliance act, and bills concerned with pure food and meat inspection, offered in response to the revelations of Upton Sinclair's muckraking novel, *The Jungle,* of which Roosevelt had at first been skeptical. Like his father before him, Robinson Locke was not averse to using the powers of government to restrain individuals and corporations from abuse of power — economic as well as political.

There was talk of a third term for Roosevelt — a prospect toward which *The Blade* was not unsympathetic. But when William Howard Taft, Secretary of War, opened his campaign for the presidency in August, 1907, with Roosevelt's support, *The Blade* endorsed him — another fellow Ohioan. Taft's speech at Columbus was praised for its clear-cut denunciation of the evils of the trust, "remarkable for its range, for its lucidity, for its patriotic tone, and for its utter absence of anything that might be construed as a bid for personal support."

The Democrats nominated William Jennings Bryan, for the third time, and *The Blade* predicted that the "prophet without honor" faced another defeat. Taft was described as "great of body (he weighed 330 pounds), great of heart and soul. He is good enough for Roosevelt. Isn't he good enough for YOU?" Yes, he was, and Taft carried Lucas County by some 2,500 votes—considerably fewer than TR's 1904 margin of 12,000, but still a respectable showing. TAFT AND THE FULL DINNER PAIL was *The Blade's* post-election headline.

Disenchantment with William Howard Taft as president came on gradually. The first wave of dissent among members of the Progressive wing of the Republican party who had voted for him was a consequence of dissatisfaction with the Payne-Aldrich tariff. *The Blade,* however, continued to support Taft, arguing that the Republican pledge to restore prosperity had been carried out. N. C. Wright, by now in charge of the editorial page, reviewed Taft's first year in office: "One source of much fault-finding and doubting is the uncertainty as to the ability of our president to stamp his administration with his own personality and hold it in a grip strong enough to keep it altogether on safe ground." This succinct and perceptive assessment foreshadowed the problems that were to beset the Taft administration in its latter stages.

The Blade was critical of the firing of Gifford Pinchot as chief forester in the Department of Agriculture. It backed him when he charged that the secretary of the interior, Richard A. Ballinger, had granted the Guggenheims access to reserve coal lands in Alaska. Even so, Wright continued to insist that Taft was doing a good job as president. Mistakes there had been, but these were mostly errors in politics, "and with them all, he has gone ahead, steadily, patiently, bravely, doing honestly and to the limit of his ability all he or any other man could do to carry out the pledges of his party and the expressed will of the American people."

The swing away from Taft toward Roosevelt became increasingly apparent—nationally as well as locally—during 1911. When *The Blade* polled voters, asking Republicans to express approval or disapproval of both Taft and TR, the results were overwhelming. There were 10,105 votes against Taft and only 1,841 for him; 10,430 favored Roosevelt with only scattered votes of disapproval. Walter F. Brown, the Toledoan who was chairman of the state Republican central committee, a member of the party's national committee, and who was to become postmaster general in the Herbert Hoover cabinet, announced in December, 1911, that he was for Roosevelt.

The first Roosevelt Club in Toledo was organized on January 24, 1912. In a front-page editorial, published February 26, *The Blade* proclaimed: "ROOSEVELT AND VICTORY. TAFT AND DEFEAT."

The presidential preference system for electing delegates to national party conventions was used in Ohio for the first time in 1912. In addition to Taft and Roosevelt, Senator Robert M. LaFollette of Wisconsin had substantial support—much of it from progressive Republicans who were unsure of TR's commitment to reform causes. J. A. Mathews, now chief of *The Blade's* Washington bureau, reported in April that "the boom for LaFollette is dead," which proved to be a premature conclusion. Mathews quoted Senator Albert B. Cummins of Iowa in the same dispatch to the effect that the Republicans were sure to nominate Roosevelt, which was even farther off the mark.

Particularly difficult and embarrassing for *The Blade* was the contest in the Ninth Ohio district over the choice of delegates to the Republican national convention. The problem was that the Taft delegates were none other than Edward Drummond Libbey and John N. Willys, the presidents of Toledo's two major industries of the period. Both were personal friends of Robinson Locke and were admired by N. C. Wright, his successor as editor. *The Blade* was, of course, supporting the Roosevelt delegates. There were repeated editorial references to the high regard in which their fellow Toledoans held Libbey and Willys and statements that although there was nothing the city's residents would deny them in their own right, the issue here was Roosevelt vs. Taft. Libbey and Willys, it was suggested, were being used by the local Republican machine and defeat would be a blow not at these industrial leaders but at the party bosses.

The Blade accused these bosses of a number of crimes during the primary campaign, including "the cheap political trick" of setting up LaFollette delegates in Toledo to draw off support from the Roosevelt delegates. It was alleged a week before the election that "several new high water marks for political absurdities have been set already" in the "rich man's campaign methods" being used by Taft backers. "The Ninth District primaries of 1912 are destined to live long in the memory of the hungry ward heeler and the thirsty soil who count election days as happy milestones," *The Blade* declared.

When Roosevelt came to Toledo on May 16 to speak on behalf of his candidacy, *The Blade* welcomed him with a front-page editorial, captioned THEODORE ROOSEVELT — TODAY:

> Theodore Roosevelt, first citizen of the Nation, comes to Toledo today fighting the greatest and bravest battle of his great and brave career. It is YOUR battle, fought for YOU at greater self-sacrifice, at greater risk to his own fame than ever statesman took before and against greater odds of combined wealth, special interest and organized political machinery than any other man has ever faced . . .
>
> Toledo owes it to Theodore Roosevelt to show him today that its heart is with him. Toledo owes it to itself to show the nation today that this is a people's city, a free city, unfettered by privilege.
>
> Toledo is a Roosevelt stronghold. It should fling its colors high and far today.

The Blade carried another editorial tribute on that same day — May 16, 1912. This was to a man who had been an associate of David Ross Locke and who had continued, in the quarter of a century since Locke's death, to play a key role in the newspaper's growth and development. The tribute, on the occasion of Lane's death, was entitled FRANK T. LANE, BUILDER:

> The career of Mr. Frank T. Lane covered that period, that unsung but still romantic and blossoming period, in which the town of Toledo grew into the city of Toledo.
>
> Mr. Lane's connection with the *Blade* dates from those days when the early, tentative movements toward growth, inspired by such visions as his own, became strong and definite . . .
>
> Of his quaint, dry humor, the *Blade* could tell many anecdotes. On his private, almost secret, benefactions, we could dilate . . . But we believe that he himself would rather be remembered, not for those traits that were as natural with him as breathing, but for his connection with the erection of a great and aspiring city upon the site of a small, half-lost town at the junction of a yellow river with an inland lake.

Frank Lane had been a balance wheel in *The Blade* organization throughout the Locke years. His death was a great loss, and the almost lyric editorial tribute — which may well have been written by Robinson Locke — was a richly deserved recognition of his contributions.

The Blade returned at once to the political wars, with a front-page editorial proclaiming that THE PEOPLE MUST WIN. Both its newspaper rivals — the *Times* and the *News-Bee* — were attacked in blistering terms. The *Times* was characterized as the "vapid valet" of the Toledo Republican machine, which had "fought valiantly for its masters." There was even greater contempt for the

News-Bee, "redolent of the stench of its former Standard Oil ownership and affiliation," which had "sneered at the people's struggle and fought for Taft by attempting to win Roosevelt votes for the utterly hopeless LaFollette cause." A rousing peroration declared that "privilege is fighting its most dangerous foe and fighting him with all its vicious strength. It will go to any length to beat Theodore Roosevelt."

Privilege was routed on primary election day, the people were victorious. Theodore Roosevelt won 34 of Ohio's 42 convention delegates. In the Ninth district — comprising Lucas, Wood, Fulton and Ottawa counties—the Roosevelt candidates amassed a plurality of more than 3,000 over Taft's Libbey-Willys ticket. *The Blade* was jubilant, but its joy was short-lived.

★ ★ ★

A more flagrant example of boss rule of a political party than that provided by the renomination of William Howard Taft as the Republican presidential candidate in 1912 is difficult to imagine. There was overwhelming evidence of popular preference for Theodore Roosevelt, who had defeated Taft in primary after primary and appeared to have the nomination in hand. The incumbent president did have a substantial base of delegates—most of them named by states which still held conventions rather than primaries and many of them in the South, where Republicans were few and machine politicians had a tight hold on the process of choosing delegates. The real blow to Roosevelt's hopes came, however, when the nominating convention assembled in Chicago in June. The Republican national committee, dominated by Old Guard elements, used all the advantage of organization to seat Taft delegates in virtually every instance where there was a contest. N. C. Wright and *The Blade* were horrified.

Even in states where primaries were held — as in Ohio — the process of thwarting the popular preference for Roosevelt had begun in state conventions. When Ohio Republicans convened two weeks after the primaries, they endorsed Taft for president, ignoring the strong popular vote for Roosevelt. Then they named Taft men as the six at-large delegates to Chicago. *The Blade* proclaimed it "the betrayal" and cited "three things that have been learned" from it:

> First — that the Taft campaigners are so desperately hard-up for delegates that they will have them by foul means, if fair means fail.
>
> Second — that the bosses, big and little, are ripe for the block.

Third — that the people, so long used by the politicians, must get the trick of using the politicians.

No matter what the Republican machine wanted, *The Blade* insisted, Roosevelt would be the party's real leader in the coming campaign. What happened subsequently in Chicago was a blow, but it did not shatter N. C. Wright's faith in his friend, TR. THE LIGHT WILL COME was the caption of the editorial he wrote in the wake of Taft's nomination:

> Out of the iniquity perpetrated by the Republican national convention at Chicago has grown a situation too complex for instant solving . . .
> That the progressive Republicans of the country will not, in majority numbers, support the candidacy of Mr. Taft is certain. The bitterness and shame of the stolen convention makes united support of the President impossible . . .
> Theodore Roosevelt acted in patriotic wisdom when he refused to commit his followers to any immediate action and insisted that the final decision be deferred for weeks . . . The country's faith in Roosevelt has never been misplaced. Some way, somehow, out of the chaos and turmoil of today will come great and lasting good for the republic.

The Democrats met in Baltimore and nominated Woodrow Wilson on the forty-sixth ballot. After Roosevelt's followers had returned to the same hall in Chicago where Taft had been nominated and named him as the Progressive party's candidate for the presidency, *The Blade* lost little time in making its preference among the three men clear. There was some praise for "Professor" Wilson but, Wright declared, "he is not the ideal candidate" because "his life work as an instructor, his inexperience in governmental affairs, his consistently changing viewpoint, and his continually shifting policies make poor promise for an effective national executive." William Howard Taft was dismissed in short order as the candidate of the privileged and the bosses. "And as for this newspaper," the editorial concluded, "with Theodore Roosevelt, 'We stand at Armageddon and we battle for the Lord.' "

The Blade battled bravely in that most remarkable of election campaigns—the first, and up to now the last, in which a third party contested on more or less equal footing with the two major political groups, even outpolling the party from which it had broken away. The campaign was hectic and confusing in Ohio, as in many other states. The Republican organization stubbornly insisted on the complete loyalty to Taft of all candidates—many of whom had campaigned in the primaries as Roosevelt men. One result was the nomination of three tickets for state offices and in many counties. In Lucas County the total was four, since the Independent party, while endorsing Roosevelt for president, named some candidates of its own for local offices.

Walter F. Brown, who had indicated his support of Roosevelt before the primaries, now resigned both as chairman of the Republican state committee and as Ohio's member of the Republican national committee. He formally declared his association with the new Progressive party "in the belief that it is destined to be an effective instrument in solving the social, industrial and political problems of our times." Many other Republicans of Progressive inclination followed Brown's lead.

In October—only about three weeks before the election— Roosevelt was shot by a would-be assassin, John Schrank, in Milwaukee. Although he was not seriously injured, TR was able to make only a limited personal campaign in the remaining time, and *The Blade* wanted to know WHO COACHED THE ASSASSIN?:

> The man who with a madman's patience followed Colonel Roosevelt from place to place around the country in quest of the opportunity to assassinate him, shouted: "Any man looking for a third term ought to be shot."
>
> The New York reactionary newspapers, the mental food of this madman, have virtually been saying this very thing for months . . .
>
> The responsibility for this attempt upon the life of Theodore Roosevelt rests upon the venomous malevolence of the tory organs and orators. The madman was of their making.
>
> Under the moral law, it is for them to answer for him.

The Blade's final endorsement of Roosevelt's candidacy, early in November, hailed him in eloquent phrases as THE PLAIN PEOPLE'S CHAMPION: "Not since the great Lincoln went out into the unknown places have the plain people of the republic been championed by such a man as Roosevelt. Not since the lips of Lincoln were silenced has the nation listened to such a plea for humanity and human justice as Theodore Roosevelt has made throughout this splendidly fought battle for better things."

Woodrow Wilson carried Lucas County, with 13,999 votes to 12,442 for Roosevelt. The Socialist candidate, Eugene V. Debs, got almost as many votes as did Taft—just over 5,000 each. *The Blade* offered Wilson its congratulations, which was about as warm as its relation with the new president ever became. It took great heart at another aspect of the election returns:

> The tremendous popular support given the Progressive party—a party just one hundred days old—is the plainest indication in the world that the Progressive movement is here to stay. That great vote justifies the revolt against the bosses at Chicago. It justifies every action of the seceding delegates who could not condone the great theft and it amply justifies every word and every appeal of the people who gave themselves to the cause of human rights and the program of rule by the people. To scoff at the Progressive movement is to make the greatest of errors . . . It is booked for great things. For nothing right has ever been slain, even by repeated distresses.

David Ross Locke and Robinson Locke had always been wholly unsympathetic with third political party groups—even when they might sympathize with the cause that brought the parties into being. Only in this light is it possible to appreciate the extent of the break with tradition which this decision to support Roosevelt's candidacy in 1912 represented. Probably it was less painful than it would have been in almost any other circumstances. Both Robinson Locke and N. C. Wright had supported Progressivism within Republican ranks, as had a large majority of party members in Toledo.

Wright's personal friendship with and admiration for Roosevelt was unquestionably a major factor in the decision to depart from this tradition of more than seventy years. After the election, he paid this tribute to his friend:

> The debt of gratitude the country owes him has grown heavily in these last three months. That it will be canceled, even in small measure, in his lifetime, is a matter of question. But that in the purview of history he will be accorded the rank that he has so richly won as one of the greatest and bravest and truest of American citizens, there is no shadow of doubt.

The Blade's editor had no regret about the decision to stand with Teddy Roosevelt at Armageddon to battle for the Lord.

★ ★ ★

Robinson Locke continued to spend some time in Toledo after he retired as editor of *The Blade* in 1908. He maintained an office in the building at Superior and Jefferson, where his theatrical library was housed. He also continued to write theater and music criticism for *The Blade* as Rodney Lee.

N. C. Wright and Harry S. Talmadge made few changes in the newspaper they now leased from the Locke estate. Wright was a strong editor, Talmadge a capable business man, and *The Blade* continued to grow and prosper under their management. Grove Patterson, as managing editor, headed a strong staff, which included such men as Luke Beecher and Jack Warwick, providing vigor and enterprise in covering local and state news. The Washington bureau grew in activity and prestige.

Toledo grew rapidly in the first three decades of the twentieth century — from 131,822 in 1900 to 290,718 in 1930. Five thousand people and an area of three square miles were added to the city in 1916, when the town of Tremainsville was annexed. Residential development spread in all directions from the downtown area.[40]

There were changes in city government, too. Home rule—for which *The Blade* had fought alongside Sam Jones and Brand Whitlock (with whom it agreed on few things) — was strengthened by a constitutional amendment approved by Ohio voters in 1912. Toledo adopted a new charter, and the first election under its provisions took place in 1915.

Chapter 18

The Blade in War and Peace

Woodrow Wilson's two terms as president were dominated by war in Europe — leading eventually to the United States' involvement. *The Blade* — like its political hero, Teddy Roosevelt — stood for a more aggressive position than the Wilson administration assumed after the outbreak of the war in July, 1914, though it did not urge American involvement in the fighting.

What N. C. Wright did urge was that the United States prepare for war if it wanted to preserve peace. *The Blade* was, therefore, pleased when William Jennings Bryan offered to resign as Secretary of State in the summer of 1914. Never a favorite of Wright — or of Robinson Locke — the "Great Commoner" was now assailed for his "stubborn, mollusk-like clinging to the one idea, peace-at-any-price propaganda of the ultra-pacifists," an advocate of "jelly-fish diplomacy." To keep the country out of war, *The Blade* proposed construction of one hundred submarines, twenty-five destroyers, a hundred armed aircraft, more money for coastal defenses, heavy artillery, machine guns, small arms and ammunition. Wright wanted the military to keep abreast of the latest in armaments. In 1916, citing the "effectiveness of the new machine gun in the European war," he asked: "Is the United States going to learn to use it?"

The Blade offered full information concerning war activities at home and abroad. "The A-B-C of National Defense" was the title of a series of articles by J. W. Muller, beginning in June, 1914. Another series — "What America Should Learn from the War" — was offered three months later. Its author was Theodore Roosevelt.

"This country wants no part in the hideous struggle on the other side of the Atlantic," *The Blade* declared in February, 1915, adding that "the United States wants peace — and must have peace." The possibility of American entry into the war was discussed as early as 1915, but lack of a sufficient navy, coastal defense and any well-built reserve system was cited as reasons why this country was not ready for such involvement. *The Blade* did urge attention to the need for preparedness and a plan for national defense, including the addition of a million men to the armed forces.

When the Lusitania was sunk on May 7, 1915, *The Blade* called for "strict accountability." Citizens were urged to stand behind President Wilson in this "hour of trial." Theodore Roosevelt likened the nation's neutrality to that of Pontius Pilate and condemned submarine warfare. Secretary of State Bryan, who had stayed on after his earlier offer to resign, now left the cabinet because he regarded Wilson's note to the Germans as "dangerously close to an ultimatum." *The Blade* suggested Elihu Root or Henry Cabot Lodge as his successor. It was neither Root nor Lodge, but Robert Lansing, who was named.

President Wilson proposed in October, 1915, that the nation should organize for defense, though not for war. Among those opposed was Toledo's octogenarian congressman, Isaac R. Sherwood, who urged that the army be cut to half its size, with more reliance placed on high school cadets. *The Blade*, which found the Civil War hero an embarrassment as the Ninth District's representative in Congress, reminded Sherwood that lack of preparation to deal with rebellion had resulted in four years of civil strife. "Not one of the men responsible for that nonpreparedness but knew he was 'absolutely right'," *The Blade* concluded.

The war moved closer to Toledo in a number of ways in succeeding months. It was reported late in June, 1916, that William Barber, son of Judge Jason A. Barber, had been severely wounded at Verdun. The young man, a student at Oberlin College, had gone overseas to join an ambulance service.

The Blade took heart in Toledo's reaction to a preparedness parade in the city. In the issue of June 30, Wright declared:

> Peace-at-any-price should flourish in Toledo if it does anywhere . . . We are a very busy folk, much absorbed in our daily labors, much inclined to concentrate our thoughts upon Toledo, its welfare and its growth, and to ignore the world beyond the corporation lines.
>
> But peace-at-any-price has no standing in this community. The preparedness parade of Saturday advertises the fact that Toledo believes in adequate defenses, believes in protecting the future at the cost of the present, believes in being ready for any eventuality . . .

The Blade in War and Peace

Pacifism, as it is preached in the United States, gets nowhere.

Only a few days later — on the Fourth of July — *The Blade* took another swipe at peace-at-any-price advocates in an editorial criticizing the American Peace Society as a sham, supported by rich men. There was, meantime, no lack of evidence as to where Wright's sympathies lay. *The Blade* praised the Allies' refusal of German peace offers and predicted that "we shall not be reading of serious movements for peace before 1918 and may not hear of a meeting of the peace delegates until that year is nearly over." When Verdun fell to the Germans in September, 1916, a photo of the town in flames was inserted in a *Blade* editorial, which concluded: "Now there are only blood-smeared battlements, and women and children, desolate."

The presidential election occupied increasing attention during the fall of 1916, although the war continued to be a dominant concern. On September 11, for example, *The Blade* contained five editorials. Three were directly related to the fighting in Europe. A fourth, CONGRESS AND THE WAR, discussed the need for new tariffs in view of the war's developments.

★ ★ ★

Woodrow Wilson, seeking his second term as president in 1916, was opposed by Charles Evans Hughes of New York. *The Blade*, after its brief desertion to the Progressives in 1912, was now back in the Republican fold, giving full support to Hughes. Since there was no Theodore Roosevelt in the field this time, there was no attractive alternative. When Maine went Republican in its traditional early election on September 11, *The Blade* applauded the "satisfying significance of the splendid Republican victory" in a state that had been a stronghold of Progressivism four years earlier. Fear that many who had voted for Roosevelt in 1912 might now support Wilson instead of Hughes was thus allayed.

Women, of course, were not yet eligible to vote in 1916, but *The Blade* managed to get in a plug for both the right of women to vote and for the Hughes candidacy:

> The *Blade* has long stood for woman suffrage and for a deeper interest in both local and national politics on the part of women. We are glad to note that the women who are favoring Charles Evans Hughes for President are being organized in Toledo and that they will cooperate with the Hughes party of women boosters who will be in the city on October 4. Among the distinguished guests on that day will be Mrs. Gifford Pinchot, Mrs. Raymond Robbins, Mrs. Nicholas Longworth and Mrs. Cornelius Vanderbilt.

The Blade did not wage a particularly aggressive campaign in this election, for reasons that became clearer after the voting. When Hughes came to Toledo some six weeks before the election, Wright did praise him for opposing a bill calling for an eight-hour day for railroad workers. This in a city with 8,000 to 10,000 railroad workers, who might not agree with Hughes but must admire a man who had the courage of his convictions:

> Once he has determined in his mind what is right he will stick to it, if need be, until the devil invests in winter clothes . . .
> This is exactly the kind of President the country needs. . . . We can get that kind of President only by making a change at Washington.

The reverse of this argument was used against Woodrow Wilson in an editorial a few days later, captioned THE WIND VANE. "The average opponent of Mr. Wilson," Wright concluded, "the average critic, does not quarrel so much with the President's policies as he quarrels with his vacillations. It is the one unfavorable thing in the President. It is the one thing that seems wholly foreign and un-American in the White House."

Much was heard during the campaign of the argument that President Wilson had "kept our country out of war" and should therefore be re-elected. Ten days before the election, *The Blade* took aim at this argument and two others that had been made on Wilson's behalf:

> Woodrow Wilson did NOT keep the country out of war. The United States was kept out of war by the belligerent nationals themselves . . .
> Woodrow Wilson did NOT give American labor the eight-hour day. As a makeshift, he gave a raise of wages to the trainmen, through a law which may be unconstitutional . . .
> Woodrow Wilson did NOT give the country prosperity . . . The European war rescued this country from impending panic in 1915 . . .
> These three things he did NOT do.

One local contest to which *The Blade* gave special attention was that involving Congressman Isaac Sherwood, nominated again by the Democrats, and his Republican opponent, Frank Mulholland. Wright asked his readers to SEND A BETTER MAN TO CONGRESS:

> The Ninth District needs a new type of congressman . . .
> It needs a congressman who is above trying to win votes with garden seeds paid for with public money. It needs one who is above trying to keep in office with gifts of Uncle Sam's Cook Book, paid for and distributed

The Blade in War and Peace 193

at the people's charge. It needs one who considers pork dishonest, who will vote against pork bills . . .

Mr. Mulholland is fully abreast of the day. He knows what the country and the district need now, not what they may have needed and desired in the year 1879 . . .

Sherwood was not mentioned in the editorial, but no one could have had any problem identifying him. Nor did the voters at the polls a few days later, when they returned Congressman Sherwood to Washington.

The Blade presented its summation in the presidential contest the day before the election. The caption of the editorial — IT IS A CHOICE BETWEEN MEN, NOT DOCTRINES — provided a clear indication of the stated reasons for supporting the Republican Hughes:

. . . When one party's principles mirror the other's principles, one doctrine is very much like another, the voter must make his selection according to the character of the competing candidates. In this campaign, such a choice can be easily made. In character, Mr. Wilson and Mr. Hughes are as far apart as the Ten Commandments and the policies of Machiavelli. If we elect Mr. Wilson, we endorse wavering, vagueness, a constitutional habit of keeping the right hand unacquainted with what the left hand does. Should we elect Mr. Hughes, we will have shown our preference for the use of the backbone in government, our liking for these clean-cut virtues which for more than a hundred years we have boasted of as American.

The nation's voters did not follow this advice, of course, and after an exciting election, whose outcome remained in doubt for some time, N. C. Wright provided his analysis of the reason why the Republicans had been beaten. It also suggests clearly the kinds of reservations in his mind that made *The Blade's* enthusiasm for Hughes's candidacy less than it might have been:

. . . There isn't any argument about it. The reason for national party defeat is absolutely plain. The blame and the shame lie upon the Old Guard. They, the men who wrecked the party in 1912, have again led it to defeat . . .

The Old Guard should have been sent to its political death years ago. The cleansing of the party temple, already too long delayed, must be undertaken now or never.

The Republican Old Guard managed to outlast Wright. Just two years before the death of *The Blade's* editor, they led their party to victory in 1920 with Warren Gamaliel Harding of Ohio as their candidate. For reasons that are not entirely clear, Wright made the ride with them.

★ ★ ★

Other excitement than the political kind was offered to Toledo in the fall of 1916, and *The Blade* kept abreast of it. Geraldine Farrar, the American soprano, sang the title role in Bizet's "Carmen" at the Terminal Auditorium on the night of October 16, and another renowned prima donna, Lena Cavalieri, known as "the world's most beautiful woman," came to town to hear her husband — the tenor, Muratore — sing Don Jose opposite Miss Farrar. Next day, a two-column headline on the front page trumpeted the news:

TOLEDO "ARRIVES" ON MUSICAL MAP
5,000 HEAR OPERA

Motion picture theatres were thriving, too, and the volume of advertising in *The Blade* was swelled considerably by large displays announcing the latest offerings — called photoplays. One of these was "Where Are My Children?" with Tyrone Power, billed as "the greatest American dramatic actor." No children under sixteen would be admitted, unless accompanied by an adult. There was also "The Brand of Cowardice," starring another rising young actor named Lionel Barrymore.

Regular daily comic strips were featured in *The Blade* in 1916, four years after the first ones had appeared in the Saturday Feature Section. One of these was Rube Goldberg's "It's Hard to Find a Reason for Some Things." Such popular strips as "Mutt and Jeff" and "'S Matter Pop" were also included.

★ ★ ★

The United States severed diplomatic relations with Germany in February, 1917, but *The Blade* didn't think this would lead to war. It would only "add to the multitudinous threats of war which have rained upon the United States in the last two years." Universal military training was suggested, not just as a means of being prepared, but to improve the health of young men. It would give them sounder constitutions and it would "give the United States a sounder patriotism."

The Blade continued to criticize Congressman Sherwood and several times suggested that he should resign. By March, 1917, Sherwood had changed his views and was calling for a special session of Congress to declare war on Germany. A few weeks later, President Wilson declared that a state of war existed when the sinking of

The Blade in War and Peace 195

American ships by German submarines continued. He read his war messaage to Congress on April 2. War was declared four days later. "Germany, not the United States, has made this war," *The Blade* observed.

The war efforts received full support from *The Blade*. There were stories about local military units, women in new jobs, and victory gardens. War bond drives were highly publicized. Meatless days were seen as only the beginning of the discipline of war. Conscription was endorsed as a fair method of raising troops. *The Blade* believed it was essential, since men were not volunteering in such numbers as had flocked to enlist at the beginning of the Spanish-American War.

The Blade addressed an editorial to Kaiser Wilhelm on August 9, 1917, stating why the United States was fighting the war against Germany:

> We are fighting in humanity's name to stop the piteous crimes for justice of these millions in the spirit world. We are fighting to prevent your butchers bringing the "blood and iron" cult to the United States.
>
> We are fighting to save American babies from your bayonets.
>
> We are fighting to save American women from death in the flames and from bayonet goring.
>
> We are fighting to keep you off our land and, Heaven helping, we think we can do it.

Toledo had its share of problems involving allegations against foreign-born residents. Inevitably, its large number of German-Americans were suspected of sympathy with the homeland. *The Blade* criticized no particular nationality, but did complain of those who came to this country to work, then claimed exemption from the draft on the basis of foreign birth. Wright thought too many foreigners in this country had given no evidence of trying to become Americanized. A full-page advertisement at the beginning of the third Liberty Loan drive was headlined: "Who Is the Kaiser's Spy in Toledo: The United States Government Will Soon Know Where YOU Stand." Men wearing robes similar to those once used by the Ku Klux Klan tarred and feathered several pro-Germans. A *Blade* reporter who saw the robed men described them as "sober-minded men, fairly prominent in civic affairs, and respected in their own community."

All kinds of rumors circulated in Toledo throughout the war, and *The Blade* thought many were the work of German propagandists: "This industry has been running day and night since we entered the war, being manned mostly by pro-Germans. It has damaged our cause by interfering with enlistments, increasing the number of slackers, impeding the raising of charity funds and the campaigning for Liberty Loans."

The Blade assigned a high priority to the arrest of all who were evading military service. Police raided theaters, pool rooms and dance halls in July, 1918, and arrested 440 men of draft age, including 121 who had no draft cards. Toledoans who drove their cars on Gasless Sundays were called slackers and the police took their license numbers. Idlers were rounded up and assigned to essential jobs, including work at a government nitrate plant near Toledo. Men who worked as janitors, florists, waiters, window cleaners were told to enlist or seek war positions.

★ ★ ★

One of the most dramatic events of the war on the home front was the so-called "false armistice" of November 7, 1918. It had a particular significance for *The Blade* and for its young managing editor, Grove Patterson. Always a great raconteur, he recalls what happened in *I Like People:*

> Horns and bells, horns and bells, the seemingly endless cavalcade of automobiles rolled down Jefferson Avenue past my window in the Blade office toward the river. At least it seemed endless for me, for I prayed that the din of this awful procession might pass out of my eyes and ears and mind quickly and forever. On the sidewalks and around the open motor cars, men, women, boys and girls jostled their way on bicycles and on foot, screaming in their delight. Many of them, when they passed under my window, looked up and laughed, pointed their scornful fingers and cried out the louder. Tense, tired, nervous and yet, as I remember, outwardly calm, I wondered if it would ever be quiet and peaceful again.
>
> It was on the seventh of November, 1918. Our opposition, the *News-Bee,* had put an extra edition on the street, shouting in billboard letters across the front page that the armistice had been signed and the war had come to an end.
>
> The papers were selling faster than the newsboys could take in the pennies, and in an incredibly short time the tumult was on and the roaring parade was under way. Inside the editorial rooms of the *Blade* it was deathly quiet — quiet because I had made a decision. As executive editor, it was my sole responsibility and there was no one else to whom to turn. N. C. Wright, the editor, was out of town. The *Blade,* then as now, carried the twenty-four hour service of the Associated Press; the *News-Bee* had the United Press. The *News-Bee's* extra edition had been based on a dispatch sent to the New York office of the United Press by Roy Howard, then head of the UP. Howard had good reason for cabling the dispatch

because he got the word from Admiral Wilson, in command of the American fleet in the harbor of Brest.

The authority was excellent and I have never voiced any criticism of Howard for sending the cable. Admiral Wilson had what he thought was reliable information that the armistice had been signed. The only trouble with the story was that it wasn't true. The armistice was not signed and the war was not over until four days later, November 11.

If I live to be well over a hundred, I shall never forget that heartbreaking parade of November 7. As the hours wore on, no denial or modifying word came from the *News-Bee*. No announcement of the signing of the armistice came from the wires of the Associated Press, and I was slowly perishing. The procession kept up, the tumult and the shouting rose, and nobody went home. The *News-Bee* stood pat and the *Blade* stood pat. It was the same the next day and the day after.

The town was talking and the phones were ringing. Folks were saying that apart from being a half-wit, incompetent, asleep, and cruel enough to keep on killing our boys in a war which was over, Grove Patterson was a nice enough fellow. Even some of the members of my own staff, I am convinced, seriously doubted my judgment. But in accordance with that judgment, such as it was, I stood by my silent guns and the Associated Press and ignored the tempest. After pretending for two days that the world stood still and there was no war news to print, the *News-Bee* came out with a front-page statement that it had been mistaken. In the meantime, we contented ourselves with a simple first-page announcement to the effect that when the armistice was signed the *Blade* would print the news. In a few days thousands of readers had become calm enough to think straight . . .

I remember now that I thought a long time about the best way for the *Blade* to deal with the *News-Bee* after our painfully delayed triumph. My first impulse was to write a boasting editorial, but I thought better of it. On November 12, the day after the real news of the armistice, I contented myself with three lines of not too big type at the bottom of the first page:

"The *Blade* is the only afternoon newspaper which carries the dispatches of the Associated Press."

It seemed to me that this was only a decently moderate piece of bragging by implication.[41]

This kind of humor-tinged understatement became a trademark of Grove Patterson and it helped make him immensely popular as both a writer and public speaker. His style as editor was not to lead resounding crusades against the forces of evil. Even his enthusiastic support of the Republican party did not cause him to denounce his political foes as deep-dyed villains. He had serious doubts about Brand Whitlock's sincerity, for example, but he did not openly attack Whitlock and always conceded his abilities.

One of the consequences of the false armistice was a story about the Toledoan who was awakened, months later, sometime between midnight and daybreak, by a newsboy yelling "Extry, extry!"

"Which paper have you got?" he called down to the boy in the street below.

"*News-Bee*," was the reply.

Whereupon, the story has it, the man closed his window and climbed back into bed, reasonably sure that nothing very important had happened.

True or not, the tale was unquestionably indicative of local attitudes toward the two newspapers. *The Blade* had begun the climb that would restore it to the dominant position it had once held. By 1919, *The Blade* was again the leader in circulation, with 86,032 subscribers to the *News-Bee's* 78,181. Ten years later, in 1929, *The Blade's* total had increased to 134,672 and before another decade had passed — in 1938 — the *News-Bee* had closed down, leaving the afternoon field in Toledo to *The Blade*.

★ ★ ★

A *Blade* headline announced on November 12, 1918 — the day after the armistice that ended the war had been signed: EVERYTHING FOR WHICH UNITED STATES FOUGHT HAS BEEN WON, SAYS WILSON. An editorial declared:

> Germany lies naked before the world she has despoiled and outraged for four years.
>
> Never in the world's history has the flail of heaven fallen so weightily on an arrogant, defiant nation; never has a vanquished foe been stripped so completely of ill-gotten conquests; never has a peace of such magnificent justice been won. It only remains to secure at the council table of the nations the fruits of blood, steel and courage, and the sacrifice of eight millions and a half precious lives.

There was talk of a memorial to Toledo's service men, and *The Blade* recommended construction of some kind of permanent building. Two hundred trees were later donated to be planted as memorials to those who had died in the war. When troops began to return home, *The Blade* issued an eight-page souvenir edition, with pictures, stories and a list of the 5,586 casualties of Ohio's 37th Division.

When the high cost of living became a post-war problem, *The Blade* urged an investigation. Surplus food was bought from the army and sold without profit to residents. Women were urged to boycott meat dealers and stop buying from profiteers. Wright cited "the wastefulness of Americans . . . with a resulting higher cost of what is left" in urging that everyone should save the crumbs of expensive bread. A contest on "How Do You Beat the High Cost of Living?" was sponsored by *The Blade*, which finally put the blame for high prices on the Democratic administration, extravagance, inefficiency, and too many taxes.

N. C. Wright was an early believer in the principle of the League of Nations. He suggested that the covenant would "make the world safe for democracy so long as democracy is safe for the world." He added:

> The language of the article is clear, unequivocal, lofty in utterance of just and humanitarian principles and the covenants pave the way for a practical fellowship and peace of mankind such as the world has never hitherto enjoyed — about which, in fact, it has never before more than dreamed.

When Henry Cabot Lodge and others in the Senate demanded revision of Wilson's proposals, *The Blade* suggested that the chief opposition resulted from the President's refusal to permit his scheme to be "touched or tinkered with." Somewhat caustically, Wright observed that "it remains yet to be seen whether Mr. Wilson will have to pay the price of dropping the statesmanship he has practiced in Europe to play the politician at home."

The Blade made these observations after the Senate had rejected the treaty:

> The American people want a League of Nations — if that will bring the world nearer to universal peace and not entail too heavy a responsibility and obligations upon the United States.
>
> The American people do not want a League of Nations — if that means they must dip into every quarrel, however remote, and supply in the flesh and blood of their sons the common fodder of these arguments.
>
> The cold, unpleasant truth has come home to America that to some nations late our comrades in arms, the League means not less greed and cruelty in the world, but opportunity to practice selfishness on a scale hitherto denied them. The further unpleasant truth is forced on one that Washington is well aware of these desires and aims abroad and that, while preaching the doctrine of an earth new-born, it is nourishing the suspicion that the doctrine is wrong.

These were not words to give much comfort to Woodrow Wilson's final efforts to rally public support for the beleaguered treaty to create a League of Nations. Nor was *The Blade's* role in the 1920 election at all helpful in that respect.[42]

The Blade gave extensive coverage to both political parties' national conventions. Lucas J. Beecher, now political editor, attended both. Correspondents from other news organizations included Irvin S. Cobb, Ring Lardner, Senator William E. Borah, William Jennings Bryan and Rube Goldberg. Both parties chose Ohio newspaper editors as their candidates — Warren G. Harding of Marion for the Republicans, James M. Cox of Dayton for the Democrats. *The Blade* supported Harding, even though he had the blessing of the Republican Old Guard. Jack Warwick, a staff member, wrote a series of eighteen articles on Harding — a friend from his younger days.

The Blade stayed with Harding throughout his increasingly troubled years in the White House, declaring at his death: "Despite the grumblings and scoldings and readiness to misunderstand him, he has been respected . . . He could have no better epitaph than that he lay down a course of cleanness and honesty for himself and kept the faith."

When Calvin Coolidge succeeded to the presidency, *The Blade* expressed suspicion of his ties with international bankers, who would be "bound in the nature of things to give the humble citizen of the republic the worst of it." But when, in his first message to Congress, the new President called for a tax cut, announced that he considered the League of Nations a dead issue, and insisted that Russia not be recognized until she acknowledged her debts and ceased to oppose American institutions, *The Blade* applauded. It was just what might have been expected — "calm, brief to the point of nakedness, clear as water from a Green Mountain spring, not a word wasted."

The Blade endorsed President Coolidge for re-election in 1924 over the Democratic candidate, John W. Davis, and Senator Robert M. LaFollette of Wisconsin, who had been nominated by the Progressives and of whom *The Blade* was particularly critical. "Fighting Bob" was described as the only presidential candidate in the history of the United States who "put up the white flag in time of war and the red flag in time of peace." The landslide victory of "Silent Cal" Coolidge was enthusiastically approved.

CHAPTER 19

Nearing the End of an Era

Robinson Locke died on April 20, 1920, after an operation for appendicitis. His estate was valued the week after his death at $550,000; by 1937 it was appraised at $837,476. His second wife, the actress Mabel Dixey Dunham, survived him by almost fifty years, dying on February 10, 1968, at Scarsdale, New York.

Although he had not been active in the management of *The Blade* since 1908, Robinson Locke had continued to make his influence felt in many ways. He continued, of course, to act as music and drama critic. He did much to promote and develop the Saturday edition of *The Blade*, which he saw as serving many of the purposes of a Sunday edition.

The Blade had continued to grow in size, averaging eight pages — four on Monday, twelve on Saturday, eight on most other days. Carriers distributed about half of each day's edition in Toledo; the remainder went by mail to outlying areas. Arrangements were made for daily sale of *The Blade* at hotels in New York, Washington, Buffalo, Philadelphia, Cleveland, Detroit, Cincinnati, Chicago, St. Louis, and other cities.

Sports coverage was increased to two full pages daily in 1916. World Series reports were blazoned in red banner headlines across the front page, and extra editions were published to report many sporting events. The ingenious "Birdograph" was used to report yacht races at Put-in-Bay in Lake Erie. Chartered boats then took special editions containing the results back to the big crowds at Put-in-Bay.[43]

Robinson Locke's death left *The Blade* without the innovative inspiration he had provided. Some members of the Locke family criticized him as a dilettante with exotic tastes and interests who left most of the work of producing a daily newspaper to others. There was a measure of truth in these allegations. It was equally true, however, that David Ross Locke's son shared many of the characteristics that had made the father a successful editor and publisher. Much of what David Locke had accomplished for the weekly edition of *The Blade,* Rob Locke had motivated in the daily edition. Something important was lost when he died in 1920.

Three years later, another death created further problems. Nathaniel C. Wright, who had been editorial manager for fifteen years, was a journalist of exceptional ability and experience. He had joined the Associated Press in 1893 and became its chief field correspondent in the Spanish-American War. He was later managing editor of the Indianapolis *Sentinel* and became editor and publisher of the Indianapolis *Journal* in 1903. He went to the Cleveland *Leader* as managing editor in 1904 and, with Harry S. Talmadge, operated both the *Leader* and *The Blade* after the lease had been arranged with the Locke estate.

Wright was an intelligent and dynamic editor. He gave *The Blade* a quality that was important in winning its hard-fought circulation battle with the *News-Bee.* His friendship with Theodore Roosevelt and other Progressive Republican leaders proved helpful. He was popular with politicians and others who came to know him. Wright turned down several offers to be a candidate for office, insisting that he did not believe an editor should seek political favors.

Frederic S. Buggie, who had been circulation manager, now became Talmadge's partner. The talents that had made him a success in waging a circulation war did not, unfortunately, make him the man to succeed Wright. Grove Patterson was named executive editor in 1923 and began to write his enormously popular "Way of the World" column in the same year. He was not, however, in a position to be able to solve some of *The Blade's* operational problems.

★ ★ ★

Another blow — psychological if not financial — befell *The Blade* when publication of the *Weekly Blade* was discontinued on October 9, 1924. The weekly edition had been an important part of *The Blade* for almost ninety years. It had enjoyed a national reputation during the last sixty years. Circulation had declined from a peak of 230,000 in 1913, but it still had 114,000 subscribers in 1924. Grove Patterson tells a story illustrating its ubiquity:

Nearing the End of an Era 203

In its prime the claim was made that it went into every county in America, and I well remember, after I came to the daily, that Mr. Davey, keeper of the subscription lists, offered a standing bet of five dollars that no one could name a village, town or city in America which had a post office which did not receive at least one copy of the *Weekly Blade.* On a trip through New England I had found a village in Maine which seemed to me to be the most remote and out of touch with the rest of the country I had ever visited. Upon my return, I brought the matter up to Mr. Davey, sure that I would win his five dollars. I still remember his air of confidence as he turned to the big pile of subscription books and showed me that five *Weekly Blades* were regularly going to that village.

Weekly editions of daily newspapers had, however, begun to decline in the 1920s. Sunday editions took their places in many instances, and a combination of the automobile, the radio and the movies broke down the isolation of rural and small town communities where the weeklies had thrived. Entertainment and information were now more readily available, packaged in more exciting forms.

Unexpired subscriptions of the *Weekly Blade* were taken over by a monthly publication, *Farm Life,* which was regarded as suitable for the audience of farmers, merchants and artisans David Ross Locke had begun to assemble in 1865, when he arrived in Toledo. The final editorial concluded: "Guess there is nothing more to say without getting sentimental, and this doesn't seem to be just the time for that."[43]

★ ★ ★

Surviving members of the Locke family had become increasingly concerned about operation of *The Blade* after Robinson Locke's death in 1920. None of them was directly involved in the newspaper and they were represented by Barton Smith, a Toledo lawyer, who was general counsel for the estate. Smith had become unhappy with the Talmadge-Buggie operation after N. C. Wright's death. So was Florance E. Cottrell, treasurer of *The Blade.* And so was Paul Block, owner of Paul Block and Associates — the nation's largest publishers' representative organization — which had handled national advertising for *The Blade.* Smith and Cottrell made the arrangements that brought the agreement with Block to buy the newspaper on August 25, 1926.

So, after sixty-one years of association with the Locke family, *The Blade* now passed into the hands of the Block family, who have continued as owners and publishers since that time. Next year —

1986 — this will have become as long a period as that of the Lockes' ownership — a total of more than 120 years of association with only two families.

PART III
THE BLOCK YEARS
1926-

Chapter 20

A Change at the Top

The life story of Paul Block, owner and publisher of *The Blade* from 1926 to 1941, was almost the prototype of the Horatio Alger saga of humble beginnings, hard work, and success. He was one of nine children of poor immigrants who came to the United States in 1880 from Koenigsberg, East Prussia, and settled in Elmira, New York. He became a citizen when his father, John Block, was naturalized in 1890.

Not until after his death was the fact of Paul Block's German birth revealed. Up to that time, he had always listed Elmira as his birthplace. Apparently he had regarded it as a kind of limitation on his Americanism, though he was not particularly jingoistic in his attitudes and wrote with obvious sympathy for the German people.

Not much is known of John Block, except that he seems to have contributed little to the support of his family. Four of the nine Block children died of diphtheria during the 1890s. Young Paul went to work as a teen-ager to help support the family, selling advertising for the Elmira *Telegram*. At the urging of a sales representative who made regular trips from New York City to Elmira, Paul moved to New York City in 1895 and went to work for J. Frank Richardson, a leading advertising representative to newspapers. He did well, established contacts with clients of the Richardson firm, and sent money back to Elmira to his family. When Richardson died, one of his nephews was given charge of the operation. Paul Block, who had been much more active in its affairs than had the nephew, felt that he had received unfair treatment, so, taking most of Richardson's contracts with him, he established his own firm in 1900, at the age of twenty-four. His brother, Max, who had been in the jewelry business in Buffalo, joined the firm of Paul Block and Associates in the mid-1920s. National advertising boomed in the first three decades of the 20th century; Paul Block and Associates prospered. The recession of 1907 struck hard at many newspapers and, with profits from his advertising business, Paul Block bought several of them. At various times, he owned the New York *Evening Mail,* Brooklyn *Standard-Union,* Newark *Star-Eagle,* Detroit *Journal* and Memphis *News-Scimitar,* as well as newspapers in such smaller cities as Lancaster, Pennsylvania, and Duluth, Minnesota. Still later he would become owner of the Pittsburgh *Post-Gazette.*

The image of Paul Block that prevails today is largely a product of the writings in the depression era of such men as George Seldes and Ferdinand Lundberg, who seized on various aspects of his sometimes sophomoric behavior to present him as further evidence in support of a popular thesis of the period — that the press in this country was wholly controlled by madmen and monsters. The chapter devoted to Block in Seldes' book, *Lords of the Press,* is entitled "Little Lord Northcliffe," after the Napoleonic British press lord, with whom there were some similarities.

Two of the most persistent of the impressions created by Seldes and his contemporaries deserve attention. The first has to do with the relationship between Paul Block and William Randolph Hearst — an immensely complicated matter, that Seldes and others have greatly oversimplified. A statement in *Lords of the Press* that "Paul Block is the only publisher in America closely associated with William Randolph Hearst" leads on to the declaration that "in 1936 the New York *Post* called him (Block) a Hearst stooge, which he let pass."[1] This is followed by an extended discussion of the purchase and sale of newspapers in Pittsburgh, Milwaukee and Los Angeles, involving various kinds of joint action by the two men. Here, as in other accounts since that time of the Hearst-Block relationship, is a blunt implication that Paul Block was a puppet whose actions were determined by William Randolph Hearst. It is a prime example of the kind of distortion that results when conclusions are drawn from appearances.

The relationship between Hearst and Block was indeed close, and they did collaborate in a variety of ways to serve their own individual interests. But it was based on a mutual admiration for each other's particular talents, as is clearly shown by the correspondence between them that remains available. Their friendship, which grew out of

A Change at the Top

arrangements for Paul Block and Associates to handle advertising accounts for Hearst's second newspaper in those cities where he owned more than one, led to a number of joint ventures.

Block admired Hearst as a publisher who had successfully challenged the journalistic establishment and had made money while doing so. Hearst thought highly of Block's business abilities and the success he had achieved in lifting himself up by his own bootstraps. He asked his friend to advise him how to improve the financial situation of some of the ailing Hearst newspapers — e.g., the Baltimore *News-American,* about which Block sent him more than five typewritten pages of analysis and advice after a visit of several days. In the case of the Pittsburgh *Post-Gazette,* Block took over as manager of this ailing Hearst paper in 1927 and greatly improved its position in competition with the Scripps-Howard *Press* and another, more prosperous Hearst paper, the *Sun-Telegraph.*

There were several newspaper situations in which a property for sale could not be bought by Hearst because some owners would not sell to him, but which would be available to Block. In other instances, Paul Block became nominal owner of a newspaper as a means of easing criticism of Hearst. Robert W. Wells reports, for example, in his history of the Milwaukee *Journal,* that a rumor circulated in 1928 that Paul Block was to take over the Milwaukee *Sentinel,* to "take the curse of Hearst ownership away," and that "the following year the prediction came true, although there was skepticism about whether the change was actual," especially since "the paper reverted to Hearst's ownership again."[2] The *Sentinel* was, in fact, part of the 1937 transaction by which Block became owner of the *Post-Gazette.*[3]

It can certainly be contended that, in some of these transactions, Paul Block acted as a front for William Randolph Hearst. In most of them, they would appear to have been more or less equal partners. That Block was no "stooge" for Hearst is, however, clear. And it is interesting to note that even Seldes grudgingly concedes that "to his credit it must be said that Block has never made his sheets as bad as Hearst's."[4]

One other aspect of the Hearst-Block relationship should be mentioned — their admiration for Marion Davies. It was Paul Block, in fact, who was first attracted to Miss Davies. He was a regular investor in the Ziegfeld Follies, where he made the acquaintance of a number of attractive young women. He spotted Marion when she was one of the topless "statues" Florenz Ziegfeld used above the stage (the girls were compelled to remain absolutely immobile or they were subject to arrest). Block even made a movie, "Runaway Romany," for Miss Davies, writing the script himself. An associate has described it as "the worst movie I ever saw."[5]

The relationship continued until Miss Davies began to suggest that Paul Block should marry her. It was at that point that he introduced her to his friend, William Randolph Hearst, with whom she lived for the rest of his life, though they were never married.

★ ★ ★

The other association which has persistently been misrepresented — to Paul Block's discredit — was friendship with Mayor James J. Walker, the irrepressible Jimmy who resigned his office in September, 1932, and was soundly beaten when he tried to win it back at the next election.

Paul Block assiduously cultivated the acquaintance of public figures. Paul Block, Jr., has suggested that if cafe society hadn't existed, his father would have invented it. This was due at least in part, he suggests, to the fact that the senior Paul Block was not accepted by New York's "Four Hundred" and that he sought compensation in the friendship of those who were in the public limelight.

There is, at any rate, no question that he was a close friend of Jimmy Walker. Nor any question that in February, 1927, he opened a joint stock account for himself and the mayor, from which each drew profits of over $246,000 before it was closed out in August, 1929. So when the mayor's activities came under scrutiny from the Hochstadter Committee of the New York Legislature, with Judge Samuel Seabury as chief counsel, in 1932, this joint stock account was given a great deal of attention.

Sinister implications were drawn concerning Paul Block's motives in establishing this account. Seldes quotes the New York *Post* as having reported that "Mr. Block was associated with State Senator John A. Hastings in a chemical company which planned to produce a tile for use in subway stations . . ."[6] This insinuation has been resurrected often, as it was in 1962 by Herbert Mitgang in an article in the October issue of the *Atlantic Monthly* entitled "The Downfall of Jimmy Walker."

To Mitgang, as to many others, it seemed strange that Jimmy Walker should benefit so enormously from "an investment of nothing but friendship." He found his answer, as had many before him, in Paul Block's interest "in a company seeking to sell tiles to contractors building the city's subways," adding that "there was no doubt that Jimmy Walker, riding around in his Deusenberg, had the people's transportation ever in mind."[7]

In fact, as one of the nation's top reporters, A. J. Liebling, discovered soon after the allegations concerning the sale of tiles to the city had been made, nothing in the tile plant was ever marketed. And, according to Dr. Robert Beye, the industrial chemist in charge of the operation, Paul Block had discouraged him from pushing negotiations with the city administration, insisting that because of his friendship with Mayor Walker "it would look bad if we sold the city tiles."[8]

Probably very few people believed the explanation Block gave for establishing the joint stock account when he testified before the Hochstadter Committee. Even he characterized it as sounding "a little silly or sentimental," but, as reported in the committee proceedings, he went ahead with this declaration:

> The Mayor telephoned me one day and asked if I would like to take a drive with him. It was a Sunday. I said, "I have promised my youngster" — who was only about ten — "that I would take a walk with him."
>
> He said, "Why don't you have Billy ride with us?" I said, "Well, that is fine." I knew that would please Billy because my boys liked the Mayor very much. He said he would be up in an hour and my youngster and I went downstairs . . . and we walked up and down in front of the house, and, naturally, our minds were on the Mayor, and my youngster said, "How much salary does the Mayor get?" And I told him $25,000 (laughter), which was the salary at the time.
>
> "Does the City give him a house?" And I said, "No they don't." I recall he said, "Does it give him an automobile?" And I said, "Yes, but not one to Mrs. Walker."
>
> Well, this youngster said, "Can he live on what he gets?" (Laughter) And I said, "Well, I suppose he can, but it probably is a difficult problem."
>
> And, Judge, I want you to believe me that it entered my mind then that I was going to try to make a little money for him. (Laughter; gavel).

When Judge Seabury called attention to the fact that none of the many other joint accounts Paul Block had established had involved any public official, the response was: "Positively, but this of course I figured was for my friend Jimmy Walker, rather than for the Mayor of New York — but he happened to be the mayor . . . I never received anything from the mayor in return. There is nothing he could have given me and there is nothing I would have accepted from him — nothing."

Samuel Seabury clearly did not believe Paul Block's story. Nor did the audience in the hearing room. Nor have the Seldeses and the Mitgangs and most others who have written about the account and its implications. Yet it fits very comfortably into the pattern of behavior that emerges from a careful study of Paul Block's actions, his letters, and most of the other evidence that is available. He was generous, sentimental, and impulsive in his personal relationships. When his intense desire for friendship with people of influence is added to the equation, his own explanation of why he established a joint stock account for Jimmy Walker — one that proved to be immensely profitable for both of them in that period of runaway stock market gains — becomes wholly reasonable. The cynics are not likely to accept it, nor those whose preconceptions are jolted by it, but it is typical of the way Paul Block lived his life and conducted his affairs.

Thus, his friendship for Clare Boothe Luce (then Brokaw) led him in the mid 1930s to establish a small syndicate for the purpose of selling material by some of his own writers. These included two old friends of Paul Block, with whom he played bridge, who were broke, and who wrote articles which bordered on the illiterate. But the real star attraction was the beauteous Clare, who he genuinely believed would become a great journalist. In her honor, he named this the Seebee Syndicate. But when, in the summer of 1937, she went to Europe, she left only enough advance copy to last two weeks, and when it ran out, a wire was sent to her saying that "Mr. Hearst and other clients must have copy immediately." Clare wired back: "Tell Mr. Hearst to go to hell."[9] That was the end of the Seebee Syndicate.

Paul Block once declared that his hobbies were two — "newspapers and friendships."[10] Both his private railroad car and his country home near White Plains, New York, were named Friendship. He could also be flamboyant, eccentric, autocratic. The new man in charge of *The Blade* as of August 10, 1926, was a paradoxical figure.

Chapter 21

A Stormy Transition

Paul Block bought *The Blade* for a price which the New York *Times* reported to have been $4,500,000. Lawsuits totalling almost that amount were brought against the new owner during the next two years by a number of aggrieved individuals — notably Harry S. Talmadge and Frederick S. Buggie, who had signed a contract with the Locke estate in 1924 to operate *The Blade* for the next ten years. This agreement, they contended, remained in effect, despite the sale of the property.

Under this contract, Talmadge and Buggie declared, each was to be paid an annual salary of $2,500 and to receive a percentage of net profits, which they estimated to be in excess of $600,000. Various aspects of this litigation dragged on for almost three years. After an out-of-court settlement for an undisclosed amount, Talmadge's suit for $1,340,047.61 was dismissed in May, 1929.

A highlight of the Talmadge-Buggie suits against *The Blade* was provided in August, 1927, when 27-year-old Dorothy Polk, also known as Dorothy Day, was apprehended in the stenographic rooms of the Toledo law firm of Smith, Baker, Effler and Eastman, which represented *The Blade*. Miss Polk-Day, described as a "girl detective of Detroit and Los Angeles," testified during her trial on charges of burglary that she had been hired by a detective named Walter Baker, who was employed by Talmadge and Buggie's lawyers, to obtain papers containing information he needed. She had subsequently sought out Marie Fisher, a secretary in the law office, promising her a handsome reward if she would make it possible for the girl detective to gain admission to the offices of Smith, Baker, Effler and Eastman. Miss Fisher did provide a key, but she also informed one of her employers, LeRoy Eastman, of what was going on. After Miss Polk-

Day had gone to the law firm's offices, taking a photographer with her, Eastman appeared and caught her in the act of carrying out her mission. The girl detective was freed of the burglary charge on grounds that Eastman, having had knowledge of her intention, had in fact permitted her to enter his firm's offices. Another attorney, Frank Lewis, of the firm of Doyle & Lewis, which represented Talmadge and Buggie, brought a $100,000 libel suit against *The Blade,* on the basis of stories which, he contended, charged him with having conspired in the hiring of Dorothy Polk-Day.

There was litigation, too, over arrangements for sale of *The Blade.* Louis H. Gould, a Toledo real estate agent, sued Barton Smith, executor of the Locke estate, for $250,000, alleging breach of a contract to pay him that amount for finding a buyer for the newspaper. Gould further alleged that he had found a buyer, but that Smith had used his influence to bring about the sale to Paul Block.

Many rumors circulated concerning the circumstances of the sale of *The Blade,* and some persist. One of them was renewed only a year ago by *New Solidarity,* the publication of Lyndon Larouche, perennial independent presidential candidate: that Paul Block cooperated with Barton Smith and Florance Cottrell in a kind of Masonic plot. Both Smith and Cottrell were prominent in Masonic and Scottish Rite affairs, as was Robinson Locke, but there is no tangible evidence to support this tale. Nor does there seem to be any substance to another rumor — that gangland forces, which had moved into Toledo in the 1920s, had gained virtual control of the newspaper under the management of Talmadge and Buggie, and that Smith and Cottrell arranged its sale to Block as a means of heading off this threat.

However the sale of *The Blade* came about, and regardless of the many lawsuits that resulted, Paul Block wasted no time in consolidating his position as owner and publisher. At the first meeting of the board of directors of the Toledo Blade Company after the transfer of ownership — on September 1, 1926 — two of the board's members resigned. One was Charles Locke, the only remaining member of his family involved in *The Blade's* operations; the other was LeRoy E. Eastman, attorney for the company and secretary of the board of directors. These two vacancies were immediately filled by two members of the Block organization — John H. Hertel of the Memphis *Press-Scimitar* and Michael F. Hansen of the Duluth *Herald.* Both men came to Toledo and

A Stormy Transition

remained for some time to help implement the change in ownership.[11] At the September 1 board meeting, Hertel moved adoption of this resolution:

> Whereas, the employment of Harry S. Talmadge and Frederick S. Buggie under agreement of August 27, 1924 . . . is such as to require exemplary and good moral conduct . . .
> Whereas, the conduct of said Talmadge and Buggie . . . has been and is inimical to the best interests and welfare of The Toledo Blade Company, and contrary to their duties as such employees, and a breach of their contract of employment . . .
> Therefore, each is forthwith discharged and agreements with them terminated because of the breaches thereof.

Paul Block acted with similar dispatch to retain the man he recognized as the most valuable member of *The Blade's* editorial staff. This was Grove Patterson, executive editor, who was completing sixteen years on the newspaper. His daily column, "The Way of the World," begun in 1923, was already among the most popular features, and had contributed to his widening national reputation as a writer. Patterson was in great demand throughout the country as a public speaker. He had been active in the organization of the American Society of Newspaper Editors and was chairman of its investigating committee, which had recommended expulsion of Fred Bonfils, publisher of the Denver *Post,* on charges of involvement in the Teapot Dome scandal.

Grove Patterson and Paul Block had, of course, been closely associated for a period of several years in the operation of the Detroit *Journal,* the Newark *Star-Eagle,* and *The Blade.* The story of what happened soon after August 1, 1926, is told by Patterson in *I Like People:*

> I had no definite idea what was in store for me. We all knew Paul Block was planning changes in the *Blade* organization. Just at that time E. D. Stair, owner of the Detroit *Free Press,* asked me to meet him . . . He made a flattering proposition, saying he wanted me to make a "lifetime connection" with the *Free Press* . . . I was greatly complimented by Mr. Stair's offer, but told him I wanted to think it over. I returned to Toledo to await what Paul Block might have in mind.
> I did not have to wait long. PB, as everyone in the *Blade* organization knew him, called me on the telephone and asked me to spend a weekend at his country estate, "Friendship," near White Plains, New York. There, forty-five minutes from Broadway, he had 186 acres, partly wooded and partly under cultivation, with miles of bridle paths, a private golf course, tennis courts, swimming pool and conservatories. The great brick house

stood on a knoll and was one of the loveliest houses in which I have ever been a guest . . .

Getting down to business in a short time, Mr. Block told me that he wanted me to remain with the *Blade* with the title and authority of editor. He assured me of the greatest freedom in the matter of editorial operation, policy, and personal independence . . .

I was still considering the offer of Mr. Stair . . . and held back on my reply to Mr. Block . . . As I was getting into the car to take me to the station, he said very earnestly: "When will you tell me that you are going to stay with me always?"

A few days later I wrote and told PB that Toledo was home base for me and that I wanted to be associated with him.

Paul Block's efforts to reassure the personnel of the newspaper of which he had just become owner did not stop at the executive level. When he met with *The Blade's* 350 employees for the first time on August 31, 1926, he announced that each of them who had at least one year's service would receive an insurance policy valued at up to $3,000.[12]

★ ★ ★

One more significant addition was made to *The Blade* staff in 1926: Fred Mollenkopf was hired as chief rewrite man for *The Blade* after its rival, the *News-Bee,* fired him from his job as managing editor in one of that paper's periodic house cleanings. A few months later he was made city editor of *The Blade* — a job in which for 23 years he alternately terrorized and comforted the reporters he supervised.

"Fred Mollenkopf," Grove Patterson once said, "is the best city editor in the nation." Paul Block, Jr., continues to insist that it was this man — more than any other — who was responsible for *The Blade's* winning out in the fight for readers with the *News-Bee* that ended in 1938 with the Scripps-Howard newspaper's demise. But what may be the most meaningful tribute to this remarkable man is to be found in the unanimity of the praise from those who worked with and under him. In preparing to write this history, the author talked with as many as possible of the *Blade* editorial employees who had been with the newspaper for at least thirty years. To each of them, he put this question: What two or three men among the various editors of *The Blade* were most important in terms of the success of this newspaper? Fred Mollenkopf's name was in every one of these responses, and most cited him immediately as most important.

A master at the art of using the carrot and the stick in his relationships with his staff, the stocky Mollenkopf could be

A Stormy Transition 217

absolutely terrifying when he believed someone had failed in some respect to do the job that was expected. It was in such moments that reporters occasionally spoke of him as "The Terrible Dutchman." Before they had been around *The Blade* city room for long, however, they began to appreciate that no one was more interested in and concerned about their welfare — both as reporters and as human beings — than this man whose eyes could twinkle even more easily than they could glare. "After he'd chewed you out for something you shouldn't have done, or not doing something you should have done," one longtime *Blade* staff member put it, "you still knew that it wasn't really personal, that it was only his pride in wanting *The Blade* to do the best job possible. You knew, too, that underneath that sometimes ferocious exterior, Fred was the kind of man who would do anything he could do for you if you needed help."

No one knew Toledo better than this man who was city editor of *The Blade* from 1926 to 1949. He was born in Maumee and got early exposure to newspapers when his widowed mother, Ella Mollenkopf, became a reporter for *The Blade* and later was its church and society editor. Unable to finish high school because there wasn't enough money, Fred went to work when he was in his teens as a *Blade* copy boy. He started his career as a cub reporter on the Toledo *Press,* where he learned the mysteries of the police beat. He used this knowledge later, when he took over the same assignment for the *News-Bee.*

The reason for Fred Mollenkopf's losing his job with the *News-Bee* seems to have been erased in the sixty years intervening. But whatever it was, he never forgot it, and when he became city editor of *The Blade,* he made it his own continuing assignment to beat the pants off the newspaper that had fired him. Nothing brought such an eruption from him, according to those who worked with him, as being scooped by the *News-Bee.* It rarely happened.

Symptoms of heart problems slowed him down in 1949, and after a particularly severe attack, his doctor and his wife, Therese, insisted that he slow down, and this meant moving him out of the city editor's chair. Publisher Paul Block, Jr., agreed reluctantly and asked Fred to take over the "Among the Folks" column, which had long been conducted by another *Blade* veteran, Chub DeWolfe.[13] His knowledge of Toledo and the area and his wide acquaintance made it possible for him to carry on the popular feature, which emphasized people and past events.

But the long-time city editor was never really happy with his new assignment. Until he died May 14, 1958, after a paralytic stroke, Fred Mollenkopf was still lamenting that he was no longer at his place on the city desk.

★ ★ ★

Paul Block was in charge of the operations of *The Blade* for fifteen years — from 1926 to 1941. More and more as the years passed, it was to become his particular favorite among the newspapers he owned. He spent considerable time in Toledo, occupying a suite at the Commodore Perry Hotel, which stored his personal bed and installed it in his suite for each visit. He became well acquainted with one of the city's civic leaders — Royce Martin, president of Electric Autolite. He gave of his time, effort and money to a variety of civic activities — the Toledo Symphony Orchestra, the Toledo Public Library, and the Indiana Avenue YMCA among them. Both of his sons, Paul, Jr., and William, were encouraged to spend time in Toledo and both learned about the newspaper business through exposure to the various departments of *The Blade*.

Because the affairs of Paul Block and Associates and his other newspapers demanded much of his time, the new owner of *The Blade* delegated actual supervision to Grove Patterson and Stanley C. Speer, business manager, but was in almost daily telephone communication with them. He had definite ideas about editorial policy, and as soon as he took over as publisher, *The Blade* announced a program for Toledo that appeared each day on the editorial page. It set forth these goals:

> Make Toledo an airport.
> Complete intercepting sewers and build a disposal plant.
> Improve the city's streets.
> Abolish hazardous grade crossings of railroads.
> Promote development of the St. Lawrence Waterway.

Writing most of the editorials was left to Grove Patterson and other members of the local staff. Paul Block did, however, contribute many signed editorials. Almost always these appeared on the front page, following the pattern established by his friend, Hearst. In a letter to Hearst, he explained his reason for writing these as being "to link myself up a little with the paper, especially as I do not live in the cities where the papers are published." Most of these editorials appeared in all his newspapers, though sometimes he wrote one on a local subject. Sometimes, too, one of these signed commentaries

A Stormy Transition 219

appeared in the New York *Times* and *Herald-Tribune*. Block paid for these, wanting to reach an audience of national leaders.

These signed editorials reflect a strong sentimental strain, illustrated by one of his particular favorites. It was originally published in *The Blade* on August 31, 1929, and was reprinted half a dozen times in later years. Entitled "No Circus for Jimmie," it is based on a news story about a little Iowa boy struck and killed by a truck on his way home from working to earn two tickets for that night's performance of the circus. The editorial concludes:

> There is something about the tragedies of every-day life — and they come and go in the lives of so many — that makes us a little more akin to each other. We come a little closer in human sympathy. Perhaps the people of this little Iowa town, where Jimmie died on circus day, will always be a little kinder to each other — because of him.
>
> And perhaps, too, other reckless automobile drivers will think of all children when little Jimmie Gregory comes into their minds.

Herman W. Liebert, who wrote editorials and speeches for Paul Block from 1934 until the latter's death, has said that his employer had "strong ideas and a poor prose style." He never left any doubt as to what his ideas were on any given subject, but he found it hard to express them in the form he wanted them to take.[14]

★ ★ ★

Plans for a new building were already under way when Paul Block bought *The Blade* in 1926. Its five-story home at the corner of Superior Street and Jefferson Avenue, built by David Ross Locke in 1885, was becoming increasingly inadequate. Fire had seriously damaged it in 1911. There was no convenient way to expand at that location.

So, late in 1925, the Toledo Blade Company had bought for $240,000 several lots at the corner of Superior, Huron and Beech streets, in the Vistula Addition. Architects for the new building — announced in April, 1926, by Barton Smith — were the Toledo firm of Langdon, Hohly & Gram. Paul Block lost no time in pushing ahead with construction. The Henry J. Spieker Company of Toledo was hired as general contractor. Cost of the building, which was completed in 1927, was $646,067.

The new building was opened on May 1, 1927, with festive ceremonies attended by Babe Ruth, the legendary baseball player. President Calvin Coolidge, a friend of Paul Block, touched a gold key in Washington that turned on the electricity in the new building and started the presses rolling. The three-story structure, with Moorish architectural overtones, has been headquarters for *The Blade* the ensuing years. Some structural changes have been made to keep pace with growth, and much new equipment has been installed. But *The Blade,* resisting a national trend toward new buildings removed from the city center, is near the heart of Toledo's most recent downtown development projects.

Chapter 22

The Best of Times, the Worst of Times

Paul Block announced on September 7, 1927, that he had bought the Newark Bears. These were baseball Bears — the Newark team in the International League. The owner of the Newark *Star-Eagle* and of *The Blade* paid $360,000 for his newest possession.

The principal reason he had bought the franchise, he said, was that he wanted to see that the citizens who had subscribed almost $150,000 the previous year to keep the club operating in Newark would get their money back. He would see to it personally, the new owner declared, that all those who had subscribed would be paid the amount given, plus interest.

There were other reasons, too. Paul Block was both an ardent baseball fan and a man who wanted to be identified with heroic figures in every aspect of life. Although the Newark Bears had not been particularly heroic in recent International League pennant races, they were home town heroes to the owner of the *Star-Eagle* and to many of its readers.

The deciding factor in buying a baseball team may, however, have been that 1927 had been a good year for Paul Block and the expanding interests in which he was already involved. The boom in national advertising continued and Paul Block, Inc., thrived on profits from its expanding accounts. The Newark *Star-Eagle* (bought in 1917), the Duluth *Herald* (acquired in 1920), and the Lancaster *New Era* (added in 1923) all did well. So did the most recent acquisition, *The Blade*, whose net profits and dividends had grown dramatically in the years since the end of World War I. Profits in 1921 had been $147,000; in 1925 they were $420,000. Dividends were $63,000 in 1921 and had risen to $90,000 in 1925. These continued to increase each year until 1930, when the impact of the Great Depression began to be felt.

Paul Block, Inc., which had been founded in 1908, underwent a major reorganization in 1927. The Block holdings were now split into three groups. One was the P. G. S. Corporation, formed to hold the stock of companies acquired at various times from the Hearst organization. Another, the Paul Corporation, supervised Consolidated Publishers, Inc., owner of three of the Block newspapers, including *The Blade*. It also included Paul Block, Inc., which would become Paul Block and Associates in 1930. The remaining Block properties — including, after 1927, the Newark Bears — were held by Paul Block personally.

The lawsuits that had resulted from the tangled skein of relationships involving Harry S. Talmadge, Frederick S. Buggie, Nathaniel C. Wright and Paul Block dragged along. Wright's widow, now Mrs. Elizabeth Graham, received notice from the Treasury Department in 1928 that, as a result of dealings involving the sale of the Detroit *Journal* some years earlier, she would be expected to pay about $108,000. "Of course," she wrote to Max Block in New York, "you know I never received it (a quantity of *Journal* stock), as it was just another of Buggie's schemes to defraud the government... I'm going to have a fine time proving I didn't get the stock." Mrs. Talmadge received notice that she owed a similar amount.

★ ★ ★

No dramatic changes in *The Blade's* approach to political affairs took place under its new ownership. As usual, the Republican candidate for governor in 1926 had the newspaper's support. He was Myers Y. Cooper, who lost in his attempt to deny a third term to Democratic Governor A. Vic Donahey.

Nor was *The Blade's* choice for mayor of Toledo in 1927 any more successful. He was Dr. William B. Guitteau, who had been superintendent of the city's schools. "A vote against Guitteau," *The Blade* proclaimed, would be "nothing less than a vote against the Great Forward Movement of Toledo."[15] Despite this endorsement, voters chose, by a margin of nearly 7,000, William T. Jackson, service director in the administration of Mayor Frederick J. Mery, who had declined to seek re-election.

Paul Block entered the editorial opinion picture gradually in his first year or two as owner-publisher. His early front-page editorials, appearing over his signature, must have been intended largely to

The Best of Times, the Worst of Times 223

strengthen his association with *The Blade* in his readers' minds. Some early titles included:

Universal Peace Day
Owen Young on Tolerance
High Wages, Good Business
Onward, Toledo

These included no dissertations on the virtues of motherhood, or the joys of Scouting, but they did not venture far into controversial areas. The suggestion that a relationship might exist between good wages and improved profits may not have been entirely orthodox at that time, but neither did Paul Block press it to the point of offending industrialists who might not share this thesis.

Not even the 1928 presidential election brought forth the expression of strong sentiments or convictions from Publisher Block or Editor Patterson. Early in the year, one of Block's front-page editorials, "Coolidge, the Man," paid high tribute to the incumbent President and suggested faint hope, at least, that "Silent Cal" hadn't really meant it when he declared, "I do not choose to run," for re-election that year.

Little enthusiasm was shown for Herbert Hoover when he began to emerge as the likely candidate. *The Blade* wanted to know in May whether his nomination would result in a real Republican victory in November. Some further problems were created when the Democrats chose New York's Governor Alfred E. Smith to oppose Hoover. Paul Block thought well of Smith and of his performance in Albany. Besides, he was much more nearly in agreement with The Happy Warrior than with The Great Engineer in the matter of what should be done about the Eighteenth Amendment's prohibition of the sale of alcoholic beverages. Hoover and Smith were both able men, *The Blade* concluded, but it upheld the newspaper's long-time tradition by endorsing the Republican.

Hoover carried Toledo by 78,000 votes to 45,000 as he won a landslide victory, even cracking the Democrats' long hold on the Solid South. *The Blade's* interpretation was that the voters wanted Coolidge's programs continued. It further suggested that Al Smith should not take his loss personally; he was still a man of extraordinary personality, integrity and good character.[16]

Two of Hoover's cabinet appointments swept away whatever serious reservations Paul Block may have had about the election.

Andrew Mellon would remain as secretary of the treasury, so "no wonder that nearly everyone is optimistic about his (Hoover's) future." And the appointment of Walter F. Brown (who had not always been a favorite of *The Blade)* as postmaster general made him the first Toledoan ever so honored.

★ ★ ★

Federal prohibition agents shot and killed an innocent man at International Falls, Minnesota, in June, 1929, and residents of the town on the Canadian border sent a terse message to President Hoover: "For God's sake, help us."

This gave Paul Block the kind of opportunity he relished for a signed editorial, which appeared in the New York *Herald-Tribune* on June 23 and on the front page of *The Blade* the following day. Block made a particularly effective statement of his version of the case against the Eighteenth Amendment, using "For God's Sake, Help Us!" as the title:

> We have had more than nine years of prohibition.
>
> In these nine years we have made the manufacture, sale and transportation of alcoholic beverages a crime. But we did not make drinking a crime because it was recognized that drinking could not be made criminal; and great numbers of our people, knowing that drinking is not criminal, apparently cannot be convinced that the sale and transportation of liquor is in fact criminal . . .
>
> Everyone knows what has happened. We eliminated legal liquor control. In its place we gained unregulated moonshining, rum-running and bootlegging, which found waiting an immediately profitable market. Naturally this business was taken over by gangsters and gunmen and, in some instances, by men who had been regarded as reputable citizens, all attracted by quick and easy wealth.
>
> In our efforts to maintain the prohibition law, as it stands today, we have made more severe the penalties for its violation. We have given more and more latitude and more and more money to officials in the attempt at enforcement. We have read, day after day, how they break into homes without warrants, how they tap telephone wires, how they have engaged young girls as spies in speakeasies and roadhouses. We have read how these Government agents have incited prohibition crimes in order to make arrests.
>
> We have learned how they shoot, recklessly, wantonly, cruelly, when there is no justification for shooting. . . We have seen communities terrorized by such lawlessness of prohibition agents, and we have heard from one of them in Minnesota . . . the agonized cry of the people to the President: "For God's sake, help us!"
>
> . . . International rum running is not the "root" of the evil. It is only a flower of the evil. The "root" of it is the Volstead Law as it now stands, which in nine years has grown to a tree bearing the bitter fruit of

The Best of Times, the Worst of Times

moonshining, bootlegging, poison whiskey, drug addiction, corruption of enforcement officers and murders, many of innocent people, in greater numbers than in any other civilized country.

When, in the name of common sense, will our elected officials, who know of the futility of prohibition in its present form, develop enough courage to start a reconsideration of it?

The campaign against the Eighteenth Amendment was carried on by Paul Block and *The Blade* right up to the day in 1933 when it was repealed. As the editorial above suggests, this opposition at first took the form of suggestions for reform, not for repeal. Two years later, however — in January, 1931 — when the Wickersham Commission filed its report with President Hoover, *The Blade* took issue with the majority recommendation for modification of the prohibition amendment. "We are convinced that the first job is to get rid of the present unenforceable system before attempting to force some other system upon a public which has not yet decided what specific alternative it favors," a *Blade* editorial declared. Immediate repeal was recommended. Failing that, there should be a referendum through state constitutional conventions.

★ ★ ★

The Blade had suggested in 1928, when Herbert Hoover was elected President, that few men had entered the White House under more favorable circumstances. He had the support and confidence of the public, the country was enjoying unprecedented prosperity, and all signs suggested that this happy state of affairs would continue indefinitely.

It was not, of course, an accurate assessment. Six months into the next year, the stock market began to show symptoms of weakness that culminated in near panic in October when the bottom dropped out of the vastly inflated price structure. Paul Block sought to reassure *Blade* readers that the consequences would be of limited proportions. A signed editorial, "Wall Street and Its Effect on Business," occupied most of the lower half of the front page on November 15 and concluded:

> In most of the cities and towns of this country, this Wall Street panic will have its effect. Those who own stocks and bonds and have put them away, have temporarily lost some paper profits. Good securities will again improve in value. The earning power of these people has in no way been changed or impaired and, in many instances has been increased and is being increased over the past and previous years.
>
> Do not sell this country "short" — this, the richest country in the

world, and richer today industrially and economically, than during any time in its history.

President Hoover addressed the Congress on December 4. *The Blade* approved his recommendations, especially a plan for reorganization of government departments which "betrays his impatience with muddling waste and duplication of bureaucratic work." His proposals to reduce the income tax and to continue a flexible tariff policy were also endorsed as helpful to meet the threat of economic trouble.

But none of the calls, which came from many different sources, for confidence, or belt-tightening, or other panaceas for the ills of the nation's economy stopped the decline. The titles of Paul Block's signed editorials in succeeding months provide a picture of their own of what was happening:

Restoring Business Confidence
Unemployment Relief
How to Regain Prosperity

Hard times did not, however, deter Paul Block from expanding his newspaper holdings. He signed memoranda of agreement on August 11, 1930, to purchase the Toledo *Times*. One of these was with Clara C. Dun, widow of George Dun, who had been Grove Patterson's first Toledo employer; the other was with Richard C. Patterson, who remained active in the operation of the *Times*. Mrs. Dun owned more than 1,500 shares of the newspaper's common capital stock and received $767,000; Patterson was paid $107,250 for the 215 shares he owned. The *Times,* while retaining its own staff, was to be published in the *Blade* plant — an arrangement that continued until the *Times'* publication ceased in 1975. Block's announcement of the purchase included this statement:

> Each paper will be run as a separate organization just as before, but we believe that the larger and newer equipment of the *Blade* plant will permit us to publish a larger and better morning and Sunday paper than has ever been published in Toledo.

Throughout much of the succeeding forty-five years, the two newspapers carried on a news rivalry that was sometimes intense. They often took opposite editorial positions on issues of the day. Some contended that the Block family continued to operate the *Times* primarily in an effort to defuse the allegations that Toledo had become a one-newspaper town when the *News-Bee* went out of business in 1938. In fact, *The Blade* moved quickly in the 1940s to establish its own status as an independent newspaper, providing access for all political points of view.

★ ★ ★

Paul Block sent the following notice to all *Blade* department heads on January 1, 1931:

"Please notify every regular employee of the *Blade* that all their jobs are secure for 1931.

"We believe the business depression would be ended sooner if all employers acted in a similar manner and we want to show our faith in the future of business by assuring all our employees that they have steady jobs so they may be relieved of worry and so they may continue to maintain their standard of living."

A signed editorial, "Now for 1931," appeared on the front page of *The Blade* on January 5, as Paul Block sought to expand this idea beyond his own newspaper:

> For some time economists and businessmen have agreed that at least 75 per cent of our business troubles today are a result of the mental condition of the people.
> The time has arrived when business should preach to itself to do its share of spending by continuing to invest in America's future. The first thing, therefore, is to assure our own employees that for the coming year their positions are secure.
> Such acts by employers will restore confidence to the 85 per cent of workers now employed. This, more than any other single thing, will prevent the hoarding of money that should be in circulation and such expenditures will help bring employment to a substantial number of the other 15 per cent not now at work . . .
> So, Mr. Businessman, start the New Year with a resolution to keep all regular employees on your payroll during 1931. . . . Success will come to those who lead in these efforts as it always has in the past.
> The Publisher of this newspaper has just sent word to all the men and women associated with him that their positions are definitely secure.

The response to this proposal was instantaneous and favorable. Among those who endorsed it were William Green of the American Federation of Labor, Senator James J. Davis (former secretary of labor), Nicholas Longworth, James E. Watson, Robert F. Wagner, Franklin D. Roosevelt, Alfred E. Smith, and others. It was announced a few days later that leaders of organized labor in Toledo "are universal in their expressions of gratification over the movement started by Paul Block to get employers to reassure their employees of regular employment during 1931." It was generally agreed that job security would go far toward stabilizing business and bringing a speedy return to normal conditions.

There is no question that Paul Block's effort to achieve job security was commendable and based on sound psychological theory. Unfortunately, insofar as Toledo was concerned, forces that could only lead to financial disaster were already in operation. Deposits in the city's banks had declined in 1929 by about $6,000,000. Unemployment was already a fact of life, especially in the auto industry. Willys-Overland had reduced its work force from 10,000 to 4,000 in 1929. Signs of trouble continued through 1930. Despite the assurance of a leading banker early in 1931 that "Toledo's seven state and two national banks weathered the critical year of 1930 and have embarked on a new year," the roof fell in before the new year was half over.

The Security-Home Trust Company was the first bank to go, on June 17, 1931. There were many efforts to reassure the public and to halt withdrawals from other banks, including this from *The Blade:*

> The fact that the Security-Home Bank of Toledo has closed its doors in order to preserve its assets and to prevent further withdrawals and deposits, pending an examination of the business, does not necessarily mean that the depositors will lose their money. Furthermore, the condition of the Security-Home banks has no bearing whatsoever on the condition of the other Toledo financial institutions.
>
> ... The other Toledo banks, some of which are among the strongest in Ohio, will continue to do business in the usual way.

It was a brave try, but its optimistic statements had little substance. Exactly two months later — on August 17 — four more Toledo banks closed. One of these was the Ohio Savings Bank and Trust Company, which had just completed and moved into Toledo's most impressive skyscraper, on Madison Avenue.[17] The psychological blow was almost as stunning as the financial one.

Then, early in September, a grand jury investigation was begun of what *The Blade* described as "the tangled affairs of the Security-Home Trust Co." Paul Block hailed it in a signed editorial as "welcome news to the 50,000 depositors who put their money into that bank." That editorial echoed David Ross Locke's campaign fifty years earlier against "Busted Bankers":

> This is logically the next step following the prompt and vigorous action of Attorney General Bettman who has already begun legal proceedings to force certain directors to return at once the money which they withdrew from the bank shortly before its closing . . .

The Best of Times, the Worst of Times 229

Toledo has thousands upon thousands of home owners, small businessmen, wage workers . . . who were among the 50,000 depositors in the Security-Home Bank. It is THEIR interest, their comfort and protection that we are most concerned with, rather than with the few who used the bank for heavy loans . . .

Let the probe go deep.

The Toledo banks were among the largest in the United States to fail, and the effects on the city were disastrous. Bank deposits shrank by a third, many small businesses went into bankruptcy, many individuals lost all or part of their savings. The bank crashes cost the city government more than $600,000 of its operating funds. Unemployment swelled rapidly, despite the enthusiastic reception for Paul Block's plea for job security. Toledo was, by the end of 1931, in dire straits.[18]

Chapter 23

Problems of Depression

The Blade in early 1932 devoted almost half of its front page to a signed editorial urging a nonpartisan approach to the presidential election that was to take place later in the year. Current problems, which were many and were increasing, should occupy the attention of both political parties and their candidates, Block contended.

The Blade and its publisher had endorsed most of President Hoover's actions against the nation's economic problems. Hoover imposed a moratorium on payment of war debts, increased freight rates to enable the nation's railroads to employ more men, created the Reconstruction Finance Corporation to aid troubled industries, established home loan banks to stimulate the building of more homes, won Congress' approval of the Glass-Steagall Act to encourage credit expansion, and launched public works and state aid programs to provide relief for individuals.[19]

There never was much real doubt that Paul Block would support Herbert Hoover for re-election in 1932, despite his strong criticism of the Republican party convention for its failure to take a forthright stand against prohibition. When New York's Governor Franklin D. Roosevelt was nominated by the Democrats, however, any slight chance that *The Blade* would endorse a Democrat for the first time in its history disappeared. Paul Block had a personal grudge against Roosevelt, growing out of the hearings the governor had initiated that same year in the matter of removing New York City's Mayor Jimmy Walker from office. Block contended that Governor Roosevelt had provided no opportunity for Mayor Walker to defend himself against allegations brought by Chief Counsel Samuel Seabury before the Hochstadter Committee. He resented, too, that he had been given no opportunity to offset the scorn and ridicule to which he had been subjected when he testified before the committee.

The New York State Supreme Court, in a decision that September 1, criticized Governor Roosevelt's methods and upheld Mayor Walker's contention that he was not receiving a fair trial. The court also upheld the Governor's right to initiate removal proceedings against the mayor. Paul Block's signed editorial on the front page of *The Blade* the next day hailed the decision and made his own feelings clear:

> The Mayor was given no chance to prove his innocence to the partisan charges made by Ex-Judge Seabury. Evidence — if inference and insinuations of guilt can be called evidence — had been mostly gathered at secret hearings. The minutes of these hearings were jealously guarded from Mayor Walker and his counsel.

Several editorials endorsing President Hoover appeared over Paul Block's signature during the summer and fall of 1932. A final appeal to voters on the eve of the election in November included these arguments:

> Franklin D. Roosevelt has made appeals to discontent and to sectionalism.
> Herbert C. Hoover has made appeals to common sense and to the nation.
> Franklin D. Roosevelt has varying theories for different classes.
> Herbert C. Hoover has one program for all the people.
> President Hoover has shown that he stands for all the people. He has not tried to set class against class. He has stood for the essence of Americanism — government by, for and of the people — all the people — and he should be re-elected.

The Blade was philosophical about Roosevelt's one-sided victory over President Hoover and observed that "we must deeply realize that we are Americans — a united people." Ending the depression was the big job, and Paul Block went to Washington on February 14, 1933, a few weeks before the new President's inauguration, to offer the Senate Finance Committee ten proposals:

> 1. Cooperation between the new President and Congress in devising the most effective measures to meet the country's needs.
> 2. Appointment of a coalition cabinet of Democrats and Republicans to assure the fullest measure of public confidence.
> 3. Reduction of war debts by a fixed percentage for each million dollars that a debtor nation spent in the United States.
> 4. Balancing the budget by levying a small manufacturers' sales

tax and reducing non-service-connected disability payments to veterans of the World War.

5. Remaining on the gold standard to ensure sound currency and integrity of contracts.

6. Repeal of the Eighteenth Amendment.

7. Large-scale public works programs, with preference for unemployed veterans.

8. Moratoriums on farm mortgages and reduced interest rates.

9. Higher prices for farm products, without resort to federal subsidies.

10. Readjustment of tariff schedules.

The Blade and its publisher went along with most of President Roosevelt's proposals for dealing with the nation's ills during the first six months of the new administration. Closing the banks, clamping down on hoarding and export of gold were all endorsed. *The Blade* observed of the inaugural address that "the first steps to put into force the program and principles so effectively and clearly presented" were now anticipated.

The President's call for a disarmament plan that would be acceptable to the new German chancellor, Adolf Hitler, also won *The Blade's* approval. Paul Block did express fear that "Hitler is the stumbling block" to any lasting agreement, but he was equally certain that the people of Germany "will rise and crush this present regime which is trying to make a barbaric people out of a cultured nation" once they realized that, while Hitler remained in power, other nations would boycott German goods and deny Germany credit. Interestingly, Paul Block favored recognition of Russia in 1933. Trade with the Soviet nation would be advantageous to the United States, he wrote, and it could be better transacted if the countries established normal diplomatic relations.[20]

Even the National Recovery Act did not draw opposition from *The Blade* at the outset. There had never been an experiment like it, but if such new approaches were needed to combat the forces of depression — well, why not give it a try?

Not until October, when Paul Block began to express some reservations in his signed editorials, was there any break in the support *The Blade* gave to the New Deal administration. Block was alarmed because the dollar was not being stabilized as quickly as he believed it should be; he thought business should be encouraged, not badgered and blamed for the nation's problems, and he was frightened by the $10 billion price tag on the Roosevelt recovery program. From there on, the path of the relationship between FDR and PB was all downhill.

★ ★ ★

The balance sheets of income and profit for the Toledo Blade Company for the year ending December 31, 1931, showed a net profit of $363,462.78, respectable in a year of economic depression, but a considerable drop from the previous year and a reversal of the previous decade's upward trend.

Even so, *The Blade's* financial situation was one of the relatively bright spots in the extensive Paul Block operations. A statement on August 4, 1931, prepared by the Chemical Security Corporation of New York, revealed that estimated cash available for the next thirteen months was $1,788,521, while maturing obligations during this period would amount to $3,614,925. That left an estimated cash deficit for the period of $1,826,403.

The major source of the problems was, according to the same statement, the P. G. S. Corporation, the holding company for the stock of the several newspapers acquired from the Hearst organization. P. G. S. had given purchase money obligations to Hearst as part of the cost of acquisition and, pending their complete retirement, no part of this group (included were the Pittsburgh *Post-Gazette,* the Milwaukee *Sentinel,* the Los Angeles *Press* and the Duluth *News-Tribune*) was available for any financing which might be effected for the other Block holdings.

Creditors — chief among them the Chemical Industrial Trust of New York — were insisting on a plan for rearrangement of Paul Block's affairs. Max Steuer, who was attorney for the Block interests, wrote in April, 1932, advising Paul Block that "almost three months still remains and I believe you ought to give every moment that you possibly can to a personal consideration of your affairs." Steuer wrote again in May to remind his client that "you will have to submit a report to each and every one of your creditors so that they know what your condition is in order that they should abide themselves accordingly." He added a paragraph suggesting clearly that Block had for some time tried to avoid the realities of the situation in which he found himself:

> I wish that you would make up your mind to be well. I do not personally consider that you are physically ill. This thing requires your

personal energetic attention. Your failure to give it is injuring you very seriously. You should be at your office and not talk about being sick. I do not mean by that that I do not appreciate that you do not feel one hundred per cent, but I do believe that if you will just buckle up and fight and go back to your office, and attend to business and see people face to face, and have an accurate statement of your affairs on your desk, so that you yourself will understand what your real position is, there is a very good chance of your coming out of this all right. It cannot be done by the telephone messages of friends or well-wishers, nor by substitutes. I beg of you to make up your mind nobody is going to consider friendship in this situation.

A letter from William Randolph Hearst to Steuer at this time makes it clear that Paul Block had asked for such support from him. "I will be very glad if occasion offers to testify to the exceptional abilities of Mr. Block as a journalist," Hearst wrote, "and also to the essential value of the properties he controls." The offer was not taken up.

An exchange of correspondence between Paul Block and Grove Patterson in the late spring of 1932 offers additional evidence of concern for the solvency of the Block holdings. After a June 3 telephone conversation, Patterson wrote to Block:

I feel very happy about the talk we had over the telephone yesterday. It is my understanding that you would like to have me remain in Toledo as Editor of the *Blade* for as long as you own the paper. And I know, from what you said, that you have not the slightest intention of selling it . . .
Furthermore, I feel gratified to have you tell me that if the time ever did come that for any reason you would care to sell the *Blade,* you would give me the first chance to assemble the capital, if I could, and buy it.

Block answered that he "would like this to be considered an agreement on your part, and on my part, too, to have you remain as Editor of the Toledo *Blade* as long as I own the newspaper, and I expect that to be as long as I live."

There is no record available of full details of the plan by which the Block organization's financial troubles were resolved. The Brooklyn *Daily Times,* which had been bought in 1928, was sold for $125,000 to the Brooklyn *Standard-Union* in March, 1932. Efforts were made to sell the Duluth *News-Tribune,* which had been acquired in 1930 (David Lawrence, then editor of the *U. S. Daily News* and a close friend of Paul Block, was approached to act as a go-between). Block's response to Lawrence's inquiry on behalf of R. C.

Hardy, Inc., of Duluth, was that "this is no time to sell newspapers, any more than it is real estate."

★ ★ ★

The Blade was, meantime, continuing to strengthen its supremacy over its only remaining afternoon rival, the *News-Bee*. The hiring of new staff members of superior ability contributed to this growing advantage.

Typical of these was George Jenks.

This lanky blond young man joined *The Blade* in 1933 as a general assignment reporter, having left a bankrupt semi-weekly newspaper in Bowling Green, the former *Wood County News*. He began in the next year to cover labor and affairs of federal government, launching a half-century career during which he brought distinction both to himself and to *The Blade*.

George Jenks covered almost every possible kind of event during that time. He represented *The Blade* both in Columbus and in Washington for considerable periods of time. In 1946, he was sent to the Marshall Islands for the first explosion of an A-bomb open to nonmilitary observers. He was one of a team who represented *The Blade* at the coronation of England's Queen Elizabeth in 1953, going on from London to Berlin and East Germany. He covered one of President Eisenhower's famed "good will" tours — to Pakistan, India, Turkey, Afghanistan, Iran, Morocco and Algeria.

Although he was national affairs editor for a time and filled other positions involving administrative duties, Jenks was at his best — and his happiest — reporting the news. He possessed the rare talent of being able to write a literate and incisive account that needed no revision or editing. Many of his articles are models of the reporter's art.

Early in his career at *The Blade,* George Jenks reported on the strike which began on April 11, 1934, at the Electric Auto-Lite Company in Toledo. The bitterness and violence of the struggle, which went on until June 6, focused national attention on Toledo, and reporters from all over the country came to the city to cover the strike.

The Auto-Lite Company, as it was generally known, was one of several Toledo industries providing parts and accessories to Detroit's auto producers, in whose prosperity they had shared during the post-World War boom period. Auto-Lite's net profits for 1928, after taxes, had hit a record high of more than $7,700,000. Company officials had predicted in February, 1929, that there would be big growth in its operations. But as the auto industry suffered in the 1930s, so did suppliers of parts. Wages were cut and companies like Auto-Lite took steps to combat the growing union sentiment among their workers.

The Auto-Lite employees walked off their jobs demanding new working terms; the company brought in strike-breakers and later employed 200 laid-off policemen. In a clash on April 17 between the striking workers and those who had taken their jobs, several people were badly beaten. Tension heightened, and on May 16, forty-six strikers were arrested in connection with picketing disorders. A howling mob stormed the doors of the courtroom where they were to be tried and laid rough hands on the judge in the case. The pickets were subsequently released.

The company's management shut down the plant on May 18 and Toledo's unions prepared for a general strike. Then, on May 23, a hundred workers rushed through the main gate with clubs and pieces of pipe, attacking the strikers and their sympathizers. The battle, fought with weapons including fire hoses, tear gas, and bullets, raged all afternoon and into the night. The next day, strikers attacked the factory, imprisoning 1,600 employees.

That same day, Charles P. Taft arrived in the city to serve as a special mediator for President Roosevelt. The National Guard, called out by Governor Charles D. White, also arrived on the 24th, and the next day was involved in violence at the plant that left two men dead and eleven others injured. On May 26, an Auto-Lite employee was stripped naked by the rioters and forced to parade to the downtown district. That was the same day Heywood Broun, president of the American Newspaper Guild and one of the out-of-town reporters covering the strike, was arrested by a squad of the National Guard, who finally released him when he showed a hotel room key.

The Blade had little to say editorially about the strike until May 28, when it took a sideswipe at federal intervention: "Legislation for compulsory arbitration of labor troubles has been proposed in Washington, but a voluntary agreement between the parties in direct interest is vastly preferable. On that basis, both sides will be the better satisfied and will enter into new friendly relationships in furtherance of their mutual interest." The only other comment came on Memorial Day, when it was suggested that "today is a holiday and it offers people a chance to really *think* about the strike."

A settlement was reached early in June, after National Guard troops had been withdrawn and Toledo's unions dropped the threat of a general strike. Terms of the agreement included a five per cent wage increase and recognition of the local union.

The Electric Auto-Lite strike was the first of more than thirty in Toledo during 1934 and 1935 that were to give the city a reputation as a "bad" labor town. The problem was one with which Toledo — and *The Blade* — had to deal for many years.

Chapter 24

Years of Troubles

The headline on Paul Block's signed editorial on the front page of *The Blade* of October 7, 1931, read:

> IT IS UP TO MAYOR, SAFETY
> DIRECTOR AND CHIEF TO
> RID TOLEDO OF GANGSTERS

This message followed:

> The public have known of the presence of a new gang of gunmen in Toledo for months. They have done nothing about it — waiting for something to happen. Something happened. Detroit police wanted Pete Licavoli, suspected of murder in that city. Toledo police found Licavoli — found him easily. Any day they could have found his companions, members of the new gang that has moved in on us. But they arrested Licavoli and called it a day.
> ... We call on the mayor, the safety director, and the chief of police to act today.

The Licavolis had operated in Toledo since moving in from Detroit in 1930 to take over bootlegging operations and assorted other rackets. There had been other notorious gang figures in Toledo before the Licavolis. Joe Urbaytis and his crew, for example, had robbed the Toledo post office of $1,600,000 on February 7, 1920.

Toledo's reputation as a congenial stopping-off place for criminals of various sorts went back to the administrations of "Golden Rule" Jones and Brand Whitlock, each of whom had served four terms as mayor during the sixteen years between 1897 and 1913. *The Blade,* under Robinson Locke's editorship, had railed against the notoriety attaching to Toledo as a result of the "soft on criminals" attitude attributed to both Jones and Whitlock. Every criminal for miles around, it was alleged, knew the city as a place to seek refuge from enforcers of the law. The police chief under both Jones and

Whitlock, Perry Knapp, was an ardent Tolstoyan. On the occasion of his appointment, Knapp wrote to Mayor Jones that he really didn't want to be chief of police, but that "so long as we must have Police Forces, I suppose we must have captains of Police, and about the only consolation that I can see for me in this position is that I may perhaps be of use to some poor unfortunate devil who may fall into the trap; that I may treat him with kindness, give him an encouraging word and send him on his way to try 'er again."[21] Brand Whitlock once said of Knapp that "there was not another chief of police like him," and few would argue with that.

But it was the Licavoli gang that contributed most of Toledo's notoriety in these closing years of the prohibition era. Thomas Licavoli — known as Yonnie — was head man. He came to Toledo after having served a two-and-one-half-year prison sentence on charges of running whiskey between Detroit and Canada. Two other Licavolis — his brother, Pete, and his cousin, Jimmy — came from Detroit with him. They added two Toledoans — Jacob "Firetop" Sulkin and Joseph "Wop" English — to their forces.

The Licavolis' decision in 1931 to take over the numbers racket in Toledo met with opposition from established gangster-bootleggers. One, Abe "The Punk" Lubitsky, was shot to death while driving on Franklin Avenue with two associates on October 6, 1931. Norman "Big Agate" Blatt was one of the two survivors of that assault, but he was a later casualty of gunfire.

In the liquor business, the Licavolis' number one rival in Toledo was Jackie Kennedy. The flashily handsome Kennedy undersold the Licavolis on beer and he declined to pay them for the privilege of operating his downtown club. He had to be dispensed with, but it took two attempts to eliminate Kennedy. In the first, on November 30, 1932, Jackie and his girl friend, Louise Bell, were shot down at the corner of Superior and Jackson streets as they were returning to Kennedy's club from the theatre. She died a few hours later in a hospital; he recovered.

The public demanded the arrest of the Licavolis, and a newly elected county prosecutor named Frazier Reams vowed to clean up Toledo. He was unable to gather enough evidence to secure indictments for the murder of Louise Bell, but managed to bring charges of violating the federal prohibition laws against the Licavolis. A front-page headline in the December 8 issue of *The Blade* proclaimed:

GANG CHIEFTAIN
AND 14 OTHERS
TO FACE COURT

The ensuing trial received a big play from *The Blade,* with two or more front-page stories every day. A typical headline, on January 24, 1933:

LOVE FOR BABY
BRINGS ARREST
OF LICAVOLI

Yonnie Licavoli and his associates were found guilty of the charges against them on May 10, 1933. They escaped sentence, however, when the prohibition laws were repealed in December of that year.

In the meantime, a second attempt on the life of Jackie Kennedy, on July 7, 1933, succeeded. Kennedy and his girl friend at the time, Audrey Rauls, were walking on Edgewater Drive when two men pulled up alongside in an automobile. One dragged Miss Rauls, a Toledo beauty queen, out of the line of fire while his companion pumped fourteen bullets into Kennedy.

Frazier Reams got his man that time. A total of fourteen members of the Licavoli gang went on trial for the murders of Jackie Kennedy and Louise Bell. Firetop Sulkin, alleged to have shot Kennedy, was charged with first-degree murder and Yonnie Licavoli and twelve others with first-degree murder and conspiracy. All were convicted and given varying prison sentences. Licavoli and Sulkin, along with Joseph English, Ralph Carsello and John Ric, were sentenced to life terms in the Ohio penitentiary in Columbus.[22]

Yonnie Licavoli spent the succeeding thirty-six years in prison, where he was reported to have written "prison songs" and short stories. When it was alleged that he was living a semi-pampered life, Frazier Reams investigated the charges and the warden was fired early in 1935. One of his successors was dismissed for the same reason.

There were allegations, too, that some members of the Toledo police department had been friendly with Licavoli. When Arnold Bunge, who had resigned from the county prosecutor's staff, made this allegation in speaking to the Men's Brotherhood of the Beverly Community Presbyterian church, *The Blade* urged him to testify to this effect to the grand jury. The editorial concluded:

Let's find out if there is any such collusive "arm of law or government" within the police department. Not alone to determine this, but to remove the shadow of these charges from the whole police department, we believe there is a call for a grand jury investigation.

Nothing came of this proposal, but efforts to free Licavoli from prison kept the case before the public for many years. Each time, there was a public outcry in Toledo against Licavoli's release. When, in January, 1969, he was finally paroled, *The Blade* suggested that "we might as well accept this, however reluctantly." Yonnie Licavoli had given Toledo a reputation "second perhaps only to the one Al Capone gave Chicago — as a gang-ridden, wide-open booze and gambling town in the era of prohibition, corrupting government with money and intimidating law-abiding, peace-loving citizens with guns." But, the editorial concluded:

> . . . in a way, Yonnie Licavoli had given Toledo a kind of civic purpose. The battle to stamp out the last vestiges of such gangsterism, to elect a sheriff who was honest, to give this city honest government, to make a good city in which to live and do business continued. And for a good long time, the only thing the responsible citizen of Toledo didn't want was to have Yonnie Licavoli, symbol as he was of the city's seamy past, released from prison.

The gangster era in Toledo did not quite end with the imprisonment of the Licavolis. Nor was a sheriff who was honest (at least by *The Blade's* lights) immediately elected. Only two years later — in May, 1936 — one of Paul Block's signed front page editorials demanded that O'REILLY MUST GO:

> The conclusion which his team mates on the ticket and other Democratic leaders are rapidly reaching, to the effect that Sheriff O'Reilly must resign and resign at once, is the logical conclusion that was reached by the great majority of Toledo citizens immediately after the revelation of the sheriff's continued association with the notorious gangster, Campbell.
>
> It is perfectly evident to all citizens of whatever party that the sheriff, by his failure to arrest the most wanted criminal in the United States, a man whom he admitted seeing on frequent social occasions, had thoroughly and completely disqualified himself for the high office which he had been holding and made himself totally unavailable as a candidate for re-election . . .

O'REILLY MUST GO!

Some of *The Blade's* ire in this instance, according to surviving members of the staff, grew from the *News-Bee's* having scored a scoop in the matter of the gangster's escape from law enforcement officials, resulting, it was believed, from a tip from the sheriff's office.

★ ★ ★

The years of the gangsters' most flagrant activities in Toledo were also years of stress in the city government's financial affairs, beginning with the loss of more than $600,000 of municipal funds in the 1931 bank crashes. Worse was yet to come.

Candidates for mayor in 1931 were the incumbent, William T. Jackson, and Addison Q. Thacher, a marine contractor. *The Blade* thought that either would make a good mayor. There was no doubt in the minds of the voters. Perhaps Thacher's popularity was a result of his having distributed free food — from perishable goods that had been unsold by local grocers — to some 2,000 people a day. Whatever the reason, he carried twenty-one of the city's twenty-two wards. The new mayor may soon have regretted winning. More and more property owners defaulted on their taxes, and with little tax money coming in, pressure increased to reduce expenditures.

Mayor Thacher's answer was a pay-as-you-go government operation. Three hundred jobs were cut from the payroll in January, 1932; the salaries of fire and police chiefs were reduced from $350 to $290 monthly; policemen's pay was cut from $200 a month to $150, and some city employees had to take part of their pay in IOUs.

It hardly sat well with many Toledoans that Ad Thacher had put several of his relatives on the city payroll, even as others were losing their jobs or were taking substantial pay cuts. *The Blade* defended the mayor, suggesting that these were criticisms of "the kind usually made of all city administrations, but no one will deny that the mayor has done many things for our citizens."

The mayor elected in 1933 was not, however, Addison Q. Thacher but Solon Klotz, by more than 2,000 votes. Klotz was a member of the Socialist party — the first to gain the mayor's office in Toledo. None of the city's newspapers had supported Klotz, who was a native of Toledo, an attorney, and an officer in the Council of Churches. On his first day in office, the new mayor announced that he would eliminate politics from city government. His next action was to fire 137 employees.

Nothing Mayor Klotz did, however, helped much in curing Toledo's financial ills. One of his proposals was that all municipal employees should take a month's vacation without pay, which would have saved $300,000 annually. *The Blade* opposed this suggestion because it did not apply to elected officials. Also, many city workers already had taken cuts in pay. *The Blade* urged a pay-your-taxes campaign to collect some of the $15,000,000 in back assessments on the city's tax rolls.

The Klotz administration's problems increased in April, 1934, when state auditors found evidence in the city's records that became the basis for claims that officials had spent more than $200,000 illegally. The charge involved funds spent without asking for competitive bids, or without approval by council and certification by the fiscal officer that money was available to cover the expenditure.[23]

The Blade now stepped up its campaign for adoption of the city manager form of government in Toledo, which it had advocated ever since Paul Block had become publisher in 1926. City manager government, it was argued, was the only means to solve the mounting problems which confronted Toledo. Sound business practices should be substituted for political finagling. "The time has now arrived to concentrate on a new plan of city government," Paul Block declared in a front-page editorial in June, 1934. It was specified that the plan should provide for "the city manager appointed by a small council, members to be elected by proportional representation."

The city manager plan was now more acceptable to voters, who had turned it down in 1928 and again in 1931. The proposal placed on the ballot in November, 1934, was approved by a margin of 33,000 to 28,000 votes. *The Blade* hailed the victory, declaring that the city's financial operations would be protected, preventing repetition of the "extravagance and mismanagement . . . which has been revealed during the last few years by grand juries and state examiners."

Leaders of the city's political parties were not pleased with the outcome, and they forced another vote on the plan in May, 1935. But this time the outcome was even more decisive — 27,000 in favor to 18,000 against. A nine-member council was elected at large by proportional representation in November. Mayor Klotz failed to make the top nine. John N. Edy, who had been city manager of Berkeley, California, Flint, Michigan, and Dallas, Texas, became Toledo's first city manager January 1, 1936, serving until September, 1939.[24]

The Blade supported city manager government in Toledo for the next twenty years, though its enthusiasm waned and its relations with the succession of city managers were often strained nearly to the breaking point. Finally, in the late 1950s, *The Blade* gave strong support to two successive efforts to change to the strong mayor plan of government in Toledo. When, in 1959, the second of these efforts was narrowly defeated, further attempts to effect a change were abandoned. Proportional representation — an elaborate voting system intended to provide minority representation in a council elected at large — was discarded some years earlier, with *The Blade* leading the campaign against it on grounds that it encouraged factionalism.

Chapter 25

European Interlude

Both the editor and the publisher of *The Blade* visited Europe in the 1930s, carrying on a tradition of personal interest in world affairs that had begun with David Ross Locke fifty years earlier and would culminate in 1953 in the establishment of the newspaper's own European bureau.

Grove Patterson, who had become increasingly a national figure in the last decade, was the first to make the journey, in 1932. His daily column on the editorial page, "The Way of the World," not only was one of the most popular features among *Blade* readers but also was widely reprinted. Patterson's remarkable talent for making complicated matters accessible to a wide audience was matched by skills as a public speaker that already had begun to make him one of the most sought-after in the country. This combination of talents was quickly recognized by Paul Block, who appreciated his potential as a good-will ambassador for *The Blade* and began to give him increased public exposure.

On his trip to Europe, Patterson's primary assignment was to attend the disarmament conference in Geneva. While there, he talked with Maxim Litvinov, the Soviet foreign minister, who, he reported, "had stunned the delegates by the incredible proposal that since it was a disarmament conference all the nations should disarm."

Adolf Hitler's appointment as chancellor of Germany destroyed whatever slight chance of success there had been for the disarmament conference. When it was adjourned, Grove Patterson went to Rome. He wanted to get Benito Mussolini's reaction to a treaty proposed at Geneva by the French foreign minister, Andre Tardieu, for preserving peace in the western world with the aid of an international army. He admitted that he fudged a little when, in seeking an appointment with Il Duce, he represented himself as bringing greetings from a large Italian population of Toledo that didn't actually exist. But he got the appointment.

Paul Block went to Europe two years later, in 1934. He visited Germany, Austria, Great Britain, Italy and France. While in Europe he talked with a number of important people, and was disappointed that an appointment with Hitler was cancelled by the last illness of President Hindenburg. Hitler, he told reporters who interviewed him on his return to this country, was "a male Aimee Semple McPherson who won't last."

The publisher of *The Blade* did, however, talk with Benito Mussolini, as did Grove Patterson. Both left accounts of their experiences and of their reactions to the Italian dictator, which provide an interesting comparison. Patterson's — in *I Like People* — is entitled "When Mussolini Interviewed Me." These excerpts suggest his irreverent amusement:

> ... When we arrived before the palace, the driver stopped in the middle of the street, and got out of his cab, and motioned me to wait. He approached two soldiers, carrying rifles, on guard at the entrance to the yard. After what seemed to me an unnecessarily long consultation, the driver returned, opened the door, and made known in sign language that I was to approach the gateway . . . I went through to be greeted by a large and impressive person, clothed in a truly magnificent uniform of blue and gold. Bowing formally, his face showing the remnants of a friendly smile, he directed me to the foot of a stairway that led up from the court yard into the palace.
>
> ... The stairs ended abruptly at a broad door. Since I had no instructions to the contrary, I knocked. Suddenly the door fairly flew open and three tall men in colorful Italian military dress uniforms clicked their heels, and in one rather terrifying motion thrust their right arms forward, aiming apparently at the top of my head. It was the Fascist salute. I bowed and they relaxed.
>
> ... After a bit we came to a spacious reception hall, set with a table long enough for the directors of a couple of Standard Oil companies, and furnished with huge leather chairs. We passed through and into a smaller room where an elderly white-haired man, with a singularly kind face, stood guard at a massive door. He was dressed in a Prince Albert coat, wore a white bow tie and gave me the fleeting impression that he was a retired Methodist preacher.
>
> ... Slowly he swung the great door and I passed into the biggest room I had ever seen outside a church or public auditorium. At the far end I made out the figure of a man sitting behind a small flat-topped desk. I was in the private office of the Chief of Government.

European Interlude 247

Grove Patterson then described Mussolini's office and his "long march" up to the desk, concluding with this description of the interview:

> Il Duce plied me with so many inquiries that for some time I couldn't get one in . . . Finally I managed to leap into a pause and asked him the $64 question. What did he think of the French Plan for preserving the peace of Europe? Instantly, he fairly snapped to attention, shrugged his shoulders, and exclaimed in his broken English:
> "Ze French Plan — it ees Reediculous."
> So there I had it — the answer that the Geneva conference and a score of newspaper correspondents were waiting to hear, but I was bound by my promise that everything Mussolini might say would be confidential, not to be written or repeated.

The impish sense of humor which was one of Patterson's most endearing qualities emerges repeatedly in this account. The contrast with the tone of Paul Block's dispatch to *The Blade* on August 12, 1934 — the day he met Mussolini — is dramatic. He wrote:

> I had the honored privilege of a visit with the great Mussolini today. I think it was the most interesting interview I ever had . . .
> He wore a white linen suit and instead of looking like the grim, serious, dictatorial man which his pictures usually show him to be, he was a gentle, smiling, courteous host, but with a personality which would be difficult to match . . . He was particularly interested in the conditions I found in England, which are better than elsewhere and far better than in our own United States . . .
> I cannot remember when I have had the privilege of talking so openly and frankly to a person of his rank. Certainly not with most of our executives in Washington. We talked on many subjects . . . (including) his experiences as an editor and publisher and his courageous efforts in fighting, through his newspaper, brainless and dishonest politicians.
> . . . We shook hands as heartily as if we had been old friends and I withdrew, leaving behind me a man whom I consider the greatest personality of the present century.

This paean of praise for Mussolini, the man, is followed by equal enthusiasm for his accomplishments — the railroads that ran on time, the extirpation of "extreme socialists, communists, and other radical organizations," bringing the Mafia under control. Ecstatic praise of the attitude of the Italian people and their devotion to Il Duce is followed by this comparison: "It reminds one of the mental change which came to the great majority of the American people right after Franklin Roosevelt was elected president. The only difference is that many of our citizens soon lost faith in our administration, whereas the Italian people are stronger for Mussolini today than ever before."

Paul Block was not, of course, the only American who found much to admire in what Benito Mussolini had accomplished in Italy since seizing power in 1922. The Christian Socialist minister, George D. Herron, who had been an associate of Toledo's Mayor Samuel M. Jones, had established his residence near Florence, proclaiming Mussolini's Italy Europe's only hope in the wake of the World War. In Block's case, his praise did lead to allegations of incipient fascism, which were undoubtedly heightened by his increasingly virulent opposition to Franklin D. Roosevelt and the New Deal programs.

To reporters who interviewed him when he arrived on the *Conte de Savoia* from Europe on August 29, he declared sarcastically: "I was happy to note this morning that the Statue of Liberty was still here. I was afraid the New Dealers might have torn it down and when I saw it still standing I uttered a prayer of thanks."

Yet Paul Block was not at all sympathetic with any of the exotic political philosophies floating about in the world of 1934. He summed up his own reactions in the concluding paragraph of his account of the interview with Mussolini in these words:

"After observing the conditions in the various countries I have just visited, I am convinced more than ever that what we need in the United States is 'progressive conservatism' and not communism, Hitlerism, Fascism or 'theorism,' such as we are to a degree receiving today at the hands of the young experimenters who hold authoritative positions in our administration in Washington."

What was meant by "progressive conservatism" is not at all clear, nor is it likely that Paul Block could have defined it any more precisely. He did believe that the welfare of this country — and most others — lay with its business community, which should be encouraged by the government in every possible way. He was not opposed to change and reform, but to the direction it seemed to him the New Deal reforms were taking. The assumption of many of the activists in Washington that business was to blame for the nation's ills and must be brought into line through regulatory, even punitive, government actions distressed him profoundly.

What the publisher of *The Blade* saw in Europe in August, 1934, was more a reflection of what he believed to be happening in the United States than of the conditions that confronted him there. He thought economic conditions in England were improving under the

European Interlude 249

Tory government elected in 1931, when in fact the worst lay ahead. He approved the way Mussolini sought recovery in Italy. These views became a part of the arsenal he was about to unleash against the Roosevelt Administration at home.

Chapter 26

Down With the New Deal!

PRESIDENT ROOSEVELT
DESERVES GREAT CREDIT

Those were unusual words in *The Blade*, which gave Franklin D. Roosevelt very little credit for anything that was good — especially when this headline appeared on a front-page editorial in the spring of 1935. This time, however, the President was commended "because he has frankly met the criticism of the American Federation of Labor in connection with his renewal of the automobile code and his refusal to abolish the automobile labor board."

These may well have been Paul Block's last kind words on behalf of the man who occupied the White House during the last eight years of the publisher's life. From 1935 to 1941, the intensity of his attack on Roosevelt and the New Deal mounted steadily. In its early stages, the campaign often seemed to be targeted not so much on Roosevelt as on his advisers, but there was never any real doubt as to who was held to be ultimately accountable.

WHEN WILL WASHINGTON RECOGNIZE ITS BLUNDERS? was the question asked by the headline on one of Paul Block's signed editorials on the front page of *The Blade* on April 22, 1935. It urged that steps be taken to balance the budget, that the Agricultural Adjustment Act be discarded, that 95 per cent of the present National Recovery Administration law be eliminated. "Some changes" should be made in the securities bill, and the proposed banking act should be abandoned because it would "place Federal Reserve banks in the hands of appointed politicians." To prevent Japan and other nations from "continuing to ruin some of our industries, thereby costing many workers their jobs," tariff laws should be corrected.

Down with the New Deal! 251

Paul Block was fond of writing editorials in the form of an open letter to a particular individual. In June, 1935, he addressed one of these to President Roosevelt:

> You have often stated that you like to receive constructive suggestions. May we take the liberty of presenting one that we believe meets that requirement?
>
> It is well known that the great majority of our businessmen have sincerely felt that if they were left alone for but a reasonable period, that conditions would improve, unemployment would be reduced, and that we would definitely be on the road to real recovery.
>
> Mr. President, why not give them a chance to prove that this can be accomplished? Why not give industry a period of six months in which to "make good"?
>
> . . . At the moment there is deep concern that the laws which Congress is now considering will prove harmful and, therefore, further delay business improvement.
>
> We have had our five years of depression now. Many experiments have been undertaken but not this one — to let industry alone for a few months.
>
> Will you try it out, Mr. President?

Ten days later, another signed editorial cited three specific pieces of legislation which, Block contended, would further retard recovery — the Wheeler-Rayburn utility bill, the Wagner labor relations bill, and proposed amendments to the AAA. *The Blade's* publisher argued that they should be defeated, not only because they would be economically harmful, but also because they were subject to serious challenge on constitutional grounds.

Paul Block also took to the airwaves to carry on his attack against Roosevelt, who had used radio so successfully in promoting his programs. *The Blade* printed excerpts on August 19, 1935, from a speech on a "coast-to-coast hookup" of the National Broadcasting Company. FDR's failure to carry out his platform promises was deplored. "Instead," Block continued, "almost from the day of his election, he has either followed or led in the policies suggested to him by a coterie of inexperienced professors and young lawyers, a radical clique, which, as one of them wrote, wanted to 'remake America.' " The latter reference was to a statement attributed to Rexford Guy Tugwell, a favorite target of New Deal critics. The ideas which Tugwell and other "professors and lawyers" in Washington espoused, the speech continued, were copied from countries "where Fascism, Communism, or National Socialism are in control."

The assault on Roosevelt and his program continued, with an

occasional diversion such as this comment early in 1936, after the Supreme Court had declared the Agricultural Adjustment Act to be unconstitutional: "Once again the Supreme Court has shown its courage. It is the last defense, impartial, strong and adequate, against the encroachment of a national administration which has been moving, by the route of state socialism, toward the destruction of American ideals."

With the coming of a new year — 1936 — when there would be a presidential election, *The Blade* and its publisher took renewed hope. Paul Block offered advice to the Republican party on how to proceed in this election in a signed front-page editorial on February 23:

> ... We urge the delegates selected for the Republican convention to bear all this in mind and to remember that our democratic form of government is at stake. The defeat of the New Deal is essential to safeguard American liberties and to wipe out the poisonous radical socialism which has actually been injected into our national life by the present Administration.
>
> And so if victory is more certain with a pledge of a Coalition cabinet and by the nomination of a Republican and a true Democrat to head the ticket, then it is the duty of the Republican party this year, and *The Toledo Blade* will support such a ticket with whatever force and influence it may possess.

The man who eventually became the choice of the Republican party for its presidential nomination in 1936 invited Paul Block and Grove Patterson to have dinner with him some months in advance of the convention. Both men were favorably impressed with Governor Alfred M. Landon of Kansas at their meeting in Topeka. When the Republicans met in Cleveland (Patterson was one of the Ohio delegates), Block approved of Landon's nomination. He also approved enthusiastically the choice of Colonel Frank Knox — a fellow newspaper publisher — as Landon's running mate. Another of his signed front-page editorials expressed his satisfaction:

> The ticket named by the Republican convention in Cleveland grows in strength hour by hour and day by day ... The reason is that the more the two candidates — Gov. Landon and Col. Knox — are studied, the more their qualifications become apparent ...
>
> Governor Landon is "Alf" to his barber, to the grocer, to the rich man and the poor man. He is like most of the men we know, a sincere friend, a real American ...
>
> Both men believe in the American governmental system and the Constitution ...

Down with the New Deal! 253

Landon and Knox go forth in a holy crusade for the preservation of the American form of government, American principles, and the rights, privileges and liberties of the American people.

Paul Block enlisted in that holy crusade at the outset. To his editorial artillery in its support, he added a column of "Paragraphs by the Blade Publisher," which began to appear in *The Blade* during the summer. These were largely devoted to criticism of the New Deal and President Roosevelt. Rexford Guy Tugwell appeared often in the role of villain.

Interviewed in Los Angeles in August, Block predicted that a third party ticket, "backed by so-called Jeffersonian Democrats," would oppose President Roosevelt in November. Either Albert C. Ritchie, governor of Maryland, or Alfred E. Smith, former governor of New York, would be the party's candidate. "Unquestionably Democrats who espouse the principles of Jefferson will veer sharply from Roosevelt," Paul Block predicted. "They will support the Constitution and the Supreme Court . . . The people of the United States will not stand for a dictator."

The Blade's publisher was disenchanted with Alfred M. Landon for only the briefest of moments. That was September 14, and it was personal rather than political. An account was provided in the *News-Bee* the next day:

Paul Block, publisher of *The Toledo Blade* and other newspapers, today was reported "in a huff" because he was denied the privilege of hooking his private car onto the campaign special of Gov. Alf Landon at Worcester, Mass.

An ardent admirer and supporter of the Kansas governor, Block had wired from New York, telling the governor that he wished to see him while the campaign train was crossing Massachusetts. A reply of "delighted" was received by Block from the presidential candidate.

When the special train arrived in Worcester, members of the Landon party discovered trainmen breaking the solid train to put on the Block private car. Landon's lieutenants immediately revoked the order and Block's car was left standing on the side track.

According to a report in today's *Herald-Tribune*, it was explained to *The Toledo Blade* publisher that the privilege of hooking onto the train had been denied prominent Republican leaders in New England and could not be extended to him.

"Block became so angry that he stormed off without seeing the governor," the *Tribune* reported, "despite the fact that he was urged to board Landon's private car for a conference."

Block's private car, which he had named Friendship, was a particularly prized possession. Built in 1929 by the Pullman

Company in Chicago, at a cost of $92,000, it was almost 84 feet long, weighed about 42 tons, had a dining room, observation living room and platform, kitchen, pantry, sleeping space for six people in four bedrooms, and crew quarters for two. It incorporated a number of special features which Mr. and Mrs. Block had requested, though the Pullman Company was not able to provide the air-conditioning system that Mayor Walker suggested.

Block preferred to travel in his private car, and Grove Patterson recalled in *I Like People* that "if in New York he suddenly decided at three o'clock in the afternoon that he wanted to leave for Toledo at five-thirty, the car had to be attached to the train at once, despite all the red tape, difficulties and possible delay encountered." He would have particularly resented his rebuff from the Landon campaign officials.

But his disenchantment did not last long. *The Blade* was soon back on the Landon bandwagon, publishing a barrage of editorials in his support. Many were signed by Paul Block and one touched on a theme that was among his favorites:

> WHAT THE COMING ELECTION
> MEANS TO YOUNG VOTERS
> The younger voter should take an inventory of Extravagance . . .
> The younger voter should take an inventory of Opportunity . . .
> The younger voter should take an inventory of Freedom . . .
> The younger voter should take an inventory of Society . . . (here the principal concern was with the ranging of class against class).
> There are about six million of these young people who have come of voting age since the last election. There are enough of them to go into the polls with their ballots to turn the New Deal out of the White House, and if they have regard for their own future and the future of the country, that is what they will do in November.

When in November forty-six states voted for Franklin D. Roosevelt, while only Maine and Vermont chose Alfred M. Landon, *The Blade* took the bitter blow philosophically. "The people have spoken," it conceded. "And like all Americans we bow to the will of the majority." Even so, Paul Block had his own interpretation:

> Regardless of the outcome, we cannot believe that the result of yesterday's election is to be construed as an endorsement of the New Deal in its entirety. We choose, rather, to think that the people, accepting the promise of a constructive change in the national administration, are therefore willing to go along with President Roosevelt for another four years.

Down with the New Deal! 255

Our earnest hope is that President Roosevelt will do nothing that will create class distinctions in the United States . . .

The President will not lack support for those policies that are designed for the substantial betterment of ALL the people. And *The Blade* will be in the forefront with such support.

But not long after the election — early in 1937 — the President's proposals for changes in the Supreme Court — described by all who opposed it as "court-packing" — roused *The Blade* and its publisher to new heights of anger. Beginning in February, Block attacked the plan in a series of signed front-page editorials, citing the court as the bulwark of democracy, the country's last protection against radicalism. A typical editorial, on May 19, called on the President to abandon his proposals:

It is quite probable that Mr. Roosevelt has no desire to create a one-man government. But everything he has done, from the time he endeavored to put through the NRA measure and the AAA measure . . . to his present Supreme Court proposal — all this is exactly the procedure which took place first in Italy and then in Germany and which brought dictatorship to these nations, under which liberties, free speech and a free press were entirely destroyed . . .

It remains to be seen whether the President will continue to insist on his own way at the peril of the national good. If he persists in his proposals, it will be but another indication that he places himself and his will above the well-being of the whole nation.

Paul Block returned to his appeal to the nation's youth to bring an end to what he regarded as the New Deal's excesses when he received the honorary degree of Doctor of Literature at St. Francis College in Loretto, Pennsylvania, in June, 1937. "It is the generation rising today," he said, "which will have to settle whether democracy shall survive in our country. It is young men such as you who must see to it that no individual, whether he be a President, a labor leader, or an opportunist, who may appear when the next depression comes, is permitted to assume such authority as is now vested in one man."

In August, Paul Block became owner of the Pittsburgh *Post-Gazette*, which he had operated under a special arrangement with the Hearst organization for the preceding ten years. The purchase price was $2,750,000.

The *Post-Gazette* became, almost immediately after the change of ownership, the vehicle for a revelation about the recently confirmed Supreme Court justice, Hugo L. Black, which shook the nation. Ray Sprigle, one of the nation's best investigative reporters, uncovered evidence that Black had been a member of the Ku Klux

Klan.[25] After a series of stories by Sprigle had appeared in the *Post-Gazette,* Paul Block declared in a signed editorial on the front page of *The Blade:*

> When Senator Hugo L. Black's name was first presented for the Supreme Court bench, it was stated in the Senate and published in many newspapers that he had been elected as a Klan candidate.
> Hearings were demanded by independent senators but these requests were overruled by administrative leaders.
> Instead, the vote on his confirmation was rushed through under pressure before the facts could be marshalled.
> But The Blade has dug them out and will present them in a striking series of six articles . . .

Justice Black made a radio speech on October 1, seeking to clear himself of these charges. In another signed editorial, Block replied: "The record proves that Black was a real Klansman in 1926 and preached and held with it in its un-American principles. Last evening he made it clear that he does not believe in the Klan any longer." As for Black's charge that a "planned and concerted campaign was being directed against him," Block declared: "Nothing could be more silly. I merely sent a representative down to Birmingham to get the story that was being rumored everywhere."

Hugo Black remained on the court, of course, but Paul Block and other critics of Roosevelt's attempt to increase the number of justices on the court got considerable satisfaction from the effort's defeat. The fight carried over into the 1938 election, in which the President attempted — with little success — to unseat members of his own party who had failed to support him.

Paul Block's war against any and all aspects of the New Deal continued unabated. It should be noted that although he was sometimes critical of Franklin D. Roosevelt personally, his most vitriolic attacks were directed against others in the administration — Tugwell, Hopkins, Wallace and others — whom he accused of wanting to destroy American principles.

The Blade was not, however, among the more blatantly anti-Communist voices of the New Deal period, of which the Chicago *Tribune* was probably the loudest. The success of the Federal Bureau of Investigation against organized crime in 1935 produced the proposal in one of the familiar signed editorials that "it should be ordered without delay to assign whatever force may be required to get the facts on this undercover war against American institu-

Down with the New Deal! 257

tions," for the purpose of "investigating and deporting the communists who are trying to undermine and destroy our government."

When "The Public Papers and Addresses of Franklin D. Roosevelt" were published in four volumes in May, 1983, Paul Block wrote a signed editorial which contained many quotations from these papers. The concluding paragraphs sum up his estimate of the President:

> Historians of the future may deduce much from the volumes of the President's words. But in the nation of today they paint a picture of the chief executive that cannot be denied. Here, in his own words, is revealed the record of five years of contradiction, of incompetence, of futile legislation that has aggravated the nation's troubles and healed few of her wounds.
>
> Those who have benefited politically and otherwise from the New Deal will probably close their eyes to the actions of a president such as Mr. Roosevelt has proved himself to be. But we doubt whether the nation as a whole will ever forget his efforts to pack the Supreme Court, his efforts to take more power by reorganizing the executive departments, his sponsorship of agricultural legislation which destroyed farm products and livestock, his responsibility for objectionable tax laws, his failure to say a word against sit-down strikes, his lack of cooperation with industry at a time when such cooperation could have prevented the depression.

There was no change in Paul Block's feelings when FDR became a candidate for a third term in 1940. The willful breaking of yet another precedent brought forth fresh denunciations and warnings of the threat to American principles. *The Blade* was 100 per cent for Wendell Willkie, observing of him in August: "We wish you could meet Wendell Willkie. A fifteen-minute chat with him would probably convince you that he is your kind of man because it is immediately evident that he is human, that he speaks frankly and that you can believe in him. We are confident that you would agree he is the man to meet the tremendous tasks which face America today."

During the campaign, Ray Sprigle of the Pittsburgh *Post-Gazette* discovered a relationship between Henry A. Wallace, the Democratic vice-presidential candidate, and one Nicholas Roerich, a mystic and guru. Sprigle's stories were about to be released by both the *Post-Gazette* and *The Blade* when the Democrats unearthed the information that Wendell Willkie had failed to pay for his mother's cemetery lot. Members of the Republican and Democratic national committees met and agreed to suppress both stories. Obviously, Paul

Block, who was very close to the Republican national committee, was strongly influenced by its members.

Personal elements accounted for much of Block's dislike of Roosevelt. Block had resented the role played by Roosevelt, who was governor of New York at the time, in the hearings — which involved Block, too — intended to remove Block's good friend, Jimmy Walker, as mayor of New York. Block shared the feelings of many self-made men that most New Deal social programs undermined self-sufficiency and that their methods were both wasteful and impersonal. But some of his critics were unjust to represent him as mean and uncaring. His relations with his employees at every level and his generosity to others suggested that he was sympathetic — sometimes to a fault.

On Christmas Eve, 1935, *The Blade* carried this report: "At least 1,000 bags of food, candy and toys, the gift of *The Blade* and Paul Block, its publisher, are being delivered to the homes of needy people this Christmas Eve . . . *The Blade* bags go to those who, despite all the excellent efforts of organization, are not reached by other help."

This was Paul Block's idea of charity — direct and personal. If it was inadequate at a time when tens of millions were unemployed and economic problems were not so simple as they had once been, it was still unfair to describe him as unfeeling.

Chapter 27

The End of a Century

The Blade observed the one hundredth anniversary of its founding by publishing a 112-page edition on October 24, 1936. The celebration should have taken place a year earlier, but at that time it was still believed that the first edition had appeared in 1836. It was almost twenty-five years later that a copy of the first issue—dated December 19, 1835—was discovered in a home in Pennsylvania.

Economic conditions provided little to celebrate in 1936, although *The Blade* had begun to recover from the depths of the slump in both advertising and circulation. From 1930 highs of 131,000 circulation and 12,245,200 advertising linage, the totals had dropped to 123,380 and 7,490,000 by 1933. Now, in 1936, about half of those losses had been recovered, but the picture still was something less than rosy.

Paul Block had appraised the value of *The Blade* at $4,000,000 at the end of 1935—a half million dollars less than he was reported to have paid for it ten years earlier. It was, however, the most valuable of his newspaper properties by a considerable margin. (Block valued the Seebee Syndicate, established to promote the writings of Clare Boothe Brokaw, at $500.)

It was in 1936, too, that *The Blade* came close to losing Grove Patterson as its editor. Arthur Brisbane, long-time columnist for the Hearst newspapers, died that year. For a few weeks, W.R. Hearst had tried writing a daily column himself. He found it difficult and decided to hire a successor to Brisbane. He wanted Grove Patterson, whom he had tried to lure to his newspapers some years earlier. Now Hearst invited Patterson to San Simeon, even though *The Blade's* editor had indicated that he was not interested in making a change. "We all had a delightful time in an atmosphere of quiet and peace,"

Patterson recalled in *I Like People,* adding that "the food he served is memorable yet." There was, however, no discussion of his becoming Brisbane's successor.

A memorandum from Paul Block to Grove Patterson at this time suggests that they may have discussed Hearst's interest. It states: "We agree, and with pleasure, to continue your services for a period of ten years, beginning the 17th day of March, 1936, as Editor of the *Toledo Blade,* directly in charge of the news and editorial departments of that newspaper. It is agreed that Mr. Block, publisher of that newspaper, will continue as directing head of that newspaper and all its departments. No other person shall have any authority over the editor, Grove Patterson." The salary the editor was to receive was $510 per week—about one-tenth of the amount Hearst was reported to have paid Brisbane. Of this figure, Block added the following: "Also, the above mentioned salary. I wish you to know that it is my expectation and plans to give you additional bonuses if conditions permit."

In fact, Grove Patterson voluntarily accepted a salary cut two years later, with the assurance that it would be restored as soon as possible. This was part of a general retrenchment in *The Blade* organization, resulting from conditions reflected in a statement to the board of directors of Paul Block & Associates on May 14, 1938:

> The chairman stated that because of present unsatisfactory business conditions and because of the uncertain business outlook for the immediate future it had been found necessary to cut expenses and reduce salaries of officers and employees and that he therefore considered it only fair and proper that those former employees who had been granted pensions and to which pensions these employees had never made any monetary contributions, should also sustain a reduction in the amount now paid them.
>
> Moved and seconded that pensions now being paid to all former employees be reduced to one-half their present amounts.

The war between *The Blade* and the *News-Bee* for readers and advertisers had gone on unremittingly during the twelve years since Paul Block had bought *The Blade* in 1926. Fred Mollenkopf, who had taken over as city editor soon after the change in ownership, headed a superior news operation. The staff included a number of top-flight reporters. Charles Corbin had also joined *The Blade* as managing editor during this time.

The *News-Bee* had, meantime, suffered a serious loss when its editor, Negley Cochran, left to become editor of the Scripps-Howard

The End of a Century 261

experimental paper, *The Day,* in Chicago. Grove Patterson had rejected Roy Howard's offer of Cochran's job at the *News-Bee,* and the gap in news coverage, circulation and advertising revenues grew in *The Blade's* favor.

The almost inevitable result was announced on August 1, 1938: The Toledo Blade Company had purchased the *News-Bee* from the E. W. Scripps Company. The sale price was $780,000, payable in quarterly installments beginning February 1, 1939, and continuing for twenty years.

THE BLADE'S INCREASED RESPONSIBILITY was the headline on an editorial on August 3—the day after the *News-Bee* announced its withdrawal from the Toledo newspaper scene. The editorial declared:

> The suspension of the *News-Bee* is sincerely regretted by *The Blade.* . . . We appreciate that we now have an added responsibility to the people of Toledo and vicinity and we shall not shirk it.
> . . . It will be our ambition also to add as many of the *News-Bee* workers to our staff as we can afford, especially if business starts to improve, as most of us believe it will.

Toledo had now joined the growing number of American cities in which a single owner controlled the remaining newspapers. The *Times* would continue publication for more than thirty-five years and it did provide some competition for *The Blade* in news coverage, as well as a divergent point of view on many issues. But the fact remained that Paul Block was now in a position to decide what residents of the Toledo area read in their newspapers. This situation —usually referred to as monopoly ownership—drew increasing concern and criticism throughout the country as the number of cities in which it existed continued to increase. There was, certainly, an added responsibility on these owners, and the Block family wrestled with the problem over a period of many years.

Some more or less immediate advantages accrued to *The Blade* from its absorption of the *News-Bee.* Circulation, which had fallen to 123,380 in 1933, increased to 153,300 by 1939. Advertising linage increased in the same period from 7,500,000 to 10,500,000. As in most such situations, some of the loyal adherents of the *News-Bee* continued to express regret—even, in some instances, bitterness.[26] Economic conditions at the time prevented immediate expansion of the staff and content of *The Blade,* but over a period of years such improvements did become possible, and further enhanced the newspaper's quality.

★ ★ ★

Paul Block and *The Blade* never really were reconciled with Franklin D. Roosevelt. Developments in Europe and the threat of war on a world scale did bring them closer together in the last years of the two men's lives.

Unlike Hearst or Colonel Robert R. McCormick of the Chicago *Tribune,* Paul Block was not an all-out isolationist. Despite concealing his German birth, he had bonds with the German people that often were revealed, as in this signed editorial published in February, 1940:

> ... Let us hope that before the New Year is very old, the German people will rid themselves of this irresponsible leadership. Only when this is done, when the corrupt oppressors of small nations and enemies of liberty have been repudiated by the great mass of honest, sincere and human Germans can the world find peace. May the reawakening of Germany be soon in coming.

PB had great admiration for the British people. When he returned to Europe in 1937, spending some time in London, he visited his friend Lord Beaverbrook, whom he particularly revered. He came back to the United States with a strong conviction that Great Britain must be sustained by the United States in whatever emergency might arise, though he remained hopeful that war would be avoided.

From the start of the European conflict, Paul Block accepted the proposition that the United States must help the Allies in every way possible, but he long specified that this must be "short of joining in the war." Even in the 1940 presidential election, when he strongly opposed a third term for President Roosevelt, he made it clear that the basis of his opposition had nothing to do with U.S. policy in Europe. He wrote, in May, 1940: ". . . there is another task equally vital to our nation as aid to the Allies and that is domestic recovery. It is this which Mr. Roosevelt has shown himself unable to achieve."

A year later, in the last few weeks of his life, the publisher of *The Blade* moved gradually closer to favoring the United States' direct involvement in the fighting, should that be necessary to turn back the Nazi threat. This was at a time when, according to Herman Liebert, the publisher's long-time editorial and speech writer, Paul Block was sometimes irrational, dictating editorial material to

The End of a Century 263

Liebert that was sheer gibberish. That he remained capable of clear thought on some occasions, at least, is indicated by his revising his thinking as the threat to the Allies from Hitler's Germany worsened.

In a signed front-page editorial early in March, Block had urged readers of *The Blade* to write or wire Ohio's U.S. senators, "urging them to keep us out of this war" by insisting on amendments to the lend-lease bill being debated in the Senate:

> It is in the deepest sense unfortunate that Mr. Roosevelt's administration has demanded such a bill under the excuse that all the extraordinary power which it grants is necessary in order that we may help England effectively. The fact is that no such grant of power is necessary for us to help Great Britain.
> ... American public opinion is just as dead set against our entering the war as it is in favor of our helping England. Why, then, run the additional risk of becoming entangled, so long as we can help the British without definite involvement?

Then, on April 16, *The Blade* carried this front-page editorial, signed by its publisher:

> Five weeks ago when the Senate was debating the lend-lease bill, we strongly but fairly urged that the bill be modified.
> Today we are convinced that such a measure was needed to assure those people of the countries conquered by the Nazis and those still fighting that we in America were with them in their determination that democracy should not perish.
> We have changed our mind because the situation has materially changed ...
> It is time for the people to face the facts which we cannot escape. England needs our arms to win and under the lend-lease act we have promised them to her. But she herself cannot protect the ships carrying these arms from the menace of Nazi submarines and raiders. It is therefore up to us to do so.

Ten days later, in one of his last signed editorials, Block called attention to the fact that Secretary of the Navy Frank Knox, speaking on April 24 to the American Newspaper Publishers Association in New York, had taken the position that "this was plainly our war and that we should do everything necessary to assure an English victory." This, he pointed out with satisfaction, was "in perfect accord with our editorial of the previous week," making it clear that "the war is now England's and America's war."

Paul Block contributed much to *The Blade* in addition to his signed editorials. Although he was in Toledo only for relatively brief periods of time, he was far from the typical absentee owner-publisher who had little interest except for the profit and loss statement. He bombarded editorial executives with ideas for improving the newspaper. Grove Patterson summed up the publisher's attitude toward *The Blade* in *I Like People:*

> I learned that he was mainly interested in one thing — the best possible newspaper that the best available staff could produce, whatever the cost . . . In all the years I was associated with him, he did not once suggest that the editorial department might be run for less money. I have an idea that this comes close to being a unique experience for an editor.

PB liked to experiment with new ideas — some that worked, others that didn't. He came back from his 1937 visit to London determined to introduce into his newspapers some of the things he admired most in the London *Express,* which was owned by Lord Beaverbrook. Short headlines and brief stories were tried out later that year. The response was wholly negative and these were soon discarded.

Another of his ideas, however, has had lasting success and is thoroughly familiar to today's readers. He believed that a newspaper should include a separate section devoted entirely to light material, which would then be minimized in other sections of the paper. First tried in the Newark *Star-Eagle,* it became the basis of *The Blade's* popular Peach Section.

★ ★ ★

When he died on June 21, 1941, at his home in the Waldorf-Astoria Towers apartments in New York, Paul Block was sixty-six years old. He had been publisher of *The Blade* for almost fifteen years.

His funeral services two days later at Temple Emanu-El in New York were attended by Herbert Hoover, Alfred E. Smith, James Farley, Frank Knox, William Randolph Hearst, and many leading newspaper executives and editors. Grove Patterson, who, in his words, was asked to "preach the sermon," recalls that these distinguished men occupied the front rows of the temple. But, he adds, "I was most impressed by the presence of hundreds of 'the little people,' the humble men and women to whom Paul Block had been kind, the people whom he had found occasion to help in ways of which the public would never know."

A tribute in *The Blade* of June 23, which was probably written by Patterson, cites his generosity to civic, charitable and educational institutions, then adds:

The End of a Century

Many of his benefactions were secret. The only record of these gifts is to be found in a scrapbook which he kept in his library. In it are letters from all classes of people — cardinals, bishops, financiers, widows of policemen and firemen killed on duty, the sick, the lame and aged — all acknowledging gratitude for some kind act.

Paul Block's major philanthropies were many, including the chapel at Hotchkiss School, Lakeville, Connecticut, which both of his sons attended, an endowment of the Paul Block Foundation at Yale University in 1930, providing a public lecture course to trace the relation of the newspaper to contemporary affairs, as well as substantial grants to both the Central and Indiana Avenue YMCAs in Toledo. In his will, he also remembered the red cap porters and gate men at the Toledo Union Station, among whom $500 was to be distributed.

The inscription on a memorial plaque in one of the visitors' lounges of St. Vincent hospital in Toledo is a particularly appropriate tribute. It reads:

IN MEMORY OF
PAUL BLOCK
1874-1941

"Always it was the faint cry of the humblest in distress which caught his ear and touched his heart."

Chapter 28

A Difficult Transition

That Paul Block's illness was terminal had been known for about three months before his death on June 21, 1941, and some steps had been taken to facilitate the transition that would have to be made. The change could hardly have come at a more difficult time.

Paul Block had been dominant in the affairs of his various holdings. He was the only shareholder of the Toledo Blade Company and owned most of the stock in Paul Block and Associates and the Pittsburgh Post-Gazette. Block's will bequeathed equal shares of stock in the companies to his sons, Paul Block, Jr. and William Block. The remainder and his personal effects went to his wife, Dina W. Block. She and her sons joined the companies' board of directors.

There were capable and devoted subordinates in both New York and Toledo. Block's long-time associate, Daniel Nicoll, became the key figure in the New York operations of the newspapers. A native of New York, Nicoll began working at the age of twelve, as office boy for the publisher of the New York *Evening Mail,* and went on to be circulation director, advertising manager, business manager and, finally, publisher of that newspaper. After the *Evening Mail* had been sold to Frank Munsey, he became a partner in the firm of Gilman and Nicoll, newspaper advertising representatives. Then, in September, 1926, Paul Block asked him to join his firm, and "Uncle Dan" Nicoll jumped at the chance, beginning an association with the Block family that lasted more than thirty-six years. Nicoll, who combined a courtly manner with a lively sense of humor, became a favorite of all those in *The Blade* organization who knew him.

Amos Harnish, who came out of the Pennsylvania Dutch area of Lancaster, where he had been associated with the *New Era* when it was under Block's ownership, remained in New York for many years

A Difficult Transition

before moving to Toledo. He was treasurer of the Toledo Blade Company until his death in 1969. Max Block continued as treasurer of Paul Block and Associates until 1946, and Herbert W. Moloney was named as its president soon after Paul Block's death.

The heirs apparent to Paul Block were, of course, his two sons, who were to become co-publishers of *The Blade* and the Pittsburgh *Post-Gazette*. At the time of their father's death, however, neither was in a position to assume these responsibilities, which made the transition even more difficult.

Both Paul and Bill Block had been given a thorough grounding in newspaper operations by their father. Both had grown up in New York City, had attended the Hotchkiss School in Lakeville, Connecticut, and had been graduated from Yale. Each had worked in all the various departments of *The Blade* after receiving his Yale degree.

Paul Block, Jr., insists that among the various aspects of the newspaper's operations to which he was exposed during this early period, his favorite was stereotyping. "It involved some principles of chemistry" is the reason cited for this preference — a reminder that the older of the two brothers always wanted to be a chemist. Indeed, he is probably the only publisher of an American newspaper today who holds a PhD degree in chemistry, and who maintains his own laboratory adjacent to his home. He is a recognized authority on some types of iodine substances.

Having come to Toledo in 1935, he remained with *The Blade* until 1939, spending summers in New York, where he studied for the doctoral degree in chemistry at Columbia University. He did a good deal of reporting for *The Blade,* using the name Peter Bly, and he spent some time as Washington correspondent. He went to New York in 1939 to complete his doctoral dissertation and was there at the time of his father's death. His assuming active managership of *The Blade* was further complicated when he was confined to a Massachusetts hospital for seven months with a serious leg fracture suffered in a skiing accident in early 1942.

Bill Block first came to Toledo in 1937 and followed much the same path as his brother in learning *The Blade's* operations. He was away for a few months, then returned to Toledo in 1938, remaining until 1941. The more gregarious and outgoing of the two brothers, he became active in many aspects of the community's life. "For the greatest contribution to community betterment through unselfish public service," he received the 1940 Achievement Award of the Junior Chamber of Commerce. The primary basis for the award was "creation of the Toledo Symphony Orchestra, the fulfillment of an old cultural aspiration never before made tangible for Toledo and its music-loving public." In March, 1941, Bill Block enlisted in the army and was in Officer Candidate School at the time of his father's death.

Four members of the Block family had been elected to the board of directors of the Toledo Blade Company in April, 1940. These were Paul Block's wife, Dina W.; his two sons, and his brother, Max Block. A year later, on April 15, 1941, members of the board re-elected Paul Block as president and publisher. He was present at a directors' meeting at the Block apartment in the Waldorf-Astoria Tower on June 11, only ten days before his death, at which Max Block acted as chairman.

Paul Block and Associates also took action soon after Paul Block's death to make adjustments. It named Herbert W. Moloney as president and elected Paul Block, Jr., William Block and Daniel Nicoll as vice presidents at a meeting on July 7. Two days later, the board of directors of the Toledo Blade Company elected Nicoll as a board member and chose Grove Patterson as its new president.

A tentative Profit and Loss Statement for 1941 reflected a generally healthy picture, with profits for *The Blade* estimated at $685,000. It also revealed losses incident to the sale of Paul Block's country house, Friendship, and other real estate, totalling just under $1,000,000. The other Friendship — the private railroad car — was sold for $10,000, about one-tenth of its original cost.

★ ★ ★

Responsibility for the day-to-day operation of *The Blade* during the years from 1941 to 1944 rested on the shoulders of Grove Patterson as editor and Stanley C. Speer as business manager, with Kenneth D. Tooill as managing editor. Dan Nicoll and Amos Harnish in New York were consultants to the executives in Toledo during this time.

Paul Block, Jr., who had moved back to Toledo in 1942, was appointed to an industrial fellowship on iodine at the Mellon Institute in Pittsburgh on April 1, 1943, and continued his work on that project for most of 1943 and 1944. Bill Block remained in the Army until 1946.

When Paul Block, Jr., returned to Toledo as active publisher in 1944, he made some changes. He fired several people, including

A Difficult Transition

Speer, and he began to bring to *The Blade* some of a group of younger men who were to play important parts in the newspaper's operations for varying periods of time during the next forty years.

It has been observed many times by many people that Paul Block, Jr., would win no popularity contests among readers of *The Blade*, and especially among Toledo's civic leaders. The observation is undoubtedly correct, nor would it too much upset the man of whom it is said. He has not, as has sometimes been alleged, deliberately offended almost everyone in town. Neither has he ever trimmed the sails of *The Blade* to avoid offending a particular group or individual, no matter how influential. In the process, however, Paul Block, Jr., has won for himself and his newspaper the respect of most observers — including many of those who have been offended by his and *The Blade's* positions in particular instances.

When, at the age of thirty-three, Block took over as active publisher of *The Blade,* the importance of making it politically neutral and independent was uppermost in his mind. With the demise of the *News-Bee* in 1938, he insisted, Toledo no longer had a strong Republican voice and a strong Democratic voice. It was therefore incumbent on him to establish news and editorial policies and practices that would be fair to both major parties, without weakening the established tradition of taking strong stands on political issues.

He emphasized the importance of treating the two parties equally, to the point of measuring inches of column space to be sure that each received approximately equal allotment. This policy required some sacrifice of traditional news values, and editors sometimes objected to Block's insistence that they temper those standards for determining how much space and what headline treatment the political stories should be given, and on which page they should appear. Over the years, however, the policy proved to be successful. Whatever grievances political leaders may have had against *The Blade,* they almost never complained that one party was given an advantage over the other in the news columns. Nor was gross distortion of news values required to maintain this policy.

Establishing an independent tradition on the editorial page was understandably more difficult. *The Blade* had been so thoroughly identified with support of Republican candidates and policies over such a long period of time that it would have appeared incongruous to make an overnight change. It had to be done gradually. There was another complication in the fact that Grove Patterson had been an active and prominent leader of the Republican party. His name had been mentioned several times as a likely candidate for his party's nomination as a United States senator or member of the House of Representatives. He had nominated Senator Robert A. Taft for President at the Philadelphia convention in 1940, when Wendell Willkie was the nominee. Although he was not a partisan of the violent sort, his identification with the Republican party was of national proportions.

As it happened, Grove Patterson was eager to remove himself from the daily routine of the editor's job, and in 1946 he was named editor-in-chief, free from all responsibilities except his "Way of the World" column, which had gained a national following. His reputation as a public speaker had become universal, and his value to *The Blade* as a good-will ambassador now far outweighed what he might have accomplished by remaining at his desk as editor. He went to Great Britain in 1943, at the invitation of the British Ministry of Information, to observe how the people were standing up under the heavy German bombing. His column recounted these experiences during and after his visit.

Patterson was succeeded in the editorship by a 43-year-old North Carolinian, Michael Bradshaw, who had joined the editorial page staff as an associate editor in 1945. The holder of B.A. and M.A. degrees from Duke University, Bradshaw had done further graduate work at Harvard and had taught English for five years at the University of Texas. He began his newspaper career at Durham, North Carolina, in 1933, and was subsequently an editorial writer for the Dayton *Herald*. He became its editor in 1943, then moved to the Pittsburgh *Post-Gazette*.

It was Mike Bradshaw who effected the transition from partisanship to independence on the editorial page of *The Blade* and who, in almost fifteen years as editor, gave it a distinctive quality and style. A man who loved the English language, Bradshaw often told members of his editorial writing staff that "it isn't what you say, but the way you say it, that counts." Although he did not mean that content was unimportant, his emphasis was always on effective and persuasive writing.

Over the years since 1944, *The Blade* indeed achieved a remarkable degree of political independence. As has been noted earlier, it was not until 1956 — in the second Eisenhower-Stevenson

A Difficult Transition 271

contest — that *The Blade* endorsed a Democrat for the presidency. Since then, its endorsement went to the Democrat in 1960, 1964, 1972 and 1976 — and to the Republican in 1968, 1980, and 1984. It was after the endorsement of John Kennedy in 1960 that a distressed woman reader called to voice this complaint: "Oh, why can't the Blade go back to being a nice nonpartisan Republican newspaper the way it was when Mr. Patterson was editor!"

More important than the matter of presidential endorsements in the long run, however, has been that *The Blade* has endorsed an almost equal number of Republicans and Democrats for city and county offices. A tradition of independence has been established that is obviously respected by Toledo and Lucas County residents, who repeatedly elect a high percentage of the candidates recommended by *The Blade*.[27]

Has *The Blade* been successful in carrying out the concept of a neutral and independent newspaper which Paul Block, Jr., began when he became its active publisher in 1944? He thinks it has, while adding that "most partisans wouldn't agree; most independents would."

Chapter 29

Toledo Tomorrow—and Beyond

Jesup Scott's dream a century earlier of Toledo as the metropolis of the Western world had not, of course, come true by 1945. But long after the death of that remarkable editor of *The Blade,* the idea of "dreaming the impossible dream" persisted. It emerged — and again under auspices of *The Blade* — on July 4, 1945, when a remarkable exhibit went on display in the auditorium of the Natural History Museum of the Toledo Zoo.

Toledo Tomorrow attracted so much attention and stirred so much excitement that, although it was to have closed on Labor Day, it was kept open until October 15.

Paul Block, Jr., had conceived the idea a year earlier and had commissioned an internationally known designer, Norman Bel Geddes, to produce a 61-foot model of a plan for "a beautiful, efficient city." Block knew of Bel Geddes' work for John Ringling North of the Ringling Bros. Barnum & Bailey Circus. Bel Geddes was a native of nearby Adrian, Michigan, who sometimes told others that he came from Toledo. He was enthusiastic about the commission and set to work on it with the assistance of Major Alexander P. de Seversky, noted expert on aviation, and of Geoffrey Lawford, an architect.

Toledo Tomorrow incorporated many elements that had helped make Norman Bel Geddes' Futurama exhibit at the 1939 World's Fair in New York so popular. The plan included: a central terminal in the heart of the city for air, rail and bus traffic; consolidated freight and marshaling yards; express highways, some of them underground; a business district surrounded by greenbelt parks and residential areas; relocation of heavy industry away from downtown sections.

Toledo Tomorrow—and Beyond 273

The model, built on a scale of one inch to one hundred feet, cost $250,000, all of which was paid by *The Blade.*

Not only were thousands of Toledoans attracted to the Natural History Museum for a look at Toledo Tomorrow, but visitors came from all over the country — indeed from all over the world. A noted Bolivian architect, Jose M. Villivicencio, came to study the plan. A national authority on highways, G. Donald Kennedy, praised Toledo Tomorrow for its treatment of highway problems. An "emissary of the new China" visited and declared that he was thrilled. The Indiana Civic Association sent representatives, who were inspired to envision the Maumee Valley — from Fort Wayne to Toledo — as the "wonder spot of the nation."

Life magazine offered its readers an extensive look at Toledo Tomorrow in a photographic essay titled "Future Toledo — A Prophetic Look at the Wonderful City They Could Have in Fifty Years." The *New Republic,* compared Toledo Tomorrow with plans in Britain to rebuild blitzed cities. "The kind of foresight shown in Toledo Tomorrow," Eleanor Roosevelt told readers of her syndicated column, would inspire other cities to follow Toledo's lead.

The Blade had assumed the cost of creating and presenting Toledo Tomorrow, with its promotion director, LeRoy F. Newmyer, as general manager. Stories about various aspects of the plan appeared from June to September. A Toledo Tomorrow essay competition was sponsored for schoolchildren.

Others joined in enhancing the popularity and reputation of Toledo Tomorrow. Local ministers spoke favorably of the exhibit from their pulpits. Chicago officials came to visit and pronounced themselves vastly impressed. Spokesmen for the Aetna Life Insurance Company outlined the benefits of Toledo Tomorrow to business. And on October 12 — only three days before the exhibit was to be closed — Mayor Lloyd E. Roulet proclaimed Toledo Tomorrow Day.

A visitor to Toledo Tomorrow who seemed to tie together the city's past and its hopes for the future was reported by *The Blade:*

> Like a fresh scented breeze from a glorious yesterday, Mrs. Mable Dunham Locke came from her home in New York City to attend the opening of Toledo Tomorrow. It was a safari of love which distance could not discourage.
>
> . . . The years have not laid a nostalgic hand upon her; her dreams are of the future. Toledo was a great city when she knew it best, but she wants its tomorrow to be much greater.

The woman was Robinson Locke's widow, and her visit symbolically linked the names of the two families who have owned and published *The Blade* for all but the first thirty years of its existence.

The bulky model of Toledo Tomorrow was discarded about ten years after the exhibit closed, when problems of storage and insurance were deemed prohibitive to keeping it.

But there is every reason to believe that its inspiration for Toledo lives on. Paul Block, Jr., has subsequently declared that his purpose in commissioning the Toledo Tomorrow exhibit was "to provide a shot in the arm" that might help motivate action on new civic programs. It was "a stunt," Block has said, that might help stir the public imagination.

Cause-and-effect relations are difficult to prove, but it would appear that Toledo Tomorrow did serve its purpose. As late as November, 1981, at a conference of midwestern cities, Toledo Tomorrow was recalled and given credit for inspiring cities everywhere to dream. On that occasion, *The Blade* urged citizens of Toledo to maintain a vision of their community that is always beyond their grasp.

★ ★ ★

The Blade wasted no time in seeking to follow up on whatever impetus toward civic progress that Toledo Tomorrow had generated. An editorial presentation of THE BLADE'S POLICY on January 2, 1946, outlined the newspaper's positions on national and international affairs, but placed particular emphasis on local issues:

> First and foremost, *The Blade* . . . believes that there is a great deal to be done here during 1946 to make this a more livable, a more prosperous, a more progressive city.
>
> Granted that Toledo Tomorrow was a visionary project so vast in scope that its attainment stretches into the distant future, there are many things to be done at once which can start us on our way. There's a new union station to be built. There's the present airport to be improved and a new one to be established . . . There are those two great superhighways which are going to bisect the city. There is a sound financial program to be devised and adopted . . .

It was on this last problem that *The Blade* moved at once by giving its all-out support to the proposal for a municipal tax of one per cent on all Toledo payrolls and personal incomes. The campaign had already been launched on December 9, 1945, when *The Blade* declared that the tax would be the best cure for the city's financial ills. The Philadelphia plan, which limited the tax to earnings of individuals, not those of corporations, was cited as a model for Toledo.

Municipal income taxes were relatively new in the United States in this post-war period. Only Philadelphia had adopted such a tax, and its benefits had been described in a *Blade* news story on December 6. There was immediate opposition — from organized labor and from suburbs such as Ottawa Hills and Maumee, many of whose residents worked in Toledo but heretofore had paid no taxes to support the many municipal facilities and services of which they made regular use.

Council approved the payroll tax on January 10, 1946, and *The Blade* commended its action, although suggesting that the ordinance needed some changes.

An editorial entitled TOLEDO TODAY pointed out on January 29 that "three great things" had happened to Toledo all at once. One of these was Council's approval of the payroll tax ordinance. Another was the City-County Planning Commission's release of a study recommending that a new airport be built. The third was the arrival of New York Central officials in Toledo to talk about plans for a new union station. Toledo was snapping out of "old depression debt and old depression ways," the editorial declared. "We are laying foundations for the Toledo of Tomorrow," *The Blade* asserted.

The fight over the payroll income tax was bitter. Refusals to pay the tax, pending a city-wide referendum, led to a special election on April 11.

The income tax was the first of many battles to be fought between *The Blade* and Richard Gosser, then regional director of the UAW-CIO. The CIO Political Action Committee provided the vehicle that Gosser and other labor leaders, including Lawrence Steinberg and Clayton Rusch, used to oppose the tax, and *The Blade* considered this cowardly. Gosser must "stand up like a man," not cry "anti-labor" and be a crybaby, *The Blade* insisted, continuing that he must reveal that he "has lined up with wealthy industrialists in Ottawa Hills" to oppose the payroll tax.

In the final week before the referendum, *The Blade* declared that it "is regrettable that this purely local campaign has been turned into a sort of labor dispute." This became unavoidable, it was suggested, "when PAC got into the act." Two days later, *The Blade* alleged that "PAC is leading a fight which would deny city workers the better wages and working conditions they (the union leaders) rightly think other workers should have."

The Blade wheeled out a favorite weapon on the day before the vote — a front-page editorial, two columns wide and titled GOOSESTEPPING WITH GOSSER, which declared: "Tomorrow the people of Toledo will tell these gents (Gosser, Steinberg and others) that if they want to spend 50 cents or so a week to make this a better city for their wives to live in and their children to grow up in, the PAC can't stop them."

Another editorial, THE LINEUP, appeared on the editorial page the same day. It listed two categories. One —For Toledo— included some thirty organizations supporting the payroll income tax. These ranged from the Toledo League of Women Voters, through the Toledo Central Labor Union, A.F. of L. and the Small Business Men's Association, to the 14th Ward Old Timers Baseball Association. The other category — "Agin" Everything — included only "Messrs. Gosser, Steinberg and Rusch," with a footnote declaring that "they report the PAC is against the payroll income tax, too, but the PAC hasn't held a referendum yet."

More than 75,000 Toledoans went to the polls on April 11. The outcome was close, but the tax was approved by a margin of 5,000 votes. "Never before have so many citizens fought so hard to pay a tax," *The Blade* observed. There was praise for many individuals, as well as the voting public. As for *The Blade,* it declared itself to be "still pro-labor, pro-industry, pro-anything that will make Toledo a better city."

Payroll income tax collections passed the half-million-dollar mark before the end of the first quarter. Suddenly a city that ten years earlier had been almost bankrupt found itself with ample funds to balance its budget, to improve its public services, and to make plans for projects of several kinds. Legal tests of the tax would continue until May, 1950, when the Ohio Supreme Court finally handed down the definitive ruling. For *The Blade,* it was a famous victory.

★ ★ ★

Stories about Toledo's ancient union station abounded for many years. One, which happened to be true, was that when the station caught fire in 1930, citizens assembled and booed the firemen who were extinguishing the blaze.

The Blade had been campaigning for a new union station for

Toledo Tomorrow—and Beyond

Toledo at least as early as July, 1941, but the Chamber of Commerce had begun such a drive in 1914. In December, 1943, the Chamber filed suit against five railroads serving Toledo to compel them to erect a union station to replace the one built in 1886. *The Blade* the next day gave its approval to the Chamber's action, declaring that "this is a fight in which everyone must join" — including service clubs, American Legion posts, the League of Women Voters, and others.

Joe E. Brown, the comedian who was one of Toledo's famous sons, jibed at his hometown's union station on his radio program in March, 1944. In August, *The Blade* printed a picture of a billboard that had been erected near the ancient structure. It read:

DON'T JUDGE TOLEDO
by its
UNION STATION

In November, a state public utilities inspector labeled the building a "real menace."

The Blade carried on a continuing editorial campaign throughout 1944, citing evidence of the need for a new station. There was no question of the New York Central's financial ability to provide an adequate structure, one editorial declared. Another proclaimed the inadequacy of a proposal by the railroad company to do a face-lift on the old station by providing an overhead concourse. "It is time New York Central joined in good faith with local organizations to do something important, serious, lasting," a June 22 editorial insisted.

The campaign came to fruition in 1947. William Levis, chairman of Owens Illinois, was on the board of New York Central and helped persuade the railroad to build the new station. Work began on a structure that was dedicated in September, 1950. A week-long celebration was organized by a committee consisting of Paul Block Jr. and civic leaders Milton Knight and Harlan Hobbs. Ted Mack of the Original Amateur Hour was there; so were the U.S. second army band and scores of barbershop quartets. Cy Hungerford, whose political cartoons appeared regularly in *The Blade* for many years, came over from Pittsburgh and did cartoon portraits of the notables on hand for the closing day's festivities on Saturday, September 22, including Admiral Chester W. Nimitz. There was a grand parade that day, and a beauty contest to choose Miss Union Station. Mitch Woodbury, for many years *The Blade's* entertainment editor, arranged for the appearance of a dazzling array of Hollywood stars in a stage show at 5 p.m. and 8 p.m. The show's cast included another famous Toledoan, Danny Thomas, along with four of the stars of the motion picture "Union Station": George Murphy, William Holden, Mitzi Gaynor and Marta Toren. The movie premiered in Toledo that week.

The Toledo Museum of Art sponsored a special exhibit honoring the new union station, featuring old prints and paintings in the history of transportation, including a number of Currier & Ives prints of railroads that were reproduced in *The Blade* on Sunday, September 17.

Harry Roberts was in charge of these celebration arrangements. A 35-year-old native of Pittsburgh, he had come to *The Blade* two years earlier from the Pittsburgh *Post-Gazette* to join the promotion staff. Imaginative and thoughtful, Harry Roberts was an idea man. He would move later to the news side of *The Blade* and become its executive editor for some years before his death in 1969.

Roberts' contributions to *The Blade* in twenty years were many. A. G. Trimble, a Pittsburgh novelty manufacturer, even credited him with originating the slogan "I Like Ike." He did, in any case, bring both depth and brightness to the pages of *The Blade,* along with an enthusiasm that was well illustrated in the union station celebration.

The Blade summed up its own reactions to that occasion in this editorial comment:

> Strangers may wonder why so much hullabaloo. Now there's a new symbol of what can be done to build a greater Toledo.
> Now we can *see* that all we have to do is to rid ourselves of stodgy actions and "get up" and do the big things.

It is easy enough to understand *The Blade's* satisfaction. Unfortunately, rail passenger transportation declined soon afterward, and the handsome building has become mostly a monument to a time when dozens of passenger trains stopped in Toledo daily.

★ ★ ★

Even more problems stood in the way of a new airport, and *The Blade* was for many years in the thick of the fight. Not until October 31, 1954, was the new facility dedicated and in operation.

The Blade's campaign was initiated with a series of editorials in October, 1943. The first of these pointed out that the municipal airport, situated in Wood county, was inadequate for anticipated postwar needs. A second editorial, entitled TOLEDO MUST BE TOPS IN POSTWAR AIR SERVICE, pointed out that other cities of comparable size, and some even smaller, were "ahead of us in airport facilities." Kansas City, Omaha and Des Moines were cited as examples. A third editorial commended Council for appointing a special committee to explore the airport problem, but contained a sharp reminder that "they must be speedy."

But there was nothing speedy about Toledo's progress toward a new airport at this point. For the next several years, there was much pulling and hauling over the matter of where a new landing field should be situated. *The Blade* took up this problem in 1946, declaring that "too many people are complaining that they don't want the airport near them and too many people on the Planning Commission are listening to them." This comment followed the Commission's choice of a site near Holland, which experts had characterized as "a poor third" of three sites under consideration. The first choice was a site near the Toledo-Maumee border, the second was in South Toledo near what is now Southwyck.

A year later the problem was that the Civil Aviation Authority had refused to recommend funds in its 1948 program for the Toledo airport. "We don't blame them," *The Blade* declared, citing continual waffling about the site. As a result, it was argued, the CAA "thinks they aren't serious."

Problems with the airport continued for seven years, during which *The Blade* was often exasperated. When, in 1951, the Federal Government announced that it had no funds — without which the airport could not be built — *The Blade* found little comfort in the need to "wait until next year." It reluctantly conceded that "we'll have to have Biblical patience."

That patience was further strained when, in May, 1952, Council voted to make a survey of the airport situation. *The Blade* offered a tart comment: "When Council doesn't know what to do, it just orders another survey, as it has just done!" When City Manager Arnold Finch urged in January, 1953, that a start should be made on the airport, even though the financial situation was still shaky, *The Blade* agreed that the city should "take a calculated risk," even though a "fumbling mayor and humdrum Council may again fumble the ball."

AN AIRPORT IN USE was the title of a *Blade* editorial of January 5, 1955. It praised the group of business and industrial leaders, led by William Levis, who had "cut through snarls of various kinds" to make the new facility near Oak Openings Park a reality.

There were still problems, ranging from heavy traffic on the approaches to the airport to getting a liquor license for the restaurant in the terminal. Governor Frank Lausche's policy of limiting the total number of liquor licenses meant that a new one was not available. Virgil Gladieux, operator of the restaurant concession, was forced to buy the license of Walt's, an existing bar, and to pay the premium price of $18,500, as opposed to the $600 charged by the state for a license. The city of Toledo, extremely eager to have a bar at the airport, paid the difference for Gladieux — a situation that did not please *The Blade*.

Despite the problems, it was now true that within ten years after the Toledo Tomorrow exhibit, the city now had its new union station and its new airport. They were not precisely as Norman Bel Geddes had imagined them — parts of a combined transportation terminal near the city center — but Toledo residents were pleased with them. So was *The Blade,* which had at times kept the projects alive almost single-handedly.

Grove Patterson (1881-1956) joined The Blade as news editor in 1910, rose to editor-in-chief, and left a legacy of journalistic excellence, exemplary character, and superlative public relations.

Paul Block (1874-1941) solicited national advertising for The Blade starting in 1908 and bought the newspaper in 1926. He gave his news editors great freedom, expressed strong opinions in editorials, communicated frequently with The Blade's business executives, and pulled The Blade through the Great Depression.

Above, Paul Block (left) and Grove Patterson share a meal. Below, Paul Block and a friend, Mayor Jimmy Walker of New York City, meet Donie Bush, then manager of the Pittsburgh Pirates. The occasion is believed to be the 1927 World Series, which the Pirates lost to the New York Yankees.

Paul Block, Jr., co-publisher of The Blade since 1942, has worked to maintain the quality of the newspaper and to help improve the Toledo area through his interest in projects such as "Toledo Tomorrow," The Port Authority, Medical College of Ohio and the City-County-State Office Building.

Marge Main (above) was a versatile reporter on The Blade in the years following World War II. She later married publisher Paul Block, Jr. and continued her career as director of features and women's news. She died in 1960.

The first board of the Toledo-Lucas County Port Authority, in 1955. Standing, from left, are Jerome Baron, president of Baron Steel Co.; John Hackett, attorney; Philip Gibbs, partner in a public relations firm; Frazier Reams, attorney and former congressman; John Martin, president of Dana Corp.; and Richard Gosser, international vice president of the UAW. Seated, from left, are W.W. Knight, Jr., formerly vice president of Allied Chemical; Paul Block, Jr.; and Arnold Finch, manager of the Toledo Concrete Pipe Co. and a former Toledo city manager.

William Block (above), co-publisher of The Blade since 1942, worked at The Blade in the late 1930s, but has concentrated most of his energies for the past four decades on publishing the Pittsburgh Post-Gazette.

Daniel Nicoll (below), who had been publisher of the New York Evening Mail, spent 36 years working for the Block family starting in 1926. He played an important role in the management of The Blade in the period after the death of Paul Block.

Michael Bradshaw

Harry Roberts

Bernard Judy

James McDonald

Paul Schrader

Edward Fallon

Fernand Auberjonois

Fred Mollenkopf

Donald Wolfe

George Jenks

Ray Bruner

Michael Woods

Courtesy of Toledo-Lucas County Public Library

Jesup W. Scott (1799-1874) was editor of The Blade for just over three years starting in 1844, but left his mark as a civic booster, opponent of slavery, successful land investor, and donor of land to found a university in Toledo.

David Ross Locke (1833-1888), the most powerful political satirist of his time, author of the Nasby letters, became editor, then publisher and owner, of The Toledo Blade and Weekly Blade. He helped the daily Blade grow and saw the Weekly Blade increase its circulation from 2,000 to more than 200,000.

Robinson Locke (1856-1920) trained on The Blade and, after two years as a diplomat in England, took over The Blade from his father in 1885. He quickly strengthened the newspaper's financial position and made significant contributions to the quality of the newspaper and to the community.

Courtesy of Toledo-Lucas County Public Library

The building above, at 150 Summit St., served The Blade from 1841 until 1884. The building below, which stood at the northeast corner of Jefferson Ave. and Superior St., was the home of The Blade from 1884 until 1927.

In 1929, The Blade used a variety of vehicles to deliver papers to stores and to carriers, including motorcycles (above) and trucks (below). Motorcycles were later abandoned, as were the drivers' caps.

The Blade's present building under construction (above) in 1926 and finished (below) in 1927, in Paul Block's first year as publisher. Blade operations eventually expanded beyond these walls, and the neighborhood changed its appearance also.

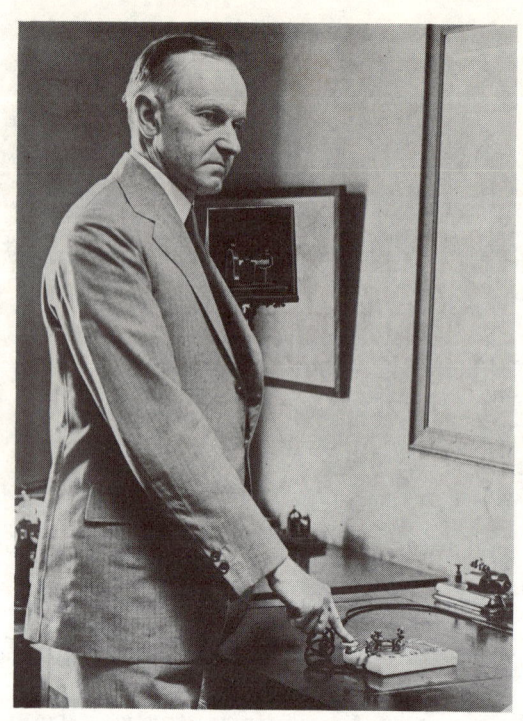

President Calvin Coolidge pressed the gold key in Washington which started the new presses in The Blade's new building in Toledo in May, 1927. The presses he started were numbered one to five, the numbers corresponding to folders (which gather, fold and cut the newspapers). In 1965, press number nine took the place occupied by presses one through five.

Chapter 30

The Blade and Mr. Gosser

It has sometimes seemed that Toledo's onetime reputation as a bad labor town stretched all the way back to the days when Colonel Benjamin Stickney and those other hardy pioneer land agents arrived at the mouth of the Maumee River to begin the development of Port Lawrence and Vistula, later to be merged as Toledo. But the fact is that despite the violent strikes that drew national attention during the depression years, Toledo has contributed some innovative approaches to the easing of labor-management problems.

The Toledo Industrial Peace Board, established in 1935, became a model for a number of cities trying to resolve labor-management differences short of the strike. The plan received considerable attention, including an article in the April, 1938, issue of *Reader's Digest,* but this publicity never quite caught up with the "bad labor town" reputation that had already been established.

The Blade gave strong and enthusiastic support to the Industrial Peace Board Plan from the outset. Edwin F. McGrady, first assistant secretary of labor, had devised it while helping to settle the Chevrolet strike in March, 1935. The plan was announced in June, while McGrady was attempting to find a solution to a walkout at the Toledo Edison Company that threatened to shut down the city. A forum representing the various elements of the community was to be established, and either side in an industrial dispute might bring its grievances to this group. The board was to have no arbitrary power and it would never order anyone to do anything. It would only discuss and advise. Thus, no employer, employee, or union would stand to actually lose anything by coming before the board.

Skepticism among both workers and employers had to be overcome. *The Blade* joined other Toledo newspapers in strong support, and when it became apparent that the panel could not continue on a volunteer basis, *The Blade* asked: "And what does Toledo propose to do about it? Is there any thoughtful, responsible citizen of this community who would vote to let the Toledo Industrial Peace Plan go by the board? We can't believe there is." Then it concluded:

> We say to City Council that this is a fundamental item of expense. It is in the nature of a public necessity . . .
> We urge the people of Toledo to join in putting it squarely up to City Council that it should take action at once to see that a great asset of this community, its industrial peace plan, should not die.

Council responded a few days later by appropriating a total of $5,625 to finance the board's operations until the end of the year. Edmund Ruffin, who had been a reporter for the *News-Bee,* became the first paid director of the Toledo Industrial Peace Board, later known as the Labor-Management-Citizens Committee.

Its successes were numerous. In June, 1942, attention was called to the fact that during that year to date, fourteen threatened strikes had been prevented, and aid had been given in settling thirteen others. *The Blade* observed that "during the six and one-half years the Board has been functioning, 219 controversies have been handled, affecting 43,399 workers, without the loss of a day's work." It concluded proudly that "Toledo's Industrial Peace Board continues to build this city's reputation as a great industrial center with a sound labor policy — a place where war work is being done without costly delays."

A year later, *The Blade* was much concerned by what it perceived as a new threat to labor peace in Toledo — a threat brought on by wartime policies of the Federal Government. When Edmund Ruffin offered his resignation as director of the Peace Board, *The Blade* lamented:

> . . . The federal government agencies have moved in on virtually every phase of the local labor field and there is nothing Mr. Ruffin is permitted to do despite his recognized skill in handling employer-worker nettles.
> . . . Toledo's Industrial Peace Board has a fair, sound and workable policy in industrial relations. The record of the present Administration is one of lamentable lack of policy in labor matters, operating mostly by political expedience. If the peace board here actually becomes a casualty of federal bureaucracy the loss will be great both from the standpoint of sound government and good economics.

The Blade and Mr. Gosser 283

Over the years, *The Blade* had built a reputation of fair treatment of the American working man. David Ross Locke had been one of the first newspaper owners and publishers to defend — even to promote — the right of laborers to organize into unions. The attitude of succeeding publishers and editors had not always been as sympathetic to labor as was Locke's, but *The Blade* had at no time joined the considerable numbers of American newspapers which fought all unions tooth and nail, attributing most of the nation's ills to labor leaders and vowing to do whatever might be necessary to prevent unionization of their own news and mechanical operations. Even in the period of the often violent strikes of the depression, neither Paul Block nor Grove Patterson had assailed labor, though sit-down strikes were criticized as violations of property rights.

Paul Block, Jr., did not want to tarnish *The Blade's* reputation for fair treatment of labor unions and their spokesmen. He had, in fact, been sympathetic with the establishment of the American Newspaper Guild unit at *The Blade* during the apprenticeship he served in the 1930s. Not long after he assumed the responsibilities of co-publisher, however, he began to be concerned about some aspects of the labor situation in Toledo. Much of his concern centered on the UAW-CIO, which was growing more powerful, and on Richard Gosser, who had moved from Detroit to Toledo to become the city's most powerful union official.

The first overt manifestation of this concern had come in the battle over the Toledo payroll income tax. Dick Gosser, *The Blade* asserted, was arrogant, he used faulty reasoning, and "he doesn't understand that improvements cost money." It was alleged that he was attempting to impose his judgment on union members who "could see no reason why they should give up the right to think for themselves just because they joined a union."

The Blade was pleased, of course, that Toledo voters had approved the tax and thus, by implication, had rebuked Dick Gosser and the other labor leaders who had fought against the tax. It suggested that the labor vote in Toledo could not be delivered by one man, or any group of men, against what *The Blade* believed to be the best interests of all Toledo residents.

Close surveillance was kept on Mr. Gosser and his activities, despite the setback he had apparently received. That was just as well, for Gosser was not a man to fall back and nurse his wounds. Two years later, in 1948, there was a national election in which Thomas

E. Dewey was expected to obliterate Harry S. Truman, and Dick Gosser took aim at a political target closer to home. The man in his sights was Homer Ramey, the Republican candidate for re-election to Congress from the Ninth Ohio district. Ramey was an affable, conservative fellow who did little to distinguish himself in Washington except to provide an occasional bit of comic relief. He seemed to be something of a fixture, but Gosser decided to try to beat him. The Democratic candidate was a very good friend of Dick Gosser's — Thomas Burke, another labor union official.

The prospect of Gosser's putting Tom Burke into Congress disturbed *The Blade,* even though it had few illusions about the calibre of the Republican incumbent. "Neither a company boss nor a union leader can tell workers how to vote," *The Blade* inveighed. More than that, if Burke were elected — a prospect described as highly unlikely — he would "be only a Charlie McCarthy for Gosser," which would not do. Burke was elected to Congress in 1948, despite these dire warnings, only to be defeated for re-election two years later by another Democrat, Frazier Reams, who ran as an independent.

★ ★ ★

The real Blade-Gosser ruckus began the next year with demands that union members be permitted to examine the books of a subsidiary agency of Local 12, UAW-CIO — the Automotive Workers Building Corporation. Before the battle was over, *The Blade* had become involved in three legal actions — as defendant in two libel suits and as financial backer of the plaintiff in a suit seeking access to the AWBC's books.

Also involved was Gosser's demand for an area-wide pension plan that would cover workers in all plants where the UAW-CIO held bargaining rights. To combat this program, a group of industrialists formed the Committee to Protect Toledo Payrolls. *The Blade* took no active part in this campaign, but was highly critical of Gosser's "fantastic area pension plan" in the course of demanding that the AWBC's books be opened to union member John W. Bolman. A front-page editorial — THE BLADE AND MR. BOLMAN — was devoted to defending this involvement. There were three ways, it was contended, in which "this newspaper has sought to discharge its proper responsibility to the community." These were:

> Its obligation to a humble citizen, an ordinary workingman, who felt he had a legitimate grievance and no way of obtaining redress.

The Blade and Mr. Gosser

... The great obligation of a newspaper to keep the public fully informed about public affairs.

... Finally, the obligation of a newspaper to serve and safeguard the best interests of its community.

From these general areas of responsibility, *The Blade* went on to make specific applications to its involvement in the Bolman suit:

> At just about the time that Mr. Bolman was bringing his charges against Mr. Gosser, Mr. Gosser was hurling his area-wide pension scheme at our industries to threaten Toledo with economic disaster. Mr. Bolman insists that there is no connection between the two and we are prepared to believe him. Certainly *The Blade* would have come as readily to his assistance without this added reason.
>
> Nonetheless, there is an unavoidable relationship, however unintentional, between the charges brought against Mr. Gosser and Local 12 officials and that pension scheme which they attempted to ram down the throat of this industrial community. This domineering labor leader was seeking greater control over the lives of our people, over the welfare of the city, and the more important he became as a public figure, the more important it was for the people of Toledo to know if he had committed financial irregularities in the management of his union.

The Blade outpointed Dick Gosser in all of the various contests in which they were engaged at the time. The area pension plan never got off the ground, although, of course, most industries were in the process of providing such benefits for their employees. Both of the libel suits were dismissed. And the courts upheld John Bolman's right to examine the books of the Automotive Workers Building Corporation.

The decision in the latter case required that a sportsmen's club in Michigan, which had been secured and maintained for a few UAW-CIO officers by way of some real estate dealings transacted surreptitiously by AWBC, must be deeded over to the Willys-Overland unit of Local 12. It also specified that the bookkeeping system of AWBC must be changed so that financial records were clear. A *Blade* editorial on November, 11, 1951, proclaimed the decision A VICTORY FOR LOCAL 12 and went on to list other beneficial results of the decision in Bolman's favor. These included:

• Gosser had given up the presidency of AWBC.

• Gosser had discontinued his hush-hush handling of financial affairs.

• Gosser had been forced to concede that "he can't run his union without regard for the laws of Ohio in defiance of the courts."

Complete as *The Blade's* victory over Dick Gosser had been in this series of contests, there were continuing fears that Toledo's reputation for bad labor relations might handicap attempts to achieve industrial growth in the 1950s. Prospects pointed toward an ongoing bitter and divisive rivalry between Gosser and Paul Block, Jr. Certainly few would have believed that, in little more than two years, the two would be allies in a number of causes and that *The Blade* would heap praise on Mr. Gosser — even to the point of defending him when, a decade later, he was sent to prison for three years.

Chapter 31

Years of Growth and Change

The decade after Paul Block, Jr., became active co-publisher of *The Blade* was a lively period of change and expansion on many fronts. There were changes in the structure of the parent Toledo Blade Company. There were changes in personnel. There was substantial growth in both circulation and advertising linage. These were good years for *The Blade* — years in which, according to some expert observers, the newspaper established a place among the most respected in the nation.[28]

Advertising and circulation figures speak for themselves. Total advertising linage in 1943 had been just over 11,000,000; by 1955 it had tripled, standing at over 33,000,000. Total daily circulation in 1943 had been 167,284; by 1955 it had increased to more than 191,000. In addition, there were now another 172,853 subscribers — readers of *The Blade's* new Sunday edition.

Many times there had been talk about the desirability of a Sunday edition of *The Blade*. There had been hesitancy for many years because the Block-owned *Times* had long published a Sunday paper, which would necessarily be discontinued if *The Blade* moved into Sunday operation. Finally, Paul Block, Jr., decided that the time had come to make the change. It was done in 1948, with Walter Graham as Sunday editor. Graham, who had been associated with the Des Moines Sunday *Register* — one of the most successful operations in the country — took charge of a staff that was at first largely made up of the people who had produced the Sunday *Times*. The first Sunday edition of *The Blade* appeared on August 1, 1948.

There had been, meantime, some changes in the corporate structure of the holdings of the Paul Block estate. In September, 1946, the several holding companies that had been formed during the senior Block's lifetime to deal with various aspects of his affairs, were combined as Paul Block, Inc. In December, carrying out a wish he had expressed before his death, the advertising-representatives firm of Paul Block and Associates was sold to its employees and executives, and it took the name of Moloney, Regan and Schmitt. Now the Toledo Blade Company became the parent firm of the Block newspapers — *The Blade,* the Toledo *Times* and the Pittsburgh *Post-Gazette.* The company maintained a New York office, under Dan Nicoll's supervision, but Toledo became the official headquarters.

The Toledo Blade Company was also involved during this period with a federal tax suit growing out of arrangements made at the time of the purchase of the Toledo *News-Bee* in 1938. The case involved deficiencies for the years 1938 to 1942, aggregating $401,393.61.

The Blade had purchased the name, circulation and other intangible assets of the *News-Bee* for $100,000, but did not acquire the *News-Bee's* plant. Two issues were involved in the tax suit. One arose from the deduction of interest on debentures issued by the Toledo Blade Company and held by Paul Block and Associates. The other had to do with the company's claim for amortization deductions amounting to $32,500 for 1938 and $78,000 for each of the years 1939 through 1942 on the cost of the covenant not to compete entered into by the *News-Bee.* While these issues covered only the years 1938 to 1942, the ultimate decision would determine the amount of deficiencies for subsequent years during the life of the contract.

The Toledo Blade Tax Case, as it became widely known, was heard in the United States Tax Court in Cleveland in 1947. The court decided in *The Blade's* favor in the matter of debenture interest, but — by a five to four vote — allowed no deduction for amortization of the covenant not to compete. The latter finding was appealed to the U.S. Circuit Court in Cincinnati, which sustained the Tax Court. A final appeal was taken to the U.S. Supreme Court which, on October 10, 1950, denied a hearing.

Increasing circulation and advertising linage brought other changes to *The Blade,* including installation of a new 8-unit high-speed press. The new equipment, capable of printing between 38,000 and 40,000 newspapers an hour, began operation at 11:32 a.m. on April 7, 1952. Donald Schelling, president of Local 27, International

Years of Growth and Change 289

Pressman's Union, pressed the button that started the new presses rolling.

★ ★ ★

The marriage of Paul Block, Jr., and Marjorie McNab Main took place on May 27, 1948, in Hollywood. It was an event of considerable importance to *The Blade.* For, until her death in 1960, Mrs. Block played an active and influential part in many aspects of the newspaper's operations.

Marge Main was a native of Cleveland and a graduate of Kent State University. She had been a reporter on the Akron *Beacon-Journal* for two years before coming to Toledo in 1943 to join the *Times* as police reporter — a job traditionally reserved for men, but opened up to women because of the war's demands for manpower. Two years later she moved to *The Blade* as general assignment reporter. She also wrote features and, for a time, covered City Hall.

After her marriage, Marge Block's impact on *The Blade* extended in several different directions, but her top priority was expanding the scope of the pages traditionally identified as those for women to widen coverage of all the things with which American women were involved in the post-war period. *The Blade* became, as a result, one of the first among American newspapers to turn away from the notion that the women's pages should be devoted almost entirely to news of engagements, weddings and occasional domestic hints. Marge Block was an avid reader of women's magazines and she brought to *The Blade* their concepts of larger photographs and better layout. A "fund of ideas" is the way she has been described by her brother-in-law, Bill Block. She put many of these ideas into practice.

Using the by-line "Marge," Mrs. Block wrote extensively for *The Blade.* From 1948 to 1960, she traveled widely, often accompanying her husband to Europe, where she ventured into out-of-the-way places and sought unusual personalities to write about. She was one of the several members of the group (which included Grove Patterson) who covered the coronation of Queen Elizabeth II of England in 1953. In 1954, she was elected to the board of directors of the Toledo Blade Company and was named director of features and women's news.

Other additions to *Blade* personnel during these early years of Paul Block, Jr.'s career as co-publisher continued to play important roles. Two of these were John D. Willey, who retired as president of the Toledo Blade Company and associate publisher of *The Blade* in 1981, and Bernard Judy, who became editor of *The Blade* in 1973. In October, 1984, Mr. Judy was named editor-in-chief, the first to hold this position since the death of Grove Patterson in 1956.

Willey, from the Boston area, had served as secretary to Senator Ralph Flanders in Washington, joined the staff in 1946 as a general assignment reporter and was later assigned to both the Columbus and Washington bureaus. He became city editor in 1952 and was named assistant managing editor two years later. Subsequently he was assistant to the publisher, was treasurer of the Toledo Blade Company, and was its president from 1969 until his retirement. Active in many community and state affairs, Willey was the moving force behind Clear Water, Inc., organized in 1965 to push the cleaning up of the Maumee River basin.

Judy, a native of Pennsylvania, came to *The Blade* in 1948 fresh from the Columbia University graduate school of journalism, where he had received his M.A. degree. He was a staff writer for ten years, covering first business, then labor. He became an editorial writer in 1959 and was named director of the editorial page in 1971. He brought a light touch and a knowledge of local affairs to the page.

In 1948 Don Wolfe moved to *The Blade,* after 11 years with *The Toledo Times,* and he was regional editor, city editor, sports editor, assistant managing editor, and columnist. Wolfe became the best known *Blade* personality since Grove Patterson. He has been a speaker or master of ceremonies at thousands of events, in addition to his service on local boards and the Ohio Governor's Commission on Alcoholism.

★ ★ ★

Paul Schrader, Ed Fallon and, of course, Grove Patterson were key news executives during this period. Each had been associated with the Block newspapers for varying periods previous to 1944.

Schrader, a native of Toledo, went to work for the Toledo *Times* as a police reporter in 1923, after being graduated from the University of Toledo. He was subsequently sports editor, news editor and managing editor of the *Times* before joining *The Blade* as assistant managing editor in 1946. He was made managing editor the next year. Schrader was active in many community organizations and developed a wide acquaintance in the area as a referee of high school and college football games for many years.

Fallon came to *The Blade* in 1940 as a copy editor, after more than twenty years in a variety of positions with New Jersey newspapers, including the Newark *Star-Eagle,* one of the Block newspapers. He became city editor of *The Blade,* later serving as managing editor until his retirement in 1969. Fallon was an active member of the Associated Press Managing Editors Association, serving on its board of directors for three years, and was a president of the Associated Press Society of Ohio.

For Grove Patterson, the period from 1944 until his death in 1956 were golden years. As editor in chief of *The Blade,* he continued to write his "Way of the World" column regularly, to travel extensively, to speak to audiences ranging from small Ohio towns to great international forums. His reputation as a public speaker became so widely recognized that *Life* magazine invited him in 1953 to write an article on the secrets of his success.

He took a particularly active part in the establishment of a sister city relationship with the original Toledo — in Spain.

He was a trustee of the Toledo Museum of Art, a member of the Toledo Public Library Board, and chairman of the board of directors of the American Press Institute at Columbia University. Honorary degrees and accolades of many sorts were conferred on him.

The one among these that probably pleased him most was the designation of one of Toledo's new post-war grade schools as Grove Patterson School, on Cheltenham Road in the Old Orchard area. He was present for the laying of the cornerstone on April 3, 1952, and became one of the two Toledo citizens for whom public schools had been named while they were still living. The other had been Edward Drummond Libbey.

On September 8, 1954, Random House published *I Like People* — an autobiographical memoir in which Grove Patterson recounts his impressions of many of the experiences of his busy and varied life. These ranged from nostalgic memories of his boyhood in the small Illinois town of Carlyle, through his years as a Big Man on Campus (though not a particularly distinguished student) at Oberlin College, and on to the long and distinguished career as a newspaperman — more than forty years of it in association with the Block family. *I Like People* reflects many of the characteristics that have always been associated with him by those who knew its author — a friendly, open attitude toward people and events, a complete absence of pomposity, and a skill as a teller of tales.

When Grove Patterson died on August 7, 1956, *The Blade*

reported that he had been called "Toledo's No. 1 Citizen." Few would have argued with that designation, and his reputation as one of the most influential journalists of his time has grown in the intervening thirty years. Posthumous honors have been many, including designation of the former Northwest Ohio Chapter of Sigma Delta Chi, Society of Professional Journalists, as the Grove Patterson Chapter in 1956, a citation for excellence in journalism by the William Allen White Foundation in 1969, and membership in the Ohio Journalism Hall of Fame in 1980.

The Blade also lost some outstanding personnel during the 1940s. One was among its best-known writers, whose full name was William T. DeWolfe, widely known as "Chub." His "Among the Folks" column had entertained readers of *The Blade* from 1928 until his death on February 9, 1948.

DeWolfe had learned the printer's trade on his father's newspaper, the Fostoria *Review*. In 1901, he walked from Fostoria to Toledo to apply for a job on the *Bee*. He got it, and subsequently worked as a reporter for the *Bee* and as city editor of the Toledo *Press* before moving to *The Blade*.

A small man with a ready smile, DeWolfe became popular with both his fellow journalists and his readers. A fitting tribute is Chub DeWolfe Park, in the island between Beech and Orange streets next to The Blade Building.

★ ★ ★

As Paul Block, Jr.'s first ten years as co-publisher of *The Blade* drew to an end, he and Richard T. Gosser, who had been unable to agree on almost anything for the better part of a decade, suddenly joined hands with other labor leaders and business executives to form the Toledo Industrial Development Council.

TIDC was announced on January 27, 1954. The appointment of William L. Batt, Jr., as executive secretary, with offices on the second floor of the Toledo *Times* building, was announced January 29. TOLEDO PRESENTS A "NEW LOOK" was the headline on a front-page editorial the same day, praising the concept and its participants:

> Behind the organization of the Toledo Industrial Development Council, which formally came into being Wednesday, lie not only months of preparation but an idea which has been tossed about in this city for years.
>
> It is the belief that the segments of a community most interested in seeking new industries and building a bigger city are those which will gain

Years of Growth and Change 293

the greatest economic benefits through its growth — wage earners, retail businesses and public utilities rather than industry itself.

The Blade lauded the heads of TIDC — Richard T. Gosser and Franz Berlacher representing the city's labor unions, Charles Ide of the Toledo Edison Company, and Michael Yamin, president of Lasalle's and the Retail Merchants Association. Another of these leaders, Paul Block, Jr., was not mentioned. Toledo's "new look," The Blade declared, "looks very good." Gosser, Berlacher and other spokesmen for labor pledged to do all they could to counteract whatever remained of Toledo's reputation as a "bad labor town," to eliminate jurisdictional fights, and to seek other ways to improve labor-management relations. The Chamber of Commerce, which had done little in recent years to try to attract new industries, pledged its cooperation with TIDC in this campaign. A Blade editorial the following day proclaimed that Toledo was "on the march."

A good many Toledoans were stunned at this clear evidence of good relations between Dick Gosser and The Blade. It all came about, Paul Block, Jr., has recalled, as a result of their mutual recognition that Toledo had serious need for new industry. Gosser did yeoman service in persuading Toledo's labor union to cooperate in these efforts, according to Block.

Good relations between Gosser and Block continued throughout the remaining years of Gosser's life and the two men became good friends. The Blade lauded Gosser when, in July, 1955, the Willys Diagnostic Clinic was opened. And when, in February, 1963, he was convicted on charges of conspiracy to defraud on charges brought by the Internal Revenue Service, The Blade's editorial comment on the verdict was headlined LAW TRIUMPHS OVER JUSTICE.

The Toledo Industrial Development Council became the Toledo Area Development Council after Paul Block, Jr., retired as its president, calling for action to revitalize the commission.

Block's active role in TIDC had another important significance in terms of The Blade's role in Toledo. This was the first time since becoming co-publisher that he had put aside the role of referee in community affairs and taken an active part in them. Almost immediately after TIDC had come into existence, Block and The Blade became deeply involved in setting up a Port Authority, with Richard Gosser again playing an important part. And other major instances of such participation by Block were to come in the next thirty years.

Chapter 32

Our Man in Europe

I have not attempted to describe scenery, and buildings, and things of that nature at all. That has been done by men and women more capable of such work than I am . . . But I was interested in the men and women of the countries I passed through, and I was interested in their ways of living, their industries, and their customs and habits, and I tried faithfully to put upon paper what I saw.

Thus wrote David Ross Locke on returning in 1881 from his first trip to Europe. He referred to the series of letters he had written to *The Blade,* which were about to be published in book form under the title *Nasby in Exile.* He had established a tradition of interest in and concern with the affairs of the world outside the boundaries of the United States which has been continued since that time.

Robinson Locke, Grove Patterson, Paul Block and others carried on that tradition after David Locke's death in 1888. *The Blade* has never been among those American newspapers — including many of its neighbors in the Midwest — which have urged that the United States should isolate itself from the rest of the world. Its editors and publishers have been interested in people all over the world, in how they lived, their industries, their customs, and their habits.

But not until after the second World War did *The Blade* have its own permanent man in Europe. Paul Block, Jr., who had visited Europe in 1946 and again in 1948, was becoming increasingly convinced that the Associated Press, on which *The Blade* relied for the account it provided its readers, left gaps in the reporting of world news. So he decided to explore the possibilities of establishing a base in London from which *The Blade's* own man could operate.

These explorations culminated in late September, 1953, but the base was in Paris rather than London. The operation began in the

Our Man in Europe

offices of the British news agency, Reuter's, on the Place de la Bourse. *The Blade's* first man in Europe was Blair Bolles, who continued in that capacity for three years. He was succeeded in 1956 by Fernand Auberjonois, who continues to write regularly from London, although officially he retired in 1982. As representatives of the smallest American newspaper to maintain its own man in Europe, these two men have given *The Blade* a unique position and an international reputation.

Bolles, who had been a Yale classmate of Paul Block, Jr., had written on foreign affairs for *The Blade* from Washington and abroad during the five years before he undertook the European assignment. He had been a reporter for the Washington *Star* and director of the Washington Bureau of the Foreign Policy Association, and was widely published in magazines such as *Harper's* and *American Mercury*. He was also the author of several books, including *How to Get Rich in Washington,* widely acclaimed at the time of its publication in 1952.

"The heyday of the newspaper foreign correspondent" is the phrase Bolles uses to describe the time when he arrived in Europe as representative of *The Blade.* Television had not yet become a major purveyor of news from Europe. American and British newspapers were concerned with what went on there in the aftermath of the war so recently concluded. Correspondents from newspapers all over the world were scattered from London to Vienna. Competition among them was fierce, but there was a bond of camaraderie as they covered the big stories, meeting in the best hotels of Paris, London, Berlin, Geneva, Rome and other capitals.

Bolles was in Vienna when Russia abandoned the occupation of eastern Austria, and at the Lancaster House conference in London where the plan for a European Army was dropped and a protocol was signed permitting West Germany to arm. He was in Geneva when President Eisenhower and Nikita Khrushchev met at "the summit."

He also enjoyed events reserved for him alone, which he then shared with *Blade* readers. Bolles interviewed the mayor of Florence in the reception hall that Lorenzo de Medici had used as his government headquarters. "We conversed in French," he recalls, "because I had no Italian and my French was no worse than his." There was a similar interview with the Cardinal Archbishop of Toledo, primate of Spain, who spoke "a sort of French, and I spoke no Spanish."

Bolles recalls that his assignment was exciting: "I had guns aimed at me in Morocco and in Egypt." It was also instructive: "In Angers, France, where Cointreau is made, I learned how to make Orange Curacao — or Cointreau — in the kitchen, with a peeled orange and a large can of alcohol and sugar (my teacher was secretary of the Communist Party in Angers, who was making his own when I called on him to ask his views about the outcome of the parliamentary elections which were in progress)."

Blair Bolles sums up the primary importance of his three years as *The Blade's* first official representative in Europe as having "brought important Europeans and important American officials (civil and military) in Europe to realize that the proprietors of U.S. newspapers are serious about gathering the news and cultivating an informed public . . . It was educational for Europeans, who suffered from a common tendency upon my arrival to think that the U.S.A. is New York City." Bolles, who recently retired as an executive of Colt Industries in Washington, D.C., says "I am glad that I was chosen to be Block's pioneer."

★ ★ ★

When Fernand Auberjonois took over from Bolles in October, 1953, *The Blade's* European operation was moved from Paris to London, where it was housed in the Fleet Street building of Reuter's.

One of the first concerns of Auberjonois (who wrote under the pen name of Fernand Fauber at the outset because *The Blade* deemed it easier for non-French-speaking Americans to pronounce) was whether he could write effectively for an English-speaking readership. Although he was bilingual, most of his writing up to that time had been in French. He was also concerned because he had never lived in the Midwest. Despite these reservations, he agreed to undertake a three-year trial run.

Auberjonois is Swiss-born, the son of Rene Auberjonois, one of Switzerland's best-known artists. He became interested in journalism while he was a geology student in Geneva, covering the League of Nations as a free-lance writer. He came to the United States in 1933 for a month's visit, but stayed on, even though he was unable to get a job as a geologist in the Texas oil industry. For the first four years, he was a news writer and editor on the staff of the Havas News Agency of France in New York. He became an American citizen and went into the U.S. Army during World War II. He was on Gen.

Our Man in Europe

George Patton's staff and sailed with the task force that landed in Morocco in November, 1942. He described the operations for his radio audience, using a transmitter on board the U.S. battleship Texas.

From 1942 to 1945, Auberjonois conducted psychological warfare activities for the U.S. Army in Algeria, Tunisia, Sicily, England, France and Germany, using the printed and broadcast word. He left active service with the rank of major, having been decorated with the Legion of Merit, the Croix de Guerre with three gold stars, and the Polonia Restituta.

On his return to civilian life, he wrote a book, *My Village, USA*, about his life in rural America. He was publishing director of *Time* and *Life* in Paris in 1946 and 1947, then resumed his activities with NBC and the State Department's International Broadcasting Division.

Auberjonois discovered soon after he had begun to report from abroad that his worries about writing in English had been excessive. "I forgot about dictionaries," he recalls, "and discovered that the big challenge in this sort of journalism is the subject matter. What does interest an audience in a place like Toledo . . . on a specific day, and how much does the reader want to know?"

Given complete freedom to choose his subjects, *The Blade's* man in Europe soon discovered that "the lone correspondent, the only representative of his paper abroad, must, like the one-man band, play many instruments." He discovered that such a reporter must "cover not only international politics but cultural events, human interest stories, urban developments, minorities, etc . . . He cannot specialize. Yet when it comes to reflecting European opinions he should make sure that he does not limit himself to government-inspired views."

It is on the basis of this combination of versatility and independence that Auberjonois has built his reputation as a correspondent over the years — a reputation of excellence that is attested to by his fellow journalists in Europe, as well as many readers of *The Blade*. Here he reminisces about some of the highlights of those years:

> I was in Berlin the morning the infamous wall went up and took pictures with a minicamera as the East German guards put up the barbed wire and brought the cement blocks. I heard John F. Kennedy shout "Ich

bin ein Berliner" at the town hall in West Berlin. I flew to Algeria on General de Gaulle's first visit there, before the army revolt, and I heard him utter the unforgettable "Je vous ai compris." I remember when Washington condemned de Gaulle for recognizing Red China. I was in Nepal when the Chinese launched a military offensive across the border; I felt quite safe since the operation was taking place in the mountains, seven days' march away.

I have seen quite a number of people killed, innocent and otherwise. I have heard the loud bang of plastic bombs. I don't think violence makes very good writing. There is a certain monotony about killing.

I have flown every conceivable airline, and types of airplanes I did not know had ever existed. I was hit in the head by a beer bottle during turbulence on a Bulgarian plane about to land at Sofia, before we had resumed diplomatic relations with that capital and that country. I was given a visa to go to Albania and was arrested and turned back ten miles inside the border, on my way to Tirana. It was a convenient way for an Albanian Charges d'Affaires to grant me a visa and have it withdrawn a few hours later.

Thanks to my association with *The Blade,* I have been given the opportunity to eat some interesting foods, like snake in China and camel in the Sahara.

I have always been to hot countries in summer and cold ones in winter. I have never seen Moscow without snow. However, I did fall on the ice in Toledo, Spain, and nearly broke my back.

Much of Auberjonois' copy was sent to *The Blade* from his London base, but few overseas correspondents have traveled more widely. In one year, 1960, for example, he covered more than 50,000 miles to provide reports on the rebuilding of Poland and Algeria's birth pangs of independence, and a special report on the border areas of India, Nepal, Afghanistan and Pakistan. He was one of the first — and few — reporters to visit Bulgaria in 1957 after the State Department removed the ban on travel there.

Although there have been exceptions, it was not the headline stories that *The Blade's* man in Europe considered to be his best work. His approach to his assignment is well summarized in a letter he wrote in 1966 to James MacDonald, who had succeeded Michael Bradshaw as editor of *The Blade,* concerning a proposed visit to South Vietnam:

I quite agree with you that the time is not right for coverage of news developments, since really nothing much is happening except in the military field.

But it has occurred to me that if I went there at some stage, I would make it very clear that we are not interested at all in military news or battlefield reporting. The purpose of such an assignment would be to write on one subject only, and that is the people we are trying to save, the South Vietnamese.

I think it is extraordinary that so little should be published about them. We don't know them. The public does not seem interested, and the correspondents who go there . . . only have eyes for the GIs.

It is the kind of reporting discussed here that *Blade* readers came to expect from Fernand Auberjonois — call it "people reporting" for want of a better term. It is not what is generally identified as "human interest" that characterized his reporting, though he is adept at handling the humorous and the unusual. What he tried to do — and with a considerable degree of success — was to give residents of the American heartland a sense of what other people are like — what they think, what they feel, what they strive toward.

His job had its share of frustrations. Like Blair Bolles, Auberjonois had to deal with the problem of his newspaper's size. Of this, he wrote to MacDonald: "The first question asked, everywhere and always, by Vatican or Kremlin or Elysee Palace, is how many papers we sell. This seems the only criterion considered when I request interviews at the top." Although he had a considerable degree of success in overcoming this problem, he says it did not go away altogether.

There were times, too, when he questioned how much interest the residents of Toledo had in what he was reporting. He wrote to MacDonald in 1968, when presidential politics and random violence dominated the scene in America: "My guess is that Europe, as a news source, ceases to be of much interest in an election year, but mainly because of our involvement in Asia. So we all over-covered the Paris Vietnam talks (one of the most ridiculous exercises I have ever witnessed) and were caught unprepared by other news. In fact, I firmly believe Western Europe could go through a major political upheaval and the U.S. would not be too interested."

But always Auberjonois' interest in people and events throughout the world restored his belief in what he was doing, and he continued to provide *The Blade* with exceptional reporting from various parts of the world. Not even his retirement brought an end to that, and his dispatches appeared regularly, except for those periods when he took refuge from the world in his Irish cottage, where he wrote poetry and worked on a biography of his father.

★ ★ ★

The Blade's reputation for providing a window on the world outside the United States is well established. The State Department has long recognized it as one of a half dozen American newspapers which have been most cooperative with various programs intended to promote international understanding. One of these programs brought to *The Blade* a considerable number of newspapermen from countries around the world to spend several weeks getting acquainted with an American city and its newspaper.

Press aides from the embassies of various countries have come to Toledo for shorter periods of time. Jim MacDonald remembers the visit in 1967 of two young men from the Soviet embassy — one of whom sought to promote *The Blade's* using material from Novisty Press, stressing the possibilities for such non-controversial material as Georgian recipes for the food page and reports on cultural topics.

Paul Block, Jr., has encouraged editors and staff members to become acquainted with Europe and the rest of the world in every possible way, sometimes with financial assistance from *The Blade*.

There has been a similar attitude toward Canada, which Block has sometimes described as the nation most poorly covered by the press in the United States. Its proximity to Toledo and the stimulation provided by the development of the St. Lawrence Seaway — with its significant implications for Toledo's port — have undoubtedly been factors in the publisher's interest in Canada and its affairs, but certainly more attention has been given to this neighbor by *The Blade* than by all but a few American newspapers.

★ ★ ★

The Blade has exhibited little of the provincialism that is sometimes represented as the predominant characteristic of the press in America. From the travels of David Ross Locke to the present, it has sought to call its readers' attention to the world outside Toledo and Lucas County. Emphasis is placed on events of worldwide and nationwide significance. It is relatively rare for a local news event to be given prominent display on the front page. Local crime news — the staple of many American newspapers — almost never appears on page one. It is treated circumspectly on whatever page it appears.

The Blade has maintained bureaus in both Washington and Columbus since the turn of the century. Their principal role has been to report matters of special interest to Toledo area residents, while relying on wire service reports for most of the breaking news. The Columbus bureau has almost always been a one-man operation, with two people in Washington who sometimes serve both *The Blade* and the Pittsburgh *Post-Gazette.*

Special writers provide readers of *The Blade* with informed reporting in a number of other areas. Not surprisingly — given the special interests of its publisher — the newspaper has been especially concerned with reporting of science and was among the first to identify a staff member as science editor.

That position has been held since 1971 by Michael Woods, whom Paul Block, Jr., describes as "the best damned science writer in the country." Woods has won many awards for medical reporting from such groups as the Northwest Ohio Heart Association (1972), the American Academy of Family Physicians (1978), and — in the same year — the James T. Grady Award of the American Chemical Society. He was made a fellow of the American Association for the Advancement of Science in 1976.

Woods most recently attracted worldwide attention with an extensive report on the health care system of Soviet Russia, which appeared in *The Blade* of Sunday, June 10, 1984. Many members of Congress praised the report as a source of information that had not previously been available to them. Soviet authorities did not agree with some of Woods' conclusions and were given opportunity to reply in the next day's *Blade.* Oleg Benyukh, head of the information department of the Soviet Union's embassy in Washington, did describe it as "a pretty big article" and added that "some very conscientious work has been put in by somebody."

Predecessor to Woods and a pioneer in science writing was Ray Bruner, who became *The Blade's* science editor in 1953. A self-taught chemist who had held research positions in industry, he wrote about science with knowledge and authority.

"Ray Bruner is unique," the American Chemical Society declared in awarding him its James T. Grady gold medal and a prize of $2,000 in 1968. He was given special recognition in 1968 by the Toledo Dental Society for his part in making fluoridated water a reality in the city. His writing about medical research won special recognition from the National Society of Medical Research in 1969.

Yet another area in which *The Blade* has provided special coverage is religion. Lester Heins, who became religion editor in 1956, had been first a reporter, then a Lutheran minister, before he returned to *The Blade.* A highlight of his career was a 25,000-mile trip to Asia, the Middle East and Africa, which was one aspect of the observance of *The Blade's* 125th anniversary celebration in 1960. One of the most ambitious reportorial assignments in the missionary field since James Gordon Bennett, in 1871, sent Henry M. Stanley into the heart of Africa to find Dr. David Livingstone, it was climaxed by attendance at the third annual general assembly of the World Council of Churches in New Delhi.

Lee Z. Steele became editor of religion news in 1968 and describes her assignment as "the best beat on the paper." In 1970, Mrs. Steele founded her own church, naming it the House of Religion, to demonstrate how easily it can be done. In May, 1980, she received a plaque in recognition of her years of "dedicated and professional service to northwest Ohio religious communities," presented by the board of directors of the area church council.

★ ★ ★

From the time when Robinson Locke — using the pen name of Rodney Lee — achieved a national reputation as a critic and reporter of the theatre, *The Blade* has provided informed coverage of the arts in Toledo. Both David and Robinson Locke played important roles in the encouragement of the visual arts that led to the establishment of the Toledo Museum of Art. William Block, during his residence in Toledo before World War II, received special recognition for his part in founding the predecessor of the Toledo Symphony.

In more recent years, informed coverage of the arts has been provided by reporter-critics such as Aline Jean Treanor and Louise Bruner. Julian Seaman during most of the 1950s stirred considerable resentment with his sometimes vitriolic reviews — especially those of performances by local musicians.

Boris Nelson has been both art and music critic for *The Blade* since 1962. He was also director of fine arts and professor of humanities at the University of Toledo until 1974. A native of Germany, who holds degrees from the universities of Heidelberg and Goettingen, Nelson has served on both the Toledo Arts Commission and the Ohio Arts Council. He has received ASCAP's Deems Taylor Award for writing about music.

And what of the theatre — the special favorite of Robinson Locke? Unfortunately, the traveling companies that once enlivened Toledo's stages have long since stopped coming, and there is little to report or criticize. *The Blade* made one significant gesture in that direction, however, devoting the entire Page One on August 31, 1983, to a reproduction of the front page of *The Blade* of December 26,

1895, when the Valentine Theatre opened, with Joseph Jefferson in the title role of "Rip Van Winkle." This was part of a "Save the Valentine Theatre" campaign against a group of downtown developers' proposal to raze the Renaissance Building in which the Valentine was located. The Valentine survived.

Chapter 33

Adventures in Politics

The Blade was among the first newspapers to recognize that reckless accusations by Senator Joseph R. McCarthy represented a threat to traditional American concepts and values. This position remained unchanged throughout the nearly four years when the senator from Wisconsin terrorized the State Department, the Army, and other branches of government — as well as individuals in many aspects of the national life.

The broadsword was never a favorite weapon of Michael Bradshaw as editor. He much preferred the rapier, and he used it with devastating effect, especially when his target was pompous and pretentious. Joe McCarthy was precisely that.

The light, satiric tone of *The Blade's* thrusts is illustrated in its comment in March, 1950, after the Senate bowed to McCarthy's demands to investigate his charges:

> Plainly enough, Wisconsin's Senator Joseph R. McCarthy is an unhappy man. And that may seem strange, since the Senate investigation of his lurid charges that scores of card-carrying Communists infest the State Department is yielding a bumper crop of newspaper headlines.
>
> Senator McCarthy's unhappiness stems from the fact that his senatorial colleagues have insisted that this be a thorough investigation, have demanded proof of the letter of his charges, have even asked that he produce files containing proof of the allegations at which he hints so darkly.

It was this kind of understatement that characterized *Blade* editorials during Bradshaw's editorship. "Let the reader draw his own conclusion, instead of hitting him over the head with it," Bradshaw advised. This comment on McCarthy in May, 1950, illustrates the technique:

What may be the most succinct comment on the charges which Senator Joseph R. McCarthy has been flinging about so recklessly of late comes from Milwaukee — deep in the heart of the senator's home state of Wisconsin.

In explaining that books written by Owen Lattimore, identified by Senator McCarthy as "Russia's top espionage agent in the United States," have become so immensely popular at the Milwaukee library during the last few weeks, a library official made this observation:

"The same sort of thing happens here whenever they show a movie based on a book we have."

Throughout the next two years, leading up to the 1952 presidential election, *The Blade* continued to carry on its attack against McCarthy and McCarthyism. During the 1952 presidential campaign, the position taken by the Republican candidate, General Dwight D. Eisenhower, in relation to Senator McCarthy, was a matter of particular concern to *The Blade*. Paul Block, Jr., was with the Eisenhower campaign train through the Midwest and he was especially concerned with this relationship. His reports suggest that he felt that Eisenhower had succeeded in positioning himself at a safe distance from McCarthy and that, as President, Ike would see that any problems concerning subversive activity in the government would be dealt with through executive procedures, thus undercutting free-lance activity in this area. He concluded, therefore, that Eisenhower would be a better candidate than Ohio's Sen. Robert A. Taft.

The decision as to which candidate to endorse in the 1952 election became a difficult one as the campaign progressed. Both Block and Bradshaw found the Democratic candidate, Adlai Stevenson of Illinois, increasingly attractive. His wit and his qualities of intellect enhanced his appeal. As *The Blade* put it in its October 17 endorsement editorial:

> The choice this year is not as easy as many people assumed it would be when our political conventions made General Dwight D. Eisenhower the Republican nominee and Governor Adlai Stevenson the Democratic nominee ... As the issues were debated, as the party realignments took place, it became less certain that General Eisenhower would be elected and doubts arose as to which was the better man.

From that beginning, Michael Bradshaw continued with a virtuoso display of another of his favorite editorial writing techniques — one perhaps best described in sports writing terms as the naked reverse. For almost two full columns, the editorial heaped praise on Adlai Stevenson, leading the reader to conclude that *The*

Blade was about to break its century-old tradition of endorsing Republicans for president. Then, in a few short paragraphs, the editorial arrived at this conclusion: "All things considered, then, it seems to us that in making a crucial decision in this critical hour, the American people can best serve the course which this country should take and other nations must follow by electing General Eisenhower as President."

The Blade was never particularly enthusiastic about President Dwight Eisenhower and was often critical of his actions and those of some members of his administration. It did, however, continue to support him against attacks from members of the right wing of his own party, and it came to his defense with great glee and considerable effect in December, 1953, when Joe McCarthy sought to enlist public support for his demands that the President act to shut off American aid to any nation engaged in trade — even on a limited basis — with Communist China. McCarthy demanded that "we refuse to give any American dollars to any nation shipping goods to Communist China so long as a single American remains in a Communist blood-stained dungeon" and urged all Americans who agreed with him to write or wire the President to that effect.

The Blade's response was immediate. Its own request for public expression on the issue appeared on the front page of the same edition that carried the story of McCarthy's appeal for letters and wires to the President. It read:

WE SHOULD *ALL* WRITE THE PRESIDENT
(And All You Have To Do Is Pick Up Your Phone)
It went on to declare:

"Since Senator McCarthy did not ask those who agree with the President to write the President, *The Blade* will make that request.

"Let's *all* write the President!

"*The Blade*, of course, supports President Eisenhower, just as it did in last year's election, and believes that most Republicans do, too. It believes, too, that this is a good time to say so.

"If you want to say that you agree with Senator McCarthy, that's all right, too. We'll forward your message.

"If you still support the President and want to tell him you do, here's how you can.

"*The Blade* wants to send this letter, signed by thousands of us here in northwestern Ohio."

Addressed to President Eisenhower at the White House, the message read: "We supported you before and we do now. We still like

Ike." Telephone numbers to call and other instructions for taking part were given. "Do it, please, before midnight tonight — *but do it,*" the appeal concluded.

The response exceeded the fondest hopes of all involved. The help of twenty-five *Blade* staff members and fourteen special operators at a telephone answering service was required to handle the 10,194 calls that jammed switchboards and trunk lines. Of the callers, 9,870 supported the President, and only 324 backed Senator McCarthy.

In an inter-office memorandum to the staff on December 7, *The Blade's* publisher characterized the project as "a big undertaking" and declared that "the untiring work of all the volunteers made it a fast and thorough newspaper job." He went on to thank all who had helped "from the switchboard operators who were swamped as never before to the volunteers from the circulation, classified, advertising, public relations and editorial departments who recorded the thousands of signatures."

Joe McCarthy was not so well pleased. "It shows how dishonest a paper can get," he declared when asked his opinion of *The Blade's* offer to its readers. He replied that he had said many times that he supported the President, and he still liked Ike. Yet, he insisted, the effect was "that anyone who signed that had to be against McCarthy." Paul Block, Jr., responded that "evidently Senator McCarthy thinks that a newspaper is dishonest if it does not follow his practice of stacking testimony in his favor."

★ ★ ★

In the long run, *The Blade* parted company with Dwight Eisenhower, and although there were several reasons for this disenchantment, the single most important factor was the President's failure to restrain Senator McCarthy and his various imitators. Particularly unpalatable to *The Blade* were Eisenhower's failure to come to the defense of General George C. Marshall and the President's acceptance of the accusations against the distinguished physicist, Dr. J. Robert Oppenheimer. So was the occasion when the President shook the hand of Senator McCarthy in the presence of Paul Block, Jr.

The Blade chose the occasion of Adlai Stevenson's campaign visit to Toledo on October 18, 1956, to break a 120-year-old tradition. "This year our support goes to Adlai Stevenson," it announced in a long front-page editorial, which continued:

Such a drastic change in political preferment calls for explanation, all the more so because four years ago we endorsed President Eisenhower. We said then, however, that of two able men, we thought he was the one best fitted for the Presidency under existing situations. Today, four years later, we say that the situation has been reversed.

The explanation for *The Blade's* change in position was not one of Mike Bradshaw's more scintillating efforts. Sometimes wordy and abstruse, it went on at considerable length to condemn the President for his failures in foreign affairs, failure to support education to meet the Soviet challenge (lately emphasized by reports of superior Russian programs), and for failure to provide the kind of leadership needed at this time. Then it declared: "Yes, we still like Ike, who has won a lasting place in American history and in the affection of his fellow citizens."

The naked reverse of 1952 is almost repeated — this time in the opposite direction — with four paragraphs at the very end of the editorial constituting the entire case for Adlai Stevenson. The argument for a change concludes:

> After four years spent largely in readjustment, it is time that we started looking ahead and going ahead again.
> And in Mr. Stevenson, now leader of the Democratic Party in his own right, we believe the United States would have a President in the liberal tradition who could give this nation and the whole free world the fresh, vigorous leadership we need.

There never was much hope — at *The Blade* or elsewhere — that the immensely popular President Eisenhower would be defeated by Adlai Stevenson, who probably would have been happier as president of a college or university than he ever was in public office. So far as *The Blade* was concerned, the importance of this endorsement had little to do with the candidate and much to do with the direction in which the newspaper was headed.

The Blade now began to be recognized nationally as an independent newspaper, even though it had been exercising a considerable degree of independence in most matters for ten years. It was a kind of political coming of age.

★ ★ ★

Some observers have insisted that the first really significant break with *The Blade's* tradition of endorsing Republicans for the presidency did not come until 1960. The basis of this is that the Stevenson endorsement in 1956 was a kind of token compliment to a man who clearly had no real chance of defeating Eisenhower and was merely an amusing aberration.

It was a different matter four years later when *The Blade,* harking back to its 1956 endorsement, recalled having said that "after four years spent largely in readjustment, it is time that we started looking ahead and going ahead," and then went on to point out that, four years having stretched into eight, "we feel even more strongly about it." What was the answer? "Jack Kennedy . . . will take a fresh look at our society, at our economy, at our national purpose in the light of all the changes fast taking place. And with that, a fresh approach to the problems of this disordered world."

This time, with Kennedy locked in a tight race against the Republican heir apparent, Vice President Richard Nixon, *The Blade's* endorsement of the Democrat was no joke to Toledo Republicans. They resented it and made their feelings known — especially after John F. Kennedy had narrowly squeaked through to victory.

The Blade has been remarkably evenhanded in its six endorsements for president since 1960. Its preference has gone three times to Democrats — Lyndon Johnson in 1964, George McGovern in 1972, Jimmy Carter in 1976 — and three times to Republicans — Richard Nixon in 1968 and Ronald Reagan in 1980 and 1984. Reagan is the first incumbent President in more than fifty years to win *The Blade's* support for re-election.

In every election since 1960 except one, the candidate preferred by *The Blade* has won. The exception was in 1972, when it endorsed the Democratic candidate, Senator George McGovern of South Dakota, although it was generally conceded that President Nixon would be an easy winner. The endorsement editorial is of particular interest because it reflects so much more sensitivity to what was going on in Washington at the time than was to be found in most newspapers:

> It is Mr. Nixon's handling of the Vietnam War that we believe will go down as a black page in the history of this country. For this war could have been brought to an end years ago — but it was not politically expedient to do so. The political timetable called for the war to be over so close to election day that the results of the peace would not have time to embarrass the candidate. And Mr. Nixon, rising to one of his most brilliant manipulations, has created a situation in which on this day, November 3, 1972, no one can be sure whether the war is on or off, whether there has been a sellout and, if so, who has been sold out.

Meanwhile 20,000 American lives have been lost; there have been losses of life and property in Vietnam, both North and South, that stagger the imagination; the world has been subjected to the sight of its strongest power dropping unprecedented hundreds of thousands of tons of bombs on one of its smallest countries.

... But what of at home? ... The stench of corruption, of cynical abuse of power, of arrogant subverting of the political processes that are marks of this Administration has never been more obnoxious than it is today.

It is not that the botched Watergate "caper," for one, is so shocking in itself; what does, or should, shock are the revelations that have emerged since that event: White House aids, surely with the knowledge of the President, crassly shuffling hundreds of thousands of dollars from one secret fund to another, sleazy campaign tactics and total disregard for the ethics of political fund-raising, and endless similarly seamy episodes perpetrated by Nixon operatives.

As has so often been the case in its endorsements, *The Blade* found relatively little to enthuse about in the candidate it chose to endorse. McGovern was "not as strong a candidate as we would like to have seen," but *The Blade* saw in a McGovern-Shriver Administration "far more hope for a return to a decent democratic society in which priorities are right and rights are respected than four more years of Nixon-Agnew."

In the ensuing three presidential elections, *The Blade* has been enthusiastic about its choice in only one — 1980. It backed off considerably in 1984, while still preferring the incumbent to his Democratic opponent, Walter Mondale.

★ ★ ★

The Blade's impact has been greatest in the politics of Toledo, Lucas County, and the Ninth Congressional district. The record for the past three decades reflects a remarkable degree of independence and, with it, imposing evidence that *Blade* endorsements have considerable influence with readers.

A post-election editorial in November, 1984, examined endorsements made since 1952 and found that in that period "we have endorsed candidates for 25 different offices — everything from the presidency of the nation down to the county coroner." In that period *The Blade* had endorsed 228 Republicans for public office, 233 Democrats, and three independents, citing these figures to support the contention that *"The Blade* has compiled a remarkably bipartisan record over the years."

Year in and year out, these endorsements have corresponded so closely to the list of winning candidates that some observers of Toledo and its newspaper have expressed concern that *The Blade* has too much influence on political decisions. In the November, 1984, general election, for example, endorsements were made in twenty-three contests, and the *Blade*-endorsed candidate won in eighteen.

There have been just enough instances of failure among candidates endorsed by *The Blade* to allay these fears. The successes and failures of candidates endorsed are well illustrated in the string of elections to Congress from the Ninth District between 1948 and 1984.

It will be recalled that *The Blade* took strong exception in 1948 to the candidacy for Congress of Thomas Burke, a labor union leader and a Democrat, resulting in the reluctant endorsement of Republican Homer Ramey. Burke won, and when he and Ramey showed up in a rematch in 1950, *The Blade* played an important part in persuading Frazier Reams, also a Democrat, to run as an Independent. With a strong endorsement by *The Blade*, the man who had prosecuted the Licavolis in the 1930s was elected. *The Blade* endorsed Reams for re-election in 1952, praising him as representing Toledo's long-time independent tradition. He was elected to a second term.

Two years later, however, *The Blade's* enthusiasm for that tradition in congressional politics had waned. It conceded that "Mr. Reams has been treated courteously in Congress, enjoys the respect of his colleagues, and has achieved personal recognition." However, "other things being equal . . . an independent is handicapped in Washington." Endorsement went to Thomas Ludlow Ashley, the Democrat, a young attorney not long out of Yale and a member of a family active in Toledo politics from pre-Civil War times. Of "Lud" Ashley, *The Blade* declared:

> What we like most about him, what has finally swung us around to his support, is Mr. Ashley's fresh outlook on so many of our old problems. He isn't chained to the policies of the past, isn't hemmed in by old commitments. We do not believe he would accept a recession as inevitable or would prefer a stalemate in foreign affairs to trying new ways to break it.

Ashley represented the Ninth District for the next thirteen terms — a total of twenty-six years. *The Blade* became somewhat disenchanted with him as a result of numerous personal problems in the early years of his incumbency, but continued to support him and to endorse him at each election until 1962. That year it expressed a preference for the Republican, Martin Janis, who had served one term in the Ohio General Assembly. Janis was described as "a local leader who exemplifies that best in forward-looking Republicanism, a practical humanitarian who finds time to serve local causes effectively." As a parting shot at Ashley, the endorsement declared that "the U.S. House of Representatives is, after all, a place for exercising mature judgment, not a playground for growing up."

The Blade found Ashley preferable to his Republican opponent in each of the next two elections. In 1968, however, it found that "it is time . . . for a change in representation from the Ninth Ohio District," going on to provide a considerably different basis for opposing the incumbent than the one suggested in 1962: "Lud Ashley has acquired a rather lordly manner of dealing with the grass roots. To the plain citizen who shares our apprehension about the war, about crime, about riots and disorder, Mr. Ashley seems downright condescending." Ben Marsh, a Maumee lawyer, was "warmly" endorsed.

After Congressman Ashley won re-election in 1968, *The Blade* endorsed his candidacy in each of the succeeding five elections, though it was not always enthusiastic. Then, in 1980, endorsement went to the Republican, Ed Weber, with this explanation:

> The Blade has supported Mr. Ashley in 11 of his 13 campaigns. We argued in recent years that it would be a mistake to turn out an incumbent just as he reached the peak of his power and influence. We have concluded now, however, that Lud Ashley has been overtaken by events, that the people of this country and this district are longing for a change, for more moderate federal policies, for less government and public regulation, for a halt to unending deficit spending, for an end to throwing billions of tax dollars at any problem that comes along — for the day, in short, when this nation will be sound and secure and satisfied again.
>
> That change will come only with the election of candidates like Mr. Weber. Whether he recognizes it or not, Lud Ashley has become chained to the policies of the past and hemmed in by his old commitment.
>
> *The Blade* endorses Ed Weber to represent the Ninth Congressional District.

Just over a quarter of a century earlier, *The Blade* had first endorsed Ashley because "he isn't chained to the policies of the past." Now it rejected him because he "has become chained to the policies of the past." The circle had been completed, and Weber went to Washington with *The Blade's* blessing.

But in 1982 he lost by a wide margin to his Democratic opponent,

Marcy Kaptur, even though *The Blade* had contended that "Mr. Weber's views in Congress best express those of the district at large." When the liberal young congresswoman ran for re-election in 1984, *The Blade* again opposed her. She defeated Republican Frank Venner by some 25,000 votes.

★ ★ ★

Some observers insist that *The Blade* has become more conservative in its political leanings in recent years, less independent in its endorsements. It is true that especially in contests for national, state and congressional offices, endorsements have tended to go to Republicans.

But, as the newspaper's editor-in-chief, Bernard Judy, sees it, there has been little change in basic political philosophy. Some of the traditional liberal remedies for the nation's problems have fallen from favor. "But," Judy insists, "we are no less interested in finding answers to problems. It's just that we think there's sometimes a need to find different answers."

All this would seem to be summed up in two paragraphs of the November 4 editorial endorsing Ronald Reagan for re-election as President in 1984:

> This nation today has no stomach, we believe, for returning to those decades when the big-spending liberal wing of the Democratic party — of which Mr. Mondale is a prime card-carrying member—applied the standard New Deal treatment of throwing billions and billions of dollars at myriad social and welfare problems, with little or no success.
>
> This is a year that this newspaper, frankly, would not have been averse to endorsing a qualified, imaginative, innovative Democratic candidate for President. But the system that party embraces for nominating candidates has, alas, followed its selection of George McGovern and Jimmy Carter with that uninspiring captive of the special interests — Walter Mondale.

Given the analyses of the 1984 election by many politicians and journalists generally sympathetic to the Democratic party, *The Blade's* position may well be seen to be about where it has always been — somewhere near the middle of the political road and, on the whole, independent of party affiliation.

★ ★ ★

One other aspect of *The Blade's* coverage of politics and elections deserves mention. It is one of the few newspapers in the United States that does not subscribe to any of the various polling services which purport to measure the results of elections in advance.

Explaining the reasons for this policy in an editorial on July 2, 1968, *The Blade* declared:

> ... To top it all, however, professional pollsters always allow themselves 3.2 per cent for "student error." But that 3.2 per cent can be either plus or minus. Thus they give themselves a range of 6.4 per cent, meaning that of two candidates they noted as even in their polls one can wind up with a range of 53.2 per cent to 46.8 per cent for the other.
>
> It is for this reason, as our readers may have noticed, that *The Blade* prefers to have its own Washington correspondents write the stories about what the polls are showing in a presidential election year rather than have figures tossed at them without an adequate explanation of where they came from and how they were taken.

Chapter 34

Past the 125-Year Milestone

The decade of the 1950s was a period of growth and expansion for *The Blade* on all fronts. Along with the increasing advertising linage from 27,000,000 in 1949 to 32,600,000 in 1959, came a rise in the number of readers of the new Sunday edition during the period — from 130,000 to 177,000. Circulation of the daily edition held relatively stable despite the growing impact of television. The installation of new presses during the decade has already been noted, and new equipment was installed in a number of other departments.

Members of the news and editorial staff — many of whom had joined *The Blade* from 1945 to 1950 — became an increasingly closeknit and effective unit. Grove Patterson's death in 1956 was a serious loss, but it was compensated for in part by the effective efforts of this new team of editors.

Toledo's future, too, looked relatively bright. Many of the city's more serious financial problems had been solved with approval of the payroll income tax in 1946, providing funds for better municipal services and for public improvements. The Toledo-Lucas County Port Authority, which *The Blade* had pushed to start, was established in 1955. It created prospects for a dramatic increase in Great Lakes shipping traffic as a result of the St. Lawrence Seaway. Paul Block, Jr., was named chairman of the authority in August, 1955.

The Blade played an important part in both of these developments. The Port Authority was, in fact, the first of three major civic projects in which Paul Block, Jr., was to take an active leadership role in the latter half of the century, leading to allegations that his involvement in municipal affairs has compromised *The Blade's* role of impartial critic or referee. Block agrees to the extent that, he insists, he would prefer to remain on the sidelines rather than become directly involved. But he adds that he has waded into these activities only when it appeared that the absence of leadership was likely to result in failure for important civic goals.

There is no question that *The Blade* has reflected its co-publisher's disenchantment with the leadership vacuum in city government. Dating back to 1946, there had been increasing criticism of city manager government in general, and of a number of individual city managers in particular, on these grounds. City manager government might provide efficiency, *The Blade* has conceded, though even that could be doubted. But manager government, *The Blade* has said, does not generate the kind of leadership that cities like Toledo must have. It encourages caution, rather than imagination, and fails to establish the line of responsibility between voters and their elected officials that is essential to the effective functioning of representative government.

The Blade took the lead in 1949 in abolishing the proportional representation system for electing members of Council. Conceding that it had supported the system when it was adopted, *The Blade* now argued that "it has taken the steam out of municipal government without eliminating political evils."

But *The Blade* believed the needed steam was not restored by the direct election of a nine-member Council, which then chose one of its number to be mayor. More and more, the city manager became the primary target of *The Blade* and, in varying degrees, of the major political party organizations. A proposal to substitute a strong-mayor form of government was placed on the ballot in 1957 and was decisively beaten, by a margin of more than 30,000 votes. Opponents of the city manager system then regrouped and began an all-out effort to overturn this huge majority in 1959, offering an almost identical strong-mayor plan.

The Blade took its place in the forefront of this attempt. Beginning in August — three months before the election — it carried on an extended editorial campaign that intensified as the election approached. The newspaper's part in the contest was considerably heightened by its editor, Michael Bradshaw, being a highly visible participant in the campaigning. Taking time off from his job, he became an active strategist among the strong-mayor forces. The City Manager League, which had gone out of existence some years after it achieved its goal of establishing city manager government for

Toledo, was reconstituted to fight for continuation of the system and to endorse and support candidates for the Council at the same election.

LET'S RUN THE CITY OURSELVES was the title of a front-page editorial on October 25, in which *The Blade* summed up its case:

> City manager government probably works all right in the smaller towns and cities but, as has been amply demonstrated here, it doesn't provide the vigorous leadership an expanding metropolitan community requires.
>
> ... They shout "politics" as though that were a dirty word. And there can be bad politics, of course.
>
> But politics, as Webster defines the term, is "the science and art of government." And so when City Manager Leaguers say that a city is better off without politics, do they really mean that Toledo can get along without any government at all?

The strong-mayor proposal made a far better showing in 1959 than it had two years earlier, but it was beaten again — this time by just over 8,000 votes. *The Blade* had lost, but it found "an ironic twist" in the fact that the election "gives dramatic proof to the major point which *The Blade* tried so hard to make throughout the somewhat hectic campaign." It found that "superficially, the City Manager League won the victory," but that the League had also "lost its political power when five of its handpicked candidates were defeated and five councilmen strongly supported by *The Blade* were elected."

The post-election editorial concluded:

> Thus we find ourselves in the uncomfortable position which we have repeatedly insisted should not exist under democratic government. Instead of looking to the City Manager League to tell them what to do as the last Council did, the new Council might well expect The Blade to give them advice.
>
> We don't believe a newspaper should have such influence in government any more than Lloyd Roulet or Howard Crosby should.[29]

The new Council was further divided by the bitter fight over the strong-mayor proposal, which had cut across party lines. Its members were five Democrats and four Republicans; five strong-mayor advocates and four who had supported city manager government. One consequence was that Council's choice of one of its number to be mayor for the next two years was a particularly messy business, resulting in the election by a 5 to 4 margin of Michael Damas, Democrat and strong-mayorite, over incumbent Democrat John W. Yager, a city manager backer. James B. Simmons, Jr., a

Democrat and city managerite, switched his vote to Damas at the last minute and was then elected vice-mayor.

The Blade didn't like the finagling that obviously had taken place over the mayoral election. Neither did it like the loss — also by a 5 to 4 margin — of a post-election attempt by Council to fire Russell Rink, a city manager whom *The Blade* had found particularly obnoxious.

★ ★ ★

Two events of special significance in the life of *The Blade* occurred in 1960. It changed its name and, toward the end of the year, it began an elaborate observation of the 125th anniversary of its founding.

A number of stories and rumors grew up around the name change, which actually amounted to no more than dropping one word from its previous title. It had been *The Toledo Blade.* Now it became *The Blade.* The action was sudden and was given little public explanation.

What was the reason? According to Paul Block, Jr., he had noticed during a several weeks' stay in Europe during the fall of 1959 that more and more European newspapers did not include the name of the city in their titles. Thus, the Manchester *Guardian* had become *The Guardian.* Most of the London newspapers were similarly identified, and on the European continent this practice was almost universal. For that matter, there were plenty of precedents in the United States — including the *Plain Dealer* in Cleveland and the *Sun* in Baltimore. Block felt that while Toledo remained the single most important concern of the newspaper, its interests were wide-ranging. Thus, it was misleading to suggest that it was a wholly local publication. Besides, *The Blade* was a distinctive name, not likely to be mistaken for another, as might be the case with a *News* or a *Tribune.*

The more Block thought about the idea the better he liked it, and, with an impulsiveness that has characterized many of his decisions, he gave instructions for the change to be made almost overnight. This created logistical problems — especially for some sections of the Sunday edition that are printed several days in advance. Even though little of this was obvious to the public, rumors began to circulate that Paul Block, Jr., had taken this action because he had been offended by the defeat in the previous November of the strong-mayor government proposal which he and *The Blade* had supported so arduously.

These stories, which took various forms, seem never to have been based on anything other than a kind of intuition grounded in wishful suspicion. The newspaper has now survived as *The Blade* for more than a quarter of a century without threat of civil uprising on the part of Toledoans — many of whom seem rather to enjoy the distinctive name of the city's only newspaper.

That *The Blade's* interests were no longer restricted to Toledo was certainly underlined by the celebration of its 125th anniversary. There was nothing in the least provincial about the series of special events that Executive Editor Harry Roberts planned and carried out with the clear intent of attracting worldwide attention to *The Blade.* Just about everybody on the staff got involved in this celebration in one way or another, but three events dramatically drew attention to the wide range of *The Blade's* interests. These were:

1) Fernand Auberjonois' visit to Nepal, India, Pakistan and Afghanistan — the borders where Soviet and Chinese interests collided — to report from the areas "where the news of tomorrow is being shaped."

2) A 25,000-mile trip by Lester Heins, religion editor, to report on the state of Christian missionary activities in the emerging nations of Africa and Asia. His coverage included reports from eight African nations and India and a special article on Dr. Albert Schweitzer from his hospital.

3) A safari of officials of the Toledo Zoo and others, led by Lou Klewer, outdoors editor, to the interior of the northeastern section of South America to bring back rare animals, fish, birds and plants for the Zoo. These included a 250-pound manatee, an armadillo, 200 tropical fish, ten flamingoes, two spider monkeys, and numerous other specimens.

Special events of many sorts went on throughout the year, including the first of a series of biennial dinners for writers of letters to the editor, a fireworks display in Walbridge Park to salute *The Blade* on the Fourth of July (unfortunately delayed by high water in the Maumee River), and a junior concert by the Toledo Orchestra that included a performance of Edwin Franko Goldman's "Toledo Blade March."

On December 19, the day *The Blade* had been published for the first time in 1835, some of the highlights of its history were reviewed in an editorial that concluded:

> Through all these years it has been dedicated to the welfare and progress of Toledo, from the time it was a small village until now that it has become a great metropolitan area.
>
> Through all these years it has resisted every effort to enslave the mind of man; to censor his newspapers, his schools or his libraries; to oppress him through bigotry or intolerance; to deprive him of the equal protection of our laws; or to deny anyone anywhere equality of opportunity.
>
> And *The Blade* will continue to do so in the years ahead.

★ ★ ★

The by-line Marge, which had become familiar to readers of *The Blade* over a twelve-year period, made its last appearance in this anniversary year. Mrs. Paul Block, Jr., whose influence on many aspects of the newspaper had been considerable, died September 30, 1960. Although much of her creative and energetic activity had gone into departments particularly concerned with women's news, she had helped stimulate a verve and an outward orientation that gave *The Blade* a quality that increasingly distinguished it from most regional newspapers.

Another change in personnel occurred in 1962, when Michael Bradshaw resigned as editor after sixteen years in charge of the editorial page. The active part in the 1959 campaign for strong-mayor government had tended to compromise his situation as editor. He took a position as editorial writer for the St. Louis *Globe-Democrat,* but returned as a contributor to *The Blade's* editorial page in 1964, continuing to write until his retirement in 1970.

At his death on October 15, 1971, *The Blade* reprinted two entire pages of Michael Bradshaw's editorials on a variety of subjects, along with a picture of the editor presenting a puppy to a Toledo man hospitalized by injuries suffered when he had tried to assist an injured dog. An accompanying editorial said of Bradshaw's tenure as editor:

> Progress does not come easily, and while those were good years for the city, they saw some stirring and rancorous civic battles. But progress did come, and much of the credit is due to Mr. Bradshaw's trenchant editorials. His robust style of writing, his deft touch, the clarity in which he mustered his arguments played a significant role in overcoming the forces of reaction and stand-pattism. He was a useful citizen and a brilliant journalist.

Successor to Bradshaw as editor was James MacDonald, who had joined *The Blade* as an editorial writer and associate editor in 1958.

A Michigan newspaperman, he had taught for several years at the University of Michigan in Ann Arbor. MacDonald made a number of contributions during his tenure — the most important, perhaps, being the set of guidelines on pre-trial publicity formulated in cooperation with the Toledo Bar Association and announced in August, 1966.

These guidelines were widely publicized in the national news media, including the New York *Times* and *Time* and *Newsweek* magazines. Designed specifically to avoid prejudicing the public, especially potential jurors, before a trial, the guidelines called for publishing the name, age and address of the accused person; how, when and where the arrest was made; the charge against the accused and the identity of the complainant, the fact that a grand jury had returned an indictment and that a trial date had been set.

Except in very special circumstances, the following types of information were not to be published:

Any prior criminal record of the accused.

Any so-called confession by the accused other than the fact that he had made a statement to police.

Any statements by officials or others construed as detrimental to the benefit of the accused.

Any names of jurors selected for a trial.

Any arguments made in court in the absence of the jury or any evidence excluded by the court.

An accompanying editorial set forth some of the reservations about the guidelines in operation:

> *The Blade* hopes to apply these standards in a practical and professionally workmanlike fashion, and still be able — at the proper time — to disclose fully to our readers all pertinent information in major crimes.
>
> It would be very naive to think, however, that our guidelines even come close to offering an ideal solution to a problem that is more difficult than most people realize. The press, like the law, has its singular tradition. Like the law, it is also a human and exceedingly complicated social institution.
>
> And that's why we have spelled out some reservations to our own rules of reporting on criminal proceedings.

The Blade had, in fact, been in the vanguard among American newspapers over a period of some years in seeking to point out the need to strike a balance between the constitutional guarantees of free press and fair trial. For instance, it had been strongly critical of the press in Cleveland before and during the trial of Dr. Sam Sheppard.

Now, however, in spelling out specific restrictions by which it would abide in most instances, *The Blade* stirred up a controversy that extended into its own ranks, pitting the editorial page staff against the newsroom. Although the guidelines, never actually rescinded, have been soft-pedaled, the philosophy of restraint and avoidance of incendiary publicity in these matters has continued to prevail.

Jim MacDonald had a particular interest in world affairs, and the editorial page, under his direction, had a strong international flavor. He maintained a close working relationship with Fernand Auberjonois throughout his editorship. MacDonald left *The Blade* in 1970 to become associate professor of journalism at Ohio State University.

★ ★ ★

Only twice in its 150-year history has *The Blade* been the defendant in libel suits that reached the trial stage, and in only one of these was the original court finding in favor of the plaintiff. This was the suit filed in May, 1962, by William D. Driscoll, a former Municipal Court judge, who charged that he had been libeled by editorials and advertisements appearing in both *The Blade* and the Toledo *Times* during the campaign in 1961, in which he was defeated for re-election.

When the suit came to trial in May, 1964, it drew considerable attention throughout the country. This was in part because the plaintiff was represented by Melvin Belli, the flamboyant San Francisco trial lawyer, who had most recently defended Jack Ruby, charged with killing Lee Harvey Oswald in Dallas after the assassination of President Kennedy.

The case against the Toledo Blade Company and Paul Block, Jr., rested primarily on an editorial in the *Times* of November 2, 1961, urging voters to defeat Judge Driscoll. A number of examples of alleged unjudicial conduct were cited, and two factual errors were involved. These were admitted, though it was contended in each instance that these were honest errors and that no personal malice against Judge Driscoll had been intended.

Conflicting testimony was given concerning threats against Judge Driscoll alleged to have been made by Clifford Quinn, *The Blade's* long-time police reporter. The line of Attorney Belli's questioning in this matter suggested an effort to imply that Quinn

— out of malice toward Driscoll — had been able to turn both newspapers against him.

Common Pleas Court Judge Geraldine Macelwane threw out the libel charge against Paul Block, Jr., after the conclusion of the plaintiff's case. She denied a similar motion in the suit against the Toledo Blade Company, ruling that a jury must determine whether malice had been involved.

The jury decided in favor of the plaintiff, and it awarded $150,000 in compensatory damages and $200,000 in punitive damages. Judge Macelwane denied a motion to set aside the award, and *The Blade* appealed to the Sixth District Court. Members of the court, which sits in Toledo, asked to step aside, and three members of the Eighth District Court in Cleveland heard the appeal. Their decision unanimously reversed the Common Pleas Court verdict. Judge Lee E. Skeel wrote for the appeals court that a careful study of the editorial and advertisements of which Mr. Driscoll complained showed that the substance of them under no circumstances constituted libel per se.

Judge Skeel's opinion drew heavily on the findings of the United States Supreme Court in the case of *Times* vs. Sullivan, which had greatly broadened areas of comment and criticism in political contests, except where personal malice could be established. "Acts and words of a judge committed and stated or announced in the performance of his duties are the subject of fair criticism and report by the public press," the unanimous opinion declared, actually going beyond *Times* vs. Sullivan in finding for The Blade Company.

Chapter 35

Affairs of the Family

A love feast that was unusual among American newspapers took place at the Commodore Perry Hotel in Toledo on the night of January 29, 1961. Nearly six hundred employees and officials of *The Blade* gathered to recognize their generally harmonious labor-management relationships. Paul Block, Jr., was the guest of honor.

The record of peace between *The Blade's* management and the nine unions in the Toledo Council of Newspaper Unions was cited by Monsignor Michael J. Doyle, chairman of the city's Labor-Management-Citizens Committee. Complimenting both Mr. Block and the union leadership, Monsignor Doyle observed that the LMC could go out of business if all local business and industry had equally amicable relations with their workers.

Stanley Raszka, chief steward of the Teamsters' unit at *The Blade,* praised the newspaper for its editorial fairness on issues involving labor. Among the gifts presented to Paul Block, Jr., was an honorable withdrawal card from the American Newspaper Guild, of which he was a member in the 1930s while employed as a reporter.

Block said that enlightened business recognized the role of unions in protecting the interests of their members by pressing their case for higher wages and better working conditions. He suggested that management, on the other hand, has its own responsibility to refuse to yield to excessive demands that would weaken the organization. He also urged that unions accept the responsibility of maintaining democratic practices within their ranks, pointing out that the secretary of labor had declared that unions must adhere to the American concepts of fair treatment of minorities.

The occasion provided a genuine expression of mutual respect, and few who attended would have predicted that in less than three

Affairs of the Family

years there would be a total suspension of operations at *The Blade*. Yet this came about on November 16, 1963, when bargaining between management and representatives of the American Newspaper Guild unit broke down and Guild members voted to strike. The other eight unions at *The Blade* respected the picket line, closing down the newspaper for the next week. The walkout was the first in *The Blade's* history.

But for events in Dallas, on November 22, 1963, this strike undoubtedly would have continued longer. But when news of the assassination of President John F. Kennedy reached pickets outside *The Blade* building, they quickly volunteered to return to work to report one of the most dramatic news stories of the century.

The strike was called off under a truce with the Guild. Negotiations were continued with its representatives and with those of several other unions. This understanding, the unions would later contend, had included an agreement that new contracts would be achieved promptly, but no agreement was reached until a year later. John D. Willey, treasurer of the Toledo Blade Company, reported to its board of directors that there had been a substantial loss of revenue as a result of the strike, which came at the beginning of the holiday season.

Short as the 1963 strike had been, and despite its seemingly amicable conclusion, considerable bitterness carried over. The mutual trust that had characterized labor-management relationships in previous years, and which had been celebrated at the dinner honoring Paul Block, Jr., now gave way to increasing suspicion and ill feeling. All this accumulated in the next three years, leading— perhaps inevitably—to the strike and lockout that closed down *The Blade* from October 24, 1966, to March 22, 1967.

How far apart the two sides were is reflected in statements made soon after the strike began. An editorial in the first issue of the Toledo *Record* — the newspaper published by the striking workers from November 9 until the conclusion of the shutdown—states the unions' position:

> It should be noted that the strike against *The Blade* and *Times* did not occur until after numerous and lengthy bargaining sessions over a five-month period failed to produce a realistic wage offer from management.
>
> This adamant attitude by management continued in the face of ample indication by the striking unions that they intended to take economic action unless major gains were achieved at the bargaining table.

At no time has management said it was financially unable to meet any of the union wage demands. It has simply declined to do so.

Willey's report to members of the company's board of directors on December 13 summed up management's position. Even after more than six weeks, he reported, several of the unions were still not ready to talk seriously and get to the heart of the issues. He could find no concrete evidence that they were willing to settle on reasonable terms. They seemed to be holding out for a two-year contract, which the company could not afford to give, he said, because it would only risk future strikes. The company wanted a three-year contract.

The company and the unions exchanged charges of unfair labor practices. Early in December, the unions alleged that the company had violated the National Labor Relations Act by refusing to provide the Toledo Newspaper Guild with sufficient data concerning wages, bonuses, and other pertinent matters to enable the Guild to adequately negotiate the renewal of a collective bargaining agreement. The Blade Company filed its charge a month later, alleging lack of good faith in bargaining because the union was simultaneously engaged in competition with *The Blade* by publishing the Toledo *Record*.

The strike newspaper, in fact, achieved support. Its peak circulation was believed to have been in the vicinity of 70,000, and it carried a substantial amount of advertising, particularly classifieds. The city's major retail stores gave it little advertising business, but some smaller merchandisers did use its columns.

Talks between company and union representatives continued off and on through December, with little progress. The standing labor committee of the American Newspaper Publishers Association entered the picture early in January. Sessions were held with both sides—first in Chicago, then in Columbus. The ANPA group remained a part of the negotiating process until February 26, when settlement talks broke off and no new sessions were scheduled. Issues remaining to be resolved, according to the *Record*, were wages, duration of contract, vacations, local union problems, health and welfare, pensions, hours, effective dates of wage increases, and parity of wages for circulation district managers and outside classified salesmen.

The Downtown Toledo Associates, concerned about the strike's impact on the community, entered the picture as the stoppage was in its fourth month. Exploratory conferences were held with representatives of the company and of the unions. Mayor John Potter and Congressman Ashley also attended these meetings.

Less than three weeks after these talks began, it was announced that a settlement was at hand. The *Record* reported on March 19 that publication of *The Blade* would be resumed on March 27 and of the *Times* on the following day. Ratification of individual contracts was expected in the next two days. The first union to sign was Stereotypers Local 39. A return-to-work agreement, including no-discrimination and no-retaliation pledges by both management and unions, was signed March 21. Picketing was ended and publication of both *The Blade* and the *Times* resumed, almost exactly five months after it had been suspended.

★ ★ ★

Although there are many ways to measure the impact of a strike, advertising and circulation figures provide the general outlines of the loss to *The Blade* from this one.

Total advertising linage in 1965—the year before the strike—stood at an all-time high of 35,363,326. The figure plummeted to 26,667,860 in 1966 and rose only slightly in 1967, when it reached 26,996,832. Not until 1968 did the figure move above the 1965 total.

Circulation for the evening edition of *The Blade* stood at 181,381 in 1965 and increased only to 182,022 in 1966. In 1967, however, it dropped by almost 10,000 to 173,523. Since that time, the total circulation for the evening edition has never risen above 175,000.

The Sunday edition was least affected during this time. In 1966, circulation reached 190,577—a high for the eighteen years of its existence. It dropped in 1967 by a few thousand—to 184,672—but immediately rebounded to an all-time high of 198,524. Circulation of the Sunday edition has continued to move upward since that time, reaching well over 200,000.

Some quite obvious conclusions may be drawn from these figures, although other factors have had their influence in relation to some of them. There has, for example, been a general downward trend in circulation among evening newspapers throughout the country. Some, in fact, have changed to morning publication to minimize the competition from television. Traffic congestion in many major urban areas has created additional problems for the delivery of evening editions.

Advertising linage, unlike circulation, made a relatively quick recovery and has risen well beyond the pre-strike figure in more recent years, reaching an all-time high of over 43,000,000 in 1979.

It is generally agreed that the most serious losses to *The Blade* from the strike came in the outlying areas of northwest Ohio and southeast Michigan, when readers get out of the habit of reading *The Blade* and turned to major newspapers in Cleveland, Detroit, and perhaps Dayton and Columbus and to improved area newspapers in such smaller cities as Fremont, Bowling Green, and Monroe.

Treasurer Willey reported to the board in April, 1967, that the strike had caused heavy losses for the first quarter of 1967, although the 1966 financial report had shown improvement over recent years. He also said that meetings were being held with department heads to discuss a general economy program to recoup strike losses. It was also proposed that some capital improvements already approved should be deferred.

Union members were, on the whole, pleased with the outcome of the strike. It had cost some of them in immediate financial terms, despite strike benefits. Some others—especially those in craft unions—had other jobs while the strike continued and suffered little in lost wages. Increased pay and improved fringe benefits were generous, and the *Record* expressed satisfaction in one of its last issues that the wage settlements placed *The Blade* among the dozen best-paying newspapers in the country.

Trying to identify a winner or loser from a protracted strike is, at best, risky. It does seem to be generally agreed that the unions manifested an unusual degree of cohesiveness and refused to be split. Some have suggested that this cohesiveness was gained at the expense of mobility, which may have prolonged the deadlock. As one news executive put it, "things just dragged on and on."

Some good things did come out of the strike in the long run. Most important undoubtedly was the determination from both sides that neither wanted to go through such an ordeal again. There has been, in fact, no serious threat of labor-management strife approaching the strike stage since 1967.

Fortunately, too, no lasting bitterness emerged. Union leaders insist that they have felt no resentment against management, either as an institution or as individuals. The company has, in the intervening years, moved forward with a variety of improvements in the quality of the newspaper and a policy of diversification that has taken it into other areas of communication.

The Toledo Blade Company now owns three newspapers, three television stations, and three community cablevision systems.

With the exception of *The Blade* and the Pittsburgh *Post-Gazette,* all these properties were acquired within the last twenty years. For a time — between 1967 and 1969 — The Blade Company owned six newspapers. Three of these were recent additions — *The Register,* of Red Bank, New Jersey, in 1965; *The Daily News* of Port Clinton, Ohio, in 1966; and *The Peninsula Herald* of Monterey, California, in 1967. Two of these were subsequently sold — Port Clinton in 1969, Red Bank in 1982; and, of course, publication of the Toledo *Times* was suspended in 1975.

The three television stations now owned by the company are WLIO in Lima, Ohio, WLFI in Lafayette, Indiana, and WDRB in Louisville, Kentucky. All three are UHF stations. The Lima station, an NBC affiliate, was purchased by the Blade Company and the Midwestern Broadcasting Corporation, which jointly formed the Lima Communications Corporation. All outstanding stock is owned by the Blade Company, as of 1982.

The Lafayette station, a CBS affiliate, was purchased in 1979. The most recent addition is the Louisville station, acquired in 1984. It is independent of network affiliation.

In the area of community cablevision, the Blade Company was something of a pioneer. It joined with Cox Cablevision to form Buckeye Cablevision on February 3, 1965, to serve the Toledo area. The stock of the Cox company was acquired between 1967 and 1974, making the Blade Company sole owner. Buckeye Cablevision now serves some 100,000 homes and is one of the top twenty systems in the country. Two other cablevision systems have been added to the company's holdings more recently—Monroe Cablevision, Inc., of Monroe, Michigan, and Erie County Cablevision, Inc., of Sandusky, Ohio.

Diversification has taken the Toledo Blade Company into other areas—including a travel agency and a job printing company, both of which were disposed of in recent years. At present, all of its holdings are in communications.

Chapter 36

In Matters Educational

The second of the three major civic projects in which *The Blade's* publisher, Paul Block, Jr., deserted the role of referee to become a deeply committed participant was in establishing a college of medicine in Toledo. Here he followed in the footsteps of Robinson Locke, who was one of the most enthusiastic supporters of the Toledo College of Medicine before it closed in 1914.

Talk of establishing — or re-establishing — a medical college in Toledo had begun at least as early as 1954, and *The Blade* had given extensive coverage to efforts in that direction. Soon after State Rep. Michael Damas had suggested the need for such a college, the board of directors of the University of Toledo had named a group of five to explore the possibilities. Governor Frank Lausche was asked to provide the $5,000,000 needed to construct a basic science building at the university — the first step toward a medical college.

Blade reporter Tom Reynders examined the project in depth in August, 1954, pointing out that it would be a bargain at the estimated cost of $40,000,000. His story also emphasized that three of the state's four major population centers were served by medical schools. Toledo and northwest Ohio were the single exception. Not much came of these early efforts.

Action began to accelerate in the 1960s as national concern about a shortage of doctors increased. One of the first proposals made to meet this problem in Ohio was to expand the Ohio State University medical school in Columbus. *The Blade* warned that this proposal "should be scrutinized very carefully." The argument offered in its behalf was that it would be less expensive than building, equipping and staffing a new college. This, *The Blade* contended, overlooked that Ohio's need for doctors still wouldn't be fulfilled. Besides, it argued, a medical school has two functions — training doctors and increasing attention to medical research — and Toledo offered a university and hospitals enough to serve both purposes.

A twelve-man committee was organized in 1960, and this group hired Dr. William R. Willard, of the University of Kentucky medical school, to study the feasibility of a medical school for Toledo. Dr. Willard's report, submitted in October, 1961, was characterized by *The Blade* as A BLUNT DIAGNOSIS. He warned that:

- To plan, organize and build all the original facilities might require as long as ten years.
- To raise the money needed for all facilities (including a 350-bed teaching hospital) would be a monumental task.
- Provision would have to be made for operating costs of $2,000,000 annually.
- The University of Toledo's graduate programs and research activities would have to be improved.

The Blade agreed that these were realistic requirements which citizens would have to keep in mind. However, it said that a medical teaching center does not have to be tied to a university and urged that land next to the Maumee Valley Hospital area should be kept in mind, as well as Scott Park, to which the university already held title. It was further noted that the university already had many unfinished projects and should not be expected to take on more at this time.

A breakthrough in planning at the state and national levels appeared to have been achieved in 1962. Various agencies made recommendations favorable to expansion of medical school facilities generally, and the establishment of a new medical school at the University of Toledo specifically. *The Blade* declared that "now it's time for Toledoans to get their plans in good order, to start preparing to present them in Columbus and Washington."

There were further delays, however, and it was more than a year later — in December, 1964 — that *The Blade*, in a story by Harvey Ford, education editor, was able to report success:

> When the Ohio Senate . . . passed the bill which created a state medical school in Toledo, it brought to a successful conclusion one of the most difficult and prolonged projects ever undertaken by a group of local citizens.
>
> The medical school is established by state law, bringing to an end the initial — or state — phase of the project. The next major step will be to seek and obtain federal funds for construction of the medical center.

The drive to locate a medical school in Toledo, the article pointed out, had gone on for more than four years, "surviving all sorts of problems and unexpected circumstances." There would be many more problems and unexpected circumstances, extending over a period of almost ten years, before the medical college would be firmly established. *The Blade* was very much in the thick of it all.

Governor James Rhodes named Paul Block, Jr., the first chairman of the board of trustees of the Toledo State College of Medicine (as it was first designated). The co-publisher of *The Blade* was a logical choice. His long-standing interest in chemistry and medical science qualified him particularly, as did his various associations with institutions of higher learning — including the University of Toledo — over a period of some twenty years. The governor also named J. Preston Levis to be vice chairman and John Skipton to be secretary. The position of treasurer was left vacant until operating funds were available.

One after another, problems presented themselves for the next several years. These included financing the school, finding its site, establishing its relationship with the University of Toledo, and developing operational procedures. The Hospital Planning Association of Greater Toledo (composed of representatives of the existing hospitals) prepared a levy proposal (in 1965) to provide financing to expand Lucas County hospital facilities. But the levy plan omitted consideration of the impact of the hospital that was to be a part of the medical school, and for this reason *The Blade* soundly condemned it, saying it ignored the teaching hospital in relation to Toledo's overall future facilities and needs. The editorial further stated that "despite *The Blade's* particular interest in seeing the new college of medicine come into being as rapidly as possible, this newspaper cannot support any last-minute, superficial plan based on satisfying every community pressure group in the sole interest of coming up with an attractive package for the November ballot." The levy lost nearly 2 to 1 that November.

The controversy over the medical school's site was resolved in December, 1965, by a panel of three distinguished medical educators. They were asked to weigh the advantages of the proposed site at the Toledo State Hospital, in the southern part of the city, against the disadvantages of its relative remoteness from the University of Toledo, where a smaller site was available. When the south side location was recommended, *The Blade* approved:

Ultimately, the outlook for fully developing that college into a major medical center depends on having considerable space to expand and accommodate other health-related facilities which will be attracted by the presence of a college of medicine.

More immediately, selection of the site clears the way for two further developments. Now, the college of medicine will be able to work on definitive site and building plans. Also, it frees the University of Toledo to proceed with its own long-range development unencumbered by its offer of a campus site for the medical school.

The problems of the college (its name was changed to the Medical College of Ohio at Toledo in 1967) were by no means at an end, although the essential elements were in place by the time when Paul Block, Jr., resigned from the board of trustees in September, 1970. Dr. Glidden Brooks, who came from Brown University, had been named president in 1966. Classes began in September, 1969, in temporary quarters at William Roche Hospital. Ground was broken in September, 1970, for the health science and teaching building, the first permanent structure on the 346-acre campus.

The planning of this building was to have far-reaching consequences for Toledo. Through the project, Paul Block, Jr., became acquainted with Minoru Yamasaki, who headed the architectural firm of Minoru Yamasaki and Associates in Troy, Michigan, and who made an indelible impression on the co-publisher of *The Blade*. As a result of their association, the pattern of the city's downtown development was largely determined even before it got under way.

★ ★ ★

In his letter to Governor Rhodes offering his resignation from the medical college board, Paul Block, Jr., observed that "as the medical school grows and particularly as it takes over a hospital from the county commissioners, the time is rapidly approaching when my service as a trustee to the school and my duties on *The Blade* will become incompatible." He referred to the need to be, as co-publisher, in a position to resume the role of referee — free to blow the whistle, as it were, at any sign of mismanagement or other failures in the college's operations.

The time for this whistle-blowing was not long in coming. In April, 1971, Maumee Valley Hospital, which the college had taken over from Lucas County, was discovered to have debts of $2,200,000. "How could the trustees of the new medical college approve of an agreement to acquire Maumee Valley Hospital without knowing what they were getting?" *The Blade* wanted to know. Questions were raised about the culpability of President Brooks, who "now professes ignorance as to the sad state of the hospital's finances." When Brooks resigned six weeks later, *The Blade* praised him for his achievements in the formative years of the college, but, it pointed out, "his long suit is not administration, financial matters were neglected, and all kinds of problems piled up."

Dr. Martin Anderson, head of surgery at the college, was named president in October, 1972, and *The Blade* thought he made a good start. Less than two years later, however, it came near to a change of heart when Dr. Anderson supported the board of trustees' naming of the new library-administration building at the Medical College of Ohio for the late Raymon Mulford, who had been an executive of Owens-Illinois, Inc.

MCO SELLS HONOR FOR PEANUTS was the headline on an editorial of May 20, 1974, in which *The Blade* described what had happened as "this chintzy deal." It was alleged that the MCO trustees had arranged it in secret in exchange for a $300,000 gift by Owens-Illinois to the college's fund-raising foundation. The upshot, *The Blade* said, was that taxpayers would put up $7,500,000 for a building to be named for a former corporation executive who had no meaningful ties with the college. One physician was quoted as having said at a meeting of the medical college faculty senate that the decision was "stupid" and "pompous" — a "classic example of businessmen treating a university as their own private preserve."

The Blade has maintained an interest — often critical — in the affairs of the Medical College of Ohio as it survived a variety of crises in developing its own identity. The achievement was not without its costs — including strained relationships over a period of years with officials of the University of Toledo. But it provides a significant study of the roles of a newspaper and an active publisher in effecting community improvements. For most observers agree that without the interest and support of *The Blade* and its co-publisher, Toledo never would have had a medical college.

★ ★ ★

The Blade has had a special interest in education from David Ross Locke's time to the present. It has been involved both in coverage of education and its problems and in educational activities of its own. An unusual number of staff members hold advanced academic degrees and/or have been encouraged to further their education in a variety of ways.

In Matters Educational

Harvey Ford was *The Blade's* education editor for some twenty years, until his death in 1977. The latitude his editors gave him was an example of the importance attached to education affairs. Ford, who joined the staff in 1946, was interested in pursuing a Ph D degree in history at the University of Michigan. He was encouraged to do so, was given the necessary time off and was granted the degree in 1951. In addition to his thorough coverage of education for *The Blade,* he subsequently became a columnist, emphasizing historical perspective on current problems.

Another aspect of the interest in education is manifested in the program *The Blade* has carried on for almost thirty years in schools throughout its circulation area — first known as Newspaper in the Class Room and more recently as Newspaper in Education. The program, now under the supervision of Mary Jane Spencer, who previously was a reporter and editor, has been expanded in several directions and now includes special courses for classroom teachers. These are offered at both the University of Toledo and Bowling Green State University.

The purpose of the program, Mrs. Spencer says, is "helping school children and adults learn to read the newspaper, while using the newspaper to learn to read better and become informed citizens." Its success is attested to by the continuing growth in numbers enrolled and by its steadily increasing quality.

Chapter 37

Liberty and Justice for All

Few American newspapers possess a heritage of support for the rights of the nation's black citizens that is as rich as *The Blade's*. More than 135 years ago, Joseph Williams was demanding an end to slavery. David Ross Locke trumpeted the cause of the freedmen from the day he joined *The Blade* in October, 1865, until his death twenty years later. Through succeeding generations of the Locke and Block families, this heritage has been stoutly maintained, though it may have taken different directions and applied different emphases from time to time.

Toledo's experience with racial strife in the post-World War II era has been less violent than that of most northern industrial cities. Editors and publishers of *The Blade* have sometimes attributed this to the newspaper's enlightened attitude toward interracial problems over the years. Those claims would seem to have been justified on the whole, though *The Blade* has been charged with waffling on some aspects of government programs in such areas as open housing, employment quotas and school admissions.

The record of the past forty years does suggest that *The Blade* has been well ahead of most American newspapers in efforts to advance the claims of blacks to rights long denied them, and at the same time attempting to minimize interracial strife. Its accomplishments in these areas are, on the whole, impressive.

The Blade began to move soon after World War II to expand its own employment opportunities for blacks. The first major breakthrough came in 1946 with the hiring of William Brower as a member of the reporting staff. A graduate of Wilberforce University, Bill Brower had spent five years as a reporter and editor on black newspapers in Philadelphia, Washington, Baltimore and Richmond before he joined *The Blade.* In the intervening four decades, he established a solid reputation as a journalist that brought him a variety of honors.

Brower wrote a series of articles on the status of the Negro in the United States in 1951 — one of the first serious efforts by a black newspaperman to examine problems that were just beginning to be acknowledged. These articles were published in book form by *The Blade,* under the title *15 Million Americans.* Twenty years later, in 1972, he followed up with a second series and was awarded a citation by the Robert F. Kennedy Memorial. Brower is also the author of a series on black voters in 1956, based on a tour of the Midwest and South, and a seven-part series on "The Black Athlete" in 1977.

Since 1976, Brower has been an associate editor and columnist. He has taught at Defiance College, Central State University (Ohio), and Temple University. He was honored in 1984 by the high school from which he was graduated in High Point, North Carolina.

The numbers of blacks on the editorial staff of *The Blade* have been greater than the national average and a persistent effort has been made to recruit black reporters and editors.

★ ★ ★

Reason and restraint have always characterized *The Blade's* approach to racial relations within the Toledo community. *The Blade* has supported the establishment of agencies such as the Board of Community Relations, set up in July, 1946, to try to anticipate sources of racial friction, and the Police Community Relations Committee, inaugurated in 1964 to minimize misunderstandings growing out of police operations. *The Blade* lauded a clinic on interracial unity at Washington Congregational Church in December, 1945, to find ways to promote equal employment opportunities for the 2,500 Negro veterans who were expected to return to Toledo after World War II. There was similar enthusiasm for a three-day institute on race relations in February, 1947.

The Blade has stood its ground in defense of racial equality through the exercise of restraint in situations where the public clamor seemed to invite a strategic retreat to another position. Two instances of this sort occurred in the 1950s — before racial strife had mounted to the proportions of the next decade.

Desegregation of public housing in East Toledo in 1953 was the first of these. Opponents called mass meetings and there were fears of racial flare-ups throughout the city. *The Blade,* after a denunciation of the segregationist spokesmen, limited its coverage of the controversy to a minimum, and even excluded letters to the editor on the subject.

Gradually, the threat of violence in East Toledo subsided and, when desegregation took effect some months later, there were no disruptions. As Reo M. Christenson, a former *Blade* editorial writer, has written: "The implications of such a course, used under different circumstances and for different purposes, are sobering. In this instance, however, it apparently paid off."[30]

A second time of trial for *The Blade's* policy on covering racial problems came in 1957. Several crimes in which blacks were said to have been involved had been reported during the spring and summer months. Then, in September, a minister's daughter reported to police that three black youths had raped her. Within the next few days, a nurse and a waitress made similar allegations.

The Blade had adopted a policy in 1944 of refraining from identifying alleged criminals by race, creed or color, and it followed that practice in this instance. The alleged rapists were identified as "three boys" and the nurse's attackers as a "dark brown man." The community was in an uproar, and *The Blade* was attacked for failing to provide adequate identification and for covering up a Negro crime wave. Refusing to yield to the pressure, *The Blade* continued to criticize those who accepted rumors at face value and who thus would fan the flames of racial hatred.

Then, as the clamor intensified and the threat of violence increased, both the minister's daughter and the nurse admitted that they had fabricated their stories. *The Blade* responded with a front-page editorial observing that "all of us have seen that racial identification in a crime story . . . clearly plays into the hands of those who would stir up animosity."

★ ★ ★

Toledo's experience with the "long, hot summers" of the late 1960s was relatively mild by comparison with the protracted violence that beset so many industrial cities of the North. This may have been because Toledo had a much smaller percentage of blacks among its population — fewer than any other major Ohio city and less than half the percentages in Cleveland and Cincinnati. Or it may have been because, as *The Blade* had so often suggested over the years, an atmosphere of tolerance and living together in peace had been created.

It is interesting to note how often *The Blade* proposed or praised dealing with racial problems with solutions based on mutual consent. In the immediate aftermath of the 1957 hoax, for example, racial trouble was a threat at Scott High School when Janet Quinn, who was black, was elected football queen. When the 600 members of the two upper classes of the school met to "talk it out," leading to apologies by students who had helped create the explosive situation, *The Blade* lauded "these young people" who "have shown their elders how people of different backgrounds live peaceably together within the rules of a democratic society."

There were other similar instances in the next ten years, before trouble did break out in Toledo. RESTRAINT—AND HELP was the caption of an editorial in July, 1964, after an incident of rowdyism following a dance at the YWCA for young blacks. Such actions must be met firmly, order maintained, respect for law secured, *The Blade* contended, but "some very wise thinking is needed on what to do about poor teen-age boys who are unable to find jobs."

Precautions were taken in Toledo to avoid the kind of trouble that was erupting in so many cities in the 1960s, and the city's black leaders played an important part in these efforts. Officials of the local chapter of the National Association for the Advancement of Colored People called a meeting to seek ways to combat lawlessness after there were five killings in the black community in the first month of 1965. The Board of Community Relations issued its annual report in June, 1965, and described Toledo's civil rights record as one to be proud of, praising the city's leaders and citizens for keeping calm.

On the night of July 24, 1967, arson, looting and violence broke out in various sections of the city. Crowds throwing fire bombs blocked the intersection of Bancroft Street and Franklin Avenue; looting was widespread. Extra police were called out in Perrysburg, Maumee and Sylvania, and National Guard troops were requested as a precautionary measure. Roadblocks were set up at the Ohio-Michigan line to prevent a possible influx of outside agitators. Disturbances erupted again the next night, but not as bad as the previous night. A scheduled speech by Dr. Martin Luther King was canceled.

The Blade remained calm in the face of what happened and the threat of what might have happened. In an editorial after the second night of trouble, *The Blade* praised the police for keeping the situation from getting out of hand, noting that off-duty officers came back in a hurry when they were called, and all were professional in their actions. This was "responsible behavior," *The Blade* said, noting that "there are more than a score of Negroes on the force, and that helped, too."

An editorial the following day gave credit to another group of Toledoans. It cited leaders of Toledo's Negro community, who had "worked alongside city officials during tense hours of vandalism and disturbance," and concluded: "This reminds people that the genuine goals of the civil rights movement call for the participation of all civic-minded men."

The major eruptions in late July were not the last of Toledo's racial troubles that year. In September, there was a string of incidents involving the stoning of police and their vehicles. And, in that same period, a proposed fair housing ordinance was put before the voters. When it was decisively beaten, Toledo's black citizens were bitterly disappointed and staged a protest march the following Sunday. *The Blade* offered this comment:

> Credit is due both to those who participated in Sunday's protest march and to the residents of the neighborhoods through which it passed for the orderly and peaceful manner in which the affair was brought off. It was apparent that the advance planning by officials of the Toledo chapter of the NAACP, which sponsored the march, and by the leaders of the Polish community paid off.
>
> . . . If anything can be criticized in that demonstration of disappointment over defeat of the city's fair housing ordinance, it was the decision by the parade organizers to march first through Fourth Ward neighborhoods. By that act, the marchers singled out our citizens of Polish descent who have long been substantial and constructive segments of this community in a way that suggested that they were the only ones who voted against the ordinance.

It would be hard to formulate a more representative statement than this of the philosophy of reason and restraint that has so consistently characterized *The Blade's* attitude toward the entire range of problems that have grown out of the accelerated efforts to achieve the goal of liberty and justice for all which David Ross Locke set out to achieve almost exactly a hundred years before the troubled summer and fall of 1967.

In some instances, at least, *The Blade's* attitude toward the struggle for racial equality has resulted in editorial positions that have seemed less than heroic — or even moderately forceful — to some blacks and others who believe that the goal demands vigorous leadership of the devil-take-the-hindmost sort. There is no means of resolving that difference of opinion.

There are mixed feelings among Toledo's black leaders about the positions *The Blade* has taken on some issues that they believe are important to their cause in recent years. But there never has been any serious reason to doubt *The Blade's* substantial service to the achievement of liberty and justice for all, along the lines it believes to be most likely to promote those ends.

Chapter 38

The Troubled Seventies

The strife that erupted in Toledo and throughout the United States in the latter half of the 1960s did not subside in the next decade. It moved from the inner cities to the college campuses. There, in some instances — the University of Toledo among them — radical students and militant blacks joined forces to demand the incorporation of black studies programs into the curriculum.

The Blade was sympathetic with some of the goals espoused by those who led the campus protests — notably the demand for an end to American involvement in Vietnam. It had no sympathy, however, with the violent methods they often employed in their efforts to achieve them. So when on May 4, 1970, four students at Kent State University were killed by fire from the ranks of the Ohio National Guard, sent by Governor James Rhodes at the request of university officials, *The Blade* expressed sorrow but declared that the use of force to protect campuses would be necessary. When students go on rampages, as they had at Kent State, "their conduct amounts to little more than guerrilla warfare," *The Blade* contended, adding that "in that type of warfare, as in all others, people do get hurt; some may even die."

This was only the beginning of a decade in which violence and irrational conduct would characterize much of what went on in Toledo. It was not a good time for Toledo's image — never closely akin to the vision of the shining "City on the Hill" that Toledo's "Golden Rule" Jones and Cleveland's Tom Johnson had shared for their cities three-quarters of a century earlier. First, problems in the city's schools drew nationwide attention, then, a year later the violent consequences of a general strike by municipal employees —

The Troubled Seventies

including policemen and firemen. It was not the sort of publicity Toledo needed or wanted.

Events in 1978 and 1979 made for frightening pictures on televised screens across the nation by all three major networks. But the forces that erupted in those years had been simmering beneath the surface for more than a decade, heated by a combination of the city's economic problems, repeated rejections of school tax levies and militant union attitudes.

★ ★ ★

School problems began to reach crisis stage in October, 1976, when state officials announced that the entire system would have to be shut down for thirteen days, beginning on December 3, for want of operating funds. "The day of reckoning is truly at hand for the city's schools," *The Blade* proclaimed on October 22. The immediate threat of closing was seen as only a part of the problem. Without additional sources of revenue, it would be necessary to close even earlier in 1977. There was only one hope for relief — a school levy on the ballot in November, to which *The Blade* lent support, as it had for the preceding two levy attempts that voters defeated.

This one lost, too, and after the schools closed on December 3, *The Blade* saw DARK DAYS FOR TOLEDO SCHOOLS. The same situation could develop in 1977, it warned, saying that new methods of financing Toledo's schools must be found. Beyond this, however, the school system must do much more to trim costs, and the public must be convinced that such cuts had been made. More and more parents, *The Blade* contended, were becoming disenchanted with the kind of education their children were receiving. Classroom standards and teacher qualifications must be raised.

A fourth attempt to pass a school levy, in June, 1977, resulted in another defeat — "the poorest showing of four votes," *The Blade* reported. Two months later, the state auditor announced the bad news of closings for the new school year, which had been forecast in 1976. School would open on September 7 and would be forced to close the next month — perhaps as early as October 13 — for the remainder of 1977. *The Blade* characterized this as "a calamity" and insisted that "this city must find a solution for this disaster."

There was one last effort to avert this disaster. For the fifth time, voters were asked to approve a school levy. At 6.1 mills, this was the smallest of any thus far submitted. *The Blade* devoted much of its editorial page on October 30 to making THE CASE FOR THE

SCHOOL LEVY, stressing the need for an emergency infusion of new revenue to prevent the threatened closings. Emphasis was placed on damage that would be done to the city's young people if the shutdowns were permitted to occur.

The Blade saw reasons for hope: A citizens' committee had conducted an intensive analysis of the school system's problems and had recommended changes that would result in greater efficiency; Frank Dick, superintendent of schools, had announced that he would resign as of the end of the school year to remove himself as a source of dissatisfaction; and three of five school board seats were to be filled at the November election, making it possible to get some fresh thinking onto the board.

The Blade's final reason for endorsing the levy was that the school situation was detrimental to Toledo in several ways. School enrollment had declined, more and more teachers were leaving their jobs, and the real estate market was taking a beating — more houses were for sale and longer periods were being required to sell them.

Disaster seemed to be averted when the levy was approved, but the solution for Toledo's school problems was not to be as simple as that. An error was discovered about a month after the election: failure to include on the ballot a statement of the dollar amount that the tax would generate annually. The Lucas County Common Pleas Court issued an order prohibiting the school system from spending any more 1977 tax revenues except for repayment of notes.

The Blade called what had happened an "inexcusable blunder" and blamed the board of education's legal counsel. The immediate solution to the problem was seen to be uncertain, but the ultimate remedy, *The Blade* insisted, was a continuation of the spirit that had passed the levy in November and "the elimination of all influences by political parties in the selection of school board members."

The city's teachers announced on the day after the Common Pleas Court's ruling that they would refuse to return to their classrooms without assurances that they would be paid. Two days later, the Ohio Legislature enacted a bill to allow Toledo's schools to borrow money to meet its payroll. The Ohio Supreme Court reversed the lower court's ruling two weeks later and upheld the legality of the school levy approved on November 8. "This is only one hurdle to be gotten over," *The Blade* warned, adding that there would be more in the future.

This may have been one of *The Blade's* greatest understatements

The Troubled Seventies 345

in its 150-year history. The American Federation of Teachers, which had represented the city's school personnel since 1968, had decided to seek substantial improvement of both salaries and fringe benefits for its members, who had had no pay increase since January 1, 1976; nonteaching personnel had had no raise since October 1, 1975. The need for a pay increase was acknowledged, but there was a wide gap between the union demands and what the school board believed it could afford to offer.

When, after four months of negotiations, no agreement had been reached, the board announced late in March, 1978, that it was instituting a 7 per cent increase in salaries. The response of Dal Lawrence, president of the Toledo Federation of Teachers, was that the board members had "spat upon every employee." The union went to court to restrain the district from implementing the pay increase the board had approved.

All of this, *The Blade* believed, had created a situation in which the board was "entirely justified in seeing a duty to put into immediate effect as large a raise as the district's still-limited revenues will support." On the other hand, it contended, "the fight by the union leaders to bar their members from receiving a pay raise as compared with the board's action in granting it must surely raise the question in the mind of every teacher and nonteaching school employee of just which side is most interested in his or her welfare."

One week later, on April 10, the teachers' union embarked on a strike that was prohibited by the laws of Ohio. It was to continue for 22 days. As the strike began, *The Blade* called attention to the fact that "it would not be surprising" if students in the Toledo city school district "have begun to think that going to school is the exception rather than the rule." This could only have adverse impact on the specific educational efforts and goals of students at all levels, *The Blade* declared, then added: "Though it is supposed to be for the young people's benefit that the school system exists, they too often of late have seemed to be the ones whose interests get the least attention."

The strike focused national attention on attacks on homes, autos, and persons of the teachers who sought to stay on the job. The school board sought court orders to enforce the Ferguson Act, which forbade strikes by public employees and invoked heavy fines on unions and their members, and *The Blade* thought the courts did not move fast enough in this direction. When, on May 2, the strike ended, there were many reservations about the cost of a 13.5 per cent increase in salaries, the need to replace one-time-only funds that were included in the basis of the settlement, what it did to chances for winning voter approval of school levies in the future, and — a particularly devastating setback — "this abdication of professional responsibilities by the teachers." *The Blade's* post-strike editorial concluded:

> Toledo has endured more unfavorable publicity the past year from its public school system than from any other sources. For this reason alone, the end of this costly strike . . . can be greeted with, if nothing else, a sigh of relief.

★ ★ ★

But that sigh did not last long. Little more than a year later, strife and violence again shook the city. This time it grew from differences, between the city government and unions representing its employees, that led to a strike that began on the night of July 2. In the absence of police and fire protection, gangs of vandals took to the streets, setting fires and throwing anything they found at hand. Scores of blazes raged out of control. The Plaza Hotel, undergoing construction as an apartment hotel, was fire-bombed and one of its buildings was destroyed. Toledo was on national television again, and in the most unfavorable light possible.

A *Blade* editorial July 4 observed that there was "nothing for Toledoans to celebrate today." The scene was described as "total anarchy." This was "a sad time" for Toledo residents, "a shameful period for 3,500 or so municipal employees whose livelihood is made possible by tax-payers, and a day of infamy for those safety forces who thumbed their noses at the law, their duty to the city, and the welfare of this community."

The strike was ended next day under a court order imposing heavy fines on unions and their members if their illegal actions were continued. There had been other casualties of the strike. After around-the-clock bargaining sessions, Mayor Doug DeGood collapsed in his office and was hospitalized. Robbers fatally shot a TARTA bus driver, and all buses were pulled off the streets until adequate police protection could be provided. Union leaders threatened to take supervisory workers out of the Collins Park water pumping station, which would have resulted in cutting off the city's water supply.

In the aftermath of the strike, *The Blade* demanded editorially that action be taken to make such action by public employees impossible. Democratic state legislators from Lucas County were criticized for having voted for a succession of bills that "would give official sanction to public employee strikes," and *The Blade* said that only Governor Rhodes' veto had protected Ohioans from this sanction. Existing legislation prohibited strikes but offered no alternative machinery, *The Blade* pointed out, as it urged Toledo's Democratic legislators to exert their influence to enact "a sound, responsible collective bargaining bill for public employees that does not include the right to strike."

Negotiations between the city and the police and fire unions dragged on for several more weeks, although contracts with other unions had been signed earlier. *The Blade* had little sympathy for union demands. When the president of Firefighters Local 92 complained that firemen were working as "slave labor," it was pointed out that their salaries were more than $24,000, plus fringe benefits, and "if they think they are being treated as slaves, they are free to leave the 'plantation' at any time." A subsequent editorial, headlined WHO RUNS THE CITY?, declared that "it would be neither sensible nor desirable to turn over to municipal employees the right to get whatever they demand."

Toledo was to feel the effects of the events of July, 1979, for a long time. In January, 1980, *The Blade* called attention to the fact that investigation of the fire bombing of the Plaza was still going on despite the fact that "so much is known." It cited several items of evidence pointing to the involvement of Plumbers Union Local 50, which had been in a protracted dispute with the Plaza's owner over his use of nonunion labor.

Economic conditions over the next several years — rising unemployment and declining tax revenue most notable among them — created new problems. When Toledo voters rejected an increase in the city's income tax in June, 1981, many municipal services had to be curtailed drastically. Dark days continued for Toledo, yet they presaged developments that would bring the city in the 1980s to the brink of a future that looked much brighter than any of its residents had so recently dared to hope.

Chapter 39

The Arrival of Tomorrow?

Mayor Harry Kessler named Paul Block, Jr., chairman of the Toledo Development Committee on June 3, 1975. When the co-publisher of *The Blade* resigned from the committee on May 25, 1979, the city was well embarked on a program of downtown redevelopment that held out the prospect of giving substance to some of the dreams that had been dreamed ever since the Toledo Tomorrow exhibit more than three decades earlier.

On the day he resigned, Paul Block, Jr., made this statement: "It's *The Blade*. I don't do things as an individual. *The Blade* has been doing things around here for 120 years." He added that *"The Blade* is behind my successes, but not my failures."

Whoever deserves the credit — and most observers suggest that the retiring chairman of the Toledo Development Committee was unduly modest — what had been accomplished in that four-year period was indeed remarkable among civic enterprises of its kind. It was not without its ups and downs for the chairman, including a 1975 mayoral campaign in which the avowed purpose of one of the candidates was to force Block's resignation from the chairmanship. Mrs. Pamela Daoust, a member of the City Council, alleged that endorsements by *The Blade* had been dangled before Council members by the newspaper's co-publisher, although others present on the occasions in question denied that such offers had been made. Mrs. Daoust survived the primary election in September, but was defeated by Mayor Kessler in November.

Paul Block, Jr., likes to reminisce about how he came to be involved in the development committee. He was discouraged by the previous three decades' halting progress toward renewal of the downtown area. Never much impressed with the way traditional city

The Arrival of Tomorrow? 349

planners went about their work, he decided that real imagination and creativity were needed. So he arranged a telephone conversation with Minoru Yamasaki, the architect from Troy, Michigan, who had made such a favorable impression on him during construction of the Medical College of Ohio.

"Would you like me to come down and see it?" Yamasaki had asked. He came and drew up a plan, centered on a plaza one story above the ground, running between Jackson and Adams Streets, from Erie Street to the waterfront. It was this plan that Paul Block, Jr., described as "large, dramatic, even grandiose" soon after he became chairman of the TDC, adding that its development would remove Toledo from the mediocrity of midwestern towns and "put it right on the map."

Revisions and modifications of the Yamasaki concept were to be made over the years, but the architect, who was subsequently engaged to design the city-county-state office building that was to be a central part of the plan, continued to provide much of the inspiration for the effort that was essential to transforming dream into reality.

★ ★ ★

The Blade had supported downtown development for many years. In May, 1959, it had applauded announcement by local architects that they were preparing to unveil a large-scale model for a reshaped and revitalized downtown Toledo. When the model was placed on exhibit three months later, it was praised as "realistic." *The Blade* hoped that "perhaps citizens can think about the future of the downtown . . . now that Toledo has shown a willingness to experiment with pedestrian malls downtown."

The news, in March, 1960, that three companies — Owens-Illinois, First National Bank of Toledo and Owens-Corning Fiberglas — were planning major improvement in their downtown buildings was seen as reassuring, as was Libbey-Owens-Ford's plan for a new headquarters building. Progress was reported in 1964 on the Vistula Meadows project on Cherry Street downtown, and Mayor Potter was quoted as hailing this development as an indication that "we are on our way." *The Blade* hoped he was right, but pointed out that arrangements for financing weren't yet clear. "Let's wait and see" was its advice.

There were setbacks, too, and *The Blade* was especially disturbed by the decision to build the new Masonic auditorium on

Heatherdowns Boulevard, seven miles southwest of downtown Toledo. It recalled that with the exception of the Scottish Rite, represented by Robert A. Stranahan and Dr. Howard Smith, all groups at a meeting only a year earlier had been in favor of a downtown location. Stranahan and Smith gave a sentimental reason for their opposition: Forty years previously, those in charge had wanted the Heatherdowns site. It was doubtful, *The Blade* observed, that Mr. Stranahan ran the Champion Spark Plug Company that way.

Disillusionment with what was being done — or, more accurately, not being done — by city planning agencies set in at *The Blade* in the late 1960s. There were too many changes in plan and direction. Not enough of the top echelon of Toledo business and industry were behind urban renewal projects. The city should be moving forcefully on planning and construction of off-street parking structures. The city's urban renewal office should be strengthened. New problems were upcoming. What was going on was aptly described as "merry-go-round planning" and, *The Blade* insisted, it was time to quit going in circles.

When talk of building a new convention center began in 1970, *The Blade* urged that it be given top priority. But it took strong objection two years later to the proposal that the center be located on the riverfront and commended Mayor Kessler for opposing that site. "The river is Toledo's greatest single asset," *The Blade* insisted, reminding its readers that "it has long been the dream of many people to turn the riverfront into a place of beauty and enjoyment for Toledoans." This has been a persistent theme in the newspaper's approach to nearly every aspect of downtown development, and it became the organizing factor in Minoru Yamasaki's bold design of a few years later.

The Blade sent a reporter to Louisville, Kentucky, in December, 1973, to find out how that Ohio River city had gone about renewing its downtown area — a plan that centered on the riverfront. This successful effort was reported to have been accomplished largely by private interests, with the cooperation of city and state. *The Blade* noted similarities between this operation and the Greater Toledo Corporation — a private agency supported by fifteen business and banking institutions that had pledged themselves to such a joint effort. GTC's president, Leslie Barr, had successfully directed

The Arrival of Tomorrow?   351

Louisville's comeback. "If it can be done in Louisville," *The Blade* wanted to know, "why not Toledo?"

Renewal plans suffered a temporary setback in April, 1974, when one of Toledo's oldest department stores, Lamson's, closed its downtown store. "Lamson's will be missed," *The Blade* noted, little suspecting that within the next ten years the two other major downtown department stores would be closed — the Lion Store in 1980, Macy's in 1984.

★ ★ ★

When Paul Block, Jr., resigned as chairman of the Toledo Development Committee, he said that he "had hoped to finish this assignment in two years, but the task seems to be one without end." He had decided, therefore, that "there will be no more logical time to step down than the fourth anniversary of my appointment to the TDC." He could look back at that point on a record of considerable accomplishment in getting downtown redevelopment in motion. Edwin D. Dodd, chairman and chief executive officer of Owens-Illinois, who had contributed much to the success of TDC's efforts, made this statement at the time: "Mr. Block's support was all-important to this undertaking. His efforts in behalf of the downtown reflect a dedication to service of his community to which he has devoted much of his life."

The Blade reported in July, 1977, that "a new vision of downtown Toledo showing tree-lined boulevards, green space, blocks of vehicle-free plaza, and millions of dollars in new public and private investment, was revealed Monday in a meeting of the Toledo Development Committee." As a part of this plan, Owens-Illinois prepared a bas-relief of its projected world headquarters building. *The Blade* widened its editorial page to include a photograph, accompanied by an editorial headlined FROM OWENS-ILLINOIS AND TDC: BLUEPRINT FOR A NEW DOWNTOWN. And in November, the new building was hailed as "a milestone on the path to a brighter tomorrow," citing Yamasaki's earlier comment that Toledo would now be "a brand new city."

A second major change in the Yamasaki plan came about in 1978, when problems developed about the site of the new government office building that was to provide the anchor at the north end of the boulevard. This controversy involved *The Blade* and its co-publisher in a brouhaha that brought attention from well beyond Toledo.

The original proposal was for the new building to house various governmental offices to be situated on the block bounded by Jackson, Adams, Huron and Erie streets. Unfortunately, this block included St. Paul's Lutheran church, which had been there for 110 years and which could not be induced to move, despite the offer of a new church building only a block distant.

This led some critics to designate the proposed site of the new government office building as "Block's Block." There were allegations that *The Blade* and its co-publisher were "trying to run St. Paul's congregation out of their church."[31] In fact, the offer of a new building was accepted by St. Paul's board of trustees but was rejected by the congregation. As a result, the office building project was moved a block north, and the boulevard linking it with the river and the Owens-Illinois building was accomplished by means of widening Jackson Street. The resulting street was less grandiose than the original boulevard suggested by Edwin Dodd, chief executive officer of Owens-Illinois, Inc.

★ ★ ★

Mayor Doug DeGood's decision to disband the planning unit, announced a few days after Paul Block, Jr., resigned as chairman of the Toledo Development Committee, was seen by *The Blade* as "an indication that Toledo has moved from talking and planning to actual, physical rebirth." It has continued to be supportive of the spirit of that process, although it has not always approved of individual actions taken to that end. When it has dissented, the basis of its disagreement most often has been the position it has so long taken in the matter of protecting the Maumee River waterfront from exploitation in ways that threaten its value as a focal point for recreation and aesthetic enjoyment.

Thus, *The Blade* from the first has praised the role played in the development of the SeaGate Center by Owens-Illinois and Edwin Dodd. But when, in July, 1980, O-I asked the city to apply for a $7,500,000 federal grant to help finance construction of a 300-room hotel next door to the company's new building, *The Blade* objected that "the time has come for Council to say NO!" It cited the considerable help already granted to the company in relation to SeaGate and pointed out that the hotel would shut off the river from parts of downtown Toledo. "We need a hotel," *The Blade* admitted, "but not on that site."

Again, in 1983, when the city completed and opened a huge new multi-story parking garage that cut across the Vistula Meadows area from O-I's headquarters building to the northeast, *The Blade* protested the wall between the downtown and the riverfront. Its editorial startled many of its readers — a huge picture of the parking garage was spread across the entire upper portion of two pages, emphasizing its fortress-like quality in a way words alone could not have accomplished.

When the new Portside Festival Marketplace opened in May, 1984, *The Blade* joined in the general expression of enthusiasm and approval. The 97,000-square-foot structure situated south of the new hotel is seen as the catalyst in attracting stores, restaurants and — eventually — residential facilities to downtown Toledo. It is the work of James W. Rouse, creator of the Fanueil Hall Marketplace in Boston and Harborplace in Baltimore.

The Blade remains concerned about some aspects of the city's downtown redevelopment. Many gaps remain to be filled in the older parts of downtown — some of which have been almost completely abandoned in recent years — and there is still little sign of movement toward residential development in the area. *The Blade* continues to call attention to these matters, as it continues to resist plans for exploiting the riverfront area in ways that might undermine the integrity of Minoru Yamasaki's concept of greenery, open spaces and the Maumee riverfront as a place where Toledoans can enjoy the city's greatest asset.

Chapter 40

The Blade at 150

Newspapers sprang up in considerable numbers in the decade of the 1830s and they included such distinguished journals as Benjamin Day's New York *Sun* (1833), James Gordon Bennett's New York *Herald* (1835), and the Baltimore *Sun* (1837). Only a few have survived through a century and a half of continuous operation.

The Blade, in reaching its 150th birthday on December 19, 1985, joins a small number of newspapers which have achieved that age. One of these is its sister publication, the Pittsburgh *Post-Gazette.*

Journalists and scholars of journalism have a tendency to look back on these 150 years as the Golden Age of the newspaper in America. It is usually intimated — if not specifically stated — that the outlook for the future is far from promising. But *The Blade* at 150 shows no signs of imminent decline.

The Blade has been established as Toledo's one daily newspaper. The decision to discontinue publication of the Toledo *Times* in 1975 probably determined that status for the foreseeable future, although a spirited effort to start a competing newspaper was made in 1977. This was the *Daybreak Dispatch,* which remained in operation from August, 1977, to March, 1978.

Its publisher was Corey D. Garber, an ambitious young Toledoan who had sought to oust Congressman Thomas Ludlow Ashley in the Democratic party primary a year earlier and who had accused *The Blade* of unfair treatment. He formed the Garber Publishing Company and began to distribute some 120,000 copies of a free morning newspaper. Garber was reported to have had the backing of a number of wealthy Toledo residents, including at least one member of the Champion Spark Plug Stranahan family.

Garber mounted what he obviously considered to be a major

The Blade at 150

campaign against *The Blade*. When the support he had expected from major advertisers failed to materialize, he began a series of front-page editorials in which he accused *The Blade* of engaging in "unfair and potentially illegal activities . . . to kill the *Daybreak Dispatch,* to insulate the *Blade's* monopoly in the marketplace; and to protect Paul Block's enormous editorial control over this city." Exerting pressure on advertisers and intimidating carriers were among the "unfair and potentially illegal activities" of which Garber accused *The Blade.*

The last repercussions from these charges were not laid to rest until April, 1984, when Garber's anti-trust lawsuit against the Toledo Blade Company was dismissed after both sides had sought an agreement. The suit, filed in 1981, alleged monopolistic practices and unfair competition. The settlement required that Garber pay $1 to *The Blade* to satisfy a counterclaim alleging defamatory statements in speeches, newspapers and other publications.

The Justice Department had earlier empaneled a special grand jury to investigate alleged criminal violations by *The Blade.* This dragged on for more than a year, until the investigation was closed in June, 1979.

★ ★ ★

The Blade has moved, in the last five years, into a period of generational transition. Both Paul Block, Jr., and William Block, after more than four decades as co-publishers of *The Blade* and the Pittsburgh *Post-Gazette,* continue to be active in the newspapers, making day-to-day decisions and shaping long-range planning and policy. Each continues to act as publisher of the newspaper in the city where he lives, but major decisions about either newspaper are made jointly.

The Blocks, unlike many newspaper families, have continued in the third generation to maintain an active interest in the operation of the newspapers, rather than an eagerness to dispose of them and invest in more lucrative enterprises. Three of the sons of the co-publishers have begun to play active roles, and all three were named members of the board of directors of the Toledo Blade Company in December, 1984. William Block, Jr., who was publisher of the Red Bank *Register* for a time before its sale, joined *The Blade* in 1982 and is now director of operations. Paul Block, Jr.'s twin sons joined *The*

Blade in 1980 — John Robinson Block is Sunday editor, Allan Block is director of electronic planning.

Another new member of *The Blade's* executive staff is John Harms, longtime Detroit newspaper executive who was named president in 1982 to succeed John Willey after his retirement.

There is — perhaps inevitably — some uneasiness among staff members about the direction in which generational transition may take *The Blade*. There have been a number of changes in key personnel recently, though hardly more than on other newspapers. The rumor factory — a particularly busy aspect of all newspaper operations — has predicted more changes than have actually taken place.

An exception should be noted in relation to a succession of executive editors in recent years, some of whom have remained for periods of only a few weeks or months. The position has been vacant since October, 1984, and Bernard Judy, subsequently named editor-in-chief, has assumed some of the responsibilities previously assigned to the executive editor, while continuing to supervise the editorial page operations.

★ ★ ★

The Blade has seemed to some to be engaged, during the first five years of the 1980s, in a search for its own identity. No revolutionary changes have taken place, nor is there evidence that any such changes are likely in the immediate future. The newspaper's conception of itself was accurately stated in 1966 by Ed Fallon, the managing editor: "We try to make *The Blade* a truly metropolitan newspaper: to make it the only newspaper a person really needs to read to be well-informed."

Anyone who reads *The Blade* with any regularity must note its adherence to this concept. Its efforts to fulfill this function have, in fact, brought criticism from some observers. More emphasis should be placed, they contend, on coverage of state and local news; money spent to maintain a European presence might, for example, be better invested in a second man in the Columbus bureau.

The Blade has paid little attention to these criticisms. Most recently — during 1984 — its own reporters have continued to be present at the sites of major news events, rather than depending on wire service coverage. Both the Winter Olympics in Sarajevo and the summer games in Los Angeles were reported by *Blade* staffers — Lynda Brooker from Sarajevo and Tom Loomis, sports columnist, from Los Angeles. Later in the year, as the famine crisis in Africa worsened, a two-man team was dispatched there — Michael Woods, science editor, and George Joseph Tanber, staff writer. Beginning on November 18, they reported regularly on both the natural and human elements of widespread starvation. John Nichols wrote accompanying articles to provide an overview of the problems and the answers proposed.

The Blade has never been a crusading newspaper. Its consistent philosophy has been that its responsibilities are best served by means of thorough and consistent attention to public business. Paul Block, Jr., contends, for example, that a principal reason why Toledo has been relatively free from graft and corruption in public affairs is *The Blade's* watching and reporting the activities of public officials so thoroughly.

Beyond that — as Michael Bradshaw put it during his editorship — what is important in terms of editorial effectiveness is the attitudes a newspaper helps to create among its readers over a period of years, not the kind of overnight change that most crusades try to bring about. *The Blade* has adhered to these tenets in the past, and there is little evidence of any immediate change.

This philosophy probably accounts in part for the fact that *The Blade's* name has been absent from the ranks of prize winners in national competitions — of which the Pulitzer Prizes are best known — which have placed increasing emphasis on the crusading variety of journalism.

In many categories, however, *The Blade* has been a consistent award winner. Especially notable have been those of the American and the Ohio bar associations for various aspects of the reporting of trials and the approach to reporting news in all areas of the law.

Five times during the years from 1962 to 1969, the Ohio Bar Association cited *The Blade* as the top newspaper in the state for its coverage of law and courts. Twice — in 1965 and again in 1967 — the American Bar Association's Silver Gavel Award was presented to *The Blade* "for outstanding contributions to public understanding of the American system of law and justice." *The Blade's* formulation of a voluntary code of fair practice in coverage of criminal news to guard against prejudicing the rights of the accused was the basis for the 1967 award.

Michael Woods, science editor, has been a consistent winner of both national and state awards. Among these have been first prize in 1983 in the annual journalism awards of the American Academy of Family Physicians; first place in the 1982 competition sponsored by four national radiological organizations; the James T. McGrady Award of the American Chemical Society for "interpreting chemistry to the public" in 1977, and a number of awards in state competitions.

Boris Nelson, arts editor, was awarded a $1,000 first prize by the American Society of Composers, Authors and Publishers for articles published in *The Blade* during 1970. The Ohio Arts Council presented *The Blade* an award for media support of the arts in 1978.

Duane Croft, associate editor, received the Sigma Delta Chi national award for editorial writing in 1967. Ralph H. Johnson, editorial director, was awarded the Pulliam Fellowship, given by the Sigma Delta Chi Foundation, in 1983. The award carried a $10,000 grant which permitted Mr. Johnson to study the impact of national and international trade on the Midwest, Ohio, and Toledo.

Members of *The Blade's* photography department have been consistent winners in both national and state competition, and many other individual staff members have been recognized for outstanding work in a variety of categories. The newspaper has been cited by consumer groups and many others for meritorious performance. And, in 1977, *The Blade* Building was designated by the Society of Professional Journalists, Sigma Delta Chi, as a historic site in American journalism, honoring David Ross Locke, the newspaper's editor from 1865 to 1888.

★ ★ ★

The Blade has not specialized in the kind of grand scale promotional activity by which many newspapers seek to call attention to their beneficence. It has maintained involvement in a variety of public activities — some of which have become traditional in Toledo.

Much the best known of these is the Old Newsboys Goodfellow Association, founded in 1929, although its beginnings go back to Toledo's first charity newspaper sale in 1907. Ray Kest, *The Blade's* longtime circulation manager, was the moving force in this undertaking until his death in 1964. "Feed people first, investigate later" was the philosophy Kest once expressed in relation to the Old Newsboys' efforts, which provided food, clothing, toys and other comforts for the city's poor. Beginning with an annual street sale of a special edition newspaper just before Christmas, with leading citizens who had once sold or carried newspapers taking to the streets again, the association grew into a wide-ranging charity organization that staged a variety of fund-raising events throughout the year. *The Blade* contributed $5,000 in 1965 to the Ray Kest Old Newsboys Goodfellow Scholarship fund, established to honor the man who had given so much of his time and energy to this undertaking.

Many of the community activities which *The Blade* has sponsored have been oriented toward participation, often providing instruction or information. In sports, there has been an annual ski school at Mount Brighton, Michigan, and a baseball clinic with members of the Toledo Mud Hens International League baseball team as instructors. There have been poetry contests, recipe contests, and even a contest to choose the Mud Hens' bat boy.

Inexpensive tours of Ohio college and university campuses for graduating high school seniors have been sponsored by *The Blade*. So have a food fair and a children's book fair. A speakers' bureau provides Blade staff members to speak to groups of many kinds. A travel forum brings a series of travel films to Toledo each year.

Sometimes *The Blade* joins with others to sponsor special events. Thus, in 1969, the Boston Pops Orchestra, with Arthur Fiedler conducting, came to Toledo under joint auspices of the Toledo Orchestra and *The Blade*. A seminar on citizens' rights was co-sponsored with the Toledo Bar Association in 1983; for many years, *The Blade* has sponsored a free arthritis forum in conjunction with the Arthritis Foundation of Northwest Ohio.

Numerous high school athletic and educational events are sponsored, including *The Blade* relays each spring. School traffic safety awards are distributed through the Green Banner Safety program. A number of newspaper-related seminars are held each year.

The emphasis has been on widening the range of activities and interests available to Toledo area residents of all ages. Their purpose includes an element of calling attention to *The Blade*, but a low-key quality has minimized the promotional aspects in favor of encouraging community involvement.

★ ★ ★

The Blade continued to improve and expand its physical plant during the last fifteen years and to make changes in its equipment. These reflect management's response both to the continuing growth of the newspaper and to the need to keep pace with technological developments that have changed so many aspects of newspaper production.

They also reflect a commitment to maintaining *The Blade's* downtown location. After nearly sixty years at the intersection of Superior, Beech and Orange Streets, there is no intention of moving.

To this end, *The Blade* building has been expanded several times. Storage for newsprint in the basement of the building was increased in 1970 and a transportation system for newsprint was installed. A new boiler room was installed as an addition to the south side of the building in 1982 to provide gas-generated heat, replacing steam heat that had been supplied by the Toledo Edison steam plant. The newsroom was redesigned and redecorated in 1985 and the mailroom was expanded on the south side of the building to facilitate the operation of inserting advertising materials. A new inserting machine has been added to one already in use.

There have been several major equipment changes, beginning with the introduction of an Itek copy processing system — generally known as "cold type" — a computer system for production, news and classified advertising departments. This installation required three years — 1975 to 1978. It has been followed in 1985 by a new Atex copy-processing system, enabling reporters and classified advertising salespersons to enter copy on video display terminals.

A Letterflex platemaking system was installed in 1982, providing the ability to control the quality of plates, which are made of steel backing and photosensitized liquid polymer. An extensive program of improvements in *The Blade's* presses was carried out in 1984-85. Page size was changed to enable *The Blade* to offer standard advertising units to national and regional advertisers.

Recent circulation figures reflect *The Blade's* continuing physical growth. Reports of the national Audit Bureau of Circulations and continuing in-office reports suggest that circulation for the daily edition has stabilized at about 165,000 (the most recent monthly figure is 164,487) after declining from a peak of 193,000 in 1953, following a national trend. During the same period, however, the Sunday edition of *The Blade* has gained dramatically — from some 160,000 in 1953 to 222,500 in November, 1984 — an all-time high.

Despite increasing competition for advertising — especially national advertising — *The Blade* has shown a healthy growth in total linage. The total has been above 40,000,000 in most of the last ten years, compared with the 31,000,000 linage in 1953.

Continued expansion of the parent Toledo Blade Company into diversified media properties provides a further strengthening of *The Blade's* financial status. Both the television and cable operations have continued to expand in recent years.

★ ★ ★

What, finally, can be said of *The Blade* — its past and its future — on this occasion of its 150th birthday? On the whole, there seems to be little to add to what has been recorded in these chapters.

The Blade does not, as has been noted earlier, believe in political polls. Nor does the author believe in going out among readers of *The Blade* or to those who might be designated experts in their judgment of newspapers, seeking data on which to base some sort of concluding assessment. The statement from Edwin Emery's *The Press in America,* quoted earlier, is indicative of the esteem in which the newspaper is held by many such observers.

One of *The Blade's* particular strengths is, surely, that it has never been owned and managed by individuals who have seen themselves as being engaged in a popularity contest. Many people in Toledo dislike Paul Block, Jr., for the positions *The Blade* has taken on a variety of issues. This could also be said of David Ross Locke in his time. And of Jesup Scott and Joseph Williams. All of these men have sought the respect, not the affection, of their readers. That respect has been almost universally granted — however grudgingly on some occasions.

This is a rich heritage for a newspaper embarking on the last half of the second century of its existence. It imposes a heavy obligation, too, on the generations following those who have established this reputation of *The Blade*.

NOTES

PART I

1 Taft, William Howard, *The Toledo Blade, Its First One Hundred Years,* pp. 2-7.

2 Winter, Nevin O., *A History of Northwest Ohio,* Lewis Publishing Co., New York, p. 82. Cited in Taft, p. 27.

3 Barclay, Morgan and Glaab, Charles N., *Toledo: Gateway to the Great Lakes,* Continental Heritage Press, Tulsa, pp. 25-26.

4 Ibid., pp. 39-40.

5 Taft, p. 25.

6 *Blade,* May 16, 1837. Cited in Taft, p. 108.

7 Waggoner, Clark, *History of Toledo and Lucas County,* Munsell & Co., New York, p. 695.

8 *Biographical Cyclopaedia and Portrait Gallery of the State of Ohio,* II, p. 572. Cited in Taft, p. 30.

9 *Gateway,* pp. 26-27.

10 *Blade,* Oct. 17, 1872. Cited in Taft, p. 30.

11 *Gateway,* pp. 17-18.

12 *Blade,* Oct. 21, 1846. Cited in Taft, p. 31.

13 *Gateway,* p. 27.

14 Taft, pp. 15-16.

15 *Blade,* July 22, 1850. Cited in Taft, p. 95.

16 Taft, p. 45.

17 *Blade,* Oct. 20, 1862. Williams County is located on the Ohio-Indiana border and was at the westernmost edge of the congressional district.

18 Klement, Frank L., *The Limits of Dissent,* The University Press of Kentucky, Lexington, pp. 156ff.

19 Cited in Taft, p. 173.

PART II

1 *Reminiscences of Nasby,* Toledo *Sunday Journal,* November 18, 1894.

2 *Toledo Weekly Blade,* Promotional pamphlet issued by the Toledo Blade Company, 1885.

3 *Blade,* February 26, 1840. Cited by Taft, p. 50.

4 Taft, p. 51.

5 *Ibid.,* pp. 53-54.

Notes

6 *Ibid.*, p. 55.

7 George P. Rowell, *Forty Years an Advertising Agent*, p. 258.

8 *Ibid.*, p. 100.

9 Paul Buck, *The Road to Reunion*, pp. 20-21.

10 The reference is to Jefferson Davis, president of the Confederacy, and two others prominent in Confederate affairs.

11 Taft, pp. 269-270.

12 "Some Little Account of the Founder of the Toledo *Blade*," pamphlet published after Locke's death in 1888.

13 John M. Harrison, *The Man Who Made Nasby, David Ross Locke*, p. 168.

14 Taft, pp. 288ff

15 *Ibid.*, pp. 320-321.

16 *Ibid.*, pp. 326-327.

17 *Ibid.*, pp. 328-329.

18 Harrison, p. 249.

19 *The Morals of Abou ben Adhem* comprised a series of satirical sketches written by Locke and published by Lee and Shepard, Boston, in 1875. Abou was represented as a Persian philosopher, several hundred years old, who had established himself in a New Jersey village where he dispensed advice on many subjects.

20 John McElroy was managing editor of the *Blade*. He wrote a series of articles about life in Confederate prisons for the *Weekly Blade*, which were subsequently published in book form under the title *Andersonville* (see p. 107). He was later with the *National Tribune* in Washington, D.C.

21 James Parker Locke had achieved some fame as a cornetist, having studied with a leading teacher in Boston at the expense of his uncle, David Locke. He was best known for his ability to play two cornets simultaneously.

22 The Draconian (now Toledo) Club was founded in 1875 by a group of leading citizens who met regularly for an evening of discussion or other entertainment. It was Locke who proposed that the club be named for Draco, Athenian lawgiver, sixth century B. C., whose name is remembered for the particularly barbarous code of laws he promulgated.

23 For the best study of this controversy, see Chester M. Destler, "The Toledo Natural Gas Pipe-Line Controversy," *Historical Society of Northwest Ohio Quarterly Bulletin*, XV (April, 1943), 76-110.

24 Taft, pp. 287-288.

25 David Ross Locke died in the period between January and August, 1888, but it is doubtful that he had much part in editorial decisions at this time.

26 Taft, pp. 390ff.

27 Frank G. Carpenter. Unidentified newspaper clipping, 1895. Locke Papers, Hays Library, Fremont, Ohio.

28 *Ibid.*

29 THE BLADE did not, in fact, issue a Sunday edition until 1947. The Toledo *Times,* also owned by the Block family, had previously published a Sunday paper.

30 Taft, pp. 305-306.

31 *Ibid.,* pp. 302-303.

32 *Ibid.,* pp. 375-376.

33 *Ibid.,* p. 432.

34 Brand Whitlock wrote several novels which received considerable critical attention — much of it favorable — in the first two decades of the twentieth century. Best known are *The Turn of the Balance,* which exposed prison brutality, and *The Thirteenth District,* a study of corruption in politics.

35 Brand Whitlock, *Forty Years of It,* p. 130.

36 Robinson Locke was married July 15, 1886, to Katherine King of Toledo. She died in 1894.

37 Thalheimer changed his name to Talmadge several years after completion of the lease arrangement with the Locke family.

38 Taft, p. 44.

39 Grove Patterson, *I Like People,* p. 84.

40 Barclay and Glaab, *Toledo: Gateway to the Great Lakes,* pp. 95, 101.

41 Patterson, pp. 118 ff.

42 Taft, pp. 509ff.

43 *Ibid.,* p. 310.

PART III

1 George Seldes, *Lords of the Press,* p. 67.

2 Robert W. Wells, *The Milwaukee Journal,* p. 214.

3 Seldes, pp. 67-68.

4 *Ibid.,* p. 70.

5 Interview with Herman W. Liebert by John Robinson Block, Yale University, April 14, 1977.

6 Seldes, pp. 68-69.

7 Herbert W. Mitgang, *Atlantic Monthly,* October, 1962, pp. 103-104.

8 New York *World-Telegram,* May 24, 1932.

9 Liebert interview.

10 Seldes, p. 69.

11 Hertel's nephew, John Grigsby, a member of *The Blade* staff, recalls that his uncle visited the Grigsby home near the end of the time he remained in Toledo and reported some aspects of his part in the transfer of ownership.

12 Taft, p. 257.

13 P. 295, this volume

14 Liebert interview.

15 *Blade*, September 13, 1927. Cited in Taft, p. 502.

16 *Blade*, November 7, 1928. Cited in Taft, p. 476.

17 *Toledo: Gateway to the Great Lakes*, p. 134.

18 *Ibid.*, p. 134.

19 Taft, p. 478.

20 *Ibid.*, p. 480.

21 Samuel M. Jones Papers, Toledo-Lucas County Public Library. Knapp to Jones, October 21, 1902.

22 *Gateway*, pp. 148-150.

23 Taft, pp. 504-506.

24 *Ibid.*, pp. 507-508.

25 Sprigle was a star reporter for the *Post-Gazette*, whose work sometimes appeared in *The Blade*. His best-known series was a pioneering report on the American Negro, for which he tinted his skin and represented himself as a black.

26 As late as 1950, some Toledoans still recalled the "good old days" of the *News-Bee*, though most Scripps-Howard newspapers had by then moved well to the right politically. Even in the summer of 1984, a carry-out clerk at a Toledo grocery store suggested that a history of the *News-Bee* would be even more interesting than one of *The Blade*.

27 Figures giving specific information are cited in later chapters.

28 Edwin Emery, *The Press in America*, p. 667: "In Ohio, Publisher Paul Block, Jr.'s Toledo *Blade* advanced rapidly in the 1950s in comprehensive news coverage, community leadership, and independence of opinion . . . The *Blade* also was one of the few American dailies to have a European correspondent."

29 Lloyd Roulet was owner of a jewelry company, Howard Crosby of a real estate firm. Both were prominent in the Republican party and in the City Manager League.

30 Reo M. Christenson, *Midwest Journal of Political Science, Vol. II, No. 3, August, 1959, p. 238.*

31 Michael Castranova, *Ohio Magazine*, April, 1979, p. 46.

SOURCES

Most of the materials used in this book are from THE BLADE itself. Microfilm files of the weekly, tri-weekly and daily editions from 1835 to 1985 have been used extensively. So have clippings and other materials filed in THE BLADE library, as well as records of the Toledo Blade Company and of Paul Block and Associates. Some of Paul Block's personal papers have also been examined.

Other primary sources included two collections of papers: the Robinson Locke collection at the Rutherford B. Hayes Memorial Library in Fremont, Ohio, and the letters of Samuel P. Jones at the Toledo-Lucas County Public Library.

Two unpublished manuscripts have been used extensively. One of these — William Howard Taft's dissertation on the first one hundred years of THE BLADE — is acknowledged in the preface. The other is a biography of Samuel M. Jones, titled Sam Jones and the Golden Rule, by John M. Harrison and Harvey S. Ford.

The author has interviewed many individuals. John Robinson Block's interview of Herman Liebert, one-time associate of Paul Block, which took place at Yale University on April 14, 1977, has been especially helpful.

Notes to the three parts of the book acknowledge additional secondary sources. Of these, most extensive use has been made of these three:

Charles Nelson Glaab and Morgan J. Barclay, Toledo: Gateway to the Great Lakes.

John M. Harrison, The Man Who Made Nasby, David Ross Locke.

Grove Patterson, I Like People.

INDEX

A

Adams, Charles F., 28.
Akron Beacon-Journal, 289.
Altgeld, John P., 158.
American Farm Journal, 106.
American Mercury, 295.
American Protective Association, 147.
Anderson, Dr. Martin, 334.
Andrews, Samuel, 32.
Arliss, George, 143.
Arnold, S. G., 42.
Arthur, Chester A., 126.
Ashley, James M., 51, 61, 64ff, 83, 96ff, 109, 125.
Ashley, James M., Jr., 149, 152.
Ashley, Thomas Ludlow, 68, 311ff, 327.
Atlantic Monthly, 210.
Auberjonois, Fernand, 295ff, 226, 319.
Austin, James, Jr., 167.

B

Backus, Abner, L., 46.
Ballinger, Richard A., 181.
Banks, N. P., 39.
Barber, William, 190.
Barrymore, Lionel, 194.
Bartley, Rudolph A., 160.
Batt, William L., Jr., 292.
Battelle, J. B., 126.
Beaverbrook, Lord, 262.
Beecher, Lucas J., 162, 200.
Bel Geddes, Norman, 272, 280.
Bell, Clark, 111.
Bell, Louise, 239.
Belli, Melvin, 322.
Benton, Thomas Hart, 21.
Berdan, John, 8.
Berlacher, Franz, 293.
Bernhardt, Sarah, 143.
Beye, Dr. Robert, 211.

Bissell, Edward, 4, 11.
Black, Hugo L., 255.
Blaine, James G., 128, 135, 145.
Blanchard S. S., 13, 16.
Block, Allan, 356.
Block, Dina W., 266.
Block, John, 207.
Block, John Robinson, 356.
Block, Marjorie M., 289ff, 320.
Block, Max, 205, 222, 267.
Block, Paul, 124, 177, 203, 205ff, 287, 294.
Block, Paul, Jr., 210, 218, 266ff, 287, 294, 305ff, 315, 330ff, 348ff, 355, 357, 361.
Block, William, 218, 266ff, 302, 355.
Block, William, Jr., 355.
Bolles, Blair, 295ff, 299.
Bolman, John W., 284.
Bouton, Emily S., 113, 138, 142ff.
Boutwell, George S., 94.
Bowling Green Wood County News, 235.
Bradshaw, Michael, 270, 298, 304ff, 320, 357.
Brisbane, Arthur, 259.
Brooker, Lynda, 356.
Brooklyn Daily Times, 234.
Brooklyn Standard-Union, 208, 234.
Brooks, Dr. Glidden, 333.
Brough, John M., 73.
Brower, William A., 336.
Brown, Joe E., 277.
Brown, John, 47.
Brown, Walter F., 162, 163, 181, 186, 224.
Bruner, Louise, 302.
Bruner, Ray, 301.
Bryan, William Jennings, 165, 180, 189.
Buchanan, James, 38, 43.
Buck, Paul, 87.
Buckeye Cablevision, 329.
Buggie, Frederic S., 202, 213, 222.
Bundy, Major James M., 111.
Bunge, Arnold, 240.
Burke, Thomas, 284, 311.
Burnside, General Ambrose, 72.

Index

C

Campbell, James E., 145.
Campbell, Mrs. Patrick, 143.
Carter, Jimmy, 309.
Case, Frank M., 66.
Cass, Lewis, 9, 28.
Cavalieri, Lena, 194.
Chaflin, George D., 105.
Chase, Salmon P., 37, 53, 97.
Chicago Tribune, 89, 256, 262.
Christian Statesman, 102.
Cincinnati Commercial, 83.
Clay, Henry, 14, 19, 28, 33, 35.
Cleveland, Grover, 128, 135, 145.
Cleveland Leader, 161, 202.
Cleveland Plain Dealer, 176.
Cochran, Negley D., 157, 172, 178, 260.
Colfax, Schuyler, 98.
Columbia Telescope, 17.
Columbus Ohio State Journal, 126.
Columbus Ohio Statesman, 11.
Comly, General James M., 126.
Commager, General Henry S., 109.
Coolidge, Calvin, 200, 219, 223.
Cooper, Myers, Y., 222.
Corbin, Charles, 260.
Cortland County Democrat, 82.
Corwin, Thomas, 13.
Cottrell, Florance E., 203, 214.
Cox, George B., 162ff.
Cox, James M., 200.
Coxey, Jacob, 146.
Coy, Cyrus H., 115ff.
Craig, John, 148.
Croft, Duane, 358.
Crouse, Hiram P., 157.
Cummins, Albert B., 182.
Curtis, Charles Locke, 128, 162.
Czolgosz, Leon, 179.

D

Damas, Michael, 317, 330.
Daniels, W. J., 4.
Davies, David T., 166.
Davies, Marion, 209.
Davis, John W., 200.
Dayton Empire, 72.
Dayton Herald, 270.
DeGood, Doug, 352.
DeSeversky, Alexander P., 272.
Des Moines Sunday Register, 287.
Detroit Free Press, 28.
Detroit Journal, 177, 208, 215, 222.
Dewey, Thomas E., 284.
DeWolfe, William T. ("Chub"), 217, 292.
Dodd, Edwin D., 352.
Donahey, A. Vic, 222.
Douglas, Stephen, 45, 50, 60.

Doyle, Msgr. Michael J., 324.
Dreiser, Theodore, 144.
Driscoll, William D., 322ff.
Dubuque Times, 90.
Duluth Herald, 214, 221.
Duluth News-Tribune, 233, 234.
Dun, Clara C., 226.
Dun, George, 226.
Dunne, Finlay Peter, 173.
Dustman, F. L., 162.

E

Edwards, Paul, 46.
Edy, John, 243.
Eisenhower, Dwight D., 37, 305.
Elmira Telegram, 207.
Erie County Cablevision, 329.
Everett, Dr. Wilson, 4.

F

Fairbanks, Abel W., 9, 13, 15, 21, 27, 29, 30.
Fallon, Edward P., 290.
Farm Life, 203.
Farrar, Geraldine, 194.
Fillmore, Millard, 28, 32, 43.
Finch, Arnold, 279.
Finch, Robert H., 157, 159.
Findlay Hancock Jeffersonian, 77, 94.
Fiske, Minnie Maddern, 143.
Foraker, Joseph B., 120, 145, 149.
Ford, Harvey, 335.
Fremont, John C., 37, 43, 59.
Fremont Lower Sandusky Whig, 42.

G

Garber, Corey D., 354ff.
Garfield, James A., 113.
Gladieux, Virgil, 280.
Gleason, A. W., 106.
Goodrich, Calvin, 167.
Gosser, Richard T., 275, 283ff, 293.
Gough, John B., 104.
Gould, Louis H., 214.
Graham, Mrs. Elizabeth, 222.
Graham, Dr. Hosmer, 29.
Graham, Walter, 287.
Graham, William A., 34.
Grant, Ulysses S., 65, 93, 95, 98.
Graves, Edward A., 13, 15.
Greeley, Horace, 93, 107.
Green, Charles C., 163.
Griffin, Charles P., 130, 149.
Guilbert, W. D., 162.
Guitteau, Dr. William B., 222.

Index

H

Hale, Thomas, 81, 82.
Halstead, Murat, 120.
Hamilton, J. K., 130.
Hanna, Mark, 149, 180.
Hansen, Michael F., 214.
Harding, Warren G., 193, 200.
Harms, John, 356.
Harnish, Amos, 266.
Harper's, 295.
Harrison, Benjamin, 135.
Harrison, William Henry, 10, 12, 24.
Hastings, John A., 210.
Havas News Agency, 296.
Hayes, Rutherford B., 108, 138.
Hearst, William Randolph, 208, 218, 233, 259, 260.
Heins, Lester, 301, 319.
Helper, Hinton R., 49.
Henry, Arthur, 144.
Herron, George D., 150.
Hertel, John H., 214.
Higgins, E. A., 105.
Hinkle, John N., 154.
Hitler, Adolph, 232.
Hoadley, George R., 120.
Hone, Parks, 148.
Hoover, Herbert, 223ff.
Hosmer, Hezekiah L., 11, 24, 27, 36.
Hosmer, Stephen T., 31.
Howe, Franklin T., 142.
Huber, J. M., 81.
Hughes, Charles Evans, 191.
Hungerford, Cyrus, 277.
Huntley, G. W., 166.
Hurd, Frank H., 108.
Hurin, Mary Locke, 139.

I

Ide, Charles, 293.
Indianapolis Journal, 202.
Indianapolis Sentinel, 202.
Irving, Pierre, 8, 9.
Irving, Washington, 8.

J

Jackson, William T., 222, 242.
Janis, Martin, 312.
Jenks, George, 235.
Johns, E. B., 162.
Johnson, Andrew, 75, 76, 88, 109.
Johnson, Lyndon, 309.
Johnson, Ralph H., 358.
Johnson, Tom, 154.
Jones, John Paul, 85, 105, 165.
Jones, Samuel M., 68, 149ff, 238.
Judy, Bernard, 290, 356.

K

Kaptur, Marcy, 313.
Keeler, Coleman I., 4.
Keller, Carl, 168.
Kendall, Amost, 25.
Kennedy, G. Donald, 273.
Kennedy, Jackie, 239.
Kennedy, John F., 271, 309.
Kessler, Harry, 348.
Kest, Ray, 358.
Ketcham, George B., 149.
King, William R., 34.
Klewer, Lou, 319.
Klotz, Solon, 242.
Knabenshue, A. Roy, 113.
Knabenshue, Samuel S., 113, 142.
Knapp, Perry, 239.
Knox, Col. Frank, 252, 263.
Koch, Alfred, 218.

L

LaFollette, Robert M., 182, 200.
Lamb, Sylvester, 164.
Lancaster New Era, 221, 266.
Landon, Alfred M., 252
Lane, Frank T., 86, 106, 113, 115, 140, 142, 183.
Lang, A. E., 169.
Larouche, Lyndon, 214.
Latimer, P. E., 32.
Lausche, Frank J., 330.
Lawford, Geoffrey, 272.
Lawrence, David, 234.
Lee, Robert E., 75.
Levis, J. Preston, 332.
Lewis, Frank, 214.
Libbey, Edward Drummond, 143, 182.
Licavoli, Jimmie, 239.
Licavoli, Pete, 239.
Licavoli, Thomas (Yonnie), 239.
Liebert, Herman W., 219, 263.
Liebling, A. J., 209.
Life, 273, 291, 297.
Lincoln, Abraham, 45, 50, 71, 87, 94.
Lincoln, Robert T., 135.
Lloyd, Henry Demarest, 132.
Locke, Charles, 214.
Locke, David Ross, 51, 77, 78, 283, 294, 302, 334, 336, 361.
Locke, Henry, 110.
Locke, James Parker, 111.
Locke, Otis, 139.
Locke, Robinson, 106, 110, 126, 128, 140, 147, 187, 201, 214, 238, 294, 302, 330.
Locke's National Monthly, 106.
Lodge, Henry Cabot, 190, 199.
London Express, 264.
Loomis, Tom, 356.

Index

Lorain Times-Herald, 176.
Los Angeles Press, 233.
Lucas Robert, 3, 7.
Luce, Clare Boothe (Brokaw), 212, 259.
Lundberg, Ferdinand, 208.

M

McBain, Daniel, 13, 15.
McCarthy, Joseph R., 304.
McClelland, George B., 59, 71, 73.
McCormick, Col. Robert R., 262.
McCune, Robert, 102.
McElroy, John, 113.
McGovern, George, 309.
McGrady, Edwin F., 281.
McKinley, William, 146, 236, 179.
McKinnon, W. D., 163.
McMaken, Gen. William V., 154.
McRae, Milton A., 172.
MacDonald, James, 298, 320, 322.
Macelwane, Geraldine, 323.
Major, Guy C., 147.
Manchester Guardian, 318.
Marsh, Ben, 312.
Martin, Royce, 218.
Mason, Stevens T., 7.
Mathews, J. A., 182.
Maumee Express, 10.
Maumee Miami of the Lake, 21, 18.
Maumee Times, 31.
Mellon, Andrew, 223.
Melvin, James, 149.
Memphis Press-Scimitar, 208, 214.
Mery, Frederick, 222.
Milan Times, 42.
Miller, Dr. A. P., 85.
Milwaukee Journal, 209.
Milwaukee Sentinel, 233.
Minneapolis Journal, 154.
Mitgang, Herbert, 210.
Mollenkopf, Fred, 216, 260.
Moloney, Herbert W., 267.
Monroe Cablevision, 329.
Morse, Samuel F. B., 24.
Mott, Richard, 27, 37.
Mulholland, Frank, 192.
Musical America, 142.
Mussolini, Benito, 245.

N

Nasby, Petroleum Vesuvius (pseudonym of David Ross Locke), 77, 93, 113.
Nast, Thomas D., 95.
National Broadcasting Company, 296.
Nelson, Boris, 302, 358.
Newark Star-Eagle, 177, 208, 215, 221, 264, 290.
Newmyer, LeRoy F., 273.

New Republic, 273.
Newsweek, 321.
New Solidarity, 214.
New York Evening Mail, 111, 208, 266.
New York Evening Post, 54, 208.
New York Herald-Tribune, 218, 224.
New York Times, 111, 218, 321.
New York Tribune, 107.
Nicoll, Daniel, 266.
Nimitz, Adm. Chester W., 270.
Nixon, Richard M., 309.
Novisty Press, 300.

P

Palmer, Andrew, 3, 8, 10, 15.
Parker, Alton B., 180.
Parks, Lysander K., 119.
Patterson, Grove, 175, 196, 202, 215, 226, 245, 252, 259, 261, 268, 283, 290, 294, 315.
Patterson, Richard C., 226.
Pelton, Alonzo D., 45, 77, 78, 100.
Pennington, William, 49.
Perrysburg Fort Meigs Reveille, 31.
Phelps, Edward L., 66.
Phelps, Ralph, 261.
Phillips, Wendell, 92.
Pierce, Franklin K., 33, 98.
Pinchot, Gifford, 181.
Pittsburgh Chronicle, 79.
Pittsburgh Post-Gazette, 208, 209, 233, 255, 256, 267, 270, 288, 301, 329, 354, 355.
Pittsburgh Press, 209.
Pittsburgh Sun-Telegraph, 209.
Polk, Dorothy, 213.
Polk, James K., 19, 20.
Port Clinton Daily News, 329.
Port Lawrence Herald, 3, 11.
Potter, Emery D., 4.
Potter, John, 327, 349.
Power, Tyrone, 194.
Pratt, A. M., 108.

Q

Quinn, Janet, 339.

R

Ramey, Homer, 284, 311.
Raszka, Stanley, 324.
Reader's Digest, 281.
Reagan, Ronald W., 309, 313.
Reams, Frazier, 68, 239, 284, 311.
Red Bank Register, 355.
Redpath, James, 114.
Reed Alexander, 86.
Reynders, Tom, 330.

Index

Rhodes, James, 332.
Richardson, J. Frank, 207.
Ritchie, Frank, 253.
Roberts, Harry, 271, 319.
Roerich, Nicholas, 257.
Roosevelt, Eleanor, 273.
Roosevelt, Franklin D., 227, 230, 236, 248, 253, 262.
Roosevelt, Theodore, 171, 173, 179, 180, 183.
Root, Elihu, 190.
Roulet, Lloyd E., 273.
Rowell, George P., 85.
Ruffin, Edward H., 282.
Rusch, Clayton, 275.
Russell, Charles E., 152.
Russell, Lillian, 143.

S

Schimansky, O. K., 142.
Schrader, Paul, 290.
Scott, Jesup, 17, 15, 22, 35, 112, 129, 361.
Scott, Winfield, 15, 21, 33, 59.
Seabury, Samuel, 210, 230.
Seaman, Julian, 302.
Seldes, George, 208.
Shannon, Wilson, 13.
Shepard, Charles A. B., 126.
Shepard, Dr. Sam, 322.
Sherman, John, 48, 93, 97, 194.
Sherwood, Isaac R., 108, 192, 193, 194.
Simmons, James B., Jr., 318.
Skeel, Lee E., 323.
Skipton, John, 332.
Smith, Alfred E., 223, 227, 253.
Smith, Barton C., 162, 203, 214.
Smith, Dr. Howard, 350.
Speer, Stanley C., 216, 268.
Spencer, Mary Jane, 335.
Sprague, Charles H., 40.
Sprague, T. Spencer, 40.
Sprigle, Ray, 255, 257.
Steedman, James B., 51.
Steele, Lee Z., 302.
Steinberg, Lawrence, 275.
Steuer, Max, 233.
Stevens, Thaddeus, 92.
Stevenson, Adlai E., 37, 305.
Stewart, Gideon T., 38, 40, 90.
Stickney, Benjamin, 4, 7, 281.
Stowe, Harriett Beecher, 35.
Stranahan, Robert A. 350.
Sumner, Charles, 92, 107.
Swain, William M., 25.

T

Taft, Charles P., 236.
Taft, Robert A., 270.
Taft, William Howard, 165, 173, 180, 185.
Tanber, George Joseph, 357.
Taylor, Zachary, 15, 21, 28, 31.
Thacher, Addison Q., 242.
Thalheimer, Harry S. (later Talmadge), 161, 177, 213, 222.
Tilden, Myron H., 12.
Tilden, Samuel J., 109.
Time, 297, 321.
Toledo Commercial, 97, 108, 109.
Toledo Daybreak Dispatch, 354.
Toledo Gazette, 3, 8, 10.
Toledo News-Bee, 157, 161, 168, 172, 175, 177, 196, 197, 198, 216, 226, 234, 260, 269, 282, 288, 292.
Toledo Press, 292.
Toledo Record, 325.
Toledo Register, 16.
Toledo Republican, 29, 32.
Toledo Telegram, 126.
Toledo Times, 64, 172, 176, 226, 288, 289, 290, 322, 327.
Tooill, Kenneth D. 268.
Treanor, Aline Jean, 302.
Truman, Harry S., 284.
Trumbull, Lyman, 57, 90.
Tugwell, Rexford Guy, 251.
Tyler, John, 14, 21.

U

Urbana Collustrator, 4.
Urbaytis, Joe, 238.
U.S. Daily News, 234.

V

Vallandigham, Clement L., 72, 93, 98, 108.
Van Buren, Martin, 27, 28.
Venner, Frank, 313.
Vernam, Clarence, 177.

W

Waggoner, Clark, 38, 40, 71, 108, 109.
Waite, Morrison R., 67.
Walbridge, Heman D., 86.
Walker, James J., 210, 230, 258.
Wallace, Henry A., 257.
Ward, J. M., 44.
Warwick, Jack, 200.
Way, George B., 4, 7, 8, 9, 13, 19.
WDRB, Louisville, 329.
Weber, Ed, 312.
Webster, Daniel, 28, 32, 33.
WFLI, Lafayette, 329.
White, Charles D., 236.
White, William Hansford, 113.
Whitlock, Brand, 68, 145, 158, 238.

Willard, Dr. William R., 331.
Willey, John D., 289, 325, 328.
Williams, Joseph R., 4, 6, 8, 9, 31, 36, 64, 336.
Williams, Thomas, 96.
Willkie, Wendell, 257.
Willys, John N., 182.
WLIO, Lima, 329.

Wilson, Blacque, 177.
Wilson, Woodrow, 127.
Woodbury, Mitch, 277.
Woods, Michael, 301, 357.
Wright, Nathaniel C., 161, 177, 202, 222.
Yager, John W., 317.
Yamasaki, Minoru, 333, 353.
Yamin, Michael, 293.

HONOR ROLL

The following 223 people have, as of 1985, provided at least 25 years of continuous service to The Blade. The list includes one-third of the newspaper's full-time personnel and is presented in order of seniority.

Herman N. LaPorte
Ross T. Wetherald
John N. Grigsby
Paul Block, Jr.
Raymond P. Jankowski
Donald Wolfe
Seymour D. Rothman
William Block
Jeanne M. Walker
Mary K. Durivage
Bernard S. Rachuba
James R. Stewart
Frank A. Sosko
Ernest J. Okonski
George R. Dansack
Floyd C. Davis
Paul A. Gschwind
Donald Kroggel
Bernice Bourdeau
Louis Tomczak
Clifford J. Garling
James A. Bailey
Lloyd H. Ransom
Virginia Jankowski
Mildred Benson
Joseph E. Augustine
David E. Morris
William D. Hahnlen
Howard L. Burkhardt
Kenneth E. Rieger
John R. Smestad
Bruce G. Sinner
Jack D. Bigelow
Michael J. Pompili
Thomas D. Komisarek
Ralph A. Fata
James E. Richardson

Warren R. Wanamaker
Stephen Bartha
Charles Conner, Jr.
Hildagarde W. Condon
Robert P. Bauerschmidt
Richard J. Markowiak
Byron G. Morris
John G. Fern III
Robert M. Planck
Robert L. Murphy
John J. Weislak
William A. Brower
Robert G. Speck
Jerry P. McLaughlin
Earl F. Martin
Harry E. Brannan
Harold R. Wolfe
Melvin F. Nottage
Robert J. Brandon
Helen M. MacKay
Joseph F. Walles
Marvin A. Manore
Donald E. Nulton
Bernard F. Judy
Kenneth J. Himes
Mary Jane Spencer
Richard J. Merrill
Chester A. Sullwold
Richard G. Jeffery
Eugene J. Davis
Gerald E. Momsen
Roy E. Felty
Louis V. Hogan, Jr.
Arnold J. Herzig
Leonard C. Rossman
Donald F. Ganss
William H. Woodward

Edmund Vogel
Edward G. Lagger
Jack H. Rower
James R. Seymour
Waylon E. Dickey
George Mays Leow
Donald Miller
Robert E. Maley, Sr.
Albert W. Nyitray
Robert K. Beilhart
John R. Jolley
Ruth A. Gimple
Lee Z. Steele
Evelyn M. Alexander
Donald R. Kubicki
Leonard Newman
Theodore Bishop
Kathleen G. Loomis
Claude L. Beck, Jr.
Robert W. Morris
Robert L. Van Scoy
Signe Walstrom
William Balla, Jr.
Richard M. Bernhard
Richard C. Knoth
Richard J. Thatcher
Charles E. Urie
George L. Antoine
Tommie J. Armstead
Joseph R. Berlin
James E. Loomis
Richard F. Tegatz
Clarence O. Meyer
Albert H. Bryant
John E. DeVaul
Carl J. Aldrich
Wilfred B. Roberts III
Thomas H. Ross

Robert W. Dailey
Charles M. Kozina
John T. Craney
Charles T. McGowan
Mary A. Powell
Ethan B. Remley
David W. Newman
Leroy Gagle
Emil J. Zach
Homer T. Martin
William R. Gentner
Charles W. Cocke
Gus G. Matthews
Robert D. Abbott
John F. Wright
Edwin F. Seymour
Paul L. Feck
Thomas J. Loomis, Jr.
Donald J. Flory
Charlotte R. Conner
William W. Krum
Robert C. Ganss
Janet E. Connin
Stanley W. Frankowski
Fred W. Meyer
Richard D. Mesnard
Edith J. Damschroder
Vernon L. Hehl
William F. LaPountney
Frederic D. Nofziger
Paul A. Jakubowski
Robert R. Kyle
Kenneth C. Carr
James L. Bialorucki
Lee Merkle
Arthur P. Brust, Sr.
Robert E. Drager

Marvin F. Elling
John E. Marker, Jr.
Vernon F. Glenn
Lorne R. Trainor
Sidney Goldberg
Carl R. Parrish
Herbert M. Knowlton
Edric G. Costain
Robert M. Gray
William A. Shay
Edson Whipple
Donald H. Jahns
Harry R. Smith
George Melvin Leow
Robert R. Faylor
Richard Parthemer
Carlton P. Manzek
Richard E. Rhodes
Edward P. Jacobs
Ronald R. Thompson
Peter Drome
George S. Rettig
Dorothy J. Edgington
Robert W. Conboy
Nancy K. Gould
Marvin E. Blackburn
Francis Blust
Steve C. Kaifas
Paul W. Pierce
Johnnie W. Browder
George D. Markham, Jr.
Richard W. Matthias
Verna R. Duncan
Howard E. Beck
James B. Regenold
Charles B. Cannon, Jr.
Thomas L. Stough

JoAnn M. Andersen
Edward T. Roberts
Salvador Hernandez
Terry W. Roberts
Dorothy Rainie
Thomas E. Ostertag
Frank R. Timm
Carol L. Barber
Richard Garris
Lyle S. Grosjean
Ronald F. Hojnacki
Louise C. Seibert
Vernon G. Brubaker
Thomas R. Duris
Jacqueline Rutkowski
William J. Rokicki
Don N. Schwartz
Joseph B. Blowers
Harold J. Brownlee
Henry H. Quilter, Jr.
Donald L. Ellison
Robert Stebli
Donald P. Zbierajewski
Philip M. Grote
James A. Huth
Donald R. Strayer
Lehr K. Whitney
Thomas C. McLean, Sr.
Mary A. Warr
Charles M. Hansen
Harold L. Twaddle
James C. Lind
Ralph B. Spradlin
Burruss C. Drennen
Alvah C. Querry
Walter T. Fritz
Robert W. Kavanaugh

PN 4899 .T65 B534 1985